Personality and the Cultural Construction of Society

MELFORD E. SPIRO

Personality and the Cultural Construction of Society

PAPERS IN HONOR OF
MELFORD E. SPIRO

Edited by David K. Jordan and Marc J. Swartz

THE UNIVERSITY OF ALABAMA PRESS

Tuscaloosa and London

Essay Index

Copyright © 1990 by
The University of Alabama Press
Tuscaloosa, Alabama 35487–0380
All rights reserved
Manufactured in the United States of America

∞

The paper on which this book is printed meets the minimum
requirements of American National Standard for Information Science-Permanence of Paper for Printed Library Materials,
ANSI A39.48–1984.

Library of Congress Cataloging-in-Publication Data

Personality and the cultural construction of society : papers
  in honor of Melford E. Spiro / edited by David K. Jordan
  and Marc J. Swartz.
      p.   cm.
    Bibliography: p.
    Includes index.
    ISBN 0–8173–0469–X (alk. paper)
    1. Personality and culture.   2. Ethnopsychology.   3.
  Spiro, Melford E.   I. Jordan, David K.   II. Swartz,
  Marc J.   III. Spiro, Melford E.
  GN504.P47   1990
  155.8—dc20   89–32993
                                                       CIP

British Library Cataloguing-in-Publication Data available

TO MELFORD E. SPIRO

Contents

Contents

Acknowledgments

We cannot list all of the many friends and well-wishers who have given us their time, sympathetic advice, and help at various stages in the preparation of this volume, but we are grateful to them all. Especially prominent among them were the following: George Devereux (University of Paris), Cora Du Bois (Harvard University), A. L. Epstein (University of Sussex), Meyer Fortes (London School of Economics), Gerald Hyman (Alexandria, Virginia) Waud Kracke (University of Illinois, Chicago Circle), Richard A. Krause (University of Alabama), George P. Murdock (University of Pittsburgh), Michael D. Murphy (University of Alabama), Manisha Roy (Wrentham, Mass.), Simon Ottenberg (University of Washington), Steven Piker (Swarthmore College), and Milton Singer (University of Chicago). George Devereux, Meyer Fortes, and George Murdock passed away while the volume was in preparation.

We are also grateful to the Office of Graduate Studies and Research, University of California, San Diego, for a publishing subvention, to George Ericksen for preparing the index, and to our UCSD colleagues M. Schmalowitz and D. Woo for their unfailingly helpful logistical advice.

Personality and the Cultural Construction of Society

Introduction

Anthropology has addressed itself to only a few questions over its history, but these few are fundamental for an understanding of humanity. It has always asked what is universal in the human condition and what variable, and how societies exert the grip they have on their members. It has examined the ways in which symbols take on meaning, how children learn to be adults, and the similarities and differences between the sexes. Such questions are not always (or even usually) explicit, but in the end they underlie much of the work done by most anthropologists.

Now and again an anthropologist will raise new aspects of these questions and, more than most of us can, will advance our attempts to provide answers. Melford E. Spiro is such an anthropologist. This volume of essays is intended to extend his advances in a variety of areas that relate to culture, personality, and social life. Not all of us agree with everything Spiro has written, but we all agree that our work has benefited from his wide-ranging interests and findings. We also agree that, by focusing attention here on the problems he has addressed, the approaches he has used, and the theories he has developed, we may be able to extend and strengthen his contributions.

The editors have divided the essays here into four broad groups that roughly correspond to several main foci of Spiro's own research. The first relates to the nature of explanation in anthropology. The second deals with the relationship between culture and personality as they are expressed in gender roles, the Oedipus complex, personality configurations, and dreams. The third considers religion and symbolism, with attention to the role of symbols in human motivation. Some chapters examine questions Spiro has raised with respect to the data he collected in his own fieldwork, drawing on information about quite different societies or developing different answers. The chapters in the final section address issues relating to the management of aggression and the application of power in human societies and, more broadly, in primate ones. Here attention focuses on leadership, charisma, and the range of social skills involved in social manipulation.

Our volume salutes a great anthropologist. It does so less by praising him (although praise is certainly in order) than by showing how powerful the influence of his work has been. If our chapters discuss issues of interest and importance to him and address areas in which he has been a prime theorist, the reason is that these issues are of interest and importance to us as well, for they are central to the discipline of anthropology.

PART I: NONTELEOLOGICAL FUNCTIONALISM

How are human forces harnessed to make social life possible in its variety of forms, and what prevents or limits deviance enough for us to be able to cooperate usefully? The usual anthropological answer, of course, is that social conformity and participation come about because participants in a society possess a learned and shared culture.

But as Spiro has suggested (e.g., 1961c), actors must not only share beliefs, values, and perceptions but must also actually use them as guides for their behavior. An important part of Spiro's work has been concerned with explaining how parts of culture come to enter into actor's perceptions and motivations and how the participation in such institutions as rituals, monasteries, chieftainship, and even collective agriculture contribute to the continuation and operation of society as a whole. The explanatory scheme he uses is what he calls "nonteleological functionalism" (Spiro 1961c). Nonteleological functionalism is discussed here in whole or in part by several authors, who seek to put it into perspective and to extend it in various ways or who take issue with it in the hope of seeing how it might, like all our best theoretical schemes, someday be transcended.

Kevin Avruch sets Spiro's nonteleological functionalism in the perspective of the history of anthropology, paying particular attention to the differences between Spiro's formulations and those of other noted theorists. An important and distinctive characteristic of Spiro's functionalism is its insistence on discovering causes in personality processes. One of Spiro's most fecund concepts in such analysis is the "culturally constituted mechanism of defense," which links personality and culture and is accordingly central to the identification of causes.[1] Avruch examines the development and application of this concept in Spiro's study of Burmese monks. The elegantly simple idea has two parts. First, as they learn culture and participate in some of its institutions, individuals acquire psychological needs, including conflicts that produce painful tensions. Second, these needs can sometimes be met through participation in other culturally based institutions. Culture both giveth and taketh away. Functionalism, in anthropology, is inevitably

2

associated with the famous "British school" of the middle of this century, and Avruch emphasizes the importance of Spiro's departures from British functionalism.

Michael Meeker begins with Spiro's attack on Malinowski's assertion that the Oedipus complex is absent from the Trobriand Islands. Meeker asks how different theorists came to interpret the same data so very differently. He sees the rhetorical strategies adopted by different interpreters as the key to understanding their findings. Unlike anthropologists today, theorists at the turn of the century exhibited a rhetorical impulse to redeem their own visions of the humanity by discovering in "primitive" societies what they regarded as absent but desirable in their own. Malinowski's Trobriand interpretations, for example, may have been guided in part by his impulse to see tender, loving parental figures as a normal part of some human society albeit not his own.

Pursuing this line of thought, Meeker argues that Durkheim was heavily influenced by a strong moralism and a keen sense of living in an age of science. He tended to give pride of place to moral sensibilities rather than to scientific discourse. (Ironically, Durkheim found himself defending his position by reference to scientific discourse itself.) Freud dealt with the same ethnographic data (in *Totem and Taboo*), but he took the view that religion could most easily be understood by analyzing ambivalence in the associations of neurotic patients. Seeing morality itself resting on human ambivalence, Freud, while differing from Durkheim, nevertheless addressed the wellspring of human morality, the very problem that Durkheim stressed in the analysis of the Australian material. Meeker's paper, taking as its point of departure the Spiro-Malinowski "debate," in the end gives us a powerful analytic tool for interpreting many other disconcerting points of disagreement between honorable observers.

In the third chapter Gananath Obeyesekere also deals with the general question of how scholars come to regard material as they do, and also like Meeker, he selects Durkheim as a specific example and culturally constituted defense mechanisms as the specific issue. Obeyesekere brings two insights to Durkheim's work. First, Durkheim was far more of a psychologist than most modern followers have tended to assume, and second, he was a much more modern psychologist than we might expect to find him. In fact, Obeyesekere is able to discover in Durkheim's work foreshadowings of many of the ideas later developed by Kardiner, Spiro, and other contemporary writers on the psychological understanding of human life. Modern social theory, Obeyesekere shows, stresses the psychology of human motivation as a major source in the causation of culturally mediated behavior despite a tendency in some quarters to regard it as peripheral.

David Jordan uses Spiro's form of functional analysis to examine the sectarian religious practices of Taiwan. Jordan explores an elaboration of the approach to take into account dysfunction. There is no reason to believe, Jordan argues, that all is always for the best: a eufunction can have dysfunctional aspects and a dysfunction eufunctional ones. Human action and custom depend less on eufunction alone than on a kind of "vector sum" of the various eufunctions and dysfunctions involved. Turning to Spiro's important distinctions among *types* of functions, and considering them in light of the contrast between eufunctional and dysfunctional aspects, he enlarges the scheme and shows that his extension helps us understand why an institution such as a Taiwan divination sect is more compelling to some group members than to others and why "miracles" play a central role in sect activity.

In the section's final chapter, Marc Swartz concentrates on the concept of "status," an idea which plays a central role in Spiro's nonteleological functionalism, since Spiro's analysis uses the analysis of status requirements and benefits to establish the link between individuals and social systems. Swartz regards statuses as cultural constituted means for the distribution of culture, and he demonstrates that at least some kinds of Swahili behavior— "aggressive speech," in his example—can be fruitfully explained in terms of the statuses of those involved and the cultural content of these statuses. By taking as the point of analytical departure the cultural elements that define statuses and guide behavior within them, Swartz is able to account for (1) the kinds of aggressive speech that occupants of different statuses do and do not use, (2) the people to whom they do and do not direct the speech, and (3) the bases for the effectiveness of the aggressive speech.

PART II: CULTURE AND PERSONALITY, GENDER ROLES,
THE OEDIPUS COMPLEX, AND DREAMS

The second section begins with an article by Roy G. D'Andrade entitled "Culture and Personality: A False Dichotomy," whose title recalls one of Spiro's earliest papers (Spiro 1951). D'Andrade reviews various relationships between culture and personality. He notes that the causal/functional relationship (wherein personality "needs" find expression in culturally constituted institutions) has received considerable attention, but another important sort of relationship, "overlap," has been neglected until very recently. In this relationship, adumbrated by Spiro in his famous 1951 paper, the same learning serves both culture and personality. D'Andrade makes clear that schema theory in cognitive anthropology provides a vital new basis for understanding this overlap relationship better by focusing attention on cultural schemas (folk models) on the one hand and individual functioning on the other. The schema focus provides not only an approach to the ways

4

in which individuals do things but also to their reasons for choosing the goals they do.

Gender and sex have emerged in recent years as critical to our understanding of the human condition. The biological sources of gender and sex differences are obviously crucial, but so are sources that are only indirectly biological, that is, based in biology but slightly removed from that base. The "indirectly biological" universal include those deriving from the lengthy dependency of human infants and from the role of women as child-bearers and nurses. In his book *Gender and Culture*, Spiro suggests an important possibility: what we find ethnographically as universals in sex roles may derive (1) from directly biological differences, (2) from universal experiences rooted in such things as human dependency and the biological role of mothers, and (3) from the interaction of these with each other. Spiro's enduring interest in the apparent universality of the Oedipus complex has much to do with the role of this conflict in producing universalities of sex- and gender-based differentiation of social statuses. Several chapters in this volume deal with gender, and of these, several consider the fascinating problems of interpreting the Oedipus complex.

Raymond Fogelson approaches the puzzle of the universality of the Oedipus complex with data from a society in which women's positions are often regarded as very powerful. The Cherokee, like the Trobrianders, are matrilineal, and their kinship system, like that of other matrilineal systems, includes important mothers' brothers and politically powerful mothers. Fogelson examines Cherokee historical data from the eighteenth and nineteenth centuries in an effort to discover whether the Oedipus conflict was visible in this society and, if so, what form it might have taken. The historical data do not provide a definitive answer concerning the historical Cherokee Oedipus complex itself, but, Fogelson concludes, they do strongly support Spiro's view that there is a limit to how far cultural variation can influence what is apparently rooted in panhuman biology and panhuman childhood experience.

George and Louise Spindler attend equally to males and females in their report on the results of years of work among four quite different societies. They support Spiro's kibbutz finding that the sexes differ substantially in their attitudes and their value emphases, and the authors agree that the biological components of differences are inseparable from cultural ones. In all four societies they find that women view social and cultural change far more favorably than men do. In the societies less fully transformed by "modernization," women are more oriented to the new and "modern," while in Germany, as in Spiro's kibbutz, the women express a longing for traditional roles and relationships. Somewhat paradoxically, then, women, more than men, want to move away from the status quo. This statement is apparently true whether the status quo is more nearly traditional in their view or represents a considerable departure from tradition.

The Spindlers describe this finding as being explainable by one or (most likely) both of the following hypotheses. First, women favor change more because in most or all social systems they receive fewer rewards than men do and therefore are less attached to those systems. Second, domestic roles have intrinsic rewards; when these are threatened, women reassert their attachment to them. Thus any change may be desirable, but changes that lessen domestic satisfaction eventually produce an interest in returning to earlier arrangements in which the rewards were greater. The Spindlers suggest some biological bases for these hypotheses and findings, but their main conclusion is that no complete understanding of society and culture can fail to take into account the differences in perspective between men and women.

Aram Yengoyan's chapter turns from the differences between males and females, one of the most public aspects of life, to dreams, one of the most private and idiosyncratic. Focusing on the Pitjantjatjara, an aboriginal Australian society, Yengoyan is concerned to demonstrate how dreams relate to particular cultural ethos and *at the same time* express and partly resolve cultural and psychological conflicts, as psychoanalysis has shown. Yengoyan examines dreams and their interpretation by the dreamers and analyzes the relations that the dreams have with Pitjantjatjara culture, social structure, and language. He shows that the group's generally prescriptive (rather than prospective) orientation, reflected in avoiding linguistic negation, is evident also in dreaming and in dream interpretation. Furthermore as individuals move through the structural system, changes occur in their dreaming that correspond to the changes in their social and cultural position. Freud's prediction that "no" would be found to be virtually absent from dreams is confirmed for this Australian group, but Yengoyan argues that the reason is not the disjunction between a free dream life and a constrained waking life (as for Freud's patients) but rather the continuity of tendencies that also dominate both language use and culture. Yengoyan argues that it should be possible to establish general relationships between the processes of culture and social structure and those of dreaming and the interpretation of dreams by the dreamers.

The Oedipus complex and the structure of dreams are hardly the only cultural universals. It seems that each newly discovered universal phenomenon makes the notion of universality itself more provocative. Rorschach responses also seem to be largely culture free. In the chapter that concludes this section, George De Vos examines Rorschach responses and concerns himself with the implications of the culture-free quality of one particular response: the tendency of some subjects, apparently in all societies, to identify human figures in motion in the Rorschach inkblots. The answer must lie, he reasons, in universals of the interpretation of kinesic experience, experience which must then fall into the category that Spiro has identified as indirectly biological universal experiences rooted in such things as human dependency and the biological role of mothers. Exploring the implications of the relation between kinesic universals, Rorschach responses, and personality functioning, De Vos develops an impressive formulation of personality functioning in its relationship specifically to social participation and social coping (and for that matter to maladaptive rigidity in some individuals). The argument is inspired at many turns by data drawn mainly from Japan, but the message relates to universality.

PART III: RELIGION AND PERSONALITY

Religion has long been seen as lying especially near a culture's heart, and many anthropologists have devoted their attention to it. Spiro and the authors of this book have focused their attention specifically on the relations between aspects of religion and personality. The questions they raise concern the motivations for religious activity, and the relations of these motivations to nonreligious areas of experience, the nature of religious symbols, and the social and psychological consequences of religious participation. Other issues concern the social, psychological, and motivational aspects of trance behavior, identification of the sorts of people who become religious specialists, and consideration of the bases on which others can provide social and economic support for such specialists.

In the opening chapter Manning Nash, like Spiro, seeks to move beyond the limitations of traditional functionalism. Also like Spiro, he is concerned to view cultural universals as rooted in inevitabilities of the human condition—the same kinds of inevitabilities mentioned earlier in connection with the Oedipus complex: the biological, the "indirectly biological," and those that partake of both. Here Nash proposes a carefully articulated definition of religion that points directly to the empirical dimensions of belief and practice and provides especially clear boundaries to exclude certain cultural material as specifically *not* in the domain of religion. This refinement of definition allows especially precise generalizations about the relationship between religion and "existential tensions of man in society." Nash uses wide-ranging ethongraphic examples to explore the ways in which the human condition, with its "indirectly biological" constraints, seemingly inevitably gives rise to religious formulations of experience.

Robert Paul's chapter centers on the recruitment of clerics among the Sherpas. Paul further develops a theme touched on by Jordan in chapter 4 when he was concerned to explain why Taiwan sects appeal more to some people than to others. Paul begins by considering the sorts of lives led by Sherpas who become monks and how they differ from the lives of those who remain among the laity. In his approach to the problem Paul combines Freudian psychology with structuralism and symbolic anthropology in a way that is similar to, and inspired by, Spiro's habitual linking of Freudian and cultural anthropological concepts and approaches. For the Sherpas, the most salient characteristic of the monks' life is that they, uniquely, do not marry. Paul proceeds by examining the family situation that produces monks and the psychological characteristics of individuals who have grown up in this situation. He then relates these psychological characteristics to the social, and especially to the symbolic, aspects of being a monk in a way that recalls Spiro's examination of Buddhist monks in Burma. Impressively, he is able to account for 100 percent of the cases.

William Wedenoja in his chapter deals with trance behavior. Like Paul, Wedenoja examines a religious phenomenon using the same basic approach taken by Spiro in examining a similar sort of event but focusing on issues and using approaches that are not central to Spiro's work. Like Spiro (1978a, 1982a), Wedenoja is interested in trance behavior, but unlike Spiro, Wedenoja directs attention to brain physiology. Ritual trances are reported for 90 percent of all human societies, and they are part of established practice in 65 percent of the Jamaican churches he studied. They are related to the hypnotic state, which is in turn based in neurophysiology. Trance, Wedenoja argues, is, in evolutionary perspective, a normal human activity, and ritual trances are a cultural "use" of a human physiological characteristic; for individuals, trances can be understood as related to the psychological needs and to how these "fit" with what is culturally needed.

The issue of trance is further discussed by Erika Bourguignon. She is concerned with the cultural structuring and specific psychological use of this state. Her chapter provides a carefully controlled comparison of recruitment to the shaman status and to the phenomenon of being possessed in Haitian Vodoun, Nepal Taman shamanism, and the Burmese shamanism described by Spiro. The problem lies in determining the particular sorts of possession trances that occur in different kinds of statuses. Bourguignon shows that individual needs are not a sufficient basis for understanding recruitment to the shaman statuses in which trance is expected. Indeed, it is not sufficient to consider these needs even when they are taken together with an examination of social structure and the social and symbolic meanings of trance. Just as Spiro has maintained, cognitive and perceptual orientations must also be considered. The "deep structure" of personality finds expression only through the "surface structure" of local culture.

PART IV: AGGRESSION, DEPENDENCY,
AND THE SKILLS OF SOCIAL MANIPULATION

The late twentieth century has brought with it a pervasive view among anthropologists and educated laity alike that aggression, rooted in our primate biology, is one of the most important wellsprings of human social interaction, perhaps even the central one. Psychological studies have from the beginning been concerned with the psychic management of hostility and of aggressive impulses. People have come to believe that hostility and aggression, sublimated in various ways, impel not only leadership (standing at the top of the "pecking order") but also much of daily social interaction. We are discovering, however, that the situation is more complicated. One of the chapters in this section shows that aggression is only one of a wide repertoire of ways in which modern baboons deal with threat and competition. Surely also it is only one of the ways in which our ancient forebears dealt with the same conditions. Indeed, it is beginning to appear that, important as aggression is, assigning it too large a role in human affairs is worse than inadequate: it is probably dead wrong.

Closely related to the issue of aggression is the question of dependency—indeed aggression and dependency are the two psychological problems on which Spiro touches most often in his work. Dependency, of course, relates directly to the inherently social nature of the human (or more broadly primate) animal, and dependency lies in the primatological background of the section of De Vos's chapter that concerns itself with human belonging. In this final section, we see dependency again, this time innovatively linked to (of all things) charisma. The chapter here suggests that dependency, rather than aggression, may be psychologically central to the social processes that support charismatic leaders.

Shirley Strum examines the repertoire of baboon social skills. For some years Strum has been observing a troop of baboons in Kenya which she has whimsically named the "Pumphouse Gang." Her study shows that, even among baboons, aggressivity does not occupy the unique and unchallenged position often assigned to it. She finds that in the Pumphouse Gang, on the contrary, aggression is only one of several responses to threat and is no more prominent than several others as a competitive maneuver. When baboons are threatened or when they want something from other troop members, they use various types of affiliative behavior, including behavior involving "friends" and the infants of those friends, at least as prominently as they do the expression of hostility. Since human and baboon lines of evolutionary development diverged at least 14 million years ago, and since the behavior now found in both species is likely to have been present in the common ancestor, we may reasonably infer that our joint forebears too had a wider range of social strategies than a view of them as merely "killer apes" would suggest. Instead, affiliation and related modalities of action appear to be equally ancient and equally prominent, even as a means of participating in competition or responding to aggression.

F. G. Bailey moves from the primatological back to the specifically human but continues to address the same theme. If aggression is less useful than we once thought, and if it should play a smaller role in our models of human behavior than it once did, what other psychological processes should we reexamine as we rethink our models? Bailey approaches the problem specifically in the context of theories of leadership and social manipulation. He looks to panhuman psychological process for the main source of that which has been rather mysteriously labeled "charisma" and has been curiously neglected in anthropological analysis. Charisma is often regarded as a quality of leaders, but it is in fact a quality attributed to leaders by their followers. The phenomenon that requires explanation, therefore, is the attitude of followers that gives leaders a superhuman status, thereby placing them beyond accountability and making them subject to blind faith.

Bailey draws on Spiro's view that powerful unconscious forces are not only vital determinants of behavior in all societies but also the raw material from which culture and historical circumstances produce observed behavior. On this basis, he is able to advance the hypothesis that "numenification" (the manipulation of charisma) is most effective when such unconscious forces as dependency reign. Furthermore, when this situation is present, people turn to a person, a leader, and not to an institution. Leaders manipulated the unconsciously based forces of their followers, but this manipulation is often fully conscious and calculated even when the sources of the leaders' own motives are not. Leaders whose numenification is successful are viewed as superhuman, but because of this, they are expected to perform miracles. If these miracles do not occur, the leader must do something or lose power and, ultimately, position of leadership. People whose leadership is charismatically based often respond to the disaffection stemming from their failure to produce generally desired miracles by further numenification, which can serve to delay public disenchantment. The psychological underpinnings of the process, however, continue to be dependency.

The chapters in this volume can all be described as psychological anthropology. Yet it is probably a sign of the broad relevance of that subdiscipline that in the end they address the most central questions of anthropology as a whole. All of the chapters manifest the conviction that social and cultural activity is possible only when individuals are motivated to carry it out, and a study of social and cultural life therefore demands an examination of motivation. In this respect, as well as in the specific ways that have been noted in the case of each chapter, our work is inspired by and follows that of Melford E. Spiro.

N O T E

1. The idea itself derives from Spiro's friend and teacher A. I. Hallowell and has its ultimate source in the "Urfunctionalism" of Malinowski.

PART ONE
Nonteleological Functionalism

1

Melford Spiro and the
Scientific Study of Culture

KEVIN AVRUCH

In his contribution to *The Making of Psychological Anthropology* (1978b), Melford Spiro provides a précis of an ongoing intellectual autobiography. In it he describes the changes in his point of view about human nature. According to his account, in line with the "received anthropological wisdom" of the late 1940s, he began as a cultural determinist and relativist. He sought to demonstrate the unlimited plasticity of human beings and their cultures. In the course of almost four decades, many field trips, and a number of research projects, however, he has shifted from a position which derogated the existence of a panhuman, psychobiologically invariant human nature relevant for the exploration of culture to a view that makes the existence of such a human nature the foundation for a theory of culture. He now argues that motivational dispositions and cognitive orientations are both culturally invariant as well. This invariance is to be found on the level of "genotype" or "deep structure" (his metaphors) which underlie (and belie) the seemingly unlimited plasticity of phenotypic, surface structural cultural forms. This view of human nature guides much of Spiro's later work (e.g., 1982a:6–14) and is explicitly expounded in *Gender and Culture* (1979a) and *Oedipus in the Trobriands* (1982c).

The autobiography thus describes intellectual movement on an issue central to anthropology, and clearly this movement Spiro himself regards as a hallmark of his career. To this outsider the movement may appear in fact to have been well under way early in the four decades. The paper "Human Nature in its Psychological Dimensions" (1954) prefigures most of the shift, and much of Spiro's mature point of view is already present: the motivational

15

invariance, certainly, but also, with reference to Redfield, the inclination to postulate cognitive invariance as well (1954:26–27).

Nevertheless, when we consider Spiro's career in terms of an intellectual history of anthropology and not in the autobiographical terms of a personal intellectual history, another theme emerges. This theme is characterized not by movement and change but by constancy and continuity. I cast Spiro as the ever-constant defender of a scientific faith: the relevance— better, the necessity—of a psychological anthropology for the explication of culture and social systems. Or perhaps I should use the term that Spiro prefers to "psychological anthropology" and speak of the relevance of the "culture and personality" approach. That he prefers the latter term, which many regard as old-fashioned, if not seriously compromised or permanently stigmatized by the excesses of configurationalism, national character studies, and swaddling hypotheses, is a diacritic of the faith. For in this preference Spiro opposes both an academic psychology which would dismiss "the personality concept as too vague or too holistic for rigorous scientific investigation" (and perforce dismiss psychoanalytic theory by the same stroke) and a "psychological anthropology" which, becoming "little more than cross-cultural psychology," would do away with the concept of culture (1972:578).

Such a position has its adversaries. But if Spiro has remained a constant spokesman for culture and personality, the nature of the adversaries has changed. The present essay considers the changing grounds of the adversarial relationship. It sketches a part of the intellectual history of contemporary sociocultural anthropology. I will examine the development of Spiro's program for the scientific study of culture in terms of some changing foci or thrusts in the discipline as a whole. I will deal primarily with his writings on religion and with the logic of his explanations. And let me repeat, if I use the device of holding the core of Spiro's thought "constant" so as to view changes in the discipline, I do so because I find such constancy exemplified throughout his work.

THE FIRST ADVERSARY: ON STRUCTURES AND THEIR FUNCTIONS

The Boasian Heritage

In the late 1940s when Spiro began his professional career, American anthropology was already far along in developing its Boasian heritage: the "culture concept" was its orthodoxy and the centrality of culture to the proper study of man the first article of its credo. Most significantly, of course, these served to distinguish American "cultural" anthropology from its counterpart, "social" anthropology, in Great Britain. But in the United States the universal homage paid to culture did not preclude sectarian developments. What was culture, anyway—phenomenal reality or analytic construct? How ought one to study it—as science or as history? And however one answered these first two questions, how was the psychological study of the individual implicated in the study of culture (crucially or not at all)? By their responses to any and all of these questions, one could group and differentiate the major anthropologists of the time: White from Kluckhohn, White from Kroeber, Benedict and Sapir from Kroeber and White, and so on. And as a comment on the "history of science" approach to anthropology, one can use these questions to differentiate between anthropologists of this time, too.[1] While Spiro has addressed all three questions—and his response to the second is, as we shall see, unequivocal—it is with the third question—what about the individual?—that I am especially concerned here.

Given the centrality of the culture concept to the anthropological tradition in which Spiro was trained, and given his position on the crucial importance of psychology to the study of culture, Spiro might have been expected to develop his program, concretely, against the superorganicism of Kroeber and the culturology of White. And indeed a seminal early paper, "Culture and Personality: The Natural History of a False Dichotomy" (1951), is cast very much in this mode. Declaring the radical disjunction between culture and personality to be mistaken, he argued instead that they are but different labels for the same "unified process developed by individuals for the purpose of biological adaptation, social adjustment, and personality integration" (1951:46) or, more strongly, that "they *are* the individual as modified by learning" (1951:43; emphasis in the original). Very soon, however, he began to shift from this unitarian view toward a Parsonian tripartite one which asserted the analytic autonomy of personality and of cultural and social systems. Increasingly, in fact, his analyses focused on the workings of the social system, and with this shift his criticisms of superorganic and culturological approaches became implicit. Explicitly, he chose as his main adversary in this period the kind of *social* anthropology that was exemplified by Radcliffe-Brown and his followers, and they were engaged by Spiro on the field of functional analysis.[2]

Radcliffe-Brown: Society as Organism

I will not recapitulate here in great detail the many surveys and critical summaries of Radcliffe-Brown's work. But it is necessary to set forth the main points of his program. First, Radcliffe-Brown conceived anthropology to be a "natural science" of society, an endeavor having the same spirit, and the same goals, as physics, chemistry, and biology. Like scientists in these latter disciplines, the anthropologist took as a highest goal the discovery and elucidation of general and universal laws of social—rather than chemical or biological—process. His aims were nomothetic rather than idiographic. These aims justified calling anthropology a science and distinguishing it from history, which "consists primarily of idiographic enquiries" (1952:2). Biology was the science that Radcliffe-Brown used most often in analogies with anthropology, and this choice had important consequences for his natural science of society. In terms of its nomothetic accomplishments, biology was (next to anthropology) the youngest of the natural sciences. The biologist as "naturalist" working in "the field" to collect, classify, and catalogue "specimens" was not yet a distant ancestor of contemporary biologists, who worked increasingly in laboratories, much like their physicist or chemist colleagues, according to the experimental method. This similarity alone would have recommended biology to Radcliffe-Brown as a worthy exemplar for anthropology. For anthropology, freed recently from the conjectural pseudohistoricizing of the nineteenth-century evolutionists, was just beginning to realize its scientific aspirations. Radcliffe-Brown could easily assimilate the naturalist to the ethnographer (both of whom work in "the field") and could thus anticipate the first task of a scientific anthropology: collection, classification, and categorization, all in the service of ever-generalizing comparisons of forms. For the naturalist the forms were specimen organisms; for the anthropologist, specimen social structures. The phenomenal reality of the former (organisms) was evident by common sense. The reality of the latter was a matter of epistemological fiat: "Social structures are just as real as are individual organisms" (1940b:190). In short, for anthropology, as for the more mature sciences, first things come first. "We should remember that chemistry and biology did not become fully formed sciences until considerable progress had been made with the systematic classification of the things they were dealing with, substances in the one instance and plants and animals in the other" (1940:195). In anthropology, social structures had the same ontological status as substances, plants, and animals.

The biological analogy was thus important as a model of the course of disciplinary evolution. Furthermore, it led to Radcliffe-Brown's leitmotif: the comparison of society to the living organism. The organismic analogy determined the nature of Radcliffe-Brown's conception of the social system and its most important problematic. For in addition to the social "morphological study, consisting in the definition, comparison and classification of diverse structural systems, there is a [social] physiological study. The problem here is: How do structural systems persist? What are the mechanisms that maintain a network of social relations in existence, and how do they work?" (1940b:195). Thus, in his reliance on contemporary biology, Radcliffe-Brown came to view a particular sort of explanation as the sine qua non of the nascent science of anthropology: the functional explanation, which specifies the way in which any social activity, institution, trait, or form, contributes to the "harmony," "internal consistency," regulation—the maintenance—of the social system as a whole.

Here Radcliffe-Brown believed he was following Durkheim's lead, and certainly Durkheim was a functionalist. Radcliffe-Brown was less punctilious, however, in noting the increasing autonomy Durkheim had given to collective representations from social morphology (cf. Durkheim 1933 and 1915). Moreover, his insistent "functionalizing" of Durkheim obscured in practice the other sort of explanation Durkheim demanded, namely the causal (Durkheim 1938). To Radcliffe-Brown, causal explanations meant historical ones (Radcliffe-Brown 1952a:186), and these were either unavailable or trivial with respect to the nomothetic tasks at hand. Radcliffe-Brown also followed Durkheim (1938:104, 110) in dismissing the relevance of psychology for social anthropology (Radcliffe-Brown 1948:45, 1958:18).[3]

Enter Spiro. In most of his writings he has had recourse to functional analysis. In *Burmese Supernaturalism* he declared outright: "Despite the current revolt against functionalism . . . , I remain an unregenerate functionalist" (1967:7). But his use of functional explanations differed from Radcliffe-Brown's in several respects, and these differences were often formulated explicitly in contrast to Radcliffe-Brown's overall program.

The disagreement was phrased in two ways. First, Spiro criticized Radcliffe-Brown (and others) for misuse of the logic of functional analysis. In this he followed Merton (1949) and Hempel (1952, 1965). Second, Spiro sought to undo the extreme "functionalization" of Durkheim's program by Radcliffe-Brown, that is, he sought to disentangle functional explanations from causal ones. He parted company with Durkheim, of course, on the question of the level of analysis at which causes were to be sought. Indeed in his search for causes (specifically at the level of personality analysis), Spiro sometimes appears a strange, if "unregenerate," functionalist. If Radcliffe-Brown can be accused of assimilating causal explanations to functional ones, Spiro, by his own words, can be accused of the opposite: "functional and configurational explanations . . . either are ultimately causal or else they are not explanatory" (1967:65). I shall return to discuss implications of this statement later, after examining the points raised above in the context of Spiro's ethnography and its analysis.

Ifaluk and Alus

From Spiro's fieldwork on Ifaluk came a series of papers (especially 1952, 1953, 1959, 1961c) which set the tone of his own functionalism and challenged that of the social anthropologists. The earliest of these papers laid the foundation of the argument.

The people of Ifaluk believe in two sorts of supernatural beings: high gods and ghosts. The former are remote and are not significantly involved in the quotidian lives of the people. Ghosts (*alus*) are of two types, malevolent and benevolent. Malevolent ghosts cause evil: immoral behavior and illness. The people hate and fear them, and much ritual is addressed to them. Belief in evil alus is manifestly functional; it provides the Ifaluk with a theory of disease etiology and, through rituals directed at the alus (e.g., exorcism), with techniques of treatment. Moreover, since Ifaluk ethnopsychology asserts that humans are naturally "good" and "normal," belief in alus provides a cognitive explanation for the existence of "evil" and "defective" individuals. But this belief is also manifestly dysfunctional. The alus are the source of extreme worry, fear, and anxiety, especially about death. "From the point of view of the people, it would be better if there were no alus" (1952:498). Since the manifest dysfunctions appear to outweigh the alus-belief's functions, why should such a belief persist?

The answer lies in a consideration of the latent functions of alus-belief. Ifaluk culture is characterized by a strong ethic of nonaggression, and Spiro reports the absence of aggressive acts even among "persons who may be characterized as having a substantial amount of aggressive drive" (1952:498). This ethic of nonaggression, more positively of sharing and cooperation, and sanctions against aggression and for cooperation are perhaps functional for any society, but especially for the Ifaluk, about 250 people inhabiting an island of about one-half a square mile of land surrounding a square mile of lagoon. Indeed, the ethic is "a necessary condition for the optimal adaptation of a society inhabiting a minute atoll" (1952:501). Given this necessity, the latent functions of alus-belief become clear. An ethic of nonaggression, and even the absence of overt interpersonal aggression, does not negate the fact that "aggressive drives, like other imperious drives, demand expression; if they are not permitted expression they are deflected from their original goal and are either inverted or displaced" (1952:498–499). Although some inversion (introjection, he would say now) of aggression occurs, in large amounts this would provoke the destruction of an individual's personality and, if it occurred in many people, the disintegration of Ifaluk society. This development has not occurred, and so one looks for the displacement of aggression onto an ego-alien object of fear and hatred—and one finds malevolent alus.

Here we have an explanation of the latent functions of belief in alus phrased in terms of the "needs" of the individual (personality integration) and the "needs" of Ifaluk society (the adjustment of individuals within the parameters of a specific biophysical and social environment). The former are the psychological functions served by the belief, the latter its sociological functions. There is an interesting difference in Spiro's treatment of the two needs. He locates the needs of the sociological domain in the functional requirements of atoll ecological adaptation, and to some extent he specifies these (size of the population, size of the island, etc.). But the locus of the psychological need is described, somewhat cryptically, in terms of the "imperious drive" of aggression. Later (as in his autobiographical statement) they will emerge fully as part of a biologically invariant, pancultural "human nature."

Alus-belief serves another psychological function, however, apart from canalizing the displacement of innate aggression. This function involves anxiety: "The Ifaluk experience certain anxieties in childhood which establish a permanent anxiety 'set' in the Ifaluk personality. This anxiety is particularly crippling, for it is free-floating; that is, its source is unknown or repressed, so that there is no way of coping with it. In this connection, belief in *alus* serves another vital latent function for the individual, since it converts a free-floating anxiety into a culturally sanctioned, real fear" (1952:500).

The alus give the Ifaluk an explanation for their anxiety and fear and, through ritual techniques, ways of dealing with them. In sum: "For the Ifaluk individual. . . , the latent function of the cultural belief in *alus* is to protect him from psychological disorganization. Without this belief—or its *psychological equivalent*—the tensions arising within the individual, as a result of his anxieties and repressed aggressions, could well become unbearable" (1952:500–501; emphasis in the original).

In many ways this paper presents an entirely orthodox functional analysis of alus-belief in Ifaluk religion. One might expect this analysis to be quite unobjectionable to social anthropologists of the structural-functional persuasion. True, Spiro spends what might seem to them an inordinate amount of time discussing the psychological functions of the belief, but no structural-functionalist, to my knowledge, has ever denied that religion served psychological functions. Moreover, Spiro does not ignore the important sociological functions which the belief serves. Radcliffe-Brown would be pleased to see social order maintained and social solidarity enhanced on this Micronesian atoll. But a careful reading of the paper shows the differences between Spiro's functionalism and Radcliffe-Brown's. The distinction occurs at three points: (1) the careful use of functionalist terms to avoid common misuses of the logic of functional analysis; (2) location of the necessary conditions for social solidarity in a system external to Ifaluk society itself, that is, in the requirement of adaptation to a specific, external, biophysical environment; and most important (3) in the clear, if here (1952) implicit, separation of the causal from the purely functional aspects of the analysis. I will take each point in turn.

Functional and Causal Analyses

On the Logic of Functionalism. Both Merton (1949) and Hempel (1952, 1965), among others, have criticized many functionalists for their sloppy use of terms, which often led to logical flaws in their analyses. A common flaw relates to what Hempel (1965:311) called "the assumption of functional indispensability." Assume that a given cultural "item," *i*, like alus-belief, has the effect of satisfying a need (a necessary condition, *n*), like social solidarity, by which a social system, *s*, functions adequately under conditions, *c*, at some time, *t*. This formulation of a common functionalist argument is unobjectionable as long as one does not transform it into a syllogism whose conclusion asserts an *explanation* of the presence of *i* at *t* in *s*! (which is precisely what many functionalists do). For this assertion would presuppose "that only the presence of trait *i* could effect the satisfaction of condition *n*" (Hempel 1965:310). In our case, it would mean asserting that *only* belief in alus could effect the displacement of aggression, the binding of anxiety, and the maintenance of social order. While one may want to claim the functional indispensability of a given cultural item (belief, ritual, institution, etc.) on purely logical grounds to protect the validity of the syllogism, surely to do so would be "highly questionable on empirical grounds: in all concrete cases of application, there do seem to exist alternatives" (Hempel 1965:311). At most one can say that there exists a class of items, *I*, all of whose members are empirically sufficient for the satisfaction of *n*. Item *i* might be a member of this class, but so might *j* (say, sorcery) or many others. If this is the case, then we do not "explain" the presence of *i* (alus-belief) by noting its presence in *s*: to do so would be tautological. Rather, to explain *i* we must establish, either deductively or inductively, "adequate grounds for *expecting* i *rather than one of its alternatives*" (Hempel 1965:313; emphasis added). In Merton's terms, we must heed the possibility that there are "functional equivalents."

Spiro avoids the fallacy of assuming functional indispensability when, in his discussion of aggression and anxiety, he notes that alus-belief "or its *psychological equivalent*" serves to reduce tensions within the individual (1952:500–501). The importance of this seemingly minor caveat became clear in another context, almost a decade after this paper appeared. In the paper Spiro contrasted alus-belief with sorcery and witchcraft. In Burrows and Spiro (1953) he contended that sorcery was absent on Ifaluk. William Lessa (1961) questioned this assertion and assembled a fair amount of evidence, albeit largely circumstantial, which indicated that sorcery existed on the island. He challenged Spiro's overall "psychological hypothesis" about the functions of alus-belief on the basis of the existence of sorcery on Ifaluk at the time of Spiro's fieldwork.

Given the careful wording of the original article, Spiro was able to reply to Lessa with a lecture on logic. Acknowledging that Lessa's evidence cast "substantial doubt" on the ethnographic accuracy of the earlier reports and would affect his "general assessment of the Ifaluk social system and Ifaluk character" (1961c:824), Spiro argued that the existence of sorcery would not undermine his analysis at all, for the simple reason that he had never called alus-belief the *only* "item" which served psychological functions. "Nowhere is it affirmed that the belief in evil spirits is a *necessary* condition for the displacement of hostility. . . . Indeed . . . it does not even suggest that it is a *sufficient* mechanism. . . . However . . . , I consider it to be the most important" (1961c:822; emphasis in the original). This last statement addresses Hempel's comment on the "expectability" of any given item in a class of functional equivalents. Spiro argued (1952:502, 1961c:823–824) that, since alus-belief displaces hostility onto ghosts, while sorcery and witchcraft involve hostility toward living members of one's society, then once again, given the demo-ecological constraints on Ifaluk, alus-belief would be more functional than sorcery or witchcraft. Spiro relies in the latter paper (1961c) on deductive reasoning to provide adequate grounds for expecting alus, since Lessa did undermine his inductive (ethnographic) base.

Next, Spiro draws attention to some of Lessa's own logical slips. Lessa wrote that, in satisfying the functional requirements of a tiny atoll society, the Ifaluk did *not* "shun" sorcery to "turn to" the alus (Lessa 1961:820). Spiro agrees: sorcery and alus might be functional equivalents, though there is reason to expect that the latter is necessary, if not sufficient, while the former is neither. But, Spiro continues, since he had emphasized the *latent* functions of alus-belief, it would be incorrect to assert, as Lessa did, that the Ifaluk "turned to" alus to satisfy latent needs: to do so is to mistake function for cause; to propose an illegitimate teleology. If one is to search for the causes of cultural "items," one must look not to their consequences but rather to their antecedents.

On "Internal" versus "External" Requirements. While Radcliffe-Brown recognized that social systems must adapt to their physical environments (as in Radcliffe-Brown 1952:9), he focused almost exclusively on the "institutional" adaptation which occurs internal to the social system itself. Thus, for example, the "economic machinery of a society . . . is a means of maintaining a certain [social] structure"; the legal system "is a part of the machinery by which a certain social structure is maintained" (1940b:197, 199) and so on through religion, kinship, totemism, taboo, and joking relations. Put another way, the functional requirements which institution or custom serve are for the most part endogenously generated "by" the social system (e.g., the need for solidarity) and endogenously "satisfied" as well. In contrast, Spiro treats the functional requirements of Ifaluk society as generated largely in systems external to the society as such, for example, in an atoll ecosystem. The argument takes the form of a statement of necessary conditions: optimal adaptation (to environment) is possible *only if* high social solidarity is maintained (sharing, cooperation, lack of overt interpersonal

Kevin Avruch

aggression, etc.). Once again, Spiro is separating the causal from the functional. We move on to this distinction in the third point.

On Causality. Spiro's careful use of functional terms and his differentiation among sorts of functional requirements cleared the way for his specifically causal analysis of alus belief. The "causes" are to be found in systems analytically "external" to the Ifaluk social system, but Spiro chose not to elaborate further on Ifaluk's ecosystem. Rather, he focused on Ifaluk personality in a paper (1953) which built on the brief mention (1952:500) of the Ifaluk "anxiety set," formed in childhood. Here we see the explicit separation of cause from function and the identification of the former with perception and the psychodynamics of motivation. Here are laid the foundations of Spiro's program in culture and personality.

The paper begins with a rejection of naive "cultural determinism" as constituting an explanation for the continued existence in a society of any cultural "item" (belief, institution, ritual, etc.). "The mere existence of an institution as part of the cultural heritage is *not* a sufficient condition for its acceptance by members of the society" (1952:239; emphasis in the original). The "acceptance" of any cultural item by an individual implies that the item, which is part of a cultural heritage "external" to the individual, is "internalized" by him, that is, it is "learned."[4] It is not enough, moreover, simply to elucidate the functional consequences of a cultural item. Its origins (in learning) and its consequences are, analytically, as Durkheim noted, two separate issues. Thus it is true that alus-belief "does have important adaptive and adjustive consequences (Spiro 1952), but to identify the consequences of the belief with the drive for its learning would leave us in a most serious circle" (1953:242).

In this quotation Spiro sees the general problem of learning in terms of "drive." This focus is, of course, consonant with the psychological theories of learning—those of Hull, Miller, and Dollard, for example, which Spiro considers but rejects for their overreliance on simple stimulus-response models derived from research with infrahuman (nonsymbolizing) species. But the idea of "drive" raises the question of motivation, which Spiro pursues at length. First, however, there is the problem of the "stimulus" itself to be addressed, the existence and acceptance by Ifaluk of the alus. This is a problem in perception.

From the work of Bruner (1951) and Postman (1951), and implicitly from earlier work in gestalt psychology on the structuring of perceptual fields, Spiro borrows the notion of "hypothesis." This refers to "frames of reference" learned by individuals in interaction with others by which "the nature of one's world is inferred from the perception of it" (1953:245). In the case of alus, we are dealing with perceptions of beings who are threatening, terrifying, feared, and hated. And since even young children hold these conceptions, we must look to early experiences of Ifaluk childhood in which this hypothesis arises.

Spiro identifies two main sources for the hypothesis in a process of child rearing that is otherwise highly indulgent and "infant centered." The first, beginning at birth, is a daily bathing of the infant in the cold water of the lagoon. Although the baby is otherwise "the master of his environment" whose "slightest cry" in other circumstances elicits immediate adult response, this daily trauma, over which he has no control, proceeds despite his vociferous objections. This repetitive "primitive kinesthetic" perception of the world as potentially (or better: reliably) frustrating is strengthened with the birth of a sibling. With that event, the period of great indulgence is over. "The older child is now left to shift for himself emotionally; many of his cries go unheeded and many of his needs are frustrated. Thus the Ifaluk infant . . . is exposed to a highly threatening experience—the apparent loss of parental love" (1953:246–247). Examining the belief in alus, benevolent and malevolent, Spiro points to a number of "isomorphisms between this belief and the culturally patterned childhood experiences we have discussed" (1953:247). These isomorphisms include: the sex of the most vicious alus (female, as are the caretakers who bathe the infant); the kind of connection to any individual of the most potent alus, good or evil (the ghosts of one's matrilineage, as the living of one's matrilineage are the most potent individuals in the child's life); the ability of the alus to prevent or cure illness (the loved, "good" parent) or to attack and cause illness (the terrifying, "bad" parent); the seeming indiscriminateness of the alus's wrath (as the parents to a child seem indiscriminate in their rejection of him). In this way the culturally constituted belief in alus in the world accords with a child's experience of the world: it is a world dichotomized as pleasure-pain, assurance-threat, a world in which powerful, capricious, all-good or all-evil beings come to enjoy the status of a "programmatic, cognitive truth."

But if these isomorphisms account for the psychological origins of alus belief, how can we explain its persistence after childhood? If beliefs are to remain salient, charged, and capable of motivating behavior in adults—as the alus-belief does—then these beliefs must be reinforced and confirmed in their truth by experience. Thus Spiro considers some pschodynamics of Ifaluk personality. He returns to the ethic of nonaggression and the strong sanctions against expressing hostility. He notes the shame associated with a person's sense of such hostility in himself. Given an ethnopsychology that asserts the goodness of all men, whence the hostility? From the stresses of socialization and strains of everyday life, says the analyst;[5] from evil alus, say the Ifaluk. And where does the hostility go? Toward the alus. The alus symbolize all evil people, including oneself, and one is evil on Ifaluk to the extent that one experiences one's own hostility and one's ill wishes for others. Made cognitively and perceptually true by experiences of childhood, the belief in alus "continues to persist in adulthood, because it is re-created by the pschodynamics of Ifaluk personality functioning" (1953:250).

Whereas the 1952 paper was an "orthodox" elucidation of the functions, manifest and latent, of alus-belief, distinguished perhaps by a more scrupulous use of functionalist language and probably congenial to a Radcliffe-Brownian social anthropologist, the 1953 piece was something very different. It was concerned with psychological causes as distinguished from functions. It was concerned with ontogenetic (rather than phylogenetic or culture-historical) origins and with persistence. These concerns and distinctions— cause and function, origin and persistence, and cognition, perception, and motivation—are central to an understanding of Spiro's program. They recur, refined and developed again and again throughout his work. They are fundamental to Spiro's notion of adequate scientific explanation in anthropology. They are fundamental, as we shall see, to his implication of psychoanalytic personality theory in such explanation. And they serve as the adversarial ground from which he addressed a body of structural-functional anthropology.

Burmese Witches

The fairly lengthy attention I have given Spiro's earliest work is intended not only to review that important thinking but also to provide a basis for demonstrating the constancy in his thought. This constancy can be seen as we turn from the Ifaluk studies to his work on Burma, produced more than two decades later.[6] Although one can go to the monographs (1967, 1970, 1977) for evidence, a piece as short and focused as those on Ifaluk serves the purpose equally well. The piece is entitled "The Psychological Functions of Witchcraft Belief: The Burmese Case" (1969a).

According to this paper, the Burmese live in a world populated by supernaturals, both benevolent and malevolent. The malevolent (or potentially malevolent) include nats, demons, ogres, and witches. Malevolence, or hostility, is not confined to the spirit world; Spiro identifies a perceptual set, or stance, which is hostile and characteristic of Burmese interpersonal relations, as well. This stance may be summarized as "everybody hates me." In conjunction with the Burmese belief in witches, this outlook makes the Burman suspicious of all his fellows, and in conjunction with a general Burmese belief in supernaturals, the stance allows the Burman to attribute any harm that may befall him to the spirits' malevolent or punitive intentions. The perceptual set, then, both reflects and reinforces these beliefs; in terms of his psychological reality, the Burman expects harm from any quarter; in terms of a culturally constituted reality, the Burman expects this harm to emanate from supernatural sources.

Spiro reasons that, if witches do not ("really") exist, the Burmese who believe in them impute their characteristics, such as the desire to harm. If this reasoning is valid, he continues, one could suggest that the Burmese individual's perception of the hostility of his fellows is likewise imputed. At this point Spiro invokes two psychological mechanisms as an explanation. A perception (hostility) may be *generalized* from one aspect of the social field to other aspects, or segments, and a drive (hostility) may be *projected* from oneself onto others.

In order to account for the origins of this perceptual set, Spiro looks to early experiences in Burmese socialization. Here, he finds, after an initial period of nurturance, the child is coldly rejected by his parents. The child perceives his parents as rejecting—a hostile perception—and generalizes this perception to other segments of his social field. Because of the rejection, the child feels hostility toward his parents (and others). Psychoanalytic theory would lead us to expect this to be an anxiety-producing situation (i.e., one of drive-conflict) and to expect various defense mechanisms to strive to reduce this anxiety. One such mechanism is projection, whereby an ego-drive (e.g., hostility) is made ego-alien. Spiro maintains that both processes are at work. Perceiving others as hostile, the child becomes hostile to them. Feeling threatened (especially in the context of a Buddhist ethic), he projects his own hostility onto them. Moreover, a cultural belief in witches allows the immature ego to externalize its own destructive drives and to project them onto a culturally constituted belief in destructive beings. A psychological reality is transformed into a cultural reality: witches are cognized and perceived as real.

But Spiro is not only interested in explaining the (ontogenetic) origin of this perceptual set and its relation to Burmese witches. The paper is entitled "The Psychological Functions of Witchcraft Belief," and the problem of persistence is involved. Belief in witches, Spiro submits, is a culturally constituted defense mechanism that functions to keep "paranoidlike" behavior from becoming "paranoid" behavior. The latter, one presumes, would be dysfunctional with respect both to the individual Burman and to Burmese society as a whole. Belief in the existence of witches serves to bifurcate the aggressive drive into two components, a hostile component and a harmful component. Thus, although the typical Burman perceives his fellows as hostile to him, he does not perceive them as harmful to him. And although he perceives witches as harmful, he does not normally perceive them as hostile to him. It is when the two components conjoin—as in a witchcraft attack or

27

accusation—that is, when a Burman perceives a particular individual as (1) a witch and (2) hostile to him, that paranoid (i.e., persecutory) behavior is evident. Thus if a *personal* orientation is the perceptual basis for a belief in the existence of witches (an orientation that reinforces the cultural belief that witches exist), then the *cultural* belief serves to short-circuit the potentially pathological consequences of the personal perceptual set. In other words, the culturally constituted behavioral environment in which witches exist prevents (for most Burmese most of the time) paranoidlike behavior from becoming paranoid behavior. As long as the two components of aggression, hostility and harmfulness, are kept apart, Burmese personality and society are defended against pathological and disruptive consequences. The witch, as a cultural category, channels the harmful component of aggression away from oneself and away from one's fellow Burmese.[7]

There are important differences in Spiro's analyses of the Ifaluk and Burmese material. Ethnographic ones are paramount. Ifaluk ethnopsychology holds that all men are good; the Burmese holds the precise opposite. The richness of the Burmese spirit world—with its nats, witches, ogres, demons, and gods and goddesses—makes that of the Ifaluk seem meager by comparison. And of course one must consider the encapsulation of the Burmese spirit world in the great tradition of a world religion, Therevada Buddhism, which presents special problems in analysis and gives form to the substance of *Burmese Supernaturalism* and *Buddhism and Society.* The former work is concerned in part with the articulation of a Burmese (and, Spiro claims, a Southeast Asian) animistic supernaturalism and Buddhism. These two distinct religious systems are in some ways antithetical. The latter work explores the problem of different construals of Buddhism itself, within the Theravada tradition. The central problematic has to do with the canonical and normative religious system of sacred texts and the lived religion of social actors. The normative religion, with the attainment of nirvana as its soteriological goal—and whatever its philosophical appeal or metaphysical elegance—is insufficient, Spiro maintains, to satisfy crucial psychological needs. For social actors, many of these needs are more proximate than final release from the Wheel of Rebirth. The analysis then focuses on the difference between "religion-in-doctrine" and "religion-in-use" (cf. Spiro 1982b), as exemplified in the institution of monkhood and the personalities of Burmese monks. Indeed—if we may leave religion for kinship momentarily—the argument that cultural systems do not exist in splendid isolation from the minds of social actors but are crucially implicated in (and by) those minds also informs Spiro's work *Kinship and Marriage in Burma* (1977).

Nevertheless, the structure of the analysis of the Burmese material, the logic of its development, the explanatory apparatus employed, and its thrust are, in my opinion, in line with, and remarkably similar to, those of the Ifaluk papers of the 1950s. Here again is evidence of constancy.

Social Systems and Personality

The theoretical work of the first period—that period which I explored using Ifaluk ethnography—reached its zenith in two papers published originally in 1961 (Spiro 1961a, b). Two other important papers which followed these, one on cultural defense mechanisms, to which I alluded above (Spiro 1965a), and the other on problems in defining religion (Spiro 1966b), used material from fieldwork in Burma and began to address issues with which I will deal in considering the second set of Spiro's adversaries. In the 1961 papers, however, Spiro formulated most forcefully and programmatically his thoughts on the relationship of personality to social systems, and in both papers he explicitly addressed a Radcliffe-Brownian "British structuralism" on the demerits of systematically excluding "psychological variables" from analyses.[8] Both papers build explicitly upon the distinction between cause and function and between origin and persistence, in the argument for including "motivation," psychologically construed, as the crucial variable in the analysis of social systems.

"Social Systems, Personality, and Functional Analysis" (1961b) takes as its central problem questions of social control and social conformity, that is, *the* questions of structural-functional anthropology. Given that "adequate" amounts of social control and individual conformity are necessary conditions for the continued existence of any social system—though the range of "adequacy," especially its minima, is rarely specified—part of the question becomes "how must individuals behave in order to conform?" as well as "how is control maintained and conformity induced," often with the tag "by the social system?" Many social philosophers have addressed these questions—Rousseau, Hobbes, Marx, Freud, Durkheim, and others. With these questions Spiro begins, first by dismissing the position of a naive cultural determinism (cf. 1953) which holds in effect that people perform the "activities" of their social system "because it's part of their culture" (1961b:94). This assertion does not take us very far; indeed, as explanation it is compelling only in that it may ultimately be recast as tautology. Spiro notes that, with respect to the control-conformity question, "what a person *must* do in order to participate in a given social system is not identical with what he *can* do, [and] it may be inconsistent with what he would *like* to do" (1961b:99; emphasis in the original). The problematic of social conformity is now rephrased in terms that emphasize potential conflict, conflict "between" person and social system. Spiro quotes Erich Fromm: "In order that any society may function well, its members must acquire the kind of character which makes them *want* to act in the way they *have* to act as members of the society. . . . They have to *desire* what objectively is *necessary* for them to do" (in Spiro 1961b:103–104; emphasis in the original).

In this way the second question ("how is control maintained and conformity induced?") now becomes "how is 'duty' transformed into 'desire'?" And Spiro begins by considering the tag which is often appended, namely "*by* the social system" itself.

A social system may usefully be considered in terms of its component parts: subsystems (e.g., a kinship system), institutions (e.g., the family), and roles (e.g., "father" or "mother" within the family). While social groups in a society cohere in institutions, and institutions in subsystems, if our interest now lies in understanding a *person's* transformation of duty to desire, we must direct our attention to the level of role. "The role . . . is the smallest unit of a social system; the operation of the social system, ultimately and most directly, depends on the proper performance of roles" (1961b:98). To this statement a sociologically oriented theory such as structural-functionalism would raise no objections. In order then to explain proper role-performance, such a theory might invoke a notion such as "norms," which are learned and which operate "on" the individual with a Durkheimian "moral force." Since moral force by itself might not be sufficient to induce conformity (though it will be argued as going a long way), such a theory would seek also to specify special techniques of social control, positive or negative "sanctions," which would carry the force of reward or punishment with them. Together, norms and sanctions explain the proper performance of roles.

Leaving aside "moral force" for the moment, we see that Spiro agrees that sanctions are part of the explanation. He agrees that such sanctions, what he calls "extrinsic social control," are universal. He denies, however, that they are always, or even often, of paramount importance. And he notes that in any case this sociological theory, "despite the anti-psychological bias of many of its proponents (Radcliffe-Brown . . .), is essentially a motivational theory. No social sanction can *compel* a person to conform; it can only *motivate* him to do so" (1961b:102; emphasis in the original). To the extent that extrinsic social control ensures proper role-performance, we are dealing with "extrinsic cultural motivation"; insofar as we are dealing with motivation at all (and especially if sanctions act to oppose an individual's personal motives), then the analysis of conformity cannot "avoid the concept of personality" (1961b:103). The concept of the smallest unit of a social system does double-duty. It is a way of speaking sociologically and psychologically at the same time; analytically it articulates personality with social systems (cf. Avruch 1982:99–102). The place of role in the analysis of a social system is then immediately clear. Spiro must, however, specify its place in an analysis of the personality system. He does so by arguing that, since roles are learned, we must look first to a model of learning and second to a context of learning. His model of ontogenetic learning is undergirded by concepts from psychoanalytic theory, especially "cathexis." The context is socialization.

Viewing personality as a motivational system, Spiro begins by designating "drives" as independent variables (cf. Spiro 1953:242). A drive is defined as "some felt tension or discomfort . . . in a psychological, not a physiological, sense" (1961b:100–101), which the organism continually strives to reduce. A "goal" is some cathected object that reduces the drive. That "act" which is instrumental in the attainment of a goal becomes behaviorally patterned. Because of man's noninstinctual behavioral plasticity, the range of goals that can reduce drives is potentially great. A number of these goals, however, if cathected, would be dysfunctional with respect to the persistence of a social system, and the same is true of the acts by which they are attained. The attainment of certain goals via certain acts is thus proscribed; other goals (acts) are reinforced; and still others are prescribed, by agents of socialization in the course of passing on a "cultural heritage." Thus a "canalization" occurs such that drives are connected to certain goals; this drive-goal connection is termed "needs." Goals are cathected; it is necessary also for needs to be cathected if their satisfaction is to reduce (psychologically prior) drives. And this, writes Spiro, "is the function of child-training. In the process of socialization, children acquire not only drives, but they acquire goals as well; they learn which objects or events—the culturally prescribed goals—are drive reducing" (1961b:105). Socialization, then, transforms culturally stipulated goals into personally cathected ones, and a need can now be defined as the personal cathexis of a culturally stipulated goal. Needs replace drives as the appropriate independent variable in describing cultural motivation (cf. Spiro 1953). However, Spiro adds a qualification which is fundamental to his program. For while both needs and cultural goals, arising in socialization to particular cultural heritages,

> are parochial, most human drives—because of their rootedness in a common biology and in common conditions of social life—are probably universal. Hence, it is generally not too difficult to demonstrate (on a fairly high level of generality, of course) that the quite diverse goals of different societies, as well as the roles which are instrumental for their attainment, are functionally equivalent; they serve to gratify the same drives. [1961b:104]

The implication is that, if knowledge about needs is necessary to *describe* (or, to foreshadow, "to understand") a culture's motivational system, knowledge of drives is necessary to *explain* cultural motivation. Thus any "description" of needs and cultural goals is essentially an ideographic endeavor, part of "the ethnography," *while the analysis of the connection between needs, goals, and drives is nomothetic.* (And the theory that guides the analysis is psychoanalytic theory.)

In any event, the above quotation makes clear how roles are implicated in the personality system. Since behavior is motivated, and since psychological needs must be satisfied (i.e., prior drives must be reduced) if a personality is to remain integratively functional, the performance of certain behaviorally patterned and culturally stipulated acts—roles—depends on their satisfaction of personal needs (or the expectation that they will do so). When goals attained in the performance of social roles do satisfy personality needs, then "not only are the functional requirements of individual and society satisfied simultaneously, but the functional requirement of each is satisfied by an attribute of the other; that is, personality drives serve to instigate the performance of social roles, and the performance of roles serves to gratify personality drives" (1972:590).

This quotation is a masterpiece of teleological reasoning. Two systems, personality and social, are implicated in their mutual dependence for the satisfaction of their respective, ultimate, requirements: functional integrity. But as it stands, the statement also commits the sins of teleology. We must deal directly with notions of purposiveness, with the philosopher's hornet's nest of intentionality.

Teleology and the Unconscious

The critique is most easily mounted against teleological analyses of social systems: how, it is asked, can one speak of a monolithic, systemic intentionality when the system is composed of an aggregate of diverse, and some perverse, individuals? Radcliffe-Brown sought to circumvent the criticism by invoking the "think of society as an organism" analogy. But the point is precisely that societies are *not* organisms. Perhaps we should use Hempel as our touchstone here, not the least because, as his citations suggest, Spiro would have done so.[9] Hempel writes of the danger of assimilating such functional analyses as those found in biology to the social and behavioral sciences. The danger stems from mistaking "function" in an empirically demonstrable self-regulating system (e.g., an organism) for "purpose." In the social sciences, "psychologically, the idea of function often remains closely associated with that of purpose, and some functionalist writing has no doubt encouraged this association, by using a phraseology which attributes to the self-regulatory behavior of a given system practically the character of a purposeful action" (Hempel 1965:321). He adds that this "attribution of purposes is an illegitimate transfer of the concept of purpose from its domain of significant applicability to a much wider domain, where it is devoid of objective empirical import," in which case "the attribution of purposes . . . has therefore no scientific meaning" (1965:327–328).

Spiro would very likely agree with this statement, but his strategy seeks to make this criticism not germane to *his* analyses. For we may recall that (in the quotation above) "personality drives serve to instigate the performance of social roles" so questions of purposes and intentionality are deflected from social systems to personality systems. This assertion has one great advantage. Societies are not organisms, but personality is "situated in" human beings. And human beings, even if they are massively symbolizing creatures, are organisms qua "creatures." Thus such concepts as "goals," "motives," and "purposes," applied to personality, may yet remain within a "domain of significant applicability" and may yet possess "scientific meaning." That is, they may do so if Spiro is able to avoid another sort of illegitimate teleology, the unwarranted attribution of motives to the "organisms" themselves. And he does so by invoking the fundamentum of Freud's insights, the unconscious.

Spiro invokes the unconscious in the context of his functional argument. The argument asserts "that personality plays an important part in the operation of social systems because, by motivating the performance of social roles, it enables the social system to serve its social functions" (1961b:108). But the hoary problem of intentionality remains if personality functions are conceived only as manifest ones, those recognized by the individual. Spiro is able to extend the explanatory range of manifest functions by refining Merton's (1949) paradigm. Merton conflated " 'intention' and 'recognition.' As he defines them, manifest functions are those which are both intended and recognized, while latent functions are those which are neither intended nor recognized" (Spiro 1961b:123, n. 7). Spiro separates intention from recognition and is thus able to speak of manifest functions, some of which have consequences that are unintended from the actor's point of view. This distinction, it should be noted, does no violence to a philosopher's notion of intentionality, since several have pointed out, for example, that "behavior which is intentional under one description of it, need not be intentional under another" (Von Wright 1971:26; see also Anscombe 1957). But even the idea of manifest unintended consequences will not empower our explanation fully; moreover it is not enough simply to invoke latent but *unintended* functions—as Merton defines "latency"—since then we would once again face the problem of unwarranted attribution of motives (by their intentions) to the actors. Instead, Spiro completes his refinement of Merton's paradigm by speaking of latent functions which are, "under one description" of them, *intended.* Can such a creature exist? Spiro replies, of course, "that the paradox of an intended but unrecognized function is apparent rather than real, becomes clear when one considers that motives may be unconscious, as well as conscious. In short, manifest (recognized) functions are served by the performance of roles when at least one of the motives for their performance is conscious; latent (unrecognized) functions are served when at least one of the motives for their performance is unconscious" (1961b:108).

In pursuing the idea of unconscious motivation, Spiro returns to socialization. Drives, goals, and acts are canalized—and needs are engendered—at some psychic cost. For although a cultural heritage provides for need by prescribing those acts (roles included) which satisfy them, at the same time, (and often necessarily with respect to the persistence of the social system) "it prohibits other means which this relatively plastic and imaginative animal may come to prefer. Moreover, it may completely prohibit any conceivable (manifest) expression or reduction of certain drives. But motives do not disappear simply because they are prohibited" (1961b:109). That is, while they *may* disappear from the manifest, recognized, or conscious awareness of actors, so that we must speak cautiously of intentionality, they reappear—repressed—in the unconscious. And as "imperious drives" they must be reduced if the organism is to remain integratively functional.

Intentionality is thus rendered latent but remains teleologically defensible. Indeed, by using the notion of unconscious motivation, and the host of psychodynamic processes implicated by postulating the unconscious, Spiro is able to claim that more than a teleologically functional explanation has been offered. For once we grant the validity of unconscious motivation, then, in Hempel's words, "explanation by reference to motives, objectives, or the like may be perfectly legitimate in the case of purposive behavior and its effects. *An explanation of this kind would be causal in character*, listing among the causal antecedents of the given action, or of its outcome, certain purposes or motives on the part of the agent, as well as his beliefs as to the best means available to him for attaining his objectives" (1965:327; emphasis added). Thus Spiro is able to claim that he has achieved the paragon of scientific analysis à la Hempel, namely a causal analysis. Not only is his separation of cause from function—contra Radcliffe-Brown—now complete, but he has, by implicating personality and its psychodynamics, shown that functional explanations "either are ultimately causal or else they are not explanatory" (1967:65, and see 1968a:559–560).

Of course, in reading the last part of Hempel's statement, which refers to the motives of the agent and "his beliefs" about the "best ways available to him for attaining his objectives," one may want to argue that Spiro speaks well beyond the brief that Hempel provides. It is crucial, then, to grant the *validity* of unconscious motivation, with its latent though intended consequences, in order to expand the range and "domain of significant applicability" of such ideas as "agent," "purpose," "motive," "belief," and "best ways" of attainment (the last are often faute de mieux, psychoculturally speaking). There are reasons to suspect (and some of them will be adduced soon) that Hempel himself might be reluctant to grant this validity to the unconscious. But Spiro, most assuredly, is not (Spiro 1961b:113–114).

Social Control and Conformity

"Social Systems, Personality, and Functional Analysis" concludes by returning to the problem of social control and conformity, the transformation of desire into duty. To the "extrinsic social control" of social sanctions Spiro adds two other types. "Intrinsic social control" refers to much of our discussion of (intrinsic) cultural motivation, whereby culturally stipulated goals are cathected (becoming needs), and conformity is achieved in role-performances which satisfy these needs. This type of motivation is based on "id-ego" need, Spiro asserts, and in turning to the superego of the Freudian trinity, he discusses, finally, "internalized cultural motivation," by which "proper"performance of roles satisfies the no less imperious needs of the superego. "To put it in the terms we have been employing, if extrinsic control is achieved (in the case of positive sanctions) by the cathexis of the social sanction, and if intrinsic control . . . by the cathexis of the cultural goal, internalized control is achieved by the cathexis of the cultural norm" (1961b:117).

Put simply, violation of (or the intent to violate) norms which have been internalized in the superego during socialization arouses "moral anxiety." Psychoanalytically understood, such anxiety is a drive as powerful as any libidinal one and must be reduced. Whether the agents of socialization are themselves "introjected," the norms also being internalized, in a super-ego (producing "guilt-oriented" cultures), or whether only the norms are internalized (producing "shame-oriented" cultures), the basis for conformity is the same: the reduction and avoidance of moral anxiety. Thus Spiro rein-terprets the Durkheimian "moral force" of a society's norms (see above). He concludes by again asserting the ineluctable *motivational* character of our most important variables, by searching for causes among the functions.

The Problem of Nonconformity

"Culture and Personality: An Overview and Suggested Reorientation" (1961a) begins where "Social Systems, Personality, and Functional Analysis" (1961b) left off: "Instead of merely asking how the social system influences the development and structuring of personality, we are now equally interested in how personality affects the functioning of social systems" (1961b:121). Spiro recommends that the conceptual status of personality be

changed from explanandum, as it was in older culture-and-personality theories (and in a Durkheimian derived social anthropology when it was considered at all), to explanans, from dependent to independent variable
(1972:585).

As the earlier explication of the tripartite modes of social control might
suggest, Spiro had now rejected his early (1951) unitarian view of culture
and personality in favor of a Parsonian classification (1972:589, n. 5). He
once again addressed the social anthropologists directly—Radcliffe-Brown,
Firth, and Gluckman—on the defects of rejecting psychological explanation;
such rejection "can only lead to truncated, if not false, theories" (1972:583).
His discussion of Gluckman's "rituals of rebellion," in particular, presents a
critique of a nascent symbolic anthropology, repeated in more detail in an
exchange with Edmund Leach (Spiro 1966b, 1968b) which I shall consider
later.

Perhaps most important, this paper contains a discussion of social non-
conformity. Cultural norms may be "irksome" or not sufficiently internalized;
social structural constraints may deny certain individuals or groups access
to valued roles (e.g., discrimination against American blacks); or a drive may
have no means of culturally stipulated satisfaction because "the drive itself
is culturally disapproved" (1972:592). This discussion allows Spiro to extend his functional analysis in the direction of explaining social change,
viewed in the context of the breakdown of social controls. "Frustrated
drives . . . provide one motivational source for social-cultural change
. . . [and] an important motivational basis for the disruption of social systems" (1972:595-596).

But these remarks are offered as "preliminary suggestions" for the
study of change, and Spiro returns quickly to his major concern, that of the
persistence of social systems. The rest of the paper contains a sketch, developed later (Spiro 1965a), of the "various mechanisms of ego defense,"
notably repression, displacement, and sublimation, to which Freud pointed
in his investigations of the unconscious. These "culturally constituted defense
mechanisms," as Spiro terms them, become fundamentally important in his
later analysis of Burmese folk religion (1967) and the Theravada Buddhist
institution of monkhood (1970). In this context, however, their importance
lies in the fact that they deflected Spiro from a full-scale consideration of
social change in favor of an elaboration of the bases of persistence.

In 1966 Spiro published a paper on problems in the definition and
explanation of religion. According to the view that I develop here, it is a
transitional paper. On the one hand, he recapitulated arguments which he
had distilled earlier (1961a, 1961b). He addressed his adversaries again,
criticizing Durkheim for the vacuous notion of "the sacred"; Evans-Pritchard
for refusing to offer any substantive definition of religion; Firth for his re-

luctance to allow the "inner states" of participants in ritual within the anthropologist's purview; and finally Radcliffe-Brown for his misuse of functionalist logic. First, Spiro writes, Radcliffe-Brown once again confused function with cause by an illegitimate transformation of religion from a sufficient condition for the satisfaction of a structural requirement (social solidarity) to a necessary one. Not only, then, is an explanation of religion's origins invoked when it should not have been, but the explanation of persistence is botched. Second, even if we grant the structural-functional epitome, that the function of religion is to produce social solidarity, we should relize that we have then "explained" social solidarity, not religion. (For in that statement religion is the explanans and social solidarity the explanandum.)

On the other hand, the concerns of this paper point forward: a few thrusts at Leach on the nature of cultural symbols and their explanation would occasion a further exchange (Leach 1967, Spiro 1968b) and did foreshadow some of the themes championed by Spiro's next adversaries. More explicitly, Spiro himself spoke of transition. In his autobiographical essay he wrote of "the influence of Max Weber, whose religious sociology I became acquainted with only after returning from Israel. The *Protestant Ethic* opened my mind to a point of view and method of analysis which were revolutionary and enormously exciting . . . ,[and his other work] stimulated an interest in Asia and Asian religions" (1978b:346).

In the conclusion of the 1966 piece Spiro noted that, although the paper was concerned mainly with the sociological and psychological functions of religion, it did not touch upon the "crucial problems," Weberian-inflected ones of suffering, redemption, and theodicy. Broadly put, these are problems of "meaning," and they began to concern a variety of anthropologists when, in the late 1950s and 1960s, many turned completely away from the concerns of the structural-functionalist's program. Spiro took on these problems, but we cannot say that he has significantly wavered from his earlier construals of functionalism.

The Problem of Self-Regulated Systems and Social Change

It is time to take stock. In arguing for the inclusion of a psychodynamic psychology in the study of culture, Spiro opposed not so much the culturology of White or the superorganicism of Kroeber as the social anthropology of Radcliffe-Brown. Focusing on the operation of social systems, Spiro met Radcliffe-Brown on his own ground, that of functional explanation. Meticulously applying the logic of functional inquiry, Spiro sought to disentangle function from cause. In this way, methodologically as well as epistemologically, he was able to respond to charges of "psychologism" or "psychological reductionism" with logical appeals for recognizing the prior problem of motivation. This theme is a central one. "The functional requirements of group existence are satisfied not by the *existence* of customs but by their *performance*" (1968a:563; emphasis in the original). And performance—indeed the very operation of sociocultural systems—"is, in the last analysis, a motivational problem" (1972:605).

Because he chose Radcliffe-Brown's ground, Spiro ended, perhaps paradoxically, by making his most important contributions to Radcliffe-Brownian problems: not to "social solidarity" per se, nor to sibling unity, lineage solidarity, and so forth, but to elucidating the bases on which these granite structural "principles" stand (or fall): the processes by which social control is maintained and conformity induced. In this sense, his elaboration of culturally constituted defense mechanisms is an epochal achievement. But although any psychodynamically informed theory will not slight process for structure, we must yet return to a point raised earlier and ask to what extent the elaboration of these defense mechanisms slighted change for persistence.

Spiro himself might argue that it is a question not of slighting but of priorities. Or (more probably), slipping into his adversarial mode, that, while *other* sorts of functionalism might not be able to deal with change (cf. 1972:585), *his* sort certainly can. Indeed, I have cited above some of his "preliminary suggestions" for investigating the sources of change: drive-frustration and need-frustration due to the constraints of cultural norms or social structures and the various stresses of acculturation (see also 1968a:562–563). He has even, in the last publication cited, indicated that there is a need for culture and personality research to devote more attention to cognitive and perceptual variables in studies of change. Clearly, then, a theory of change is implicit in his theory of persistence, and if so, the most we can say is that he has neglected to pursue substantively, that is, ethnographically, these particular ramifications of the theory. Perhaps. But there is another question. Is it an adequate theory of change?

We return to our touchstone, Hempel. In my earlier discussion I emphasized that Spiro was able to avoid the pitfall of mistaking "function" for "purpose" by designating *personality,* "located" within a demonstrably self-regulating organism, as the relevant, inferentially self-regulating system for explaining the operation of social systems. In this way he deflected the problem of purpose or intentionality from the level of social system, where it is problematic, to personality system, where (as "guiding" an individual's behavior) it may be reasonably presumed to belong. And by postulating the unconscious and sundry "regulatory" mechanisms associated with it— ego defense mechanisms—Spiro was able to extend the range of "significant applicability" of (latent, unconscious) intentionality to empower his explanation.

But for all his care in following Hempel's strictures regarding the logic of functional inquiry, there is one stricture that Spiro did not follow. It may well be "reasonable" to presume that personality, organically situated, is a self-regulating system. Nevertheless, in the *absence* of empirically determined, operationally defined, and at best quantitatively expressed ranges within which regulation or equilibrium can be said to occur, *and* criteria which specify the total ranges of viability of the system (beyond which equilibration is no longer possible), we are seriously limited in an ability *to treat the self-regulatory nature of the system itself as a hypothesis* subject to empirical confirmation (cf. Hempel 1965:323–326). Simply put: *how much* "frustration" does it take to activate a defense mechanism? How much frustration does it take to "overpower" a defense mechanism? At what point does a personality system, pushed beyond its range of viability, dissociate or change?

Of course, "simply put," these sorts of questions seem simpleminded, Baconian, even vulgar. It is as if I were demanding for personality a sort of formulation of "carrying capacity" similar to the ecologist's. We are accustomed to softer, more qualitative, "clinical" assessments about such matters. And here perhaps we can afford them. But the problem arises when one strives to implicate self-regulating personality systems in the explanation of *change* in social-cultural systems. Now the need to specify reference values (defining equilibration) and goal ranges (defining ranges of total systemic viability) becomes acute. Simply put: how many frustrated drives in how many individuals are needed to activate self-regulatory processes? How many such frustrated drives in how many such individuals before the culturally constituted defense mechanisms are overpowered? At what point, then, will the social system cease to function or undergo change? Again, I seem to be demanding an empirically determined, operationally defined, and quantitative figure or range that represents the carrying capacity of a social system. *Yes.* This figure is necessary because without it functional analysis may serve heuristic functions but not explanatory ones—scientific ones—à la Hempel; without it functionalism becomes a "final cause" teleology of the Aristotelian kind (i.e., according to Hempel, the metaphysical kind).

These are strictures that Spiro did not address. He writes of "optimal adaptation," "sufficient" cathexis of goals, of the points at which "cultural pathology will become so extensive that social life is no longer viable" (1961b:103), and so on, but never (to my knowledge) does he confront directly Hempel's dictum "it is of crucial importance to establish appropriate hypotheses of self-regulation in an objectively testable form" (Hempel 1965:317). The personality systems' lack of such specifications compromises their ability to explain change in social-cultural systems. For if such "empirical criteria are lacking" in these hypothetical self-regulating systems, then "in other cases of self-regulating systems"—social-cultural ones—the "attribution of purposes . . . has . . . no scientific meaning" (Hempel 1965:327–328).[10]

To my knowledge, in one paper Spiro attempts to deal substantively with social change in the context of his functional analysis (Spiro 1973).[11] Noting that specific sociological changes have occurred in postcolonial and postindependence Burma—increasing political factionalism, brutal crime, political violence, and insurgency—all of which suggest a generalized weakening of social control, Spiro seeks their origins. Did they have their roots in changes in Burmese psychological character brought about by the deleterious effects of British colonialism, as some students of colonialism suggest? Spiro argues against this interpretation. Examining historical accounts of precolonial Burma, he finds that Burmese character was highly aggressive. But he also identifies a variety of culturally constituted and socially sanctioned institutions—from warfare and the treatment of criminals to "entertainments" of various sorts (cock and buffalo fights, races, etc.)—which served as channels to sublimate and neutralize hostility and aggression. Many of these were proscribed by the British, as warfare was, and vanished as British standards of sport and penology replaced Burmese; the latter never regained their precolonial importance even after the country achieved independence. In their absence, then, or in much weakened forms, drives of aggression and hostility sought their reduction in other acts: in crime, insurgency, and so forth. Thus the character of Burmese personality has remained constant, while exogenous forces (the British) changed the character of the social system; thus changed, it was open to other changes caused by ongoing processes (drive reduction) at the level of the personality system.

This study, Spiro contends, can stand as a "test" of his central hypothesis, that social institutions serve psychological functions. One is testing a relationship of covariance; and since personality remained constant while the disappearance of certain social institutions was accompanied by increasing social disorder along various axes, the hypothesis "seems (albeit indirectly) to have [been] confirmed" (1973:295). I shall not quibble over methodological problems, for example the practical difficulties which might arise in using historical texts (often composed by colonialists with their own goals and biases) to make the sorts of "depth" personality assessments that Spiro's model demands. I shall only observe here that considerable controversy often surrounds the clinically phrased personality assessments presented even by trained ethnographers using personality-sensitive "instruments" of one kind or another. Beyond such quibbles, the fact remains that this study did not address the Hempelian strictures: reference values and ranges of systemic viability were not empirically and independently determined nor operationally defined. And realistically speaking, how could they be?

Spiro seems uneasy here and much less assured than usual. His main point seems to be that in order to study change one must "add" history onto functionalism; this assertion is hardly startling and taken by itself might even seem naive (cf. Barth 1967). Spiro, however, is enlisting history by using it in a specific way. He writes:

> . . . I have attempted in this paper to demonstrate the method-
> ological utility of history in the assessment of theories concerning the
> psychological functions of social institutions. A rigorous, that is, *ex-*
> *perimental,* demonstration of the validity of functional (or, for that
> matter, *causal*) explanations of institutions is of course *impossible* in
> the study of social groups in their natural settings. But natural societies
> have an important dimension that has typically been ignored in func-
> tionalist studies, and this dimension—history—can be used as the
> equivalent of the crucial dimension of an experimental study, namely,
> the control group. [1973:294–295; emphasis added]

To my question, then, of the adequacy of Spiro's theory of change we might respond with Spiro's own doubts about the adequacy of tests designed to confirm or disconfirm it. And if one is doing anthropology according to Hempelian rules and standards, such doubts weigh heavy and loom large. One message that may be gleaned from the passage quoted above is that the anthropologist working within these rules and standards must work as rigorously, ingeniously, and scrupulously as he or she can. But with the "experimental method" as one's exemplar, one must always be prepared to labor as a scientific citizen of the second class.[12]

The Demise of Structural-Functionalism

If throughout this chapter I have stressed Spiro's differences with Radcliffe-Brown, I should close by noting a fundamental similarity. Both men take anthropology to be a science whose concerns are nomothetic and whose goals are *explanations* of sociocultural systems and their institutions. Both men invite evaluation of their work according to these goals. And because both men shared those goals, it seems to me that Spiro's engagement with structural-functional anthropology—on the necessity of including psy-chological variables in the explanation of sociocultural systems—was ex-ceedingly productive. Both social anthropology and psychological anthropology benefited from this engagement of adversaries. But even while Spiro pressed on and refined his attack, the nature of his adversary changed.

For by the 1950s the sturdy house of structural-functional anthropology

41

had begun to crumble, beset from within by some of Radcliffe-Brown's own students and followers. Broadly speaking, these fell into two camps. The first attacked Radcliffe-Brown for his inability to deal with and explain social change; the second for his neglect of the "other side" of Durkheim—collective consciousness and collective representations—the symbolic. Again speaking broadly, each camp pursued certain sorts of problems. The first focused on politics and law, often influenced by Gluckman (e.g., Bailey), or on kinship (Van Velsen), or on religion (Abner Cohen) assimilated to politics. One would place Barth, and the "early" Leach and Turner, in this camp as well. Several took their focus, contra Radcliffe-Brown and like Spiro, to be the individual actor in a social system, with questions of motivation being raised—why are "siblings united" if they are? But these questions were linked to a primitive, often unacknowledged, psychology: man—as political or economic actor—seeks to maximize power or profit, as in the work of Leach and Barth, respectively. Victor Turner (and others) bridged the two camps; his earliest work on the Ndembu bore the stamp of Manchester orthodoxy (Turner 1957), while his later work (beginning with Turner 1967) dealt increasingly with the interpretation of symbols.

The second camp, then, dealt with the "collective representation side" of the *Elementary Forms of the Religious Life* or with Durkheim's interests in primitive classification systems: the work of Mary Douglas is exemplary here. One would have to count as well the great impact of Lévi-Strauss's work (on "later" Leach and Needham, for example), with its injection of Cartesian antibodies into the scholarship of British anthropology.[13]

The first camp constituted a potential adversary that Spiro never fully addressed. But we should recall that he shared with Radcliffe-Brown a concern for explicating the bases of conformity, and his contributions to the study of social change were not a major part of his work. With the second camp, however, Spiro placed himself in an adversarial position: with Lévi-Strauss on the nature of myth (Spiro 1979); with Leach on the interpretation of cultural symbols (Spiro 1966b, 1968b), with Needham on some defects of structural analyses (Spiro 1963). And increasingly, Spiro addressed a growing number of American cultural anthropologists (influenced variously by Lévi-Strauss, linguistics, natural language philosophers, and continental "post-structuralists"), who also took the analysis of cultural symbols to be their central task: in America, Goodenough, Geertz, and Schneider, immensely influential in their own right and through their respective students.

In many ways, these latter anthropologists have presented Spiro with a more serious challenge than Radcliffe-Brown. First, because Radcliffe-Brown and Spiro, whatever their differences, take anthropology to be a science whose goal is *explanation*, while the "symbolists" (to give them a name to which all would undoubtedly object) are less ready to accede to

Hempelian rules or standards in the pursuit of their anthropology. Some would say that the goal of this anthropology is not explanation (either in the deductive-nomological sense or in the inductive-probabilistic sense that Hempel champions), but, hermeneutically, some form of *understanding*.

The second reason why the symbolists' challenge is serious is that, while Radcliffe-Brown and other structural-functionalists merely dismissed Freud, several of the symbolists have sought to appropriate him. I shall return to this point in the next section.

To bring into view the distinction between "explanation" and "understanding," let us turn briefly to Evans-Pritchard, who repudiated Radcliffe-Brown in the 1950 Marett Lecture.

In his programmatic *Theories of Primitive Religion* (1965), Evans-Pritchard presents us with a catalogue of past errors. He first rejects nineteenth-century evolutionist views of religion, both for their conjectural nature and for their reliance on psychology, whether cognitive (the "intellectualism" of Tylor) or affective (the "emotionalism" of Marett—and Freud). He renounces any essentialist definition of religion, saying that, for "the social anthropologist, religion is what religion does" (Evans-Pritchard 1965: 119–120).[14] He repudiates the "too slick" pragmatism of functionalism, à la Malinowski or Radcliffe-Brown. And finally, at the essay's conclusion, he derides the scientist who is also a nonbeliever for seeking some "theory" that purports to "explain" religion. Religion "can truly be grasped only from within," and the scientist who is also a believer seeks not to explain (away?) religion but rather "to understand" it (Evans-Pritchard 1965:121).

THE SECOND ADVERSARY: ON SYMBOLS AND THEIR MEANINGS

Symbolist Anthropology

Now, it would be dangerous, wrong, to have Evans-Pritchard "stand for" all those who eschew explanation for understanding. Evans-Pritchard draws the distinction on the basis of a profound and personal religious belief, something that is (at least evidently) lacking in many others. But the things which he pursues (understanding from "inside"); the things which he avoids (essentialist or even formally denotative or ostensive definitions of religion); and the things which he rejects (explanation either causal or teleological) are all found to some extent in the writings of other symbolists as well.

It would be misleading, too, to take my generic label "symbolist" to the point where it extinguishes all differences in a diverse and ornery group of scholars. The broad distinction between British social and American cultural anthropology remains germane, for example. One needs only to consider Mary Douglas, who assimilates everything in her path to "society," while David Schneider does the same for "culture," to see this distinction in action.[15]

Finally, it would be misleading to give the impression that the symbolists have effectively swept all opposition from the field—even leaving Spiro aside for the moment. In the United States the spirit, if certainly not the letter, of Radcliffe-Brownian functionalism has been transformed and appears vigorous. Now embellished with such cybernetic ideas as "negative feedback," it presents itself as systems analysis in the "new cultural ecology." And—to take one representative from the field—this work has taken into account the full range of Hempel's critique of the older functionalism, if with only partial success (see Rappaport 1968 and 1979, esp. chaps. 3 and 5).

In Great Britain, meanwhile, the symbolists face an older tradition, recrudescent despite Evans-Pritchard's criticism, that of the "intellectualism" of Frazer and Tylor. Here religion and magic are seen as cognitively instrumental, giving believers an explanation of world and cosmos in terms of superhuman agency and by extension a religious/magical technology by which humans believe they can exert a measure of control over world and cosmos. The work of Horton (1960, 1967) may be taken as representative of the "new intellectualism." Skorupski provides a précis of the differences between the intellectualist position (which, with some modification, could hold for Spiro's culture-and-personality theory as well) and that of the symbolists:

> If the key concept of intellectualism is "theory" then the key concept of the alternative approach is "symbol"; and the understanding of magic and religion which is sought is not causal but hermeneutic. . . . Whether or not it [the symbolist approach] grants that there *is* a level at which rituals (magical or religious actions) are instrumental it claims that at the level at which understanding of them is to be sought they are not instrumental at all: they must be grasped as symbolic, expressive, as "showing" and "saying" rather than "doing" [Skorupski 1976:12; emphasis in the original].

The symbolists, then, deny not that religious action or beliefs can have (à la Horton) instrumental, literal meaning but only that "literalism" is mistaken in holding that this literal meaning is the only one to be understood. With this position Spiro, but for different reasons, and by invoking the unconscious, would agree. But the symbolists also contend, in part following Evans-Pritchard, that the problem of understanding is one of "decoding" or "translation," with little "searching for causes which produced the overt, surface form of ritual beliefs" (Skorupski 1976:18). With this position Spiro would strongly disagree.[16]

Explanation and Understanding

By now we have gained some sense of the differences among the symbolists and any one of a number of forms of instrumentalism, whether intellectualist, psychoanalytic, or structural-functional. In a volume entitled *Changing Perspectives in the Scientific Study of Religion* (1974), editor Allan Eister seems to find signs of a sea change. Whereas, he writes, the older (instrumentalist) tradition sought

> to define religion in terms of the object or objects "toward" which it is taken to be directed or in terms of distinctive attitudes or postures towards those objects . . . , others have moved on to ask, not so insistently what religion *is*, but, rather, how language that is called religious is used. . . . they have turned attention away from the substance or "content" explicit in religious belief systems (or implicit in rites or cultures and the like) and toward symbols having their own reality as cultural artifacts regardless of what they "express" "point to" or stand for (that is, symbolize). [Eister 1974:2; emphasis in the original]

Among the "modern scholars" who have "moved on" Eister includes Whitehead, Kenneth Burke, Eliade, Leach, and Mary Douglas. We could certainly add Geertz, Schneider, Sahlins, and others to the list. In any case, Eister contends, religion can no longer be seen as a "generic phenomenon," and religions are no longer "readily identifiable" (Eister 1974:3).

Several related themes, typically phrased as dichotomies, can be discerned in Skorupski and Eister's remarks: "theory" versus "symbol"; "explanation" versus "understanding" (translation or decoding); religion as a generic, definable "object" versus religion as a "language" with which "to say" something about something, and so on. These themes are related as strands of a larger problem: what constitutes the "scientific study of religion" or culture or anything else, for that matter? Posed in this way, the question forms part of an ongoing debate in the philosophy of science, characterized by Von Wright in these terms:

> Two main traditions can be distinguished in the history of ideas, differing as to the conditions an explanation has to satisfy in order to be scientifically respectable. The one tradition is sometimes called *aristotelian*, the other *galilean*. . . . the galilean tradition in science runs parallel with the advance of the casual-mechanistic point of view in man's efforts to explain and predict phenomena, the aristotelian tradition with his efforts make facts teleologically or finalistically understandable. [Von Wright 1971:2–3, emphasis in the original]

In the nineteenth century the battleground on which the two traditions engaged was history: ought it to seek explanation (*Eklären*) or understanding (*Verstehen*) as its goal? Increasingly, as they came into their disciplinary own, the social and behavioral sciences became implicated in the debate. Von Wright notes the many ambiguities on this point in the works of the masters themselves, Marx, Weber, Durkheim, and Freud: the "tensions" between a "causalist" and "hermeneutical-dialectical" orientation—between, in his words, a conception that "explanation consists in making phenomena . . . intelligible rather than predictable from knowledge of their efficient causes" (1971:8). For anthropology, in Evans-Pritchard and Kroeber's day, the tension was expressed in the debate over whether anthropology was itself "history" or "science." Nowadays the lines are more broadly drawn, between the natural sciences and their methods, on the one hand, and the "human" or "moral" sciences, on the other.

Seen in its historical perspective, the debate shows the swing of a pendulum: in one period one tradition seems to reign—but with dissenters ever present—and in the next period, in what the dissenters sometimes dramatize as a counterrevolution (e.g., Rabinow and Sullivan 1979), the pendulum swings the other way, and our journals and anthologies seem filled, for a time at least, with the new orthodoxy. In a complex way these swings correlate with the temper of debate in the fractious community of philosophers. And the debate there is such that social scientists have a surfeit of champions to represent them: Hempel, Nagel, or Popper (to name a few) on one side and the "later" Wittgenstein, Winch, or Kuhn (to name a few) on the other. In the course of the debate, a sort of progress is made. But it is progress, in Geertz's words, "marked less by a perfection of consensus than by a refinement of debate. What gets better is the precision with which we vex each other" (Geertz 1973b:29).

What Von Wright calls the "galilean tradition" appears in the social sciences as one or another form of positivism, characterized by three tenets. The first is

> *methodological monism,* or the idea of the unity of scientific method amidst the diversity of subject matter of scientific investigation. [The] second . . . is the view that the exact natural sciences, in particular mathematical physics, set a methodological ideal or standard which measures the degree of development of all other sciences, including the humanities. [The] third . . . is a characteristic view of scientific explanation. Such explanation is, in a broad sense, "causal". . . . The attitude towards finalistic explanations . . . is either to reject them as unscientific or to try to show that they can, when duly purified of

'animist' or 'vitalist' remains, be transformed into causal explanations. [Von Wright 1971:4; emphasis in the original]

The symbolists' response to these tenets is more or less vehement but uniform. The symbolists reject them.

Spiro's Critique

Spiro, of course, does not reject these tenets. This is the ground of adversarial engagement. But if he met Radcliffe-Brown on the field of functionalism, he meets the symbolists—naturally enough, given the exposition above—on the field of "symbols and their meanings." In one important way, however, the terms of engagement have changed radically. Spiro and Radcliffe-Brown shared the same conception of what anthropology was and of the goals it ought to pursue. The symbolists reject this conception and these goals. Against the symbolists, then, Sprio has not only been obliged to argue for the relevance or necessity of psychological explanations to supplement sociological ones; he must first argue for the relevance and necessity of explanation itself.

In engaging the symbolists Spiro has put forth, at various times, four different though related positions. The first (Spiro 1969b) questioned the conceptual validity of a separately constituted subdiscipline, "symbolic anthropology." The second attacked particular theories of sociocultural symbolism (Spiro 1979c). The third position held that the symbolists' approach and certain instrumentalist ones (e.g., functionalism) are, or ought to be, compatible and not contradictory (Sprio 1979b). The fourth position, finally, was Spiro's own construal of the place of symbols and their meanings in anthropological analysis (Spiro 1982b). I will, of necessity briefly, elaborate on each position.

1. As a discussant at the 1969 meeting of the American Ethnological Society (Spencer 1969), Spiro commented on a number of papers—by Turner, Douglas, Schneider, Swartz, and Peacock, and others—that were devoted to "forms of symbolic action." Put in other, more usual contexts, "sessions on kinship, religion, values, and so on," the papers would all be judged "excellent." But as part of a proceeding devoted to symbols and anthropology, they left him "with a feeling of disappointment—even frustration" (Sprio 1969b:208). Upon reflection, Spiro writes, these feelings seemed to arise from a disquiet about the way in which the burgeoning interest in symbolic anthropology was unfolding. The papers gave, for example, little sense that others, "ancestors," within anthropology and outside it, had grappled with symbols before. Where, he asks, were the references to White, Warner, Hallowell, Roheim, or Sapir; to Cassirer, Langer, Freud,

or Piaget? "It is as if, rather breathlessly, we were all, for the first time, discovering America . . . , entering a brave new world on whose soil no anthropological foot had, until recently, ever tread. In fact, however, the terrain is filled with many ancestral tracks, some of them well beaten at that" (Spiro 1969b:209).

Related to this historical myopia was a more central problem. Never, Sprio asserts, was "symbol" defined. Nowhere was a coherent theory of symbolism put forth. The result was that each paper seemed to mine the vein oblivious of the others, each insular, each within its own idiom. Moreover, in this conceptual miasma Spiro thought he could discern in the various and idiolectical usages of "symbol" and its cognates a much older idea, "what used to be called (in the old BAE Reports and in the old ethnographic monographs of the American Museum of Natural History) 'culture' " (Spiro 1969b:211). Recalling Molière's Monsieur Jourdain and his Teacher of Philosophy, Spiro avers that perhaps anthropology had been speaking symbols all the time, since the day of Tylor at least, without knowing it. Indeed, he seems barely to refrain from echoing the gentleman's thanks to his mentor: "I am infinitely obliged to you for having taught me this." Instead he does the gentleman one better. Until symbolic anthropology addresses its central issues, analytically and theoretically, it risks being taken for old Gallo in very new bottles marked Rothschild Mouton Cadet. Until then, "perhaps we would be wise to reread *The Interpretation of Dreams*" (Spiro 1969b:214).

2. Spiro's hyperbole (which I have taken the liberty of enhancing) might well be traced to a rather specific perception of neglect: certainly he has been speaking symbols all along. In "Culture and Personality: The Natural History of a False Dichotomy," he wrote that the

> crucial characteristic of human intelligence [is] the capacity for delaying response—without which there could be no culture. . . . [Man has this capacity] by imaginatively entertaining alternate modes of response and choosing that response that will most effectively satisfy his needs . . . , [and] this requires the capacity for representation, the ability to transcend the immediate and to conceive of a nonimmediate future . . . [And this] presupposes the use of the *symbol*. [Spiro 1951:27; emphasis in the original]

Of course, in reading this passage one can see immediately the reasons for the later symbolists' neglect. (The reasons would be similar with respect to their neglect of Leslie White.) Following Freud (in the subtext one reads of "delaying gratification," "reality testing," "secondary- vs. primary-process thought," cognitive "ego functions," etc.), Spiro harnesses his theory of symbolism to the engine of instrumentalist, psychological functionalism. If this commitment to psychological functionalism is the reason for the symbolists' neglect, it is also the basis for Spiro's critique of the symbolists' approach.

His critiques take two forms. Either (as in Spiro 1969b, discussed above) he accuses the symbolists of having no general theory by which the meanings or functions of symbols may be "deduced from established theorems" (Spiro 1968c:392),[17] or he criticizes those alternate theories that are offered. In turn, the latter critique takes two forms. Sociologically derived theories of symbolic action or belief—Gluckman's on rituals of rebellion (Spiro 1972:601–602), Leach's on the nature of natives' ignorance of paternity (Spiro 1966b, 1968a, 1982c:59–60)—are criticized for their neglect of psychological variables. On the other hand, "psychological" theories of symbolism and Lévi-Strauss's structuralism, with its assumption of Boolean mind, are criticized for their neglect of sex and aggression (in mythic texts that are manifestly obsessed with both; Spiro 1979c). The work of cognitively oriented ethnopsychologists, for example those interested in the componential analysis of kin terms, is criticized for its truncated view of the "psychological reality" of the informants—a view that limits the meanings of kin terms to their referential and taxonomic meanings. These ethnopsychologists are taken to task for their neglect of affect and motivation (Spiro 1977:11–23). More generally, the emic approach of the cognitivists is criticized for being a "descriptive and relativistic inquiry whose interest begins and ends with the parochial" (Spiro 1967:6). Whatever virtues its methodology possesses for pursuing ethnography, it cannot produce science.

I should add, or course, that many symbolists would respond by rejecting Sprio's notion of what "science" entails or of what the "human sciences," in any case, entail. The cognitivists, drawing on the model of linguistics, would in particular reject a Hempelian view of explanation and the role of prediction in scientific accounts (e.g., Goodenough 1981:54–59).

3. These critiques are tempered by Spiro's belief that the symbolist approach is not incompatible with, or contradictory to, his own. "Despite the polemical opposition between symbolic and functionalist approaches, there is not intrinsic opposition between them. On the contrary, I would say (to paraphrase Kant) that functionalism without symbolism is blind, and symbolism without functionalism is lame" (Spiro 1979b:323). Elsewhere Spiro has written that hermeneutics is "the important meeting ground for anthropological and psychoanalytic theorizing" (Spiro 1979c:5) and in yet another place that the distinction between interpretation (understanding) and explanation is a "false" dichotomy" (Spiro 1982b:64). As to the last position, other symbolists have argued similarly but for reasons very different from Spiro's and ones that he would probably not find congenial (see Ricoeur 1976: chap. 4).

To see why Spiro thinks that there is no intrinsic opposition between a symbolic approach and his own, we need to examine more closely his construal of symbolism. We must now turn to A. I. Hallowell.

4. Hallowell's pioneering work on the self and its behavioral environment (Hallowell 1955c: chap. 4, 1976: chap. 9) provided psychological anthropology with a dimension lacking in the more orthodox readings, or applications, of Freud: a phenomenology bound inextricably to the concept of culture. Hallowell demonstrated "that action is not so much a function of the objective properties ('stimuli') of the environment, whether physical or social, as of their *meanings* for the actor. . . . perceptions are not mediated through perceptors alone, but through cognitive orientations that organize and confer meaning on them. . . . these . . . orientations are acquired in large measure from the actors' cultural symbol system" (Spiro 1976:609; emphasis in the original). Hallowell was not merely interested in the cognitive dimension, however, as was a generation of anthropologists who sought to distinguish emics from etics. He spoke as well of a "motivational orientation . . . of the self towards the objects of its behavioral environment with reference to the satisfaction of its needs" (Hallowell 1955c:100) and of a "normal orientation"—values, ideals, and standards—which lent to consciousness the critical dimension of self-appraisal and judgment. Clearly, such phenomenological "orientations" can quite easily be assimilated to a psychodynamic theory which postulates ego, id, and superego functions. And in the work of Spiro they were.

Spiro's Symbology

One way to look at Spiro's work is to see it addressing a particular problem generated by Hallowell: the relationship of cognitive and normative orientations to the constraints of motivational ones. Many sorts of behavior by which the self satisfies its needs would disrupt the social order. There must therefore be some sort of adaptive fit between a personally constituted behavioral environment, characterized in large part by the demands of imperious drives, and a culturally constituted one, characterized by the demands of orderly, effective, and moral intercourse with nature and other humans. We have returned to the problem phrased earlier as the transformation of duty into desire. We can come at it now from a different angle and speak of the problem of articulating private, personal symbol systems with public, cultural ones.

One of Spiro's main criticisms of the symbolic approach is that, although it devotes a good deal of time to elucidating the meanings of symbols, it has not devoted nearly equal attention to explaining the efficacy of symbols. How, or why, do symbols work? The identification of certain symbols in a larger complex as "key" (Ortner 1973), "epitomizing" (Schneider 1976), or "dominant" (Turner 1967) ones is certainly an important step. But to Spiro it is a step in the coherent organization of an *ethnography*, and one must seek to move beyond this point, to *theory*. Given the nature of magico-religious symbol systems, the question of "how symbols work" can be re-phrased: "Why do individuals believe and act on their beliefs?" In answering, Spiro begins in much the same way that he started his exploration of conformity (see above). Spiro (1961b) rejected, first, a naïve cultural determinism and, second, any recourse to the view that "norms" acted on individuals with a Durkheimian "moral force." Here he begins by rejecting the position, accepted since Durkheim, that "the coercive power of cultural symbols on the human mind [may be taken] to be a self-evident truth" (Spiro 1982b:45).

In this paper Spiro directly addresses the problem of "collective representations" as it emerged from Durkheim's *The Elementary Forms of the Religious Life*. Spiro himself calls this paper a "somewhat extended and delayed commentary" on his 1969b piece, discussed above. It is also, however, an extension of his (1966b) work on defining religion. For there, in contrast to others (e.g., Evans-Pritchard) who would do without any definition of religion, Spiro offers a nominal-analytic one, in which *the* defining attribute of a religion is posited as belief in "culturally postulated superhuman beings" (Spiro 1966b:96). This (1982b) paper is, among other things, an extended explanation of why superhuman beings were so chosen.

The analysis begins by asserting two points which certain symbolists would immediately dispute. The first is that to understand cultural symbol systems it is necessary to attend to "mind" (private meanings) as well as "culture" (shared, public meanings); more specifically, it is incumbent on us to understand how the mind *works* (Spiro 1982c:43 and 1982b:46; but cf. Geertz 1973b:10–13). Second, Spiro distinguishes two broad domains of culture, the "mythicoreligious and ritual systems" and the "technicoeconomic" ones. The distinction is crucial, since, he contends, the former is based to a large extent on primary-process modes of thought, the latter on secondary-process modes (Spiro 1982b:53; but cf. Dolgin, Kemnitzer, and Schneider 1977:7, 22, 34–36). I will emphasize here that these two points are central to the development of Spiro's analysis but that their assertion puts the analysis instantly at odds with, and beyond, the concerns of most symbolists.

Focusing upon primary-process thought, Spiro proposes several parallels: the world of a dreamer, where primary process reigns, and the world of a believer. "The dream world is a *reified* world. . . . dream images are believed by the dreamer to *be*, rather than to *represent*, the persons and events they signify" (1982b:53; emphasis in the original). In religion, too, images in the mind are reified; moreover, they are *externalized* as well. Persons and events are taken to be real not because they are, as in a dream, privately and idiosyncratically experienced as real but because they are shared, public, and acquired "images" of a cultural tradition. They are proclaimed true and confirmed true in a culturally constituted behavioral environment in which the self lives and by which the self lives and by which the self understands life. An individual's "belief in the correspondence between the mythico-religious world and his mental representation of it is confirmed by the consensual validation of his fellows" (1982b:57).

But whatever the correspondences between dream world and mythico-religious world, two other bases must be invoked to explain the believability of the latter. The first, a motivational one, rests on what William James would call the "cash value" of religious beliefs (cf. Evans-Pritchard 1965:48). They satisfy needs, both cognitive and emotional, especially with regard to Weberian problems of explaining suffering and unfairness and providing techniques with which to overcome them. Second, in addition to a motivational predisposition to believe, there is, so to speak, a cognitive template on which belief may be built: the universal, biological givens of the childhood of *Homo sapiens,* prolonged helplessness and dependency. As a result, "cultural systems, when viewed ontogenetically, are not the first resource from which social actors construct their representational world" (1982b:59).

Even before the acquisition of language, which makes possible the formation of a *culturally* constituted conception of the world, the infant begins to build a *socially* constituted conception of the world. The latter arises from interactions with parents and parental figures. The helpless child is completely dependent on these strange, all-powerful, nurturing and frustrating figures. Prior to the development of object constancy and secondary-thought-process reality testing, the images of these parents are bound up in primary-process thought. At first the parents are but an extension of the infantile self. Even when externalization begins, primary-process thinking still reigns. The parental images are "split" into all-good and all-bad entities, to relieve the great tensions of love and (destructive) rage being focused on the self-same entity—a sort of infantile solution to the problem of theodicy. In addition, the infantile self, battered by a constantly frustrated sense of self despite "the omnipotence of thought," tries desperately—ritually—to beseech, control, and manipulate these powerful figures, to satisfy its needs.

Although in normal development, secondary-process thought (ego functions) begins to rein in primary-process id functions, the template is already set:

> If one considers the typical mythico-religious world—with its gods and demons, saviors and satans, redeemers and destroyers—then it

becomes apparent that the *socially-constituted* images which young children form of the powerful beings comprising their family world are highly similar to the *culturally-constituted* images which, at a later stage, they form of the powerful beings comprising the mythico-religious world. . . . we may say that children are cognitively pre-adapted to believe in the reality of the superhuman beings that are represented . . . in the external collective representations of mythic narratives and religious ritual, as well as in the mental images which children form of them. [Spiro 1982b:61–62; emphasis in the original]

Manifestly, then, three sorts of symbolic transformations are effected: infantile symbols are mapped onto isomorphic adult ones; privately experienced symbols are mapped onto culturally shared and experienced ones; and unconscious concerns (dependency, for example) are transmuted into conscious ones (e.g., as in prayer or supplication).

However, religious symbol systems have a latent deep structure. Spiro returns to dream work and its symbolism, where symbols (à la Peirce) are frequently transformed into icons. In this manner and in others (e.g., condensation), symbolic distortion may function as a disguise in the service of expressing forbidden desires. Thus a discussion of tropes leads into one on ego defense mechanism, and Spiro develops this subject into a view of religious symbols as *objects* (cf. Eister 1974:2; Dolgin et al. 1977:22) by means of which culturally constituted defense mechanisms are able to do their personality-integrative work—much as private symbols, in dreams, are worked through displacement, condensation, and so forth so that repressed and painful desires may be expressed. Chief among these are desires relating to dependency and aggression.

Thus the believer in benevolent and malevolent superhuman beings is able both consciously to gratify dependency and aggressive drives in culturally appropriate ways (e.g., prayer or sacrifice) and simultaneously to gratify unconsciously these needs in regard to their parents (gratification that would be inappropriate if it were directly expressed by adults). Whatever the value of examining "religion-in-doctrine" and its symbolics may be, then, the value of examining "religion-in-use" is clear. Such was the message of *Buddhism and Society*. Religion "is a means for the symbolic gratifications of . . . powerful infantile needs . . . , [thereby sparing society] the highly disruptive consequences of their direct gratification" (Spiro 1982b:70).

This paper, refined with references to a Saussurean deep structure, to Peirce, and to tropes, and undergirded by an even stronger reliance on psychoanalytic theory, is in a direct genetic line with the earliest work on Ifaluk. It may be taken to signify the constancy of Spiro's thought, the contention with which I began this essay.

The Symbolists' Response (?)

We must consider the ways in which the symbolists might respond to the four positions I have adumbrated. I shall be brief.

1. Is symbolic anthropology merely old wine in new bottles? Certainly not, if one considers the change of emphasis from the arch-utilitarian view of symbols found in the work of White, Malinowski, or Radcliffe-Brown.

2. Does symbolic anthropology lack a theory of symbolism? (1) Only if one continues to reject a sociogenic theory in favor of a psychogenic one (Leach?). (2) Only if one accepts Spiro's Hempelian notion of theory (Geertz?). (3) Of course not: vide linguistics (Goodenough?).

3. Are the two approaches compatible? Certainly not, if one rejects the causalist-functionalist program outright.

4. What about psychoanalytically derived explanations of symbolism? (1) Insofar as one adopts a "mechanistic" causal-functional view of psychoanalytic theory, one is merely perpetuating (retrograde) (bourgeois) (reactionary) (nineteenth-century) (etc.) notions of science. (2) Psychoanalysis does indeed have something to offer—in the way of understanding, not explanation. But to appreciate this point, let us seriously treat the work of Freud as itself the text.

This last statement I will take as the final riposte to Spiro's program. I will not develop it at this time. But one sees, in much of Lacan's work, in Ricoeur (1970, 1974), Derrida (1978), Schafer (1980), and a host of others, the "interpretive turn" grinding inexorably toward Freud, himself now conveniently pegged as, for example, that "master shaman" (Shweder 1980:65). Certainly the shaman himself is much to blame: the case of *Dora*, by itself, can occupy a legion of deconstructionists for a millennium. But I would wager a guess that, when Spiro spoke of the "meeting ground" that hermeneutics can provide for anthropology and psychoanalysis, he had something else in mind.[18]

How to reconcile two views opposed to each other such that the one holds "it is the job of the anthropologist to uncover the reality behind the appearance" (Spiro 1979c:5), while the other holds that behind the appearance is only more appearance, "thickly" embedded, and—as in the Indian story of the infinite line of turtles holding up the world—behind that yet more appearance, "all the way down" (Geertz 1973b:28–29)? How to reconcile a program that seeks to go beyond interpretation and understanding to explanation, "not only of a culturally parochial, but also of a trans-cultural provenance" (Spiro 1982b:50), with a program that asserts that, if such "transcultural" explanations could be found, they would likely be trivial? How to reconcile a commitment to nomothetic goals with one aimed at proceeding from one genre of "local knowledge" (Geertz 1983) to another? In earlier works Spiro wrote of hermeneutics as a meeting ground for his sort of anthropology and that of the symbolists. More recent works—dealing with the conceptual status of cultural relativism in the discipline—show him to be less optimistic about such a meeting (Spiro 1984, 1986). Indeed, he sees in the supremacy of the hermeneutic approach great peril for the future of anthropology. In an earlier day, the "crisis" in anthropology was often expressed as the disappearance of the primitive world which scientists studied. For Spiro, the current crisis lies in the disappearance of the scientists themselves.

CONCLUSION: RETROSPECT AND PROSPECT

It is sometimes said nowadays, of an older sort of anthropological monograph, that, in its zealousness to portray a culture or society as an "integrated whole," it bent its own data into fanciful shapes or procrustean molds, embellishing here, neglecting there, and so on. An essay such as the present one, aimed at organizing the data of a personal intellectual biography in the context of an entire discipline, runs very much the same risk. Thus, for example, by focusing on Spiro's work on religion, I have neglected his studies of the kibbutz. Moreover, given my own ethnographic interests in Israeli society, I had, in the past, read this part of Spiro's corpus most attentively.

The kibbutz books (Spiro 1956, 1958, 1979a) are important to Spiro's (1978b) autobiography in that they—or, more concretely, the first two as completed by *Gender and Culture*—demonstrate for him the great truth of the stubborn, precultural invariance of human nature, even in the crucible of the self-reflexive consciousness of a utopian community. And they are important too in following changes in his thinking about the functions of socialization. According to the social learning theory on which he relied earlier (Spiro 1961b), socialization functions to promote the acquisition of culturally appropriate needs. Now Spiro argues that socialization works for "the acquisition of cultural norms that ensure the gratification of precultural needs by culturally prescribed means" (Spiro 1979a:87).

In positing the "precultural," Spiro does not have in mind a simple redaction of sociobiology—"one gene, one vote." The precultural encompasses not only genetic factors but experiential ones. The "experiences" to which Spiro refers are those of long-term dependent human infants raised in human families. These experiences are panhuman and hence universal: constituent of a universal human nature. But cross-culturally speaking, not all human families (to take but one dimension of variability) are similarly structured in all respects, and therefore the universality of certain motivational dispositions (say, that of incest and the concomitant Oedipus complex) does not entail their invariance at the level of either their cross-cultural expression or their resolution.

But here again we are concerned with the changes in Spiro's thought throughout his career, and I have chosen to stress the constancy. Framed by his writings on religion, the constancy is perhaps best seen as a concatenation of theoretical commitments—to psychoanalytic theory and functionalism—and a methodological stance: to the hypothetico-deductive canons of Hempelian science. And these are as much in evidence in *Oedipus in the Trobriands* as they were in his earliest papers on Ifaluk.

Earlier, in my discussion of Spiro's functionalism and his theory of social change, I drew attention to the limitations of his program when measured against Hempelian ideals. I believe it is a limitation that Spiro himself recognizes. Of course, I can (very much in keeping with the rules of this particular genre) end on a Panglossian note and assert that future advances in, say, that vigorous congeries the "cognitive sciences," will see us out of the thicket. Perhaps. But certainly it will have to be a cognitive science divorced fully from cultural behaviorism or merely idolatrous methodologism—a science unafraid of grappling with mind or meaning, motivation or affect. And one can look forward to seeing Spiro engage the new adversaries to whom such a science will give rise. But this last thought aside, the Panglossian stance seems to me affected.

In part, at least, the limitations I noted are themselves a matter for debate and well within Spiro's terms. One ought not, for example, try to force the study of culture and social action into methodologically aseptic "laboratories" in order to mimic the experimental method. To do so achieves not mimesis but parody. To do so is to do violence to the natural settings— the family, the village, the ward—in which culture is lived (see Spiro 1977:xiv).

To be sure, some limitations remain—those having to do with unoperationalized assumptions about personality and society as self-regulating systems. But whatever the limitations (and on second thought I am not sure Spiro would be as docile in acceding to them as I imagine), Spiro has chosen to pursue his own vision of anthropology as the science of culture. For him there is, at the bottom, one final, damned turtle, on which the whole enterprise rests.

NOTES

1. Assuming that anthropology has its versions of phlogiston theory, we seem less likely to discard and replace them unequivocally, relegating them to the brief

"historical" sections of our textbooks. On the other hand many of us are quite prepared to believe that any theory of culture different from the one we hold is merely a version of phlogiston theory.

2. In the discussion which follows, I focus on Radcliffe-Brown's brand of functionalism, not Malinowski's. Although Spiro has gone into print contesting some of the latter's work (Spiro 1982c), he would remain in basic agreement with Malinowski's contention that culture is instrumental in the satisfaction of human needs; he disagrees with Malinowski's elaboration of this point. Nevertheless, for my purposes, Spiro's disagreements with Radcliffe-Brown are the most pointed and fruitful.

3. I say this despite some apparent contradictory evidence from Radcliffe-Brown himself. In a 1935 paper, a rejoinder to Alexander Lesser on the true meaning of functionalism, Radcliffe-Brown wrote: "Dr. Lesser speaks of the functionalist as stressing 'the psychological aspects of culture,' I presume that he here refers to the functonalist's recognition that the usages of a society work or 'function' only through their effects in the life, i.e. in the thoughts, sentiments and actions of individuals. The 'functionalist' point of view here presented does therefore imply that we have to investigate as thoroughly as possible all aspects of social life, considering them in relation to one another, and that an essential part of the task is the investigation of the individual and of the way in which he is moulded by or adjusted to the social life" (1935:185). Do we have Radcliffe-Brown here endorsing the relevance of psychology for social anthropology? I think not. For he is here proposing a Durkheimian psychology, similar in form to the epistemology which begins and concludes *The Elementary Forms of the Religious Life*. There Durkheim argued that the elementary categories of human thought (cognition)—space, time, cause, number, class, and personality—are "born in religion [society] and of religion [society]" (1915:9). It is, in short, a "psychology" in which society is the explanans and individual personality— in its affective, cognitive and perceptual aspects—the explanandum. So too is Radcliffe-Brown construing the individual only as one molded by or adjusting to "social life." This position is the reverse of Spiro's "suggested reorientation" for culture and personality, which seeks to make personality concepts the explanans for social system and culture (1972:585). Once again, Radcliffe-Brown's "psychology" conflates cause (individual motivation) with function (the requirement for individuals' conformity to sustain social solidarity). I shall return to this point several times.

4. I should note that the equation of learning with internalization reflects the unitarian view of culture and personality espoused in Spiro (1951). Later he distinguished among several "levels" of learning as he moved closer to a Parsonian model and further refined the cognitive and psychodynamic aspects of this theory (Spiro 1961a, 1961b, 1966a).

5. And perhaps as well from the imperious *mammalian* drives of the organism.

6. Or consider his exchange with Leach on virgin birth (Spiro 1968b) or his most recent attack on Malinowski (Spiro 1982c).

7. Or part of it, anyway; cf. Spiro (1973). In *Burmese Supernaturalism* Spiro defines the perceptual basis of witches and nats. The former are based on a perception of self, the latter on a perception of parents.

8. Both pieces were written before the impact of Lévi-Straussian structuralism had been fully felt. By "British structuralism" Sprio meant what was commonly called—and what I have called—"British (structural-functional) social anthropology." But Spiro wanted to preserve a less parochial meaning for "social anthropology," as he was to argue that his form of culture-and-personality theory is legitimately part of a genuine social anthropology (cf. Spiro 1972:581, 604).

9. And more directly and personally, on the evidence that Spiro assigned Hempel to his graduate students, including me, at the University of California, San Diego.

10. Of course Spiro has published "quantitatively informed" papers, e.g., Spiro and D'Andrade (1958) and Spiro (1965b). But in the former paper, Spiro relies on Whiting and Child's (1953) scalar ratings of sorts of variables (e.g., "satisfaction of dependency/oral/aggressive drives"), which do not directly address the problem of the self-regulating nature of the system: i.e., reference values and ranges of systemic viability. (On 1965b, see n. 11.)

11. Another paper (1965b) dealt with long-term structural change in an evolutionary perspective. Although it may be assumed that the institutions in the types of societies that Spiro treats are themselves functionally integrated, this paper is not a functional inquiry per se but a causal (evolutionary) one. More germane to the line of argument I have developed here, then, is his 1973 piece.

12. To put the matter differently: any questions we have about the adequacy of ways of testing the validity of Spiro's theory of *change* arise because of prior questions about ways of testing his theory of *persistence*. I refer here to my earlier comment: Hempel might well be reluctant to concede that the notion of the unconscious and its processes is valid.

13. And one would want to note as well the influence of Levy-Bruhl, as in Evans-Pritchard's work.

14. Mary Douglas (1981:31–34) has noted some parallels between Evans-Pritchard's thought and Wittgenstein's. Evans-Pritchard's position on the definition of religion—that religion is to be found in the "usage" ordinary folk make of the religious; religion *means* what they *do*—recalls Wittgenstein on the meaning of definitions. Such a stance also brings us close to Geertz's view of the definitional problem (Geertz 1983:75).

15. In the discussion which follows, given the constraints of space, I cannot hope to do justice to the full range and diversity of symbolist thought and especially ethnography. For an introduction, I refer the reader to Keesing (1974). I should note also that my category "symbolist" encompasses his tripartite division of these theorists as "cognitivists," "structuralists," and "symbolists" (proper). His division is more sensical and sensitive to the differences among them. I can plead here only the virtue of brevity.

16. It is instructive to compare Skorupski's British casting of the symbolist-instrumentalist dialogue with Sahlins's Franco-American one (Sahlins 1976).

17. The quotation comes from a caustic review of Douglas's *Purity and Danger* (1966), which should be consulted, in this context, in its entirety.

18. Or consider Victor Turner's "Encounter with Freud," in *The Making of Psychological Anthropology* (1978). Turner celebrates the *style* of Freud's thinking

"rather than his actual inventory of concepts and hypotheses" (Turner 1978:582). He uses Freudian notions of defense mechanisms, sublimation, repression, and so on metaphorically to gain insight into public ritual behavior. Freud taught him, he tells us, that symbols may be multivocal, polyvalent, or polysemic, that is, "overdetermined." Turner might have learned as much from a quirky reading of St. Augustine.

2

Natural Objects and Substitutive Acts

The Symbolic Process in the
Anthropologies of Durkheim and Freud

MICHAEL E. MEEKER 🐚

MICHAEL E. MEEKER 🐚

THE CONCEPT OF THE PRIMITIVE IN MODERN ANTHROPOLOGY

I had the privilege of reading an early version of *Oedipus in the Tro-briands* shortly before it was published. While I had come to know Spiro's work well when I studied under him at the University of Chicago, the manuscript provided me with a sense of discovery even though it did not touch the main area of my ethnographic interest and involved problems of family and childhood which had not previously attracted my attention. In my opinion, the success of *Oedipus in the Trobriands* lies in its reexposure of an anthropological debate to the subtlety of a Freudian analysis. As a result, it brings to light unwarranted exclusions which invest our inherited intellectual paradigms.

Malinowski was himself one of the first anthropologists to draw upon psychoanalytic concepts in developing interpretations of ethnographic materials. His argument that the Oedipus complex did not exist among the Trobrianders was not intended as a refutation of Freud's ideas (Malinowski 1955:77). He maintained rather that a "matrilineal complex" involving the boy, his sister, and his mother's brother took the place of the Oedipus complex. Malinowski was engaged then in the adaptation and modification of Freud's discussion of the Oedipus complex to the Trobriander context. In the process he was attempting to show that anthropology might not only draw upon psychoanalytic theory but also contribute to it (Malinowski 1955:123–24).

Despite Malinowski's positive attitude toward psychoanalysis, Spiro shows that his discussion of the Trobriander family entails a dilution of Freud's arguments to the point where their logic is broken and their force is lost. Malinowski shifts the problem of Oedipal conflict away from the central figures of the family, the boy's mother and father, to secondary figures, his sister and his mother's brother (Malinowski 1955:76). With this shift, the coordination of the boy's hostility toward the father with his sexual desire for the mother—an essential feature of the Oedipal triangle as originally conceived—is eliminated, since the mother's brother has no sexual preroga- tives over the sister. Thus the Oedipus complex is not just reworked as a "matrilineal complex" but largely disarmed as a theory of the problematic grounds of personal identity. According to Malinowski, the love of the child for both father and mother in the Trobriands is freed from the taint of unconscious desires (Malinowski 1955:72–74, 83). In this way, the foundation of personal identity in the early experience of the child is stabilized by parental devotion and support. In illustrating the various ways in which Malinowski's interpretation is not only ethnographically suspect but also theoretically flawed, Spiro brings to our attention many indications of repres- sion and ambivalence in the attitudes of the Trobrianders toward parental figures. This emphasis refocuses our attention on a disorder or instability which, in various formulations, Freud repeatedly uncovered in his investi- gations of human behavior and subjectivity.

The features of Malinowski's thinking with which *Oedipus in the Tro- briands* is concerned illustrate a characteristic "weakness" in the composition and interpretation of anthropology in the first part of this century. During this period, which I shall identify as the period of "modern" anthropology, ethnographers and ethnologists often suggested that a deficiency or defect in their own biography or civilization was absent from native society. In general, "modern" anthropological formulations tend to focus on the way in which the definition of self by family or community among "primitive" peo- ples contrasted with a problematic relationship between self and society in the anthropologist's own experience. This contrast is often perceived nos- talgically in the sense that the "primitive" represents for the "modern" anthropologist a lost experience of familial or communal wholeness.[1] In this manner, problems of human subjectivity and behavior, such as those which Freud brought to our attention, are presumed not to exist in "primitive" society and so are conceived as the peculiar problems of the "modern" age.[2]

The idealization of a primitive society by anthropologists was very likely of considerable importance in the anthropological reception of Freud's ideas.

Certainly, the instance of Malinowski, one of the greatest of what I have termed the modern anthropologists, suggests that this is so. Although he was entirely familiar with Freud's work, Malinowski overlooked clear signs of repression and ambivalence in attitudes of the Trobrianders toward parental figures. In doing so he revised the Oedipus complex, less because Trobriander matrilineality required such a revision than because he had an impulse to discover in the people that he studied something that he felt to be missing in European society and culture, in this case a loving paternal figure who is not resented and a devoted maternal figure who sustains. That is to say, Malinowski's misperception of the Trobriander family is not just a personal misperception but also a disciplinary one.

In this chapter I shall provide additional evidence of such a disciplinary misperception by comparing Durkheim's and Freud's accounts of symbolic processes in primitive society. Durkheim's *The Elementary Forms of the Religious Life* and Freud's *Totem and Taboo*, both studies of the ethnography of the Australian Aborigines, were published within a few years of one another. Both look upon these peoples as exemplars of primitive man. Both are concerned with elaborating the anthropology of a primordial social origin. Both posit three evolutionary stages of social thought: the totemic cults and taboo systems of primitives, the religions of great civilizations, and the conceptions and procedures of modern science. Finally, both books address the question of how primitive totemic cults and taboo systems bear on the authority and legitimacy of scientific discourse and practice.

While these works have much in common, the first had an enormous influence on the thinking and practice of anthropologists during the first half of the twentieth century, while the second has been viewed with much skepticism and some discomfort by most anthropologists. The different reception given the two books very likely results from Durkheim's and Freud's very different approaches to what they regarded as primitive religion.

For Durkheim, the character of primitive religion resolved questions about the decline of moral values in contemporary civilization. Arguing that scientific discourse and procedures had directly descended from this primordial social morality, he concluded that science would eventually prove fully adequate as a replacement for religion.

For Freud, however, primitive religion did not reveal the presence of what was absent or lacking in his own place and time. Comparing primitive religion with the thoughts and behavior of children and neurotics, he deepened rather than resolved questions about human subjectivity and experience. And placing primitive religion in the lineage of scientific discourse and procedures, he even raised a question about whether the latter differed from the former in kind or only in degree.

The positions which Durkheim and Freud took with regard to the relationship of primitive religion and modern science follow from their analyses of primitive religion as a symbolic process. In this sense, each of their respective studies takes the explicit form of an attempt to pin down the essential character of a symbolic process by means of an examination of its most archaic form, that is to say, what they took to be primitive religion.[3]

When their two parallel studies of primitive religion are compared, we find that Durkheim's sociological approach suppresses certain features of symbolic processes which were brought into focus by Freud's psychoanalytic analysis. This difference in their evaluations of symbolic processes results directly from their contrasting conceptions of the relationship of the primitive to their own contemporary society. Durkheim attempts to discover in the primitive the presence of what was absent or lacking in his own time and place. This is the strategy of what I have identified as modern anthropology. Its weakness lies in its resolution of problems of human subjectivity and behavior by means of an idealization of the primitive "other." Freud, however, does not look for a resolution of the problems of his own time and place in the primitive "other" but rather invokes the latter in order to dramatize these problems as primordial features of human subjectivity and behavior.

DURKHEIM: THE PRIMORDIAL SOCIAL ORIGINS OF MODERN SCIENCE

Living in an age in which scientific and technological advances had brought about drastic social changes, Durkheim was nevertheless by temperament and conviction a moralist. To affirm his personal sensibilities, Durkheim was obliged to think and to write as a man of his own time, to express the centrality of moral sensibilities in human affairs by means of systematic investigations whose results were subjected to procedures of verification. Thus he is the founder of sociology, a new kind of science whose object was itself society, the realm of moral sensibilities. But Durkheim was not content with submitting an inner commitment to the academic idioms and methods of the age in which he lived. He was fascinated by—and vulnerable to—the authority of these idioms and methods. This attraction did not in any way qualify or diminish his inner commitments. On the contrary, it drew him into the project of demonstrating that the apparent authority to which science laid claim was in fact an authority that resided in society itself. In this way, he responded to the allure of science as a source of power and truth by affirming that its criteria of objectivity and rationality derived from the priority of human relationships and interactions. Accordingly, in his later years, he attempted to demonstrate that the basic categories of conceptual thought, categories which were the very foundation of scientific specification and differentiation, arose not from an intuition of the laws of nature but from representations of a moral reality inherent in society. This attempt resulted in a curious anthropological study of primitive religion.

In *The Elementary Forms of the Religious Life*, Durkheim examined the cults and rites of the Australian Aborigines with the intent of discovering the "most primitive and simple" form of religion. In doing so, he was not much concerned with making a contribution to ethnology but hoped instead to reach sweeping conclusions about the place of religion in the evolution of human subjectivity. In the opening pages of his book, he announces this method of determining the essence of human experience by examining the primordial origins or institutions:

> Every time that we undertake to explain something human, taken at a given moment in history—be it a religious belief, a moral precept, a legal principle, an aesthetic style or an economic system—it is necessary to commence by going back to its most primitive and simple form, to try to account for the characteristics by which it was marked at that time, and then to show how it developed and became complicated little by little, and how it became that which it is at the moment in question. [Durkheim 1961:15–16]

Durkheim will examine the cults and rites of the Australian Aborigines to determine an elementary form of religion. And once such a determination has been made, so it is claimed, he will have located the essence of religion in human groups, an essence that is only "developed and complicated" in modern society, not altered in its nature. Given the scholarly prejudices of his day, it is not surprising that Durkheim identified "totemism" as the primordial form of religion. At the time, the problem of primitive religion was widely conceived to be a problem of describing and interpreting totemic beliefs and practices.

For Durkheim, the distinctive feature of "totemism" was the employment of animal and plant species as the names or emblems of their clans. He envisioned the earliest form of religious belief and practice as involving a process of collective representation. The following points recall the phases of his interpretations in the second book:

1. Among the Australian Aborigines, animals and plants are endowed with a sacred character and are displayed in religious ceremonies.

2. Why are animal and plant totems sacred? Animals and plants are employed as the names or emblems of clans. Their sacredness is not directly related to the animal and plant itself but indicates the priority of the experience of social attachments and dependencies (the clan) which they represent. These social attachments and dependencies are revealed and enhanced during religious ceremonies when the representations of totemic animals and plants are displayed.

3. Why are animals and plants used to represent social attachments and dependencies (the clan)? Because of a similarity between individual experience of animals and plants and individual experience of social attachments and dependencies, the two are merged and confused so that the former can be employed to represent the latter.

4. What is this similarity? Social attachments and dependencies constitute a moral reality that lies outside the individual like a material object and imposes itself on the individual like a physical force. Similarly, animals and plants are natural objects outside the individual. As such they are appropriate symbols of a moral reality which acts on the individual from the outside.

5. How is this interpretation confirmed? The primary sacred object of the Australian Aborigines is the churinga, a piece of wood or a bit of stone. A likeness of the animal or plant that serves as the totem of the clan is placed upon this object. When this material object inscribed by the sign of a natural species is displayed, the priority of social attachments and dependencies is intellectually and emotionally brought into focus and reaffirmed in individual experience.

Having argued that the primordial representation of society employs species of animals and plants, Durkheim proposes that the representation of more and more complex forms of society is the precondition for the classification of natural objects within spatial and temporal frames. Thus, for Durkheim, science and rationality have their origins in the representation of human attachments and dependencies. Primordially, our sense of a unity and order in nature is not derived from the contemplation of natural laws. The categories of conceptual thought are a dimension of the representation of a moral reality. Science is our way of knowing, but a moral reality is that which we know. Sketching the evolution of human thought in broad strokes in the closing pages of his book, Durkheim suggests that, as society becomes progressively more developed and complicated, religion emerges from totemism and science emerges from religion.

DURKHEIM: THE SYMBOLIC PROCESS OF PRIMITIVE RELIGION

The preceding paragraphs provide a synoptic view of the significance which Durkheim attributed to "totemic" representations. In what follows, I will examine a brief but crucial segment of his argument in detail.

The Elementary Forms of the Religious Life consists of three "Books," each exceeding 200 pages in length. The first book introduces the reader to Durkheim's concepts of primitive religion as they differ from other contemporary theories. The second book specifies the most "elementary forms" of religion among the Australian Aborigines and develops an account of their "origins." The last book reviews the details of Aboriginal cults and rites and illustrates how they are consistent with the interpretations of the "elementary forms." However, a section entitled "The Totemic Principle is the Clan, but Thought of Under a More Empirical Form," which appears toward the end of the second book, is virtually the foundation of this massive work. There, in the course of a few pages, Durkheim attempts to determine the form and content of what has been isolated as the "most simple and primitive" religious representation to be found among the Aborigines.

As we have seen in the quotation above, Durkheim's method consists of returning to the primordial origin of an institution, explaining its most primitive and simple form, and then showing how it gradually developed and became more complicated. The first step, the formulation and interpretation of the primordial origin, is therefore a crucial one. As Durkheim notes: "One readily understands the importance which the determination of *the point of departure* has for this series of progressive explanations, for all others are attached to it" (Durkheim 1961:15–16; italics added).

The section "The Totemic Principle is the Clan, but Thought of Under a More Empirical Form" is in effect Durkheim's "point of departure." Here in a few paragraphs he attempts to identify the essential characteristics of totemism, religion, and science by analyzing the representation of the Aboriginal clan by emblems of an animal or a plant. Faithful to the principles of his method, he observes: "When the idea of the totem, the emblem of the clan, is given, *all the rest follows*" (Durkheim 1961:262; italics added). If indeed Durkheim's determination of the totemic emblem is accepted, all else that follows in his study must be accepted.

His argument has two phases. 1. The totemic emblem is evaluated as a sign which constrains and determines individual subjectivity; 2. The features of this sign as an object of nature confirm that it represents a reality which is external to the individual. These two phases are then followed by an analysis of the most primitive form of totemic representation: the tattooing of the totemic emblem on the body of the clansman. Let us follow Durkheim carefully move by move.

AN EXTERNAL SIGN CONSTRAINS AN INTERNAL SYMBOLIC PROCESS

Durkheim begins by asserting that the totemic emblem does not just represent existing social sentiments but serves as a creative force to bring them into being: "the emblem is not merely a convenient process for clarifying the sentiment society has of itself: it also serves to create this sentiment; it is one of its constituent elements" (1961:263, 1960:329).

An internal state is to be given form by an external sign. In this respect, the sign, as a part of a symbolic process, does not signify a wish or desire. Rather it is external to the individual and serves to give form to the individual's internal feelings and emotions. Thus Durkheim's first step imposes a hierarchy: outside over inside. A sign on the outside determines a sentiment on the inside.

In claiming that an external sign creates an internal state, Durkheim seems to deny the possibility of individual intellection, emotion, and expression. His analysis of the emblem suggests instead the sheer mechanical determination of individual subjectivity by the totemic emblem. In the line that follows, however, Durkheim suddenly revises this initial impoverished formulation and allows for the possibility of individual intellection, emotion, and expression apart from the authority of the emblem. But in making this revision, Durkheim attempts to retain the authority of the emblem over the internal state of the individual.

Durkhiem begins by announcing the necessity for communication of internal states. Thus he turns to the issue of individual intellection, emotion, and expression but only to discover how they can be conjoined and merged: "In fact if left to themselves individual consciousnesses are closed to each other; they can communicate only by means of signs which express their internal states" (1961:262, 1960:329).

Communication involves the expression of an internal state. We shall find that this communication takes the form of a symbolic process within the individual that is governed by the external totemic emblem. Durkheim will conceive the display of the totemic emblem as a primary, dominant symbolic process which shapes a secondary, subsidiary symbolic process within the individual. He begins by first stating a condition which is placed upon communication: "If the communication (Fr. *commerce*) established between them [individual consciousnesses] is to become a real communion, that is to say, a fusion of all particular sentiments into one common sentiment, the signs expressing them [individual consciousnesses] must themselves be fused into one single and unique resultant." (1961:262, 1960:329).

The lines begin with the condition: communication (*commerce:* social relationships or interactions) is to be a communion. Note that Durkheim has not explained why an individual symbolic process should take the form of a communication or why this communication should take the form of a communion. Rather his analysis proceeds under the condition that individual symbolic processes must be a communication which is a communion. Thus the results of his analysis of individual symbolic processes are guided by the value which he wishes to attribute to them.

The insistence that communication must be a communion leads Durkheim to place two conditions on individual symbolic processes. First, the expression of internal states by external signs is to lead to the fusion of "particular sentiments" into "one common sentiment." Second, this end can be accomplished only if those external signs which express internal states are "fused into one single and unique resultant." Thus the creation of a communion ("one common sentiment") among individuals is conditional upon their expressing their internal states by the same sign ("one single and unique resultant").

Having placed conditions on what the symbolic process internal to individuals must be, Durkheim next describes the fulfillment of these conditions: "It is the appearance of this [the fusion of individual signs into one single and unique resultant] that informs individuals that they are in harmony and makes them conscious of their moral unity. It is by uttering the same cry, pronouncing the same word, or performing the same gesture *in regard to some object* [the emblem] that they become and feel themselves to be in unison" (1961:262, 1960:329–330; italics added).

The individuals of the clan all respond to the display of the totemic emblem by "uttering the same cry, pronouncing the same word, or performing the same gesture." As they become aware of their identical responses to the emblem, they are informed ("prendre conscience") of their moral unity so that they become and feel ("se mettent" and "se sentent") themselves to be in unison.

Thus a dominant external sign (the totemic emblem) determines the form and content of subsidiary individual intellects, emotions, and expressions. This external sign (the totemic emblem) represents a reality outside individuals. It is not the product of individual intellects, emotions, and expressions but is imposed instead as an external reality that determines their form and content.

So then Durkheim has evaluated the primordial sign of human subjectivity—the point of origin of primitive totemisms, ancient religions, and modern science—as a sign which does not arise from human dreams and wishes but on the contrary determines their form and content. The totemic emblem is an elementary sign of an authoritative external reality, an elementary sign under which human life takes shape and evolves. For Durkheim, then, primitive religion symbolizes an external reality, not an internal desire.

A SOCIAL REALITY IS REPRESENTED BY AN OBJECT OF NATURE

Durkheim now takes a further step in his interpretation of the totemic emblem which does not in any way follow from his previous assertions. It is of interest, however, because it reconfirms the conclusion just reached.

Certain insidious movements permeate the lines that we have been reading. In the last quotation above, for example, Durkheim has casually called the display of the totemic emblem as the display of an "object" (*objet*). This is the clearest hint that he will eventually give the totemic emblem the value of an object in nature which represents a material constraint and a physical force. In this respect, the emblem as sign will be identified as an object of natural science (as it was understood about the turn of the century), a natural science of material constraints, physical forces, and laws of cause and effect.

First we discover that a material object is an especially appropriate representation of the group because "social phenomena" resemble external material objects: "In fact, it is known that social phenomena are born, not in individuals, but in the group. Whatever part we may take in their origin, each of us receives them from without. So when we represent them to ourselves as emanating from a material object, we do not completely misunderstand their nature" (1961:263–264, 1960:331).

Second we discover that an external material object represents society because society operates as a force from outside the individual: "If the moral force sustaining the believer does not come from the idol he adores or the emblem he venerates, still it is from outside of him, as he is well aware. The objectivity of its symbol only translates its externalness" (1961:264, 1960:331).

Because society is like a physical force and a material constraint, society can be represented by an object, a bit of wood or a piece of stone, an animal or a plant.

Primordially *a moral reality is like a physical force and material constraint;* therefore, representations of a moral reality are the primordial origin of concepts of the physical and material. Thus the sign which represents society appears as an object of science. The significance of this claim is to be found in the enthusiasm for science during the late nineteenth century. During this period, many, perhaps most, learned individuals viewed natural science itself as an authoritative and definitive representation of an external reality and, in this sense, a representation that did not arise from human dreams and wishes but rather reflected external constraints and forces beyond human desires. This is no longer the prevailing view of the natural sciences in the late twentieth century. The natural sciences are now more typically seen as human projects and, as such, projects which take shape and unfold within the context of a social history rather than within the context of a pure discovery.

Durkheim's identification of the totemic emblem as an object of science must therefore be seen in the context of his own time. This identification reinforces his claim that the primordial sign of society represents a reality external to and beyond human desires and, in this respect, a reality which has the power to determine the form and content of human subjectivity.

TATTOOING: A SIGN OF SOCIETY SUFFICIENT UNTO ITSELF

At the end of the brief section we have been considering, Durkheim reaches conclusions as to why animals and plants (the former more than the latter) are used as emblems of clans. Animals and plants, the natural objects of the Australian landscape, are "closer" to the Aborigines than the stars of the firmament, other potential candidates for collective representations. Animals have a "likeness" to human beings that exceeds that of plants; therefore the totems of the Aboriginal clans are generally animals and not plants. However, before reaching these final conclusions, which easily flow from his argument as it has progressed, Durkheim pauses to consider the most primitive form of emblem and the most primitive form of society. These passages are interesting because they follow logically from Durkheim's earlier analyses and yet reveal the emptiness of his claims.

Durkheim begins these passages by diverting our attention to the most primitive form of totemic emblem, one that is even more primitive than the wooden or stone emblem inscribed with a figure of an animal or a plant: "But there is one sort of emblem which should make an early appearance *without reflection or calculation:* [one which as we have seen plays a prominent role in totemism; it is] tattooing" (1961:264, 1960:332; italics and line omitted by translator have been added).

A tattoo is a mark on the body which identifies the individual with a social group. It is the most primitive form of emblem, even more primitive than the totemic emblem, and as such, it involves no "reflection or calculation." This assertion is consistent with Durkheim's preceding arguments, since the earliest emblem cannot arise from individual reflection and calculation. It must come from outside human subjectivity, not from inside it. If we read on, we find that the tattoo is indeed a representation so primitive that it does not represent—it merely "is."

> The best way of proving to one's self and to others that one is a member of a certain group is to place a distinctive mark on the body. The proof that this is the reason for the existence of the totemic image is the fact, which we have already mentioned, that it does not seek to reproduce the aspect of the thing it is supposed to represent. It is made up of lines and points to which a wholly conventional significance is attributed. Its object is *not to represent or bring to mind a determined object,* but to bear witness to the fact that a certain number of indi-

viduals participate in the same moral life [1961:265, 1960:331; italics added]

The most primordial of emblems is a sign that does not represent and has no meaning save in its reference to a moral life. Take away society, and the sign cannot signify. But Durkheim's argument is on the verge of collapse. The tattoo does represent and does have a meaning if in fact it refers to a moral life held in common. And if we examine how this moral life is represented and given meaning, we will presumably discover reflection and calculation. Thus the emblem that is distinctively associated with the most primitive society would itself be implicated in human subjectivity. In what follows, Durkheim manages, however, to avoid this collapse.

Having described the most primitive form of emblem, he now described the most primitive form of society. The example is the Aboriginal clan:

> The clan cannot be defined by its chief, for if central authority is not lacking, it is at least uncertain and unstable. Nor can it be defined by the territory it occupies, for the population, being nomadic, is not closely attached to any special locality. Also, owing to the exogamic law, husband and wife must be of different totems; so whenever the totem is transmitted in the maternal line—and this system of filiation is still the most general one—the children are of a different clan from their father, though living near to him. Therefore we find representatives of a number of different clans in each family, and still more in each locality. [1961:265, 1960:333–334]

The most primitive form of society, the clan, is deficient in all the features that we generally associate with a moral life. It is not associated with an authority or with a territory. It is not even coordinate with the familial ties of husband and wife, father and children. Indeed, in his effort to emphasize that the clan is a zero-degree society, Durkheim even omits the fact that mother and child would indeed belong to the same clan. He insists that the clan is a society whose members have no more than a sign in common:

> The unity of the group is visible, therefore, only in the collective name borne by all the members, and in the equally collective emblem reproducing the object designated by this name. A clan is essentially a reunion of individuals *who bear the same name and rally around the same sign.* Take away the name and the sign which materializes it, and the clan is no longer representable. Since the group is possible only on this condition, both the institution of the emblem and the part it

takes in the life of the group are thus explained. [1961:265–266, 1960:334; italics added]

The primordial society is a society whose moral life is without form and content save for its representation by a name or a sign. Take away the name or the sign and there is no society. Thus we have arrived at a primitive sign (the tattoo) which does not represent except in its reference to a moral life and a primitive moral life (the clan) that does not exist apart from its representation by a sign. Durkheim has purged the problem of human dreams and wishes from the symbolic process but the only benefit is a dubious conclusion.

The tattoo is the primitive emblem of a primitive clan, but there is nothing in this primitive origin, neither meaning nor moral life. For the sign cannot signify without the prior existence of society, and society cannot exist without the prior signification of the sign or rather, virtually nothing save for that thing before our eyes: Durkheim's text, wherein we find a moral desire which writes itself as the object of science.

DURKHEIM: THE DECLINE OF MORALITY IN THE AGE OF SCIENCE

At the outset of his study, Durkheim announces his intention to demonstrate, as a truth of science, the priority of a moral reality. In book 2 he finds such a demonstration in an elementary form of collective representation among the Australian Aborigines, and in book 3 he shows how the character of Arboriginal cults and rites is broadly consistent with his interpretation of the totemic emblem. Then, in the concluding pages of his study, he reaps the fruits of his efforts. Appealing to the essence of primitive collective representations, Durkheim diagnoses the religious symbolism of all times and places as an expression of the essential moral grounds of human identities and relationships. By such an affirmation, he can insist on the existence of a moral reality apart from the past "particular" symbols which have expressed it: "Thus there is something eternal in religion which is destined to survive all particular symbols in which religious thought has successively enveloped itself" (1961:474).

With this conclusion, Durkheim is able to announce a "moral remaking" in his own time and place:

There can be no society which does not feel the need of upholding and reaffirming at regular intervals the collective sentiments and the collective ideas which make its unity and its personality. Now this moral remaking cannot be achieved except by the means of reunions, assemblies and meetings where the individuals, being closely united to one another, reaffirm in common their common sentiments; hence

Natural Objects and Substitutive Acts

come ceremonies which do not differ from regular religious ceremonies, either in their object, the results which they produce, or the
processes employed to attain their results. [1961:474–475]

This announcement of a new civil religion of the modern age is a
moment of triumph. Durkheim has in his grasp a goal that has guided the
construction of his entire book.

But just at this moment of triumph, when his project is almost finished,
his conviction in what has been demonstrated falters. What had been shown
to be a governing principle of collective life since its earliest origins can be
only dimly perceived and experienced in his own time and place: "If we find
a little difficulty to-day in imagining what these feasts and ceremonies of
the future could consist in, it is because we are going through *a stage of
transition and moral mediocrity*" (1961:475; italics added).

Modern collective representations that should be creating, shaping,
and sustaining moral sensibilities are somehow deficient. This having been
said, Durkheim seems to forget his arguments about the compelling external
authority of the totemic emblem as he hopes for a moral revival: "But this
state of incertitude and confused agitation cannot last for ever. A day will
come when our societies will know again those hours of creative efferves-
cences, in the course of which new ideas arise and new formulae are found
which serve for a while as a guide to humanity" (1961:475).

What is somehow presently absent or lacking in the scene of Durkheim's writing, his own life and times, is to be discovered in a future society.
But this future society anticipates a symbolic process of a very different kind
from that which Durkheim discovered in the totemic emblem. It is a society
based, not on a compelling external authority but on an intellectual invention
("new ideas will arise"), a society that does not indicate what is universal
and invariant but is only temporary ("which serve for a while") and a society
that does not depict a reality but only serves as an image ("a guide to
humanity").

DURKHEIM VERSUS FREUD: SYMBOLIC DESIRE,
SUPPRESSED AND RECOGNIZED

Freud also looked on the beliefs and practices of the Australian Aborigines as exemplary of a primitive religion, but unlike Durkheim, he did not
seek to discover in primitive religion what was absent or lacking in his own
life and times. On the contrary, he compared the beliefs and practices of
the Australian Aborigines with the subjectivity and behavior of deficient or
defective members of his own life and times, that is to say, with children
and neurotics. For Freud, the beliefs and practices of primitives, like the

73

Michael E. Meeker

subjectivity and behavior of children and neurotics, all had in common "the overvaluation of psychic acts" (Freud 1918:206).

Freud's approach seems at first glance to have much in common with the nineteenth-century view of primitive religion as a product of logical error and mental confusion, a view which Durkheim was energetically contesting.[4] However, on close inspection of *Totem and Taboo*, we find that Freud's views are not exactly like the "pre-Durkheimian" anthropological theories of the previous century. That this is the case is clearly apparent from his suggestion that the scientist has a certain kinship with the primitive, the child, and the neurotic. Freud does not insist on an absolute contrast between, on the one hand, the overvaluation of psychic acts and, on the other hand, scientific discourse and procedures. He observes that a "fragment" of the belief in the omnipotence of thought, which he attributes to the primitive, the child, and the neurotic, is carried over even into scientific attitudes (Freud 1918:115). In this respect, Freud suggests that scientific discourse and procedures are inherently double or divided. They refer to an outside of fact and reality, but they are touched by an inside of wish and dream.[5] Thus he has a view of symbolic processes, whether those of totemism, religion, or science, which brings into focus a conflict and tension between outside reality and inside desire. This position is very different from that of Durkheim in *The Elementary Forms of the Religious Life*. There we find a view of totemism, religion, and science as symbolic processes which are definitively shaped by an external reality wholly apart from individual subjectivity.

To illustrate Freud's contrasting approach to symbolic processes, I shall examine passages which play a key role in the organization of *Totem and Taboo* much as the passages which analyze the totemic emblem play a key role in the organization of *The Elementary Forms of the Religious Life*. I am referring not to Freud's famous interpretation of totemic cults and rites in terms of his theory of the primal horde, which appears at the end of his book, but to his less-known analysis of a case of "touching phobia," "délire de toucher," which appears nearer the beginning. Freud presents the case of "touching phobia" as a prelude to comparing taboo systems to neurotic behavior. As Freud himself indicates in his preface, this comparison, the details of which are worked out in the first two chapters, constitutes the definitive accomplishment of his study.[6]

TOUCHING PHOBIA: SYMBOLIC PROCESS AS BLOCKED DESIRE

The opening chapter of *Totem and Taboo* is entitled "The Savage's Dread of Incest." There Freud argues the case for comparing the traditions and institutions of the Australian Aborigines and other peoples with the

74

thoughts and actions of his neurotic patients. In the second chapter, entitled "Taboo and the Ambivalence of Emotions," he outlines direct analogies between the taboo systems of various primitive peoples and the neurotic compulsions of his patients, and he proposes to use the psychoanalytic understanding of the latter to develop an interpretation of the former. He then initiates this project by providing an example of the psychoanalytic approach. Here Freud presents what he calls "the history of a typical case of touching phobia":

> In the very beginning, during the early period of childhood, the person manifested a strong pleasure in touching himself, the object of which [his genitals] was much more specialized than one would be inclined to suspect. Presently the carrying out of this very pleasurable act of touching was opposed by a prohibition from without. The prohibition was accepted because it was supported by strong inner forces [love for those who imposed it]; it proved to be stronger than the impulse which wanted to manifest itself through this act of touching. But due to the primitive psychic constitution of the child this prohibition did not succeed in abolishing the impulse. Its only success lay in repressing the impulse (the pleasure of touching) and banishing it into the unconscious. Both the prohibition and the impulse remained; the impulse because it had only been repressed and not abolished, the prohibition, because if it had ceased the impulse would have broken through into consciousness and would have been carried out. An unsolved situation, a *psychic fixation*, had thus been created and now everything else emanated from the continued conflict between prohibition and impulse. [Freud 1918:40–41; italics added]

The origins of touching phobia lie in an experience whereby the satisfaction of a desire is forbidden. This leads to a striving to recover the lost pleasure while respecting the prohibition on its fulfillment. The result is what Freud calls a "psychic fixation." Thus Freud moves from a depiction of a primitive experience (of childhood, of neurotics, of humankind) toward a theory of subjectivity and behavior.

In what follows, Freud describes how the psychic fixation results in attempts to find "surrogates" for what is forbidden but desired. These surrogates take the form of "substitutive objects and actions." Here Freud arrives at a model of a symbolic process. The prohibition is not surmountable; it blocks the attainment of what is desired, but the impulse persists, and substitutions for what is forbidden proceed relentlessly. The result amounts to a "compromise." The prohibition remains in force, what is desired is never attained, but the logic of substitutions moves nevertheless to narrow, without

ever crossing, the gap between surrogate object and action and the fulfillment of the original desire:

> The transferability and reproductive power of the prohibition reflect
> a process which harmonizes with the unconscious pleasure and is very
> much facilitated through the psychological determinants of the uncon-
> scious. The pleasure of the impulse constantly undergoes displacement
> in order to escape the blocking which it encounters and seeks to acquire
> surrogates for the forbidden in the form of *substitutive objects and
> actions*. For the same reason the prohibition also wanders and spreads
> to the new aims of the proscribed impulse. Every new advance of the
> repressed libido is answered by the prohibition with a new severity.
> The mutual inhibition of these two contending forces creates a need
> for discharge and for lessening the existing tension, in which we may
> recognize the motivation for the compulsive acts. In the neurosis there
> are distinctly acts of compromise which on the one hand may be re-
> garded as proofs of remorse and efforts to expiate and similar actions;
> but on the other hand they are at the same time substitutive actions
> which recompense the impulse for what has been forbidden. It is a
> law of neurotic diseases that these obsessive acts serve the impulse
> more and more and come nearer and nearer to the original and for-
> bidden act. [1918:42; italics added]

A pleasure is forbidden at a point of origin and is therefore sought
elsewhere. There ensues a search for a surrogate by a strategy of substitutions. Something stands in for that which is desired. But what is put in the
place of the thing desired is not genuine. The desire persists, and another
substitution takes place as another surrogate takes the place of an abandoned
surrogate. The result is a psychic fixation with a kind of expressive power.
It has a "transferability" and "reproductiveness" which "wanders and
spreads." In effect, Freud has given us a model of a symbolic process, one
that he will eventually employ to interpret the taboo systems of a primitive
religion.

I shall not consider just how Freud uses the case of touching phobia
to analyze taboo systems, nor shall I consider the place of these passages in
Freud's evolving psychoanalytic project.[7] Neither of these issues is of immediate concern here. For the present purposes, the issue is rather the way
in which Freud's formulation of the symbolic process differs from Durkheim's
formulation.

The most striking difference is, of course, Freud's emphasis on an inner
subjective desire (délire de toucher) as opposed to Durkheim's emphasis on
an external objective authority (*churinga*). However, this difference is
merely the most obvious contrast between a formulation which brings out

the features of a symbolic process which turns upon matchings which are mismatchings and a symbolic process of exact copies and direct derivations. For Freud, the substitutive objects and actions of the neurotic feature a strategy of expression, one that is governed by a law of blocked desire. As the neurotic moves from surrogate to surrogate, a promise of fulfillment is enhanced, even though the false and ungenuine status of each substitutive object and action remains unaltered. Whether one accepts or rejects the Freudian theory of incestuous desire and parental prohibition, this is a powerful model of a symbolic process as problematically meaningful.

For Durkheim, on the other hand, the totemic emblems and body tattoos of primitives have a completely authoritative meaning to the extent that the symbolic process itself is impoverished and reduced to a representation of but one thing. When the emblem is displayed, it produces in individuals a unity of response, the same cry, word, or gesture. When these responses are perceived by these individuals, they experience the same internal sentiment. Thus totemic emblems, social communication, and internal states are derived from, and copies of, society, their single and unique referent. As for the most primordial form of human subjectivity and behavior, the tattoo carved upon the body, it is a symbol of society sufficient unto itself. The tattoo represents a society which consists of nothing more than a human group represented by the tattoo. There is no motivation (no impulse in Freud's terms) behind the sign and no difference between sign and its referent (no prohibition in Freud's terms). The primitive sign/society simply "is."

Durkheim's reduced and impoverished account of a symbolic process does not result from the failure of his imagination or the weakness of his logic. On the contrary, Durkheim is driven to his formulation of the emblem and tattoo by his stance toward primitive society as an embodiment of what was absent and lacking in his own time and place: the full and direct immediacy of human attachments and dependencies. This stance forces Durkheim to discover in primitive society the full presence of what he himself had never experienced. To see how, I shall suggest that *The Elementary Forms of the Religious Life*, as a symbolic process, features a slight case of "touching phobia."

First let us consider how touching phobia resembles a mode of writing. The substitutive objects and actions which express a forbidden desire have the properties of signs which take the place of what is absent or lacking. That is to say, they resemble a mode of writing, which figures its representations as a full and direct presence.[8] This writing is composed as an attempt to close the gap between itself and what it represents. Thus it is marked by a forbidden desire. Like all writing, such a writing consists of a movement from sign to sign and in this sense is constituted by substitutive objects and

77

Michael E. Meeker

actions. Even though this kind of writing might be styled "neurotic" or "diseased," it does not consist of a haphazard and frenzied series of adoptions and abandonments of first one and then another inadequate representation. It takes the form of a carefully composed strategy. The substitutive objects and actions are designed to approach progressively what would be represented as fully present even though they never attain it. In this respect, the movement of such a mode of writing aims to close the gap between what is represented and the inherent absence and lack which marks the vehicles of its representation. But while the gap is narrowed, it is never closed. As a consequence the writer of this mode of writing is afflicted by guilt and disappointment. What would have been found in a strategy of substitutive objects and actions is regretfully and even shamefully absent.

This view of touching phobia as a kind of writing is especially reminiscent, not of all of Durkheim's writing, but specifically of *The Elementary Forms of the Religious Life*, that book which has been most influential on the practice and thinking of anthropology during much of this century. Durkheim intends to show that, in primitive society, human attachments and dependencies are fully present as a primary, dominant reality and that the evolution of human subjectivity can be understood in terms of the representation of this primary, dominant reality. In the course of hundreds of pages, he moves toward the image of the totemic emblem as confirming that human attachments and dependencies are fully present in primitive society. Then, in the course of hundreds of pages, he portrays the successive evolution of primitive cult and rite, ancient religion, and modern science from this totemic emblem. But at the conclusion of this brilliant study, disappointment immediately follows triumph. What has been shown to be a reality in primitive society is not present in Durkheim's own time and place. In the face of this absence, Durkheim anticipates future projects of representation which might revive and restore what once was.

Durkheim's slight case of touching phobia leaves us to speculate what anthropology might be today had our intellectual ancestors been more inclined, like Freud, to see the primitive "other" as a dramatization of problems in their own life and times and less inclined, like Durkheim, to search in other times and places for an ideal that could not be found in their own experience.

NOTES
1. This particular strategy of composing and interpreting ethnographic materials that I have attributed to much of early twentieth-century anthropology reverses an

earlier mode. In the works of nineteenth-century anthropologists like Morgan and Tylor, what is deficient in the "savage" (cf. "primitive") other, that is to say, his superstitions and fantasies, affirms the adequacy of what is found in the self at home, namely rationality and civilization. For example, Morgan (1877:5–6) notes that "all primitive religions are grotesque and to some extent unintelligible," and Tylor (1871:I, 23) notes that "these principles [of savage religion] prove to be essentially rational, though working in a mental condition of intense and inveterate ignorance." In some nineteenth-century writers, perhaps not in Morgan and Tylor, these uncontrolled thought processes become an explanation of the savage's misery and poverty, which are contrasted with the comfort and plenty of a progressive, industrial society. Just why the earlier mode of writing and reading ethnography was abandoned and replaced by its inversion is an interesting, and no doubt complicated, problem but one that need not concern us here.

2. In what follows, the terms "primitive" and "modern" will always be used in this special sense; quotation marks, which indicate that the terms are not to be taken at face value, are always implicit.

3. In fact, Durkheim's and Freud's analyses of the symbolic process, and not their specific theses about relationship of religion and science, most attracted or repelled later generations of anthropologists.

4. Durkheim subjects this kind of interpretation on the part of Frazer and Mueller to an extended criticism in book 1 of *The Elementary Forms of the Religious Life.* Their position was similar to that of many other authors of anthropological studies in the late nineteenth century. See n. 1 above.

5. Freud's view in this respect is not very different from the contemporary view of science as a project aimed at the mastery of nature but driven by social forces.

6. Freud himself notes that his analysis of taboo systems in terms of their resemblance to neurotic behavior was more definitive than his analysis of totemic cults and rites in terms of his theory of a primal patricide: "The two principal themes, totem and taboo, are not treated alike here. The problem of taboo is presented more exhaustively, and the effort to solve it is approached with perfect confidence. The investigation of totemism may be modestly expressed as: 'This is all that psychoanalytic study can contribute at present to the elucidation of the problem of totemism' " (1918:x).

7. The quoted passages are embedded in Freud's theory of sexuality and childhood and studded with the special terminology to which this theory gave birth: prohibition, impulse, the unconscious, repression, displacement, etc.

8. My formulation of this problem has been influenced by Derrida (1976) and also by his article on Plato's *Phaedrus* (Derrida 1982). I have also drawn upon Culler's discussion of theories of reading and writing (1982), and I found especially helpful Hertz's discussion of Casaubon and textuality (1979).

3

Culturally Constituted Defenses and the Theory of Collective Motivation

GANANATH OBEYESEKERE

CULTURALLY CONSTITUTED DEFENSE MECHANISMS: AN INTRODUCTION

One of Melford E. Spiro's major contributions to psychoanalytic anthropology is the notion of "culturally constituted defense mechanisms." In his psychoethnography, Spiro has applied this idea to the study of religious systems, especially Burmese Buddhism. The theory or ontology of culturally constituted defenses is in turn related to the problem of normality and abnormality, which, according to Spiro, is not psychobiologically given as a universal but must be contextualized within each culture. But this contextualization, he argues, does not lead to a naïve relativism or particularism, for certain universal functions help us to measure or access the degree of deviation from what is "normal." These functional criteria are three: affective, cognitive, and perceptual distortion, based on what is held to be normal for each dimension of these behaviors within a particular culture (Spiro 1965a:104). These three criteria are an operational reformulation of the Freudian notion of "reality testing" (since Freud himself never operationalized reality). But reality, it should be remembered, is culturally constituted, and this notion helps us to overcome the naïve idea that cultural beliefs that seem alien to the West must necessarily be abnormal in another context. "Beliefs and rituals which characterize the behavior of religious actors in non-Western societies, though phenotypically identical with beliefs and behaviors which may characterize abnormal individuals in our society, are not necessarily (or even usually) abnormal when sanctioned or prescribed by the religious systems of the former societies and taught to the actors as part of their cultural heritage" (1965a:105). Psychotic beliefs and religious practices, Spiro argues (as Freud did earlier [1907]), may be substantively similar to one another or structurally similar (isomorphic), but they differ radically in terms of the cognitive, affective, and perceptual functioning of the individual.

At this point "culturally constituted defenses" enter the picture. They are, from a comparative viewpoint, replacements for the psychotic fantasy. "In the case of the schizophrenic, the actor resolves his inner conflict by constructing private fantasy and action systems; in the case of the [Buddhist] monk, however, the actor uses culturally constituted fantasy and action systems (Buddhism) to resolve his inner conflicts" (1965a:107). According to the logic of Spiro's analysis, the culturally constituted fantasy acts "to preclude the outbreak of pathology" (1965a:107). Unlike individual fantasy (or defenses) that are invented or activated by the individual to deal with his neuroses-psychoses, the cultural fantasy or defense may *not* have been devised teleologically by the culture for the specific task of psychic defense. It has existed prior to the individual, but it can be used by him as a replacement for psychotic fantasy. Thus Rorschach records of Buddhist monks reveal "pathological" features such as "latent homosexuality," "above-average fear of female or mother figures," pathologically regressed expression of aggressive and oral drives, and so forth (1965a:107). Yet "as a culturally constituted defense, the monastic institution resolves the inner conflict of Burmese males, by allowing them to gratify their drives and reduce their anxieties in a disguised—and therefore socially acceptable—manner, one which excludes psychotic distortion" (1965a:109).

Spiro carefully elucidates the implications of his argument: "Left exclusively to their own inner resources, many of these subjects would have become, I believe, genuine psychotics" (1965a:108). For this reason one could justly say that culturally constituted defenses are replacements for psychotic fantasy, converting what is potentially abnormal into the normal—from the point of view of universal functions—and the culturally acceptable. Insofar as psychic problems arise from infantile conflicts, cultural defenses are ultimately related to these and constitute, in Spiro's analysis, their sublimation. An example from his later work: the dependency needs of the monk are satisfied in the monastic life by the lay donor, who acts as "a giver of nourishment, a provider of nurturance" (1982a:340). This is the continuation of the infantile situation. Furthermore: "The monk can regress and reenact the role appropriate to that infantile period. . . . With his shaven head and eyebrows (required by the Rule) he acquires a foetalized appearance consistent with the psychological foetalization" (1982a:340). The replacement of fantasy by culture helps achieve the continuity of the childhood need or conflict into adult life. The object or goal to which the drive is directed is changed from private defense and fantasy into culturally constituted defense.

The intellectual genealogy of culturally constituted defense mechanisms is well known and needs little emphasis. Freud himself in "Obsessive Actions and Religious Practices" (1907) saw ritual as a defense against anxiety, and in his later (and finer) work *The Future of an Illusion* (1927) he viewed religious belief as a projection of familial images into the cosmos. But the major innovator is Kardiner (1946), who fused the two lines in Freudian thought—defense and projection—into a single concept, labeled "projective system." This idea has in turn been further revised by others (Cora Du Bois, John Whiting), but the outlines of the Kardiner model are with us today. Kardiner's departure from Freud is less with his idea of projective system than with the larger model in which the projective system is enshrined. In order to make the notion of projective system anthropologically (or sociologically) relevant, he linked it to key independent and intervening variables. These are "primary institutions" or the standardized (if not normative) childhood disciplines in a particular society that in turn produce—in a social sense—the "basic personality structure," and this intervening variable is again linked causally with "projective systems," or those beliefs that canalize private fantasy into public culture. As defenses and projections, they are rooted in pathology and infantile conflict.

> Projective systems are established under the influence of the pleasure principle, avoidance of pain or expediency. The conclusions on which projective systems are based are not inherent but are a *record of traumatic experiences*. Projective systems are therefore *excrescences from nuclear traumatic experiences within the growth pattern of the individual*. Just as the character structure of the individual has a large component of these projective systems, so the basic personality in any culture contains them. The fewer the anxieties in the growth pattern, the simpler the projective system (Comanche). It is these systems which have given rise to the complaints of the "irrational" factors in society. *Their purpose is adaptive, to relieve the mutilating effect of painful tensions.* [Kardiner 1946:39; italics added]

I will discuss in my conclusion Spiro's own contribution to this line of argument and explore some of the problems that arise from the sociological retranslation of Freud that Kardiner initiated. First I want to note that, while the genealogy of "culturally constituted defenses" itself is clear, not so with the genealogy of the larger sociological model sketched above. The major thrust of this paper is to trace the genealogy of the Kardiner type of model, one that is used by most psychoanalytic anthropologists—Erikson, Whiting, and Spiro—whether or not they are aware of its antecedents. Briefly, it postulates the idea of standardized child-training practices endemic to a particular society. These produce common motivational structures that in turn are expressed and objectified in cultural defenses or projective systems. Three key domains are activated in this model: society, personality, and culture, and, thus it can be argued, psychoanalysis can be brought into the sociological fold.

Where does this model come from? Let me take my inspiration once again from Spiro's seminal article "Religious Systems as Culturally Constituted Defense Mechanisms," where he says:

> Since the range of beliefs, values, and rituals related to supernatural beliefs and events is enormous, it is obvious, as Durkheim observed long ago, that no belief, value, or ritual is intrinsically identifiable as "religious." Since the "religious," on the contrary, is a quality of being attached to almost any instance of these three dimensions of religious systems, the latter, to use a modern idiom, are in large measure projective systems. [1965a:100]

The original quotation from Durkheim to which Spiro implicitly alludes is the following:

> . . . every religious force, comes to be outside of the object in which it resides. It is because the idea of it is in no way made up of the impressions directly produced by this thing upon our senses or minds. Religious force is only the sentiment inspired by the group in its members, but projected outside of the consciousnesses that experience them, and objectified. To be objectified, they are fixed upon some object which thus becomes sacred; but any object might fulfill this function. In principle, there are none whose nature predestines them to it to the exclusion of all others; but also there are none that are necessarily impossible. Everything depends upon the circumstances which lead the sentiment creating religious ideas to establish itself here or there, upon this point or upon that one. Therefore, the sacred character assumed by an object is not implied in the intrinsic properties of this latter: *it is added to them.* The world of religious things is not one particular aspect of empirical nature; *it is superimposed upon it.* [Durkheim 1954:229]

It is clear from this quotation that Durkheim, like other fin-de-siècle thinkers such as Tylor and Freud, saw religion as a kind of projection. But for Durkheim it was also a projection of a group sentiment, objectified and externalized, onto "things" that then become sacred. Moreover, it is clear from *Elementary Forms* that the religious sentiment springs from the collectivity. Thus we have here a model that is remarkably close to Kardiner's insofar as it deals with the collectivity and the collective sentiment that is projected onto "religious ideas"; and these in turn take on a life of their own. Kardiner's achievement was a bold synthesis of Freud and Durkheim. He was well aware of Durkheim's work, as is evident in Kardiner and Preble, *They Studied Man* (1961), but also, I think, he saw both as foreshadowing his own theory. If Kardiner is a kind of Durkheim, Durkheim also had a psychological orientation not unlike that of Kardiner. This little-known aspect of Durkheim's thought I will explore in the following section.

DURKHEIM AND THE THEORY OF COLLECTIVE MOTIVATION

For British social anthropology Durkheim was the exemplar of anti-psychologism. Evans-Pritchard confidently stated the position: "[Religion] is a creation of society, not of individual reasoning and emotion, though it may satisfy both; and it is for this reason that Durkheim tells us that a psychological interpretation of a social fact is invariably a wrong interpretation" (Evans-Prithcard 1965:46). But this view, dear to British anthropology, seems the very opposite of the equally famous French-oriented view stated by Lévi-Strauss: "Men like Tylor, Frazer and Durkheim were psychologically oriented although not in a position to keep up with the progress of psychological research and theory. Their interpretations, therefore, soon became vitiated by the outmoded psychological approach which they used as their basis" (1963:206). Strange as it may seem, both views of Durkheim, I believe, are correct: he was both sociologist and psychologist. His sociology required a psychological or motivational theory. The psychology Durkheim used was not anchored to a systematic theory, as Lévi-Strauss recognizes, but this aspect does not render it any the less important. On the contrary I shall argue that Durkheim *had* to use psychological variables in sociological analysis because they had analytical utility in his theoretical thinking and were a practical necessity for resolving some of the problems he faced in his empirical studies, both in *Suicide* and in *Elementary Forms of the Religious Life*.

Durkheim's methodology is well known, and it will suffice here merely to state its outlines. Inspired by his teacher Boutrouz at the Ecole Normale Supérieure and by Comte's positivism and notion of the hierarchy of the sciences, Durkheim sought to carve out for sociology a domain parallel to that which he thought existed in the other sciences. Sociology is the study of social facts that emerge from society or the collectivity which, in turn, is a phenomenal reality, sui generis, emerging from the interaction of a plurality of actors. Society as a collectivity cannot be studied in relation to individuals, since the interaction of individuals produces a phenomenon of a totally different nature based on the maxim that the totality is something more than the sum of its parts. Social facts are "things" ("les choses") and possess the same status as observables in other disciplines. They are characterized by exteriority (i.e., they exist independent and outside of the individual consciousness), by constraint (they impose control over the individual), and by materialization (they are often embodied in material things like a church or a churinga). The method of analyzing social facts is in terms of efficient causes and functions, the latter being essentially an item's reference to the fulfillment of the needs and goals of the social system.

Rules neatly spells out the relationship between the individual and society:

> Society is not a mere sum of individuals. Rather, the system formed by their association represents a specific reality which has its own characteristics. Of course, nothing collective can be produced if individual consciousnesses are not assumed; but this necessary condition is by itself insufficient. These consciousnesses must be combined in a certain way; social life results from this combination and is, consequently, explained by it. Individual minds, forming groups by mingling and fusing, give birth to a being, psychological if you will, but constituting a psychic individuality of a new sort. It is, then, in the nature of this collective individuality, not in that of the associated units, that we must seek the immediate and determining causes of the facts appearing therein. The group thinks, feels, and acts quite differently from the way its members would were they isolated. If, then, we begin with the individual, we shall be able to understand nothing of what takes place in the group. In a word there is between psychology and sociology the same break in continuity as between biology and the physico-chemical sciences. Consequently, every time that a social phenomenon is directly explained by a psychological phenomenon, we may be sure that the explanation is false. [1938:103–104]

Now we know the reason that Durkheim shuns individual psychology. For him the group is a phenomenological reality in itself, and group phenomena must be explained in their own terms rather than reduced to another (lower) level of individual psychology. Yet in what sense can Durkheim speak of the group as thinking, feeling, and acting differently from the individual? Does this notion entail the concept of group mind? Durkheim resolves the problem by stating that individual minds, when they interact, also constitute another emergent and equally significant phenomenal entity: the collective consciousness. The actual term is not used in the above passage, but it is clearly stated in a footnote he added to it, where he elaborates the notion of a "psychic individuality of a new sort." "In this sense, and for these reasons, one can, *and must*, speak of a collective consciousness distinct from individual consciousnesses" (1938:103n). Durkheim recognized that the col-

85

lective consciousness is a psychological phenomenon but one of collective or social psychology rather than of individual psychology.

He recognizes the utility of a social psychology in several places in *Rules*. Individual psychology, however, is not discounted either, since "the study of psychological facts is indispensable to the sociologists" (1938:111). Lévi-Strauss was not altogether correct when he castigated Durkheim for ignorance of contemporary psychology. At the very beginning of his career he went to Germany and made himself familiar with Wundt and his school. Pierre Janet was a contemporary of his at L'Ecole, and Durkheim was familiar with his work. He was fully aware of unconscious processes, as is evident from the following quotations from his paper "Individual and Collective Representations":

> Our judgements are influenced at every moment by unconscious judgements.

> We imagine that we hate someone when in fact we love him. [1974:21]

Methodologically, individual psychology was not useful for explaining social facts, but a social psychology was indispensable.

I feel that Durkheim's notion of the collective consciousness, or conscience, has been poorly appreciated by his commentators. Even such a sympathetic commentator as Talcott Parsons has misunderstood it when he says that the "Comtean conception of 'consensus' as the focus of unity in societies is the primary origin of the famous concept of the conscience collective; this rather than any German concept of Geist is clearly what Durkheim had in mind" (1960:118–119). Nisbet (1974:102–127), who shows that Durkheim was tantalized by a social psychology, discusses the conflict between individual and collective consciousness but fails to recognize its centrality in Durkheim's sociology. Radcliffe-Brown, who borrowed most of his ideas from Durkheim, simply ignores this concept, probably because of its nonempirical nature or because it seemed close to the group-mind ideas of Gustave Le Bon and others. Pocock, for example, does not see it as an analytical concept at all: "His 'collective consciousness' is, then, not a postulate or hypothesis but simply a descriptive term arrived at polemically and by analogy" (1961:37).

Durkheim is partly to be blamed for the misunderstanding of this concept. Though the idea appears as early as *The Division of Labor*, it is not very clearly spelled out there. "The totality of beliefs and sentiments common to average citizens of the same society forms a determinate system which has a life of its own; one may call it the collective or common conscience" (1964a:79). The characterization of the collective conscience as a belief cum sentiment prompted Bohannan to view it as synonymous with culture (1964:77). However, Durkheim almost never used it in this sense in any of his later writing. Elsewhere in *The Division of Labor* he sees the collective consciousness as a social fact existing prior to the individual and independent of him. "It is, in effect, independent of the particular conditions in which individuals are placed; they pass on and it remains. Moreover it does not change with each generation but it connects successive generations with one another. It is thus an entirely different thing from particular consciences, although it can be realized only through them. It is the psychical type of society" (1964a:80). This is essentialist language, and P. Q. Hirst in his brilliant critique of Durkheim's epistemology justly notes its vitalist implications (1975:120, 163). But I shall demonstrate later that Durkheim in his empirical work used collective consciousness as a theoretical concept rather than as a vitalist or essentialist notion. Even in *Division of Labor* a different and more nominalist view of the collective consciousness is found side by side with the vitalist (1964a:105). In *Rules* he does not deal with this term explicitly, yet it is indispensable to *Suicide*, which we will now consider.

In *Suicide* Durkheim's general thesis is stated in purely sociological terms and does not make much sense. In egoistic suicide the general thesis is that lack of social integration leads to high suicide rates; hypotheses based on this thesis are framed and tested with respect to religious, familial, and political society. If the general hypothesis is true, then a high degree of societal integration should lead to a low suicide rate. But in fact high societal integration can lead to another form of suicide, namely altruistic suicide (manifested in the West in military societies). Given Durkheim's own methodological prescriptions and assumptions regarding scientific analysis, this outcome simply would not do, since "x" and "not x" produce the same result. The logic of the argument can be saved only if the implicit and hidden assumptions of Durkheim's thought are laid bare and both egoism and altruism are seen to be intervening psychological variables, manifestations of a collective consciousness. Thus the independent variable is societal integration; it results in egoism (intervening psychological variable), which in turn causes the high suicide rate (dependent variable). Conversely, a high degree of integration causes a sense of altruism, which then results in (unspecified but presumably) high suicide rates. In several places Durkheim explicitly dealt with the "suicidal aptitude" of a society but denied that they should be sought in individual motivation, finding them instead "in the nature of the societies themselves" (1966:299).

But if suicidal aptitude is not an individual motivation, it is a collective one; it is the collective motivation that produces individual motivation, a thesis spelled out in detail much later in *Elementary Forms*. In *Suicide*, Durkheim thought that society itself must have a center of motivation:

Because society is the end on which our better selves depend, it cannot feel us escaping it without a simultaneous realization that our activity is purposeless. Since we are its handiwork, society cannot be conscious of its own decadence without the felling that henceforth this work is of no value. *Thence are formed currents of depression and disillusionment emanating from no particular individual but expressing society's state of disintegration.* [1966:214; italics added]

Individual and idiosyncratic motivations are only "incidental causes"; "egoism is its generating cause." This statement is equally true of anomie and altruism; they are currents of feeling created by society. Underlying these notions of collective motivation is a fundamental analytical presupposition: that the collectivity has a source of motivation, the "collective consciousness." Commentators have noted that the French *conscience* encompassed the English "conscience" and "consciousness." In *Division of Labor*, the idea of conscience is more important than that of consciousness; this work was also characterized by essentialist or vitalist notions of "conscience." But four years later, in 1897, when *Suicide* was written, the idea of a center of consciousness in society rather than a societal conscience prevailed, though it was never explicitly formulated as a causal (intervening) variable. Given Durkheim's avowed goal of a positive social science dealing with observables, it would be difficult to justify attributing causal significance to such intangibles. However, once a psychological variable manifests itself as a *rate*, then one is dealing with a different order of reality, observables, or social facts as "things." Durkheim's dilemma at this time was to formulate a methodological program for a natural science of society in *Rules*, on the one hand, and as a practicing social scientist to analyze a complex body of data on suicide, on the other. The simplicity of the methodological rules does not fit the complexity entailed in social analysis. To his credit, Durkheim was not satisfied with a mere empirical correlation; he had to ask the basic question pertaining to reflexivity and meaning: *why* do people commit suicide under certain social conditions?

The question of *why*, which I treat as a problem of meaning and a fundamental human articulation, must necessarily imply intentionality or motivation and reflexivity. Yet Durkheim refuses to accept a theory of individual motivation, since to do so not only would be nonempirical but, even more important, would negate his intention of carving out a specific domain for social science—a domain of social facts, of a collectivity sharply differentiated from the domain of the psychologist and the biologist. His solution was to postulate a collective consciousness specific to the domain of social science. Furthermore, the idea of *why*, of meaning, never emerges in *Rules* and emerges only implicitly in *Suicide*. For social facts are things, observables out there, having an existence outside the individual or collective will, rather than, as Weber saw, meanings which relate to existential issues of human species life and mediated through consciousness.

In spite of his antipsychological bias, Durkheim had a psychological theory which was basic to his essentially conservative view of human society. This theory was consonant with his theoretical (functionalist) view of society as a finely equilibrated organism, based on part-whole relationships, geared to fulfilling or satisfying the needs or requirements of the social system. He presents his theory of the relation between human needs and the functioning of the sociopolitical order in his discussion of anomic suicide, where he notes that, during economic crises such as booms and depressions, there is a disturbance in social equilibrium, which in turn increases the suicide rate.

Human needs, says Durkheim, are both acquired and physical. The latter pose little problem, but there is a serious problem of regulation in relation to acquired needs, appetites, or desires (emotions and drives). No internal regulatory mechanism can set a limit to these needs, either in the human organic constitution or in the psychological constitution. In a sentence reminiscent of Freud's (later) characterization of the id, Durkheim says: "Our capacity for feeling in itself is an insatiable and bottomless abyss" (1966:247). In contrast, purely biological drives are finite and satiable among both humans and animals. Bilogical nature, everywhere the same, possesses internal mechanisms that control our (biological) *drives,* but there are not such controls in the sphere of human *needs.* Thus the passions, theoretically illimitable, must be limited. Moreover, proper societal functioning (equilibrium) requires that these passions, needs, and emotions be controlled relative to the class position of the individual, his profession, and his general social situation. Such regulation of needs must come from outside the body or mind "from an authority which they respect, to which they yield spontaneously" (1966:249). This is, of course, society, which acts either directly or "through the agency of one of its organs" (p. 249). "It alone has the power necessary to stipulate law and to set the point beyond which the passions must not go" (p. 249).

This regulatory function "fixes with relative precision that maximum degree of ease of living to which each social class may legitimately aspire" (p. 249). To use Lewin's terminology, the levels of achievement are harmoniously blended with levels of aspiration. Although Durkheim insists that nothing is immutable about this scale and that it must vary according to time, place, and history, he nevertheless assumes an equilibrium model of society, a functional mode of explanation, and a conservative political view of human society.

Now Durkheim can relate his theory of needs to that of anomic suicide. When booms and depressions or similar crises occur, there is a declassification of the social life. In depressions individuals from a higher stratum are pushed into a new, lower (unfamiliar) position; the reverse occurs in booms. "At the very moment when traditional rules have lost their authority, the richer prize offered these appetites stimulates them and makes them more exigent and impatient of control. The state of deregulation or anomy is thus further heightened by passions being less disciplined precisely when they need more disciplining" (1966:253). Thus passions are unleashed during booms and depressions because the norms regulating passions are no longer operative. Those who are pushed to the new position or class, it is implied, have not yet assimilated or cannot assimilate the values of that class; the old values no longer operate; the passions are laid bare; and the individual hurtles to his doom. Unhappily Durkheim does not tell us why the response to this situation must necessarily entail suicide rather than, or in addition to, homicide or various other kinds of antisocial behaviors and personality disorders, although, I shall presently show, an answer is implicit in his theory.

Durkheim's ingenious and largely plausible theory of needs poses problems for the sociologism enunciated in *Rules* and its application in *Suicide*. The causes of suicide lie not simply in anomie defined as the deregulatory function per se but also in the human passions, needs, and emotions that are laid bare as a consequence. In anomie, human needs, no longer under normative control, exist in a free-floating manner, one might say, and these instigate the suicidal response in *individuals*. Thus needs or personal motivations, far from being fortuitous, are central to anomic suicide though unrecognized as such by Durkheim himself. Nevertheless, as I noted earlier, Durkheim seemed to postulate collective motivations as the intervening cause of suicide and they manifest themselves in society as currents of depression and so forth.

How can we reconcile these "social currents" (as Durkheim labeled them in *Rules*) with the notion of unregulated needs or emotions in situations of anomie? Durkheim, not recognizing the problem, could not provide an answer. Yet such an answer can be inferred from his own account. *The social currents of depression and disillusionment are themselves the products of these personal emotions and needs, which, removed from their normative moorings, can no longer be related to human problems of meaning and existence and perforce must result in depression and disillusionment and constitute a major motivational impetus for self-inflicted death.* When we spell out Durkheim's theory in a manner that he could not, the problems of collective motivation are locked into problems of social regulation or deregulation, as the case may be, and also into the fundamental problems of the personal needs and motivations of the individual.

It is now time to consider in more detail Durkheim's use of the term "collective conscience" or "consciousness," its analytical utility in sociological analysis, and the phenomenological reality which the term designates. Let me start off with an examination of his important essay on "Collective and Individual Representations" (1974), written in 1898, soon after *Suicide*. In this paper Durkheim was explicitly arguing against the biologism of nineteenth-century thinkers like Maudesly and James who, he claimed, reduced ideas, including collectively held ideas, to the working of the brain and ultimately of its cells. Such reductionism was abhorrent to a man who was attempting to delineate a special domain for sociology. It is less well known, since it is not explicitly stated by him, that Durkheim was also arguing against the psychological reductionism of Mill, with whose work he was thoroughly familiar. Biologism, Durkheim felt, was dangerous because it denied autonomy to culture, or, in Durkheim's terminology, to "collective representations." He felt that social scientists need not concern themselves with the operation of the brain; they need assume only the existence of mind. But the assumption of "mind" in place of brain must not imply a mentalistic or psychological reductionism where, in Mill's fashion, "mental laws" were substituted for social laws. Why is this the case? Inasmuch as individual ideas or representations are independent of the brain cells but rather presuppose mind, collective representations (collectively held ideas) are independent of the mind, since they presuppose society, which, in turn, is a new reality sui generis. If individual representations are created by the mind, collective representations are produced by society.

Much of Durkheim's argument, it seems to me, is directed against Mill, who in his *System of Logic*, book 6, deals with "the logic of the moral sciences." Mill argues that social science is rooted in psychology, the science that deals with the "elementary laws of the mind," and ethology, "the ulterior science which determines the kind of character produced, in conformity to those general laws" (1856:445–446). The latter is an "exact science of Human Nature" (p. 446). Social science is built on the foundations of these sciences of individual man. "If, therefore, the phenomena of human thought, feeling, and action, are subject to fixed laws, the phenomena of society cannot but conform to fixed laws, the consequence of the preceding" (p. 445). Prediction, however, would not be possible in sociology, as it is in astronomy, because "the circumstances . . . which influence the condition and progress of society are innumerable, and perpetually changing; and though they all change in obedience to causes, and therefore to laws, the multitude of causes is so great as to defy our limited powers of calculation" (p. 456). This reductive thesis is neatly summed up in the chapter dealing with his critical appraisal of the experimental method in social science.

The laws of the phenomena of society are, and can be, nothing but the laws of the actions and passions of human beings united together in the social state. Men, however, in a state of society, are still men;

their actions and passions are obedient to the laws of individual human nature. *Men are not, when brought together, converted into another kind of substance,* with different properties; as hydrogen and oxygen are different from water, or as hydrogen, oxygen, carbon, and azote, are different from nerves, muscles, and tendons. Human beings in society have no properties but those which are derived from, and may be resolved into, the laws of the nature of individual man. [p. 458; italics added. See also Pocock 1961:34–35 and Popper 1963:80–99]

Durkheim reacted against this and postulated the following notion: men *are* in fact, when brought together, converted into another kind of substance, a new reality, a collectivity or society which is the domain of sociology. Karl Popper's comment about Marx applies equally to Durkheim: he also affirmed "the autonomy of sociology" [Popper 1963: (2) 88, 90].

Nevertheless, several fundamental questions remained unanswered, the most important one being: if collective ideas or representations are independent of mind, how are they generated, and how do they change? Individual representations are for the most part nonproblematic: my ideas are directly generated from my mind. But what about collective ideas—in what sense could we say that they arise from society without the mediation of mind or consciousness? How does a collectivity generate collective ideas? It is with respect to this problem that we note the fundamental analytical utility of the notion of "collective consciousness": this agency is responsible for the formation of collective representations and their changes through time. We now can formulate the paradigm implicit in almost all of Durkheim's work (see the figure below).

| Collectivity or | → | Collective | → | Collective |
| Social System | | Consciousness | | Representation |

To take out the concept of a collective consciousness would be to reduce cultural or collective ideas to a mere 'reflex' of the social structure. Durkheim saw this point clearly in "Individual and Collective Representations" (1974), where he examined Fustel de Coulange's work on Roman religion. He argued that the origin of the Roman pantheon could not be understood without an awareness of Roman social structure, but the myths and rituals of the religion transcend this structural dependence; the one does not reflect the other. Thus collective representations are not a mere epiphenomenon of the social or political structure. Radcliffe-Brown, who borrowed Durkheim's ideas, simply ignored the latter's concept of a "collective consciousness," which probably struck him as vague, smacking of notions of group mind and the discredited ideas of people like Gustave Le Bon and of other vitalists and essentialists. In doing so Radcliffe-Brown relegated religion to an epiphenomenon of the social structure. But Durkheim had no doubt regarding the analytical utility of his concept. In one of his last papers, on "The Dualism of Human Nature" (1964b) he wrote that collective ideas are due to "that singularly creative and fertile psychic operation—which is scientifically analyzable—by which a plurality of individual consciousnesses enter into communion and are fused into a common consciousness" (p. 335).

The last quotation brings me to an important aspect of Durkheim's thought: the notion of a collective consciousness is not merely an analytically important concept; this concept itself has a phenomenological reality which he elucidates. Collective consciousness is quite unlike Freud's typological model of the mind: it is doubtful whether ego, id, and superego can be directly translated into "things" or into empirically identifiable phenomena. But presumably, for Durkheim, as for empiricists and positivists in general, the conceptual terms of science must be rooted in sense experience. Thus the term "collective consciousness" not only was a concept indispensible for analyzing group ideas or collective representations but also referred to a specific empirical reality: there *exists* an agency in society which can be designated by that term.

> To be sure, it is likewise true that society has no other active forces than individuals, but individuals by combining form a psychical existence of a new species, which consequently has its own manner of thinking and feeling. Association itself is also an active factor productive of special effects. In itself it is therefore something new. When the consciousness of individuals, instead of remaining isolated, becomes grouped and combined, something in the world has altered. [1966:310]

If one agrees that the collectivity is an independent order of reality different from the sum of individuals, one can also admit that a collective consciousness can exist as a reality sui generis, separate from the sum of individual consciousnesses. If one grants analytical and empirical status to the former, one must also necessarily grant similar status to the latter. Only two elements are required: that of the individual (a person with consciousness) and that of an interacting plurality of individuals. These elements go to constitute a collectivity and at the same time a collective consciousness.

Consider a well-known Durkheimian statement regarding religion: "Religion is in a word the system of symbols by which society becomes conscious of itself" (1966:312). Here we have a notion of reflexivity that is strikingly at variance with the mechanical notion of culture implicit in his notions of exteriority and constraint in *Rules*. But for Durkheim the reflexive nature of society was no metaphor: it is the product of an active agency capable of motivation. Immediately following the above statement is this one: "It is the characteristic way of thinking of collective existence. Here then is a great group of states of mind which would not have originated if individual states of consciousness had not combined, and which result from this union and are superadded to those which derive from individual natures" (1966:312). And then later: "We refuse to accept that these phenomena have as a substratum the conscience of the individual; we assign them another: that formed by all the individual consciences in union and combination" (1966:319). Given the primacy of collective motivation in Durkheim's sociology, he does not hesitate to label his discipline a species of social psychology: "We see no objection to calling sociology a variety of psychology, if we carefully add that social psychology has its own laws which are not those of individual psychology" (1966:313). Lévi-Strauss's pejorative assessment of Durkheim as a psychologist and Evan-Pritchard's favorable view of him as a sociologist par excellence are reconciled in this statement: he is both in his concern for the individual as well as the society. This concern is nicely expressed in one of his last papers, "The Dualism of Human Nature": "Although sociology is defined as the science of society, it cannot, in reality, deal with human groups that are the immediate objects of its investigation without eventually touching on the individual who is the basic element of which these groups are composed. For society can exist only if it penetrates the consciousness of individuals and fashions it in 'its image and resemblance' " (1964b:323).

CRITICAL REFLECTIONS ON CULTURE AND DEEP MOTIVATION

My own critical reflections on the Kardiner-Durkheim model, and on the idea of culturally constituted defenses, must necessarily be schematic and speculative. I can only ask a few key questions regarding these issues. I have no answers, although all of us interested in employing psychoanalysis in sociocultural analysis must eventually confront them. My basic criticism relates to the empiricist application of this model, although this must also be qualified. Kardiner, it must be remembered, noted that the concept of basic personality was an "operational tool" (1948). Durkheim never used this term, but his idea of definition and of a presupposition-less social science spelled out in *Rules* came close to Bridgman's idea of operationalism (1936:5–15). Durkheim's *Suicide* is a strict operational or "scientific" application of the model. This statement is less so in the more speculative work *Elementary Forms*, where the same model is placed in the rich ethnographic context of Australian aboriginal religion. The model tends toward historicization in this later work. So with Kardiner. In spite of formal statements regarding operationalism, Kardiner's *practice* tends (somewhat shakily no doubt) toward a historicist (i.e., ethnographic) application or contextual embodiment of the formal paradigm.

94

Nevertheless, I believe the very strengths of the model hide its real weakness. If Durkheim wanted to carve out a domain for sociology, Kardiner in the same vein wanted to convert the theory of individual motivation in Freud to one of collective motivation, consonant with Durkheimian sociologism (and the empiricism of *Rules* and *Suicide*). Thus the key term, basic personality structure, was inferred from standardized and empirically observable child-training practices. This shift not only brought psychoanalysis into the domain of sociology but also converted Freudianism into an empirical social science, since the notion of child-training practices was analogous to Durkheim's idea of social facts as "things."

I do not think it necessary any longer to carve out a domain for sociology (social science) in order to affirm its autonomy. In fact Durkheim's contemporary Weber, influenced by German hermeneutical thinkers, made this point well when he said that "it is not the 'actual' interrelatedness of 'things' but the conceptual interrelatedness of problems which define the scope of the various sciences" (1949:68, first published in 1904). A domain does not exist out there in empirical reality; it exists by virtue of our cognitive interest in a subject (1949:64). So is it with Freud. Inasmuch as one can regard Weber as an imperfect Durkheim, as Parsons (1937) did, one can think of Freud as a failed positivist, as Grünbaum does (1984). Or one can, with Ricoeur in his brilliant *Freud and Philosophy* (1970), make a case for a more phenonmenologically and hermeneutically oriented Freud. I shall leave others to debate what Freud *really* was. I believe we all appropriate our ancestors, and my appropriation of Freud is a hermeneutical one in the manner of Ricoeur's. I like it that way in terms of my own cognitive interest in the relationship between culture and deep motivation.

In terms of this interest in culture and deep motivation, I see a striking difference between those who employ a Durkheim-derived, Kardiner-type model and Freud himself. The *turn* in Freud's thought, parallel to the turn in Heidegger and Wittgenstein, came very early when he realized that it was not so much the *fact* of parental seduction but fantasy (or the meaning of seduction) that determined the neuroses. Masson (1983) may well be correct in saying that this theory led Freud to ignore actual cases of seduction and child abuse in Victorian Europe. But this does not resolve the issue at the heart of the problem: not empirical reality ("facts") per se but the *meaning* of that reality for people is significant for both culture (Weber) and neuroses (Freud).

The Kardiner relation between antecedent, interviewing, and consequent variables makes little sense in terms of the Freudian ontological turn. If fantasy, rather than reality or fact, determines neurosis, what is the relationship between child training, personality, and projective systems? In *Little Hans*, for example, the father was a "good guy"; yet Hans developed a terrible fear of him, which was projected into his horse phobia. Kardiner's model operates differently; if something like a horse phobia exists in the culture, it must mean that the fathers in that society are mean! It seems to me that, if one wants to postulate a connection between deep motivation and culture, one must move away from the empiricist preoccupation with child training to the *meaning* of the child training and the manner in which the values of the culture are communicated in infancy by the socializing agents. It may well be that the cultural defense or projective system is not something related to an adult basic personality but something activated in different forms and ways in early childhood itself.

Here I have some reservations regarding Spiro's culturally constituted defense mechanisms. Spiro seems to realize the mechanistic and arbitrary relation between Kardiner's three variables, but his own solution is not radical enough. Spiro recognizes that cultural defenses are not just defenses against nuclear traumatic experiences but *sublimations* thereof (1982a:338–343). Now, sublimation is exemplified in Freud in the activity of the artist, such as Leonardo da Vinci in *Leonardo* (1910b). Here childhood sexual drives are transformed (sublimated) into the drive for research. "Owing to his very early inclination towards sexual curiosity the greater portion of his sexual instinct could be sublimated in a general urge to know and thus evaded repression" (1910b:132). But the trouble with Freud, as Ricoeur discerningly shows, is that sublimation is one of his least developed concepts. Freud did not even devote a special paper to the subject (Ricoeur 1970:483–493). One of Freud's clearest discussion on sublimation occurs in his paper "On Narcissism: An Introduction," where he distinguishes between sublimation and idealization:

> Sublimation is a process that concerns object-libido and consists in the instinct's directing itself towards an aim other than, and remote from, that of sexual satisfaction; in this process the accent falls upon deflection from sexuality. Idealization is a process that concerns the *object*; by it that object, without any alteration in its nature, is aggrandized and exalted in the subject's mind. Idealization is possible in the sphere of ego-libido as well as in that of object-libido. For example, the sexual overvaluation of an object is an idealization of it. In so far as sublimation describes something that has to do with the instinct and idealization something to do with the object, the two concepts are to be distinguished from each other. [1914:94]

Sublimation has at least one consistent feature: it entails the radical transformation of the aim of childhood drives, especially sexuality (1908:187). But culturally constituted defenses do not seem to operate in quite that way. For example, the monk has dependency needs of an intense sort: he satisfies them in his relation to lay donors. The result in Freudian terms is a change of object ("idealization"); the monk is shifting from the nurturant parent to another, but it does not entail the transformation of the drive. Furthermore, in Freud the transformation of childhood aims in sublimation is so thorough that it cannot be treated as a replacement for psychosis. It is meaningless to say that Leonardo's art is a replacement for psychosis or that it "precludes the outbreak of pathology," since the sublimation has been thoroughly integrated as a component of the artist's very being. Now, I am convinced that cultural defenses do operate, at least in some persons, as something analogous to sublimation. But by the same token we must look at the manner in which monasticism has been integrated, through various mechanisms that we do not yet know, into the monk's very being, transforming childhood aims into a higher calling. Only when sublimation *fails* do cultural defenses become replacements for psychoses.

The idea that cultural defenses may substitute for psychoses creates other troublesome problems also. A psychosis is blatantly pathological. But a cultural defense is not, because for Spiro it is acceptable to the culture. This and the cultural "idealization" of the object makes the cultural defense "normal." Normality and abnormality are also specifiable according to pan-human criteria that could apply to situations of cross-cultural variability. "For a Western man to believe that he is the reincarnation of some ancestor is to commit severe cognitive distortion" (1965a:105). By that token, persons in the West who believe in reincarnation must be abnormal! Freud, in contrast, had no truck with the idea of normal and abnormal; everywhere in his work he blurs this distinction. Spiro does imply that cultural defenses or symbolic forms, by warding off cognitive and perceptual distortion, provide avenues to communication with others in the culture and also help minimize the alienation of the sufferer. But this interesting relation between the sufferer (the person employing the defense) and others in the culture is reified into universalist criteria of normality and abnormality applicable to all cultures.

Let me be brash and conclude that it is not necessary for a psychoanalytic anthropology to play with such binary distinction as normal-abnormal, relativism-universalism. Instead we should develop the idea—suggested by Spiro himself—that cultural defenses are products of sublimation and *not* replacements for psychotic fantasies. When we shift our ground in this way, we begin to ask a series of interesting questions regarding the manner in which infantile drives and conflicts are transformed, in various complex ways and at various levels of remove, into those symbolic forms known as culturally constituted defenses.

4

Eufunctions, Dysfunctions, and Oracles

Literary Miracle Making in Taiwan

DAVID K. JORDAN 〜〜〜

EUFUNCTIONAL AND DYSFUNCTIONAL ANALYSIS

This chapter takes its inspiration from Melford Spiro's article "Social Systems, Personality, and Functional Analysis" (1961b). Like much of his work, it considers the functions and motivations of social behavior. By "function" we usually mean eufunction. Human customs nearly always also involve dysfunctions, and the present paper attempts to expand Spiro's scheme of functional analysis to incorporate dysfunction by presenting most human activity as both eufunctional and dysfunctional, a sort of vector sum of causes producing a wide range of effects. I begin with eufunction.

To explain the persistence of a custom or institution (as against its origin), we must refer to its functions, Spiro argues. For Spiro, following Merton, a human institution may have manifest or latent functions. Unlike Merton, Spiro contrasts manifest and latent (a distinction he refines into conscious and unconscious, recognized and unrecognized), with two other, orthogonal oppositions. In the full scheme, a function may be recognized (conscious, manifest) or unrecognized (unconscious, latent), but it may also (and separately) be intended or unintended, and it may be personal (psychological) or social (sociological).[1] Only on the intended functions, conscious or not, does responsibility for institutional persistence fall, but in his article Spiro demonstrates that all eight permutations of these dichotomies are meaningful. One example he gives is Sioux warfare (pp. 111–113), which brings individual prestige (an intended, recognized, personal function) and

98

protects Sioux society from enemies (an intended, recognized, social function). But an important human drive is hostility, which has aggression as a means of its reduction. It would be destructive to focus aggression upon group members, including ego. Accordingly, an unrecognized but intended personal function of Sioux warfare is the reduction of an individual's hostility, while an unrecognized and unintended personal function is the deflection of aggression from the self. An unconscious, intended, social function, the analysis continues, is solidarity, while the deflection of aggression from the in-group is an unintended, unrecognized social function.

Spiro's analysis makes us realize how complex social behavior becomes when one takes unconscious motivation into consideration and how essential it nevertheless is to consider unconscious motivation in a methodical way.[2]

One of the central human drives, as noted above, is hostility. This notion was a cornerstone of the analysis of Sioux warfare. Another cornerstone is dependency. So important are these two that, in Spiro's models at least, they inevitably get pride of place. Not all individuals experience dependency or hostility to the same degree or in the same way, and different individuals obviously use different cultural resources in relieving these impulses. One important institution for their relief is religion. In a variety of papers and books, Spiro has shown how religious systems serve his full typology of functions by providing the "raw material" for behaviors that are psychologically satisfying and socially either harmless or eufunctional.

But religious systems can have dysfunctions as well as eufunctions. One dysfunction is a tendency to generate interpretations of the world that are somewhat discrepant from mundane experience, potentially producing dissonance. At least some religious customs thus require a more or less constant system of legitimation by which the believer can justify his belief to the nonbeliever, or to semibelievers, and by which he can specifically neutralize the nonbeliever's objections and reduce dissonance for himself. Dealing analytically with dysfunction as well as eufunction allows us both (1) to account for the tremendous variation in saliency of various customs making up the same cultural system and (2) to approach the problem of "change" that has always troubled functionalist analysis.

A CASE EXAMPLE: SECTARIANISM IN TAIWAN

In China miracles are one device by which religious legitimation is accomplished. By "miracles" I mean any events that believers interpret as demonstrating that something is happening in violation of the nature of the mundanely known universe. A miracle, naturally, is in the eye of the beholder, and the definition includes magic tricks believed by observers to be "real." In China miracles are the stock in trade of various priests and exorcists who peddle liturgy for a living.

In recent years I have been concerned with sectarian societies in Taiwan (Jordan 1981, 1982, 1983; Jordan and Overmyer 1986). Since miracles are part of the way in which they attract and hold members, they can provide the context for an example. Membership in a sect is a self-conscious undertaking, and it is unusual rather than universal. (Much of nonsectarian folk religion in Taiwan involves the whole community and has an inevitability that makes the notions of "individual membership," "recruitment," and "retention" largely irrelevant.[3]

A sectarian society—a common Chinese name is *bayluan,* "phoenix worship"—comprises individual members engaged in meritorious religious exercises, nearly always centering on the creation of religious texts through automatic writing séances.[4] Some groups possess their own temples; others use private houses or public temples. A few economically successful sectarian organizations extend to two or more temples, constituting, in a sense, "denominations" of the sectarian religious tradition.

At least two sectarian "denominations" maintain islandwide organizations with hundreds of local congregations. One of these is the Compassion Society ("Tsyrhuey Tarng"), briefly described by Overmyer (1977); the other is the Celestial Way ("Tian Daw").[5] Both sects center on the worship of a figure known under a variety of similar names, including "the Unborn Mother" ("Wusheng Laomuu"), "the Golden Mother of the Jade Lake" ("Yauchyr Jinmuu"), and simply "mother" (*muu*).[6] The sectarian tradition in general and the sectarian tradition in combination with the Golden Mother cult in particular are late twentieth-century derivatives of much longer Chinese traditions of automatic writing and sectarian organization (Jordan and Overmyer 1986). The mother sects are generally more successful than the others, probably because they selected the nurturant Golden Mother as their object of special attention.

Participation in a sect involves acknowledging the legitimacy and authority of an automatic writing oracle that is normally its center. The oracle is operated by a medium in trance, who traces characters on a bed of sand or incense ash with a forked stick, called a *ji*. Chinese characters written by ji are clear enough for any literate Chinese to decipher, and often a number of attendants and visitors watch the process.[7] The characters are always read out loud by an official reader and transcribed by a secretary. The finished written revelations may be personal instructions to individual petitioners (regular worshipers or visitors), but in sects they are more often general mythological and hortatory texts exhorting the group to good works and congratulating it on its virtue. Such revelations may be assembled into collections and published for free distribution as books and magazines to members and to anyone else willing to read them.

Sectarian groups meet in the evening several times a month. In the Compassion Society and most other groups, membership is marked by the oracle's revelation to each regular member of a "chapel name" (*tarnghaw*). Members are appointed to positions in a hierarchy of functionaries. Since the revelation task itself requires only a few people (usually mostly men), other members (usually mostly women) spend the sessions reverently standing, sitting, or kneeling, depending upon the group. Before the medium enters a trance to begin the revelation, many groups provide a musical invocation chanted by one or more cantors. Incense is also burnt, and flowers and other offerings are presented. In most societies each of these tasks is assigned to a designated "officer," so that most members have titles and specific obligations. After the trance has ended, the newly revealed text, if it is not directed to individuals, is read out and explicated by a senior sectarian.

An evening's revelations normally come from a wide variety of divinities, usually of the ordinary, popular pantheon but occasionally from unknown minor gods known only to the group and sometimes from the Golden Mother herself. In Golden Mother sects, other gods often refer to her and to the mythology relating to her.[8]

All sectarians exhibit a strong tendency to identify a benign presence who oversees their daily lives. Members of sectarian groups are expected to offer these group their primary religious loyalty. A member may be scolded by the ji oracle for consulting a spirit medium unconnected with the group. Some congregations participate in processions connected with celebrations of other temples or shrine center; if so, members are expected to participate with the sect rather than independently or with other groups.[9] Membership in a sect, in short, involves subordinating one's general religious participation to one's sectarian membership, sometimes at a social cost.

A FUNCTIONAL ANALYSIS OF TAIWAN SECTARIANISM

Returning to Spiro's scheme of intended and unintended, conscious and unconscious, and personal and social functions, we may produce a convincing analysis of the role of bayluan in the psychic and social economies of its members.[10] The consciously intended, personal function of participation is salvation or at least the gaining of religious merit toward that eventual end. The consciously intended social function (reflected in the publication of, for example, hortatory revelations) is the promotion of virtue, which turns out to mean value continuity with the Confucian past. Unintended but recognized personal functions are the avoidance of anxiety-producing behavior—people speak of behaving "better" because of their membership—and recognition (such as by holding offices). An unintended but recognized social function is the creation of social support networks, which provide financial and moral support to participants in time of crisis. (My informants report cases of emergency housing or loans; for some individuals such support can, presumably, become an intended personal function, as it does in some American churches.)

The analysis of unconscious functions is chancier, given my available field materials. The stress on dependency, particularly clearly illustrated by the success of the Golden Mother congregations and by the intimacy and frequency that informants report in their dealings with her, leads me to conclude that an intended personal function is the expression of this dependency, and an intended social function may be the relief of these dependency needs in ways that are socially valued (namely conformity to a traditionalistic society stressing socially eufunctional behaviors such as filial piety). Another intended but unrecognized personal function seems to me to relate to status anxiety. Chinese child-rearing practices involve punishment for misbehaving but little reward for conformity. The treatment of children, moreover, constantly stresses the extent to which they are "under observation" by a critical world concerned about their conformity.[11] My general model hypothesizes that these influences are conducive to generating anxiety about one's success at fulfilling the demands of a status.[12] Sectarian revelations congratulate members on their virtue, provide religiously meritorious tasks, and accept members without regard to their normally significant reference groups. The groups, in other words, reassure members of their inherent worth as the pantheon does what Chinese children wish parents would do: praise them.

Another unintended unrecognized personal function concerns hostility. Sectarian societies provide opportunity for the hortatory exhortation of outsiders to join the society or to perform good works. They provide an outlet for the expression of hostility felt toward a wide range of people, diverting the aggressive feelings generated by this hostility away from the individual.[13] Note that the act of converting the expression of aggression into traditionalistic exhortation in defense of socially approved traditional values also diverts it form socially destructive channels, thereby fulfilling an unintended, unrecognized, social function.

Given all of the eufunctional features of sectarian life, why do some Chinese not join up? One answer is that some of the features are not functional for all potential members. Not everyone requires or receives the personal satisfactions just listed as sectarian functions. Not everyone in Taiwan intends the intended functions or has personal needs effectively met by the personal functions. Even for participants, there are in fact dysfunctions. Our functional analysis is not really finished unless we also take into account dysfunctional features of the burden that one assumes in participation. If there are benefits, there are also costs.

If we envision the social world as the sum of various vectors, a compromise among conflicting forces, or the product of the joint operation of costs and benefits, we reach a "functional" analysis that must be as concerned with dysfunction at various points of analysis as with eufunction. Using Spiro's differentiation of intended and unintended, conscious and unconscious, and personal and social functions once again, we find that it can be used to guide a study of dysfunction as well as of eufunction.

Beginning with consciously recognized, personal dysfunctions, we find that members in the end contribute money, sometimes considerable amounts of money, whether to buy incense and flowers for the altars or to build a new temple. (The charge most often made against sectarian activity by nonmembers is that it diverts money from the family bank account.) Second, members find that they are subject to criticism from outsiders for being obsessively concerned with religion. Furthermore, membership, being exclusive in many sects, can also preempt participation in much folk religion, including many community rituals. The result is a certain alienation from (earlier) friends and family. These costs, while almost certainly unintended, are recognized by members and held to be unfortunate.

Some widely recognized personal dysfunctions of sectarian membership can have a eufunctional aspect as well and may in fact be intended. Membership takes time away from other affairs, mostly a dysfunction, but (especially for women) membership is also an excuse to escape from the family and its labor demands (a personal eufunction if a familial dysfunction).

Holding office in the sect or becoming practiced in its scripture or rituals brings prestige either with reference to a (hypothetical) reference group of all meritorious people or in the eyes of fellow members. But a case can be made that there is general recognition, that something is distinctly "second-rate" about this esoteric knowledge, simplified as it is from far more complex historical precedent. Sectarian chanting of Buddhist texts, for example, is not quite as prestigious as Buddhist chanting of them. Furthermore, despite lip service, esoteric traditionalistic knowledge is not in fact as widely or highly valued a commodity in modern Taiwan as the modern knowledge conveyed by the system of schools and universities and connected with the world of high-paying jobs. Physics and accounting, not geomancy and fortune telling, are widely perceived to be worthy occupations for the young.[14] Thus eufunctional prestige is dysfunctional superstition in some contexts.

Members and nonmembers also recognize some other unintended social costs to sectarian activity. Within the wider society, sectarian societies of all sorts have an unsavory reputation for attracting rebels, and indeed the most vivid Chinese popular image of a sect is that it is a rebel cell.[15]

Another recognized social dysfunction, probably unintended in most cases, is the subversion of the religious mainstream by sectarian activity. Buddhism is the commonest case in point, but for a Western observer perhaps the most vivid example may be the appearance of Jesus in ji-writing séances, so that the sectarians claim to supersede mission Christianity. Most sectarians do not deny that, if Christians took such revelation seriously, there would in the end be a dismantling of the Christian organizations and their assimilation into the ji divination groups.

Unrecognized dysfunctions, because they are unrecognized, do not enter directly into the rhetorical efforts for or against sectarianism. They are nevertheless real. At the social level, an unintended and unrecognized social consequence may be the association of traditionalist, "Confucian" morality with the overlay of sectarian liturgy and text production. To the extent that nonmembers see bayluan as superstition, such an association would erode the legitimacy of the traditionalist moral system promoted by the present government and corresponding to many of the private moralities of most Chinese in Taiwan.

At a personal level, an unrecognized, probably intended, but ultimately destructive effect of revelation societies (as of many similar religious activities) may be to divert attention into putative solutions rather than real solutions, exchanging short-term comfort for long-term efforts to cope. A common example is the use of medical treatment prescribed by a writing medium in place of more expensive, time-consuming, or uncomfortable therapy by a doctor.

Clearly unintended and usually not directly recognized is the sense of personal dissonance that is inspired in individual members by the need to suspend disbelief about the sect and its revelations in the presence of constant challenges to its claims by nonmembers. I have saved this dysfunction for last because it seems to be especially pervasive, and for many it is the prime factor which seems to determine whether they will or will not participate in sects. The dissonance associated with believing what others doubt is clearly a personal dysfunction of membership. An important concern of sect leaders (and tradition) is devoted to resolving the dissonance by providing evidence that the disbelieving world is wrong. The expectation of dissonance may be one of the principal reasons why nonmembers remain nonmembers: who wants to join up with crackpots?

This summary treatment of the eufunctions and dysfunctions of membership in Taiwan sectarian societies shows that a functional analysis proceeding along the lines suggested by Spiro in his 1961 article can be rendered yet more productive if there is a parallel consideration of the simultaneous dysfunctions of the institution under examination. In the next section I consider the problem of dissonance and dissonance reduction, which I take to be a peculiarly important issue in the functional analysis of religious sectarianism.

POSSESSION TRANCE AND DISSONANCE REDUCTION

If we simplify a bit, the central focus of bayluan sect claims to significance is the ji oracle: the written revelations and the process by which they are produced. Insiders must believe that the medium (or the stylus) is possessed by gods to produce divine writ. Outsiders believe either that the possession is by rather darker forces or (much more commonly) that there is no possession at all. The issue is resolved by evidence, and the evidence is the miraculous character of the writing. Believers point on the one hand to the self-evident "godliness" (read: traditionalism, morality, and stereotypy) of the revelation but also to differences between them and everyday writing. In China, and probably elsewhere, proof, general or specific, comes through the medium's ability to do in trance what he or she cannot do ordinarily.

Trance (dis)abilities represent enough difference from workaday experience to be especially preadaptive to the role of sacred manifestation. Possession trance occurs in various forms in Taiwan, as in China as a whole. The forms most conspicuous to the casual visitor are speaking mediums, known in the English literature by their Hokkien name: tâng-ki. These men and women, in their miraculous mode, mortify their flesh dramatically and, in their oracular mode, provide advice to inquirers.[16] Closely related to these are writing mediums, who are responsible for the production of ji text.[17] Other instances of possession and trance are not normally involved in the problems we are considering here.[18]

A speaking medium, in trance, is believed to speak with the voice of a god that is usually also thought to occupy the body of the medium temporarily. Sometimes the fact of the god's presence, rather than what he or she says, is most important. Possession of a medium allows the god to participate in a ritual or procession or to utter oracles for individual or community edification. Most commonly, a speaking medium acts as a community counselor, operating from a small storefront temple or from his front parlor.[19] The trance of a writing medium, in contrast, is most often the channel by which an organized revelation society receives divine instruction. Speaking mediums tend to be scorned by traditionally minded educated people, whereas spirit writing societies have often attracted the interest of some literati.[20]

David K. Jordan

Every medium has the logistical problem of providing evidence both of the reality of his trance and (especially) of the legitimacy of his possession. The usual way for a speaking medium to demonstrate his legitimacy is mortification of the flesh by cutting or piercing his back or forehead or by burning his arms or chest with hot incense, all without any evidence of pain.[21] For many or most, this is unusual trance behavior, occurring only on festival occasions, but period mortification is nearly compulsory if a tâng-ki is to retain credibility.

A second (and more common) way for speaking mediums to make miracles is to produce revelations that include knowledge which people believe that the mediums themselves do not have. If a medium lacks the ability to speak fluently in Mandarin, for example, or to write characters, or to compose verse, or to remember names, the production of revelations which contain any of these characteristics provides evidence that that medium is truly possessed by another, higher intelligence.

Mortification of the flesh is incompatible with the class associations of literary activity. Writing mediums seek to incorporate miracle with oracle and to produce in trance a text that not only contains expressions of divine opinion or will but also is one that the writer would be incapable of producing "on his or her own," that is, when not in trance. The miracle, then, as for speaking mediums, lies in the discrepancy between trance and nontrance abilities.

The miracle of the ji rarely lies in the actual content of the revelations[22] and rarely in the *absolute* level of literary accomplishment. What constitutes a miracle is not even consistency of the literary style or level from one medium to another in the texts attributed to a certain god.[23] Rather, the mediums' legitimacy lies in the *relative* literacy of their revelation, that is, in the agreement that the revelations they make are beyond their out-of-trance ability.

Given the role of a discrepancy between trance and nontrance performance, both mediums and believers seek to depreciate mediums' nontrance abilities as well as to magnify the virtuosity of their trance productions; the interested skeptic does just the opposite.[24] Such an amplification of the difference between abilities in trance and abilities out of it is predictable on the basis of a theory of cognitive dissonance (Festinger, Rieken, and Schachter 1956): people try to make the world the way they have publicly committed themselves to its actually being. There is nothing at all surprising about minimizing the medium's out-of-trance abilities so that his or her in-trance abilities can benefit by the comparison.

The universalization of literacy in Taiwan has cheapened traditional village hen scratching and has raised standards for possession essays. Since one would expect educated writers to produce reasonably well-turned essays, the standards of evaluation rise accordingly, and "inspired" essays, to be seen as supernatural manifestations, must incorporate features that no ordinary person, *however* literate, would be able to produce on the spot. Not only are they expected to be in verse, but the verse is sometimes expected to exhibit complexities that make its composition especially difficult.[25]

Some of the resulting productions are therefore prodigious in their form, particularly if we bear in mind the rapidity with which they are revealed. Let me cite some examples in order of their formal complexity.[26] In a typical revelation from a spirit writing society, the text may be composed in simple prose or it may be in rhymed lines, usually of five or seven characters each. Chinese syntax is free enough so that this task is not particularly difficult. Sometimes the lines are composed so that the first character of the first line, when combined with the first characters of the second and third (and sometimes subsequent) lines, forms a separate message, typically the name of the revealing god, the name of the person to whom the revelation is directed, or the name of the hall where the revelation is taking place. The process of composition is more complex but not beyond the capacity of educated Chinese, particularly given the tendency of the audience to look indulgently upon shortcomings in the syntax or small inconsistencies in the style or content.

With figure 4.1, however, we enter a new world of difficulty. The inscriptions in figures 4.1 and 4.3 were presented to me by an extremely fervent believer in the Celestial Way sect. The believer argued that the "superiority" of the Celestial Way was clear from the revelation type illustrated in these figures. He claimed that the "high quality" of these revelations had led him to join and remain in the sect. As he understood the situation and explained it to me, the revelations in figures 4.1 and 4.3 were received in columns. In that form they made little sense. In order to convert figure 4.1 from nonsense to sacred writ, it is necessary to start reading with the middle character and to follow through the text in Greek-key fashion, winding out from the middle. (Figure 4.1 adds guidelines to indicate the correct path.) The reader who proceeds in this way discovers a verse made of seven-character lines. But in addition, the last character of each line is a complex graph containing within it the first character of the next seven-character line. (The first part of the text is analyzed in figure 4.2 to illustrate.) Thus each line shares its first and last characters with the adjacent lines, a pattern that links the poem in the long chain that winds from the center of the page. The Greek-key format is in fact especially appropriate, since this interlocking feature would be less obvious in the conventional multicolumn presentation of verse.[27]

道降庶民天機文:

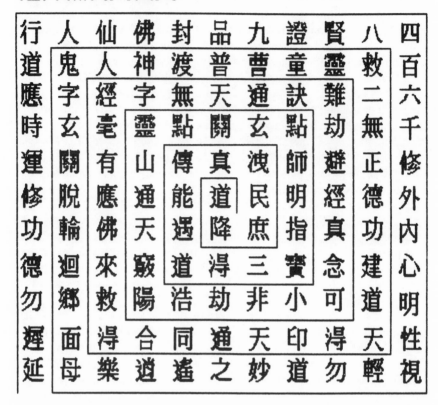

行	人	仙	佛	封	品	九	證	賢	八	四
道	鬼	人	神	渡	普	曹	童	靈	救	百
應	字	經	字	無	天	通	訣	難	二	六
時	玄	毫	靈	點	關	玄	點	劫	無	千
運	關	有	山	傳	真	洩	師	避	正	修
修	脫	應	通	能	道	民	明	經	德	外
功	輪	佛	遇	遇	降	庶	指	真	功	內
德	迴	來	竅	道	得	三	寶	念	建	心
勿	鄉	救	陽	浩	劫	非	小	可	道	明
遲	面	得	合	同	通	天	印	得	天	性
延	母	樂	逍	遙	之	妙	道	勿	輕	視

Figure 4.1. "Greek key" arrangement of Chinese text revealed in trance. Apparent gibberish becomes a religious poem when read from the middle outward (as indicated by superimposed lines). The ability to create such verses is a sign that the medium's trance is divine possession.

Figure 4.3 is the most complex revelation text I have encountered. One side of a Greek-key layout contains columns some of whose characters are in the same order as they would be if one simply took the text column by column. The message is therefore partly intelligible once we know to follow the Greek-key order. Figure 4.3, however, is gibberish until one has the solution to its puzzle. It is read starting in the middle and moving obliquely until a border is encountered. One reasonable place to start (not the only one!) is at character H3. One then reads down through I4, J5, and K6. Here one hits a border, turns counterclockwise to take in L6, and then angles up again to M5, N4, and O3, hitting a border again at P2. One makes

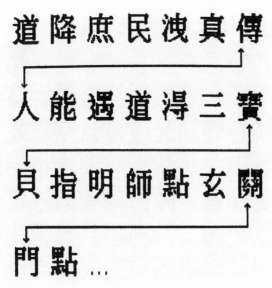

Figure 4.2. Interlocking lines of verse. The last
character of each metrical line includes the first
character of the next metrical line, as shown in this
analysis of the beginning of the text in figure 4.1.
This feature increases the sense that no human
could easily create such a verse without divine
help.

another turn to take in P1. Since that is a corner, one must turn again to
O1 before moving down to N2, M3, L4, and so on.[28] Because of the hexagonal
shape of the text, such a procedure eventually loops through all of the
characters and returns to the beginning, where one may continue round
again indefinitely, in an infinite loop. As in figure 4.1, the last character of
each verse line incorporates the first character of the next. Furthermore,
not only is the path of interpretation through the design extremely complex,
but the message closes back upon itself, with the first and last characters of
the poem interconnected just like the first and last characters of all the lines.
The verse is therefore effectively infinite, so that one may begin with any
line, progress methodically over all characters (with the same overlapping
of poetic lines), and continue round and round indefinitely, making the text
becomes a kind of infinite mantra. To the believer, the symbolism of this
closure may be as appealing as the complex coding itself. What believing
informants stress, however, is the improbability that such a text could be
written in columns by an unaided human being. What dazzles is not only
the symmetrical intricacy of the pattern of decipherment but the fact that

109

白衣大師九六天機碑文:

A B C D E F G H I J K L M N O P

1 馬苦不袠唯感豈悟終攢難吞察莫渡湖
2 牛願耕心輕知蒼臨參自空省蛇女要江
3 觀變誦田全馬個天然要衣拳男咬放奸
4 了古愛祥農客陣山神會道強忙船獄萬
5 千多臥流戀工油魂體共打真生腳末地
6 傳冰少貧輪鍋商須迷聞駕救訪後亂遊

Figure 4.3. Extremely complex revelation text read in a meander. The geometric intricacy of the reading pattern (described in the text), combined with interlocking of the lines of verse (as in figure 4.2.) virtually guarantees that ordinary people would be incapable of composing such a text, written in trance in columns. This intricacy is taken by believers as proof of the verse's divine origin, but nonbelievers see it as showing advance preparation and hence fraud.

it was revealed out of order and that the path of decipherment had to be puzzled out after the text had been set down.

Leaders of the Celestial Way have been charged by apostates (including at least one apostate medium) with faking revelations by composing them in advance, then requiring the mediums to memorize them and write them with a great flourish in ritually charged surroundings but not in a real trance and not spontaneously (Wen 1977). Such a deception is perfectly possible. It is hard to imagine that very many people are capable of composing these puzzles out of order, off the tops of their heads, while in a dissociated state. Most sectarian revelations, including Celestial Way revelations, are far less elaborate and ingenious.

Celestial Way informants were impressed not by literacy—these days anybody can achieve it—but by literary stunt driving. They were possibly (probably) also being deceived. Whether or not the remarkable puzzles were in fact composed in a trance, the attempt to present them as trance productions shows a clear and mundane awareness of the general inflation in form requirements for revelation text and of the strategic necessity of one-upping both other religious societies and skeptical outsiders in the competition for belief.

CONCLUSIONS

The exercise of examining the diversity of eufunctions and dysfunctions of the Chinese sectarian tradition enables us to see Taiwan sectarianism in relation to its individual and collective costs and benefits, to appreciate why it is more compelling to some than to others, and to understand why "miracles" should be so central a part of its activity and rhetoric. Once we see that producing revelations in miraculous forms can resolve dysfunctional dissonance in a generally eufunctional sectarianism, we can put this activity into perspective with respect to the other functions of these societies. In the general case, analysis of function as a vector sum of both eufunctions and dysfunctions improves upon analysis that considers eufunctions alone.

N O T E S

1. In some other papers, Spiro introduces additional distinctions as well. For example, in "Religion: Problems of Definition and Explanation" (1966b:109), he distinguishes between real (ethnographically discoverable) and apparent (scientifically unconfirmable) functions.

2. In a sense, many schools of social analysis, including "materialist" ones, depend upon the notion that people are motivated in unconscious ways. But functional analyses by leading spokesmen (of materialism, say) are usually unconvincing because they fail to address the problem of how unconscious motivation works.

3. For English book-length treatments of folk religion in Taiwan, see especially Ahern (1973), Baity (1975), Harrell (1974), Jordan (1972), Sangren (1987), and Weller (1987). For a book-length work on Taiwan sectarianism, see Jordan and Overmyer (1986). For folk religion in sectarian hands, see Seaman (1978).

4. See Seaman (1978) and Jordan and Overmyer (1986). Not all groups do automatic writing, but most do, and we shall presuppose such activity for the rest of this article. For other new religions in Taiwan, see a summary article by Hsiao (1972).

5. The literature on this last is large, but the most useful Chinese accounts are Lii (1948) and Su (1979). In English, see Deliusin (1972), Grootaers (1946), Jordan (1982).

6. This goddess is a historical derivative of the "Mother Queen of the West." For most Chinese she is associated with the garden where the Peaches of Immortality grow, with which she provisions a periodic banquet for the fairy world of immortals. See Werner (1932:1963f) and Cahill (1982). For her sectarian associations, see Naquin

David K. Jordan

(1976:9–18) and Overmyer (1976, 1981). Note that Chinese religion is broadly po-
lytheistic, and devotion to one god does not exclude worship of others. There are
differences in the frequencies with which appeals are made to different deities in
different personal or group pantheons, but the overlap of membership in the pantheons is substantial in fact and nearly total in theory. On the concept of personal
pantheons, see Roberts, Chiao, and Pandey.

7. Contrast other popular writing oracles, in which the characters are ambiguous.
See Jordan (1972:64–67); Swartz and Jordan (1976:644–45).

8. According to this mythology, the Golden Mother is the creator of the universe
and of humanity but is distressed to find humanity straying from the true Way and
bringing doom upon itself. To try to lead her wayward children back to her, she has
sent the buddhas of the past. The appeal is that of a mother seeking the welfare of
her children, and it asks the children to recognize her concern for them and her
superior understanding of what is good for them. Since my analysis will be strengthened by this myth and worshipers' concern with it, I will stress again that not all
sects center on the Golden Mother. On the contrary, many groups select other
"patron" gods or none at all.

9. Members of the more extreme Celestial Way condemn nearly all popular
religion as "superstition" (mishinn) and wage an unrelenting and entirely reciprocal
propaganda war against organized Buddhism, household and community rites, and
popular shrine processions.

10. Like the preceding ethnographic sketch, the summary analysis here is necessarily brief. For fuller treatment, see Jordan and Overmyer (1986).

11. The theme is common in folklore and children's literature but can readily be
elicited from informants as well. It was recently documented for school socialization
in an undergraduate honors thesis by S. Miron (Miron 1984). See also King and Bond
(1985), Li (1985), Song (1985), and Tzeng (1972).

12. See Wu (1985) and Ho (1986). Cultural traditions associated with such anxiety
might include (1) the system of elaborate etiquette designed to mask criticism and
stress recognition of statuses, (2) high cultural evaluation of titles and labels, and (3)
preoccupation with cultivating social "links" (guanshih). See Chiao (1981), Jacobs
(1980, especially chap. 3), Tzeng (1972), and Wilson (1973).

13. See Jordan (1981). For other treatments of the management of hostility through
features of Chinese popular religion, see Jordan (1983b), Li (1985), and McCreery
(1979). In Spiro's analysis of Sioux warfare, he distinguishes between the reduction
of hostility (an unconscious intended personal function) and the deflection of hostility
away from the self (an unconscious unintended personal function) and from the in-
group (an unconscious unintended social function). The same general logic applies
here.

14. See Jordan (1983a). My notes include several instances of failed students who,
barred from continuing in the higher-prestige, modernist school system, subsequently turn their attention to traditional pursuits ranging from meditation and mar-
tial arts to bayluan. Low-level (traditionalist) prestige is in these cases associated
with the corrosion of higher-level (modernist) aspirations.

15. Many Chinese use the term "White Lotus Sect" to designate such groups,

and some seem to imagine that all of them are connected through a vast underground system of authority links to create a gigantic rebellious organization. The Celestial Way, operating in secret for many years, is inevitably charged with being a "White Lotus" sect; so common and troubling is this charge that the Celestial Way initiation liturgy specifically denies such affiliation.

16. The most complete description of the cultural trappings of speaking mediums in Taiwan is Sheau (1977), but there are many shorter investigations in Chinese and Japanese. See also Liou (1975) and Song (1976). For a psychodynamic and medical analysis, see Li (1976), Tseng (1972), and Wang (1976). In English see Jordan (1972:67–86).

17. I use the term "medium" to mean both speaking and writing mediums. There is some difference of opinion as to whether the person holding the stylus—the writing medium—is possessed or the stylus itself. For our purposes it makes little difference, and I shall follow what is, for my informants, the majority opinion: namely that the writing medium undergoes possession, since clearly the writing medium goes into trance.

18. The only other major culturally valued trance behavior in Taiwan is that of the necromancer (Hokkien: *khan-bông*). See Potter (1974) for a Cantonese example. Another category of possession occurs less often and, unlike the possession of mediums, is not culturally valued. This is the "random" trance that some people suffer when they are exposed to events or places of great supernatural significance, such as temples or religious processions. The exact interpretation of this trance varies widely with context. Some instances are thought to be divine possession, as when a god is forcing a new speaking medium to adopt the calling. Others are viewed as demonic, as when procession dancers or actors are temporarily seized by the characters they are painted to represent (Jordan 1983b). Such negatively valued trances produce attempts at exorcism.

19. There are probably differences between the revelations of urban speaking mediums, who often do not know their clients, and rural speaking mediums, who normally do.

20. For example, see Doolittle (1865:II, 112–114), Graham (1961:103), Jordan and Overmyer (1986), and Shen (1941). The distinction was apparently not always made the same way in all parts of China. Even in Taiwan some tâng-ki produce written revelation, while some writing mediums break into speech. And not all writing mediums are attached to bayluan groups. Similarly, a few tâng-ki become centers of revelation societies. Elliott (1955) provides a close study of a Singapore example.

21. Several variants are part of a general repertoire of "proofs" for the speaking medium, including the ability to climb sword ladders without cutting one's feet, to walk on hot coals without being burnt, and the like. Some of these feats are extremely impressive. During my work in Bao-an the high point of the initiation of one speaking medium occurred when the new medium washed his face with boiling oil, scooped from a pan with his hands. It develops that, under certain circumstances (which may include trance), human beings are able to do so without inflicting injury on themselves. The handling of boiling oil by people in a trance is also reported by Larry Peters (personal communication) for the Tamang of Nepal. (See also Peters 1978, 1987.)

Eugene Anderson (personal communication) reports that one medium in Singapore lined up members of the community, including Anderson, and plunged the hands of one person after another into boiling oil. I do not know how hot various kinds of commonly available Asian oils actually are or how well one is protected by a layer of perspiration, but whatever the physical aspects of the matter, this is plainly a feat which people can perform without being burned and which is sufficiently contrary to everyday experience to be interpreted as an exception to the normal course of nature and hence as a sign of divine protection. It is thus more compelling and the more easily sustains belief in the legitimacy of a possession. A review of cross-cultural evidence on behavior in trance states would be burdensomely long here. For overviews, see Bourguignon (1968, 1976) and chapters 13 and 14 in the present volume. Also see Peters and Price-Williams (1980).

22. A partial exception is revelations containing the personal names of visitors. Visitors to writing séances are often impressed by this personalization, since they believe that the medium would not have known their name. In fact, such revelations rarely occur at the first visit, when visitors are normally asked their names by a sect attendant or record the information in a guest book.

23. Logically, one could argue that, if the texts are composed by gods, there ought to be consistency in the competence and style of each deity's writings, regardless of the medium. To accommodate that logic in face of obvious differences in the same god's texts from medium to medium, some believers maintain that the medium does not actually produce a text composed by a god but instead experiences the *content* of the revelation and is responsible for expressing it in words. This is not the usual view, however.

24. The same process occurs with speaking mediums, despite their having the custom of legitimating themselves through painless mortification of the flesh. For example, one speaking medium, whose possessing spirit speaks Mandarin (the official language and majority Mainland variant of Chinese), claims to have forgotten all his schoolboy Mandarin as an adult and speaks only in Hokkien (the language of everyday communication in most of Taiwan) except when possessed. Enthusiastic clients can thus mention his ability to speak Mandarin while in trance as evidence that the possessing presence is indeed the Mandarin-speaking god it claims to be.

25. Just as the boiling oil strains the ethnographer's understanding of the logistics of the phenomenon, the prodigious talent required to produce some of these compositions taxes the understanding of what is possible for a mind in an altered state of consciousness. Interesting papers bearing on this subject are Ryan and Foster (1967) and Gellhorn and Kiely (1972).

26. Since it is only the form of these that is germane to the present argument, the content is not analyzed here. Figures 4.1 and 4.3, using distinctively sectarian language, stress the blind hopelessness of the human condition and the necessity of cultivating virtue to escape disaster. Figure 4.3 incorporates more specific sectarian references. For an extensive analysis of such sectarian writing, see Jordan and Overmyer (1986) and Overmyer (1985).

27. Texts of such intricacy, called "brocade" (*jiin*) or "hidden head" (*tsarng tour*) verses, have long been playthings of the literati. To the best of my knowledge, none

so intricate has formerly been attributed to automatic writing séances. For similar "linguistic diversions" with Chinese characters, see Smith (1914:171–178). Smith's descriptions of hidden head verses suggest not that informants attributed the encoding to divine agencies but rather that they were often devised as entertainment by "educated Chinese ladies" (p. 172).

28. Accommodating the double use of the seventh character of each line as incorporating the first character of the next (here underlined), the verse therefore begins: "Tian shern gong jiah jiow sheng chwan; *jou* fang jiang hwu duh neu nan; *lih* chyang daa wen mi hwen jenn; *che* maa ching chyou bu yuann guan" ("Celestial gods pilot the barque of salvation, which navigates the rivers and lakes to save women and men; with strength they strike down the spirits who would mislead us"). The full translation is obscurely sectarian and beside the point here. The characters H3 and I3 taken together read "Tianran," the usual designation of the most recent patriarch of this sect. This name appears through a cross-reading in addition to the significance of these two characters in the text as it coils through them.

5

Aggressive Speech, Status, and Cultural Distribution among the Swahili of Mombasa

MARC J. SWARTZ

In this chapter I will analyze a form of Swahili behavior, namely aggressive speech, in such a way as to provide a basis for understanding that behavior. In the course of doing so I will direct attention to a crucial cultural process that has received little explicit attention, namely the "distribution of culture." The basic concept needed to examine it is "status" (Swartz and Jordan 1980; Swartz 1983).

A theoretical interest in status is appropriate in a volume devoted to M. E. Spiro, whose own work demands that we see society as a differentiated system whose various parts, "institutions," operate only through the efficacy of their constituent statuses. "The survival of a society depends on the operation of its social system; a social system is comprised of sub-systems which, in turn, are comprised of institutions; the functions of these institutions are served only if their constituent roles are performed. In turn, this requires the recruitment of individuals for the various statuses which comprise the social structure" (Spiro 1961b:98).

In a number of his studies Spiro's interest focuses on the individual and social consequences of being guided by the values, beliefs, and rules (that is, elements of culture) associated with such statuses as those of monks in Burma and chiefs' subjects in Ifaluk. Here attention is focused on differences between occupants of different statuses with respect to activity within a limited area of behavior and the usefulness of a knowledge of differences in their statuses for illuminating these differences. Specifically, using status

116

differences as a foundation, I will try to provide a basis for explaining observed differences among Swahili in the sorts of aggressive speech they use, the contents of that speech, and the ways in which it is harmful to its targets.

It is a truism that shared culture is a necessary basis for social life. Only if actors share understandings of what is happening, what should be happening, and who is involved can they deal with one another and the rest of the world in a way that is sufficiently productive for them to be willing and able to continue associating with one another. It is not enough for actors to have some kind of broad and general sharing; to some extent, at least, they must share the specific understandings that guide the specific behaviors called for and produced in the particular situations in which they interact with one another.

Anthropology has traditionally held that this sharing is an issue requiring little descriptive or theoretical concern, since, in some societies at least, all actors shared all culture with all others. This view was mainly implicit but was nevertheless a powerful force in anthropological thought. Only Linton's "status-role" model (1936) offered a basis for understanding social life without necessarily assuming that all members of a society shared with all others all elements of the group's culture (see Swartz 1982a:315).

The Linton model with its recent refinements (especially Goodenough 1965) contributes to an understanding of culture's ability to serve as a basis for social life through its division of a group's culture into the sets of shared understandings that constitute its statuses and roles. This model is useful in understanding the cultural basis for a group's interpersonal relations because it focuses attention on the distribution among actors of the particular elements of culture that are directly involved in the various types of interactions that constitute those relations. Linton's model—and mine follows it in this—aims at identifying and assessing the behavioral significance of particular understandings as these are shared among members of different social categories, that is, statuses, within a society.

In my view, statuses are purely cultural entities made up of separable sets of shared understandings. One of these sets concerns membership in a specific social category and provides the understandings that make it possible for culture sharers to know which individuals are status members and which are not. Another set of understandings for each status indicates its relative importance in various situations and contexts. People all occupy many statuses, and more than one is often relevant at a time, but statuses include shared understandings (that is, cultural elements) that provide some basis for knowing which are more important and which less so in particular circumstances.

The third main component of any status consists of understandings about what those in the category as defined by the first set ordinarily do (and do not do), what they are generally like (that is, personal traits, abilities, attitudes, etc.), and how to evaluate them. Understandings about what members of a status category do include the highly specific ones that, for example, enable members of the physician status to treat specific illnesses in particular patients and the much less specific ones such as that held by people in general telling them that physicians are supposed to have training and ability in treating illnesses and perhaps telling them also what special kind of physicians within the broad category to see about a particular sort of disease. These understandings also include those concerned with what sorts of possessions members of status categories have (a physician, for instance, is understood to command a certain body of knowledge, to have particular items of equipment, to dress within certain limits, to have an income of a certain general size, and so forth) and what sorts of relationships they ordinarily and/or ideally have. (For example, a physician is expected to have working relations with patients, other medical people, bankers, landlords, and others.)

"Status," as just defined, is the main concept that I use in the examination of Swahili aggressive speech here. This type of speech can usefully be divided into three different categories: badtalk, curses, and reproaches.

The category of badtalk consists of obscenities in their various forms. I call this class "badtalk" (after the Latin *maledicta*) because it includes only speech that is (at least sometimes) considered improper, indelicate, counteraesthetic, or rude. Usually those who are party to it find it so, but it is badtalk whether they do so or not as long as a substantial number regard it in this way.

Curses constitute another type of aggressive speech. Curses are specific appeals to some power (usually supernatural) to visit affliction on the target.

The third type of aggressive speech, reproaches, consists of statements accusing the target of failures, lapses, mistakes, or omissions. In other words, the target is accused of failing to meet responsibilities that are accepted by the target and/or by at least some other group members.

The Swahili themselves differentiate the three kinds of aggressive speech, just as English does. Nevertheless, as will be seen, the three types of speech have some important elements in common as well as being different enough to require separate explanations in some of their aspects. Badtalk, curses, and reproaches were chosen for study for many of the same reasons that joking and avoidance behavior have attracted attention at least since Radcliffe-Brown's classical study (1940a, 1949). Like joking and avoidance, badtalk and curses are readily observed, are often unambiguous with respect to their sources and targets, and occur frequently enough to provide a useful sample. As with the study of avoidance and joking, interest lies both in the phenomena themselves and in the implications of the findings for social life in general.

THE SWAHILI OF MOMBASA: ETHNOGRAPHIC BACKGROUND

The Swahili live on the east coast of Africa from southern Somalia to northern Mozambique. They are, and throughout their long history have been, an urban people who have had centuries of contact with Arabs and Persians as well as with the other African peoples among whom they live (Berg 1968; Salim 1973).

As part of the strict observance of the laws of the Sunni branch of Islam, outside marriage and close kinship the sexes are separated. The women spend their days alone or associate with their daughters and neighboring women, while the men go outside their neighborhoods to work. Relations between women are close and are characterized by quarreling, gossiping, and warm mutual support. In relations among men there is far more concern with dignity and the avoidance of shame (*aybu*), and the warmth found in women's relations is much less common (Swartz 1982b, 1983, 1988).

Because I could not spend time visiting with them, my information about girls and young women is much less complete than about boys and young men. For boys the period from physical maturity to financial independence is fraught with difficulty and conflict. In this society, as in many others, mature men control most material resources, and the ability of young people—especially young males, whose activities take place outside their homes—to do what they want is strictly limited by the fact that money and money-producing jobs are mainly or entirely available only through the older men of their group.

For girls and women, employment outside the home is unusual— formerly it was nonexistent—and most still spend much of their lives in the company of women kin and neighbors. For women, prestige among their peers derives importantly from possessions of the material symbols of their husbands' love—notably jewelry, expensive clothing, and expensive weddings and funerals. Some women are heiresses and use their own means to hold the ceremonies and get the favored finery, but most manage only through the resources the husbands give, as the women understand it, because they love their wives (Swartz 1982b, 1983).

There are a variety of reasons that a woman is loved by her husband; one is her virtue, especially her sexual fidelity. The virginity of an unmarried women is more important than the fidelity of a wife, but the latter is extremely important to a woman's standing and hardly less to the standing of her family, which loses prestige should she be considered other than chaste either before or after marriage.

This statement applies to all parts of Swahili society, although there are two exogamous castes. The upper caste is divided into a number of distinct but intermarrying classes. One caste consists of the descendants of slaves, and the other is composed of *waungwana*, "nobles" (that is, those whose slave-free ancestry is socially accepted). Slaves are thought to be without shame and to gossip about all sorts of things, and to use badtalk freely. Nobles are much less willing to use badtalk because of their commitment to honor (*fakhri*) and standards (*mahrua*).

As the Swahili understand it, women are constitutionally far less committed to honor and standards than men are—and for this reason, according to the understandings shared in the group, women constitute the great majority of adults engaging in emotional badtalk—and the lower classes within the nobles caste are fare less committed to honor and standards than the higher classes are.

We turn now to the use of aggressive speech as it relates to these aspects of Swahili society and culture.

BADTALK

The most common "badtalk" expression can be glossed as "Your mother's cunt." Obviously, this phrase concerns sex and suggests something improper about your mother: that her genitals exist, that they are noteworthy, and/or that you, your abuser, or both are connected with that organ in an improper way—or some such.

The phrase itself does not directly mention the impropriety of the mother's sexual activity, and there is no direct implication that the target is involved, or interested in, incest. My suggestion that this phrase, or the less common one referring to the mother's copulation (to be discussed below), implied incest or anything of the sort was greeted by informants with surprise and some distaste. According to informants, the operative part of the phrase relates to the fact that the mother's genitals exist, that they are an important part of her. The same statement holds for the reference to the mother's sexual activity. Group members understand the abuse to consist mainly in affirmation of the existence of the mother's organ and of her active sexuality.

The "mother's cunt" phrase is used by some Swahili—mainly women and children or young men—as an all-purpose exclamation of surprise, annoyance, or pain. The phrase has three forms: "kuma nyoka," "kuma nina," and "kuma mayo." All of these use the same word, *kuma*, to refer obscenely (rather than politely or scientifically) to the vulva, but they differ in the words used for "mother." *Nyoka* and *nina* are obscure, archaic words, but *mayo* is the possessive of an ordinary, current word, and the form of the phrase using that word is considered strongest.

In order to understand why the reference to the target's mother's genitals is a common insult, it is useful to begin by examining the understandings concerning mothers held by members of the Mombasa Swahili group.[1]

Survey interviews carried out in the last few years show that the overwhelming majority of Swahili sons and daughters reported that children *should* love their mothers more than their fathers (see table 5.1).

This point is in accord with discussions and observations showing that Swahili mothers are understood to be more nurturant, supportive, and warm than are Swahili fathers, and it suggests that the commonness of the "your mother's cunt" badtalk is related, one way or another, to pervasive concerns about incest. Perhaps so, but that concern does not negate the one that is more pressingly present in the Swahili's own view of the meaning of the phrase. This meaning is rooted in the shared understandings associated with the categories "woman," "mother," and "man."

One set of understandings concerns the nature of women's sexuality. In Swahili society parents and others devote a great deal of attention to controlling the sexual activities of girls and women. One of the fairly common insults that mothers use on their daughters—my data show this relationship to be the premier venue for badtalk, with the mother doing all the abusing—is to call them *mkware*, which can be glossed as something like "female with strong and constant sexual appetite." There is no corresponding term for boys and men, but there is considerable elaboration of the idea for women. So, for example, a combined curse and insult that women use on one another is: "May you get the great shame of the cat" ("Mwana kizaya ya paka").

This statement includes the insulting implication that the woman both experiences pleasure in sexual relations and is unable to restrain herself from

Table 5.1. Responses to the question, "Should children love their parents the same, their mothers a little more, or their fathers a little more?" (percent)

Informant	The Same	Mothers More	Fathers More
Son	64.3	35.7	0.0
Daughter	54.5	36.4	9.1

Note: N = 52
Source: Marc J. Swartz, "The Isolation of Men and the Happiness of Women: Sources and Use of Power in Swahili Marital Relationships," *Journal of Anthropological Research* 38(1982): 33.

wiggling her bottom as cats are understood to do when they have pleasurable sensations. This catlike movement is called "kucheza kiuno." A woman who wiggles her bottom during or after intercourse is seen as expressing sexual pleasure in a hopelessly abandoned way that is properly found, not in other people, but only in cats. Even in sexual relations with her husband of many years, it is better for a woman, Swahili men have told me, not to indicate in any way that she experienced pleasure.

Additional evidence focusing around extreme concern for the chastity of daughters and sisters and the fidelity of wives could be adduced (see Stroebel 1979:88–89), but enough has been presented to suggest the sexuality for women entails understandings involving the possibility of uncontrolled and dangerous behavior, and these understandings focus around unchecked enjoyment of sexual activity. Open reference to the mother's vulva by the badtalk word *kuma* instead of the polite and clinical *uke* encompasses, I suggest, the idea that the mother enjoys sex and is therefore likely to seek it. If, after all, her vulva is so salient a feature that it can be mentioned publicly by an indelicate term, she would seem not to be restricting the kind and amount of attention it receives and is therefore using it in ways contrary to culturally established goodness.

Insult and abuse involving reference to the mother's sexual activity itself is not as common as that referring to the equipment for such activity, but the former does occur. Children more frequently than others abuse one another by saying "Mamako atombwa," which can be literally rendered as "Your mother is fucked." As noted, the Swahili themselves see no incestuous implication in this phrase; rather, as with the reference to the mother's anatomy, the point, as they see it, is that the mother is a person whose sexuality is not restricted and concealed as it should be.

Swahili of both sexes are seriously concerned about the ability of their female kin—especially mothers, daughters, and sisters—to control their sexual impulses, which are understood to be extremely powerful. In Swahili culture, women are understood by members of both sexes to be highly emotional and to control their impulses only with the greatest effort and discipline (Swartz 1982b). Of all the impulses that women have, none is understood to be stronger or more dangerous than sex, and openly to identify a woman with her sexual parts calls attention to the possibility that she will give in to her most dangerous urges, with disastrous consequences for the reputation of those close to her.

An unfaithful wife is a serious threat to a man's prestige, but he can divorce her and lessen the damage to his reputation. A sister who cannot control herself is a serious thing, but more for her own children than for her siblings, who may have cooperated in bringing her to marriage as a virgin, which is all that the natal family can do. Most serious of all is a mother who is known to be sexually active and even promiscuous. Not only does such a mother show that her children come of at least one parent who violates an extremely important ideal—female self-control—but the very paternity of the child is in doubt, since identification of the father depends upon the mother's faithfulness, that is, upon the ability to control herself.

If a person's mother is so unrestrained in her sexuality that her genitals are publicly displayed (even if only by rude public references to them), her evaluation as a member of a community whose moral beliefs emphasize female self-control in general and sexual restraint in particular cannot be positive. By being the products of this abandoned person's sexuality and of her rearing, the children suffer damage to their reputations.

The target of the badtalk phrase, "Your mother's cunt" cannot be considered an individual whose evaluation is as positive as that of "proper" members of the community whose mothers show the restraint and discipline that is valued in women and that is, not at all incidentally, essential to a well-established paternity and for the scandal-free home that is important for an admired upbringing. The badtalk attack is particularly effective, since it is understood that, although discipline in women is essential for them to be evaluated positively, its continuing presence is always open to question because of the cultural view of women's nature.

The badtalk reference to the mother's sexual parts not only insults the target but also elevates the user by implying that his or her mother exhibits the valued restraint and discipline that would make it improper, or at least inaccurate, to publicize her genitals. This point is rather difficult to see in some uses of the badtalk phrase, since the insult to the target and the elevation of the user are simultaneous and not easily separated. The following incident, however, shows the elevation of the user with little or no assault on the target.

Two teenaged Swahili girls of the lower caste were in Nairobi walking down the street on a dull afternoon. Some boys in a car stopped to offer them a ride and some amusement. The girls were delighted at the opportunity and, seeing a girlfriend across the street who had no prospect of sharing their good fortune, smilingly shouted to her in pleasant rather than angry tones: "Fatuma kuma mayo, kuma mayo!" ("Fatuma, your mother's cunt, your mother's cunt!").

In this little incident there is no apparent basis for the users to attack the target; the target was the users' friend, and the users were not angry or frustrated. Here the aggressive speech marked an assertion of superiority without an attack, and the users were simply employing one of the most common badtalk phrases to stress the fact that they are more fortunate—a form of superiority with overtones concerning moral standing—than their friend.[2] It is not necessarily the case that the users believe their mothers superior to the mother of the target, but remember, in this badtalk phrase the target's standing as a member of the community is at issue, and the mother's reputation is important as it contributes to that standing. Any phrase asserting their superiority as members of the moral community would serve the occasion; the users simply chose one that is in common use.

The importance of the mother and, especially, of the mother's self-control as symbolized by the attention to her vulva, surely reflects a great emphasis on controlling women's sexuality, and this plays a vital part in the frequency with which "your mother's cunt" is used as an obscenity or as an insult. The view that the saliency of the mother's vulva has to do with the evaluation of the person to whom this obscenity is addressed is supported by the following incident, involving an exchange where a woman's own vulva is mentioned to indicate her less than superior standing in the community.

A Swahili woman was arguing with an Arab food salesman and angrily said "Kuma mayo" to him. The Arab, long resident among the Swahili, replied: "Why do you mention that distant cunt when there is another right here?"

As this last incident illustrates, references to the female organ are understood as attacks upon the woman whose part is referred to. This can be seen in the salesman's turning the woman's invocation of his mother's genitals back on the woman herself. "Your mother's cunt" represents an attack on the one to whom it is directed, but that attack is the more serious for involving not just the target but also the individual who is most responsible for the target's standing, according to understanding about the mother's role, and whose sexual restraint is an essential element in the target's standing as a member of the community. In addition, the promiscuity implied by the phrase casts doubt on the identity of the target's father when full membership in the group involves descent on both sides.

Users of Badtalk and Their Targets

Young men and boys are heard saying "Your mother's cunt" to one another often and with little provocation. It is heard during soccer games, as part of idle (and not necessarily heated) discussions, and among male youths working together. In my years among the Mombasa Swahili I have heard men in their thirties or older use the phrase only in great anger and even then only rarely. The other frequent users of the phrase are women. Surprisingly, it is heard most often in relations between mothers and daughters, with the daughters always, in my experience, being the targets and never the users. This observation is surprising in view of the phrase's apparent meaning for the women who use it on their own children.

A mother who says "Your mother's cunt" to her own daughter obviously attacks her daughter's standing as a decent community member, but it would seem—if indeed the phrase attacks the woman whose genitals are mentioned as well as her children—that it hardly compliments the user, since the genitals she mentions are her own.

This problem appears further in the fact that the second most common badtalk phrase among the Swahili is "Mwana haramu," "bastard" (literally "child of forbidden"), and this is also used by mothers on their children, especially their daughters. The understandings attached to being "mwana haramu" are not only of parental sin but also of faulty character on the part of the target.[3] Bastards are viewed as people who are unable to behave properly and who always cause trouble of various kinds because of their evil natures. A Swahili proverb says, "Even if you put a bastard in a basket, he will hold up his thumb." In other words, however vigorous the attempt to conceal the fact of illegitimacy, it will surely fail because of the distinctive (and undesirable) behavior of bastards.

The "mwana haramu" phrase has an alternative form which is of some interest from the standpoint of the analysis here. *Chisi* is said by informants to mean the same as the more common term for bastard, but *chisi* is almost never heard by itself and occurs only in a phrase young children use on one another in a teasing way: "Mwana haramu wa chisi, mjukuu wa ibilisi." This expression can be rather closely glossed as "Bastard of a bastard, grandchild of Satan."

Mothers use the term "mwana haramu" to abuse their young and dependent children often and without the mothers' incurring particular disapproval (although the women of the highest class in the noble caste are said rarely or never to use badtalk), but they generally do not use this kind of language in relations with their adult children.[4]

The use of "bastard" on one's own children, even if limited to younger ones, is more of the puzzling, self-referring abuse considered a moment ago. In a society with a caste division, bastardry is a particularly serious issue. The Koran allows for slave wives, *suria*, and the children of these wives are not, in the strict sense, bastards. Provision is made for them to inherit in the religious laws, but as can easily be imagined, the children of noble wives—and even more, perhaps, the noble wives themselves—are not usually pleased that the children of other women will compete with their own children for the father's bounty.

In this caste-divided society there are more than a few bastards, as the group members understand this issue, and although these children have no legal claim on the parental estate under either Koranic or secular law, some fathers have been known to be especially fond of them and to give them attention and wealth which could be reserved for their legitimate offspring. Since bastardry is such a serious issue for legal wives concerned about their own children's welfare and about themselves as the mothers of these children, it is all the more surprising that legal wives call their own children "bastards."

It will be clear that for mothers to call their children "bastards" is similar to their saying "Your mother's cunt" to the children. When young men use such phrases on one another, as we saw, they attack each other's standing as community members, and they do so by impugning the self-control of each other's mothers in sexual matters. If we exclude the interpretation that mothers are attacking themselves as much as their children when they call the children "bastard" and say "Your mother's cunt" to them, the possibility arises that the mothers are denying the tie between themselves and their children—that they are denying their children's membership in the part of the status "child" that consists of "my child." In using these badtalk phrases, the mothers seem to be saying: "You are not my child; you may be your father's child, but you are not mine."

The phrase that uses the alternative term for bastard and says "Bastard of a bastard, grandchild of Satan" is asserting either that the child is the offspring of Satan's child (perhaps his mother is a daughter of Satan) or that at least one of his real (biological) parents is a child of Satan and that the seeming parent (or parents) is, in effect, not a true parent. Mothers do not use this particular phrase very often, but it illustrates the possibility of attacking a child on the ground that his mother and/or father are not who they seem to be.

Another badtalk phrase used on children also supports the interpretation that mothers use badtalk that seems to involve themselves but that actually attacks the tie between them and their children. In this case the mother says to the child: "Matumbo yangu huzaa maradhi," "My womb has borne a disease." I take this phrase, the mother is telling the child that, whatever the child may be, he is not really her child in the proper sense and does not merit all the understandings that accompany membership in the "my child" category. This interpretation is further supported by an alternative insult for one's children, "Matumbo yangu haikuzaa," "My womb has not borne."

The interpretation that the mother denies her child his standing as such accords with the broader interpretation of the use of the mother's vulva badtalk between young people: it denies the target membership in an important status. When the mother uses this most common phrase on her child or uses the related bastard insult or says that her womb has not born, she denies the child not only the status of decent community member but also membership in the subgrouping consisting of her own children.

This idea suggests an important refinement of the hypothesis that badtalk attacks the target's membership in an important status, namely the possibility that the status membership cast in doubt by the badtalk is crucial in the relationship in which the badtalk occurs. The mother is attacking her child with badtalk that denies his or, more commonly, her membership in the status of decent community members. At the same time she is also attacking the child's membership in the category of her own children so that the foundation of their relationship is called into question.

This interpretation of badtalk as an attack on the foundation of the relationships in which it occurs is supported by another sort of badtalk: that used between young men. Here, as we will see, badtalk is again used, as in the mother-child relationship, to attack membership in a status that is vital to the relationship in which the aggressive speech occurs.

One of the main foci for the badtalk young men and boys use in abusing one another is the accusation that the other plays the passive role in homosexual relations. "Tu yako" ("your anus") and "Firi yako" ("your illegal sex," mostly used with reference to sodomy) are among the badtalk phrases used among young men, with *Hanithi*, meaning "impotent," or, more usually, "passive participant in homosexuality," being the central one. *Shoga* is a synonym for *hanithi*, indicating not impotence but solely the passive role in homosexuality and with the usual meaning that the individual looks and acts as homosexuals are expected to in this group. *Rambuza*, another word used for the passive partner in homosexual relations, may be related to the verb *ramba* ("lick"). "Firi yako" may accurately be glossed as "Your sodomy" and also "Bure yako," literally "Your free" or "Your without cost," both referring to the availability of the anus of the object of the phrase. Unlike the other phrase, "Bure yako" is sometimes used against females of the lower strata and doubtful reputation to indicate the availability of their vaginas.

Barring the extension to a small category of women, such badtalk is used exclusively among young men. It is important to note that the badtalk concerns one of the few areas of their lives where their behavior is both open to doubt and central in their relations with the peers who use this badtalk against them. Reference to the mothers' genitals similarly casts doubt on their status as proper community members, which they must be to associate with their Swahili fellows as equals. Accusations of passive homosexuality concern another important area of life that is crucial to relations among young men, since free and equal association among male peers means that those involved must be not just proper or true community members but also proper or true males. In order to meet this last requirement, the individuals cannot be seen as involved in homosexuality as the passive participant.

The Swahili distinguish sharply between proper, normal males who are quite willing to engage in homosexual practices as the active participant and feminine, "ruined" males who take the passive role in these practices.

Some idea of the seriousness of the allegation that one is a passive homosexual is evident in the fact that one of the most dangerous things a boy or man in Mombasa can do is to put his hands on the area immediately at or near the waist on another man's sides. A fight is said to be a certain result, and if the person so touched is a Hadhrami Arab, say the Swahili, the toucher will surely be stabbed. Touching the waist area at the sides, called "Tia mkono wa kiuno," is understood as a highly erotic act which, if done to a woman, will fill her with sexual desire. By touching a man in this way another man clearly expresses a view of him not as an equal but as a likely sex object, that is, as a passive homosexual.

In *Purity and Danger* Mary Douglas (1966) argues that the collapse of categories is at the heart of obscenity. This interpretation accords with the Swahili data presented here, given that understandings are assigned to categories, so that if a person is denied membership in a category, the understandings associated with that category (for example, being trustworthy or being someone who should be treated well) are also denied him. When badtalk asserts that a young man engages in culturally disfavored sexual practices (when he is said to be a catamite), the young man's membership in the category of proper males is thrown into doubt, as is the applicability to him of all the understandings associated with that category. While undermining the target, the badtalk user also implies that his own membership in the category is, where his sexuality is concerned, beyond doubt; otherwise he would himself be vulnerable when he calls attention to the target's activities.

As with the use of badtalk between mothers and children, young men's uses accord with the hypothesis that the badtalk denies the target membership in a category (here that of proper young man) and that this category membership is specifically important to the relationship in which the badtalk occurs.

Moreover, the denial of category membership takes place on the basis of failures in areas that are widely understood as being in doubt for people who otherwise meet membership criteria. We have seen that the Swahili believe that there are many among them whose legitimacy is in doubt, so that to call someone "mwana haramu" is to call attention to a possibility everyone accepts as quite a real one. To emphasize the sexuality of the target's mother, furthermore, is simply to attach to her the general understanding that many women cannot control their impulses, including (and especially) their sexual impulses. Referring to a young man as a *hanithi* (sodomite) is, in the same way, invoking a trait which is understood as possibly present in many young men, since, as the older members of the community understand it, in the past few decades members of other communities have succeeded in "spoiling" a number of Swahili boys and young men.

Badtalk, to summarize, is gratifying to the user not only because it attacks the target's membership in important statuses but also because it affirms his or her own membership in them by suggesting that he or she does not suffer from the widespread disability that is the subject of the badtalk and that denies category membership to its sufferers.

Another hypothesis supported by the Swahili material just considered is that badtalk centers on statuses that are both very broadly inclusive in their membership and relevant in providing understandings for a wide range of activities and contexts. Classification as a member of the community or not being so classified affects the whole range of understandings applicable to any individual and influences most of the interactions involving him or her. The same is true of other broad categories, such as "proper young man."

The understandings associated with being or not being classified in broad and generally relevant categories are not necessarily the most important ones in every situation, but they are nevertheless influential in most of them. Buyers are buyers and sellers are sellers, but if both understand that the other is a community member, that understanding almost surely affects their relations with one another. The same statement applies to classification as a proper young man.

Swahili badtalk, then, attacks its target fundamentally in that the statuses it denies targets, or the ways in which it gives them poor evaluations, are inclusive ones and ones whose understandings have at least some relevance as a behavioral guide across a wide range of activities.

Uses of Badtalk

Badtalk in this society provides users with a weapon that has a broad scope. The data concerning its use provide a basis for some hypotheses about the characteristics of those who are its principal users and the bases for its appeal to them.

We have seen that children, youths, and women are chief among those who use badtalk as their characteristic type of aggressive speech. In an earlier paper I argued that badtalk (obscenity) is an instrument that is most attractive to those without directly effective means of achieving their goals (Swartz 1969). In the terms of the view advanced here, badtalk is attractive on two grounds to those whose statuses do not provide them with many or powerful understandings that are practically useful in establishing relationships, in acquiring knowledge, or in getting possessions that will help them reach goals they commonly desire.

First, as we have seen, badtalk allows them to attack their target and to assert their own superiority, usually simultaneously. It should be noted, however, that badtalk is not the only way of doing these things. Young men who say "You are a poor student" or "You are an irresponsible person" to their peers do the same two things, but in fact this kind of reproach is not very common among Swahili youths or among children and women. When they are not angry or joking, they do not often voice criticisms, and when they are, they use badtalk.

The second attraction of badtalk for members of relatively powerless statuses is that it permits the expression of aggression both at the immediate target and, in addition, at those who hold the understandings that make this kind of aggressive speech "rude, inappropriate, and offensive." The use of badtalk as an exclamation of pain, surprise, or disappointment without an immediate or clear target suggests that it serves as a means of expressing emotion and of attacking those who hold particular understandings about how people ought and ought not to speak.

Among Swahili of all statuses, there is no doubt as to who is most closely associated with the understandings that make badtalk offensive; it is the mature men, who are also understood as controlling many of the practical means for reaching the goals most users of badtalk have difficulty attaining. The expressions of distaste on the faces of these men when they overhear badtalk and their frowns of disapproval when they condemn its current widespread use show that the ability of badtalk to inflict discomfort is by no means limited to its immediate targets. Thus, the very use of badtalk gives the powerless a way of expressing aggression against those in the category whose members control what they want (but do not always give it to them).

The main users of badtalk are poorly equipped for attaining those of their goals that involve independence, since independence, mainly because it involves money and such things as food and shelter, must be won from fathers who control these material things. Young men, some of the main badtalkers, are hardly more able to get what they want than young boys, also users, since money and the necessities are available only through their fathers or if they get jobs. Jobs, however, are scarce, and many youths are well into their twenties before they find worthwhile employment.

When they do find jobs, the youths are well on the way to becoming "mature men," since members of that category are understood to control their own financial affairs. The other requirement for membership in the mature men status is marriage. Given the large bride wealth in this society, young men must either get help from their fathers or wait the long period until they have saved enough from their own wages. Thus the passage from boy and young man to mature man involves basic changes in the ability to get what is wanted. The powerlessness characteristic of young males is replaced by the relative power of mature males.

For females, the situation is less clear. Women, especially the mothers, who are on a par with young men as the most active users of badtalk, are seemingly not powerless in the same way that young men are. Unlike young men, many married women who are active badtalk users have some of the material things they say they want (especially jewelry, new and fashionable clothing, and the means to stage expensive ceremonies). The women, however, get these things only through their husbands and are no more independent of their husbands (Swartz 1982b) than young men are of their fathers. For this group of badtalk users, too, there is an association between badtalk as the characteristic mode of aggressive speech and powerlessness.

If only those whose lives are importantly controlled by others regularly use badtalk, we might expect girls and young women also to use it, since they are closely controlled by their mothers as well as by their fathers. Young females of the lower caste do use such speech, but I have little data on their counterparts in the upper caste. The data I have suggest that they in fact use badtalk little, if at all. It is surely true that mature men and women *say* they do not use it. Perhaps the sexual allusions in badtalk and the emphasis put on avoiding any suspicion of sexual activity by the young women of this group inhibits them from using such aggressive speech. If so, a better statement of the hypothesis concerning the use of badtalk might be that the powerlessness of category members is a necessary but not a sufficient condition for its choice as the main form of aggressive speech for the category.

Reproach: *The Badtalk of the Powerful*

One category whose members use badtalk very little, if at all, is that of mature men, especially mature men of the higher caste and upper classes. I cannot recall a single incident in which a married and employed (or pensioned) man in his thirties or older was heard to use badtalk, and I have only one or two reports of its having happened in the memories of informants.

It is not that these men are without exclamations. One kind of sandal traditionally worn by Swahili is held on by a thong that passes between the first two toes. This thong often breaks, and these often vexatious shoes are called "viatu vya lehowla" ("shoes of lehowla"), *lehowla* being the beginning of a Koranic phrase that means: "Nothing either good or bad happens but that God wills it." Adult Swahili men can be heard saying *lehowla* in strongly emotional tones when they spill something, when they bump their toes, or when a traditional shoe fails them.

When the upper-class men do not use *lehowla* as an exclamation, they generally substitute *salala*, which is the beginning of the Arabic phrase "God send mercy and peace to the Prophet," used by the pious at each mention of Prophet Mohammed's name. Though the extent of their emotional arousal is clear from their tone of voice, even in anger the high-prestige men use *salala* or *lehowla* when other members of the society might call attention to someone's mother's privates. Certain types of men are not the only ones who use mild, religiously based alternatives to badtalk—women and children use them too—but these men rely on them to the near exclusion of other forms.

Pious references do not serve in tense or angry interpersonal exchanges even for the most prestigious men. When annoyed with, bothered by, and/or chastising someone (usually a status inferior), these men say "Huna adabu" ("You have no manners"). This sounds rather mild to non-Swahili, perhaps, but is actually quite serious, and some targets of the phrase have been observed to respond with real distress to its use. The strength of the statement depends, almost always, on the positions in the group of those who are using it and those to whom it is being applied, but when a respected superior uses it on a person who views himself or herself as an inferior, the recipient is often visibly shaken at the moment the charge is made and remains distressed for some time afterward.

The charge that one has no manners does not refer to relatively trivial offenses comparable not to saying "please"; rather it implies a failure to act as decent people do. Having no manners means, for example, failing to treat an honored person respectfully, failing to exchange greetings as the holy Koran requires, and—most commonly and seriously—not understanding that someone who has benefited from the kindness and assistance of another must return that kindness. Having no manners is a serious moral failing, not a minor violation of etiquette.

The accusation that another does not observe crucial rules for behavior takes several different forms, and all of them are used with respect to people who have won the enmity of others, especially if the accusers are high-prestige members of the society. "Huna fadhla" ("You have no sense of obligation") and "Huna hisani" ("You have no favors" or "You have no sense of returning favors") are strong, alternative statements accusing someone of having ignored the bias rules of interpersonal relations. As one informant said, "If someone says this [that is, "you have no manners"] to you, it's like dying." The same informant said that the following proverbs can be used by people—usually men—of standing in speaking to or about a person they view as failing in the reciprocity that is understood as fundamental to proper social life: "To light a lamp for a blind person is wasting fuel" ("Kumwashia tongo taa ni kumalisa mafuta") and, even more hurtful, "The gratitude (reciprocity) of the donkey is to break wind" ("Fadhla ya punda hukujambia mashuzi").

The latter proverb is explained as appropriate because, unlike all the other animals of the town (cows, chickens, goats, and sheep), which give milk, eggs, or meat, the donkey is rarely ridden and returns almost nothing for the food and care it receives.

The high-prestige men, then, focus their abuse of others on the failure to behave morally in their relations with community members generally and, most particularly, with the men themselves. These high-prestige men belong to the status category whose members control much of this society's wealth and who have authority over most other group members. They are in a position to do consequential favors for others, to help with bride wealth payments, to agree to give girls and young women in marriage, and to preside over economic transactions of importance. Their relations with one another and with younger men, women, and children reflect shared understandings, many of which call for deference and respect from their inferiors and generosity, kindness, and wisdom from them.

The understandings that lead individuals to be categorized in the high-prestige group of mature men include the importance of showing close attention to the sensibilities of others and to what is proper and appropriate. For these men to use badtalk would be to violate the membership understandings of their status or, as the group members themselves put it, would mean a "loss of respect" (i.e., a failure to meet the understandings concerning decent behavior for members of their category).

The contrast between the mature and prestigious men and younger, unestablished men is a clear one. Men and boys without wealth and without reputations for honor and reliability have little practical stake in the demonstrations of respect that are symbolized by the religiously enjoined greetings that are significant for the older men. Young men and boys who have little or no control of money, young women, or influence have little or nothing to give and therefore little or no concern about what they receive in return. These young men do not use insults or accusations such as "You have no manners" or "You have no sense of responsibility." This reproach is the characteristic mode of aggressive speech used by the senior men. Members of other status categories use it, of course, when others do not fulfill their expectations, but it is the main sort of aggressive speech only for the senior men.

Still, there are important similarities between reproach and badtalk. One hypothesis explains that badtalk is used to attack its target's membership in a status that is central to the relationship in which the badtalk is used. The same hypothesis extends to reproach among the Swahili where the target's standing as a proper participant in social relations, a person who understands reciprocity, is attacked by calling attention to his failure to understand what obligations he incurs as the recipient of favors and what ignorance or disregard he has shown for gratitude.

The very core of the relationship between the young and powerless males and the mature men involves help and generosity from the latter and a manifest willingness to return that help and generosity from the former. The reproach of the seniors focuses precisely on failure here. Also, as in badtalk, the aim in attacking the target's membership in a socially crucial status is denying him characteristics that are understood as vital to membership but not infrequently absent among those who otherwise qualify for that membership. It is understood, in other words, that many people do not have *fadhla* (reciprocity), just as it is understood that some women often have trouble controlling their impulses, that the parentage of many is open to question, and that some young men serve as the passive participants in homosexual relations.

Badtalk and reproach also share the characteristic of enhancing the evaluation of the user while at the same time attacking the standing of the target. Just as calling attention to the illegitimacy of the target implies that the user is without taint, so calling into question the target's failures in a relationship implies that the user's participation in that relationship is proper.

Despite the similarities reproach and badtalk also show important differences among the Swahili. As we saw, badtalk is characteristic of the relatively powerless, but it will be clear that reproach is characteristic of the relatively powerful, since they have the greatest interest and stake in the reciprocity and gratitude that are the heart of reproach in this society. Along the same line, badtalk attacks the target's qualifications in terms of the general understandings that provide the basis for membership in basic statuses such as those of community member or proper male, while reproach grants membership but throws doubt on the target's fulfillment of the requirements of the understandings that apply to members. Badtalk, as we have seen, assaults the target's membership in the community or the target's sexual identity and asserts, in effect, that he or she cannot be judged as decent people are. Reproach grants membership in the basic statuses but asserts that the target does not live up to the obligations of that membership.

The effectiveness of reproach depends upon the concession that the target holds the memberships at stake. That is, there is no question about the reciprocity of outsiders: Indians, Europeans, and members of other African groups are rarely charged with lack of *fadhla*. In a narrower framework, fathers tell their sons not that they are not sons but rather that they are "bad" sons (that is, that they do not meet specific requirements of the son status). This situation is very different from that pertaining to mothers, who accuse their children, usually their daughters, of not being their daughters at all.[5]

A final note about the relationship between badtalk and reproach concerns their standing in the developmental sequence of men's lives. As suggested above, there is a progression for males from the badtalk of powerless youth to the reproach of powerful maturity. This progression holds some interest for us, since it depends almost entirely on change in status.

As males are admitted to a status with more understandings useful to the gaining of their ends, they use badtalk less and reproach more. In fact, the older men who fail to establish themselves as respected, senior members of the male group are, informants say, the ones most likely to use badtalk despite their mature years. I have not myself observed any mature men using badtalk, but the few accounts of its use by such men all concern individuals who have not met all the entrance requirements—affluence, control of a family, and reputation for adherence to general understandings concerning piety and propriety—for the mature man status. This suggests that it is status membership, not age or individual qualities other than those connected with defining status membership, that determines choice of type of aggressive speech.

Curses: Strength for the Weakest

We have seen that the aims of reproach and of badtalk have important similarities despite their differences and that the two types of aggressive speech are related, for at least some of their users, in being part of the developmental cycle, at least for men. Curses differ more from the other two than either of those two does from the other. The most striking thing about curses is that their main users are members of a status which only a few members of the community ever occupy. All those who use curses as their characteristic form of aggressive speech are old people who have very limited practical means of gaining the goals they desire.

There is no necessary association between advanced age and powerlessness among the Swahili. The elderly people living on pensions or rents can be quite influential, as can those who occupy honored places in the houses of their children. The fairly rare old person who has neither wealth nor surviving close kin, however, is in an unenviable position. Old men in this situation—and there seem to be fewer of these than old women—sleep in mosques and live on the religious charity of their fellow believers. Old women without resources cannot stay in the mosques (where women are not allowed) and sleep and eat according to momentary opportunity. Regardless of sex, old people without kin and money have no one to defend them against those who may wish to bedevil them. The boys of the Swahili community—in concert with the Hadhraml Arab boys, whose families live mixed among the Swahili in Mombasa—find them easy and attractive prey. These boys seem to be mainly between the ages of ten and fifteen (older boys turn to other pursuits) and wander about the Swahili section of the city playing soccer and generally amusing themselves when they are not in school or eating and sleeping in their homes.

As recently as twenty or so years ago, the teachers in the religious schools were extremely vigorous in their use of a heavy braided whip made from banana leaf fiber (called *kikoto*). A number of now middle-aged men have told me that it was not unusual in their day for mothers to have to soak their sons' garments off their backs because of the blood from the beatings they received. When the boys got out of school, I was told, they were ready for any "mischief" and vented their emotion and energy on anyone or anything they safely could. Nowadays beatings are far less frequent and serious either in religious school or in secular school, but even now the boys are very active in their games after school and show what must be characterized as an active willingness to engage in hostile behavior.

One of the expressions of this hostility is called "kucheza shere," which means, literally, "to play ridicule." I witnessed an attack of this sort on a defenseless person, a fat, feebleminded boy of about fifteen. As I came on the scene, four or five boys about twelve years old were throwing stones at the older boy, running up and hitting him and easily dodging his slow and clumsy attempts to catch them. As they did so, they shouted "Idiot" and other names at him. He tried to chase them away, shouted "Go home," and ineffectively threw stones back at them.

According to informants, boys frequently (in the past, anyway) attacked the elderly, who are like the feebleminded boy in having neither the physical nor the social resources needed to defend themselves. Again, according to informants, these powerless elders respond to the boys' attacks not with what is here called badtalk but rather with curses. We have already seen that, although there is an association between powerlessness and the choice of badtalk as the characteristic form of aggressive speech, other understandings may militate against this choice—as they do for girls and young women.

For mature and elderly people, the public use of badtalk is associated with failure to achieve the status of a full-fledged adult. Woman may use badtalk on their daughters and occasionally on their peers within the security of their neighborhoods, but they rarely or never use it publicly. Grown men who use badtalk publicly thereby suggest that they have failed to associate themselves successfully with the dignity and restraint characteristic of the community's leading males. For both sexes, then, public badtalk is costly.

Understandings about sheer effectiveness are probably also influential.

The boys are expert and unabashed in using badtalk, and a grown person is more than likely to find himself or herself in a worse situation than before entering into an exchange of it with them. One example relates to an exchange between a boy and a Hadhrami Arab woman. The Swahili say that the Hadhrami are industrious and frugal but without manners, and the fact that the woman in the following account entered into a badtalk exchange with a boy is cited as an example of how mannerless they can be.

Boys regularly played noisy games of soccer in front of the woman's house, and her husband endlessly quarreled with them about it. If the boys saw the woman while they played, they would shout *hasili* ("jealous") at her, presumably meaning that she wanted to enjoy herself as they did. Once she got into an argument with one of the boys and called him *Hanithi*, a word that I have already considered which generally refers to the passive participant in sodomy. In response the boy shouted *Maliya* (prostitute) at the woman, to which she replied "Tu yako" ("your anus"). The boy then said "Kuma yako" ("your cunt"), and at this the woman retreated into her house.

Given the fierceness of the boys and their willingness to use badtalk freely, the old people can hope for little advantage in using it to deal with them. The use of curses, however, is slightly different. As noted earlier, the Swahili differentiate between curses (*maapiso*) and insults (*matukano*). I have neither heard reports of young people using curses nor observed them doing so. The sorts of curses old people use on their tormentors have one thing in common: they call upon God to visit various kinds of harm on those cursed. Curses are, then, a sort of prayer, and in this pious community there is a strongly held and probably universally shared understanding that prayer is effective.

The curses used by the defenseless old people include such prayers as: "God give you cholera" ("Mbwa tauni"), "God give you a great shame" ("Mwana hizaya"), "God give you enough to occupy you" ("Mbwa kupa wa kutosha"), and simply, "God curse you" ("Mwana lana"). These curses appear to have their literal meaning and, given the Swahili understanding that supernatural assistance can be invoked, may be seen as potentially effective. At the least, they do not prompt an exchange of badtalk with boys from which the adult is unlikely to profit. It may be—and my only evidence is that I have not seen them do it—that even the children in this profoundly believing society are unwilling to invoke the deity for frivolous purposes. Thus the curses offer weak, elderly victims a sort of resource to be used in their own defense. But whether or not this is so, the children do not answer curses with curses. The curse "God will defeat you" ("Mungu atakushinda") nicely summarizes the aim and hope of the powerless people who are the main users of curses of this sort.

Although curses as means of defense are used mainly or entirely by the elderly, one kind of curse is used by other sorts of people. This curse combines abuse with a call for divine intervention. This sort of curse also seems to be used less frivolously than the badtalk already discussed. An example of this combined curse and abuse is seen in an incident in which a woman struck another's child for no apparent reason.

The mother heard the noise and came out asking why the child had been struck. The attacker offered no reason, and the mother said: "You are crazy to hit a child like this for nothing." At this the attacker hit the child again and said "There, you see." The mother, enraged, said to the attacker: "God curse you and the curse is to be as you are." This was intended, informants say, both to wish something bad on its target and to make clear that the pronouncer of the curse considers the accursed as being already in a condition that shows the results of divine disfavor.

A type of expression that is fairly often found in angry exchanges between women is closely related to this type of curse. If one woman accuses the other of something that the first does not think she deserves, the accused can say *waleo*, which is based on an archaic form of the verb "to write" and means that God has written for the accuser that she be as she is (that is, angry, unreasonable, and badly behaved). There is some elaboration of this semicurse with the two other common forms ("shauri yako," "your affair"; "utaona mwenyewe," "you will see for yourself") both referring to the view that God has set a bad fate for the object of the expressions. All of these call attention to the badness of their targets and underline God's role in that condition, much as do the more active curses, such as "God make you as you are."

The users of mixed insults and curses have one thing in common with the users of pure curses: they have limited independent means for gaining the goals they want. In this curses show a similarity with badtalk. Mixed curses, however, are used not in the mother-child relationship as badtalk is, as far as I could determine, but rather between women whose relations are far more restricted in scope than those between women and their children. Women use the mixed curses on other women, but I have no evidence indicating they use curses on any of their kin or on close neighbors and friends.

Mixed curses occur in relationships that are limited in scope, then, and this is even more true for pure curses. The destitute elders have virtually no relationship with their targets—the boys who torment them—apart from the street encounters in which the curses occur. It is noteworthy that the damage intended by badtalk and reproach is limited, while the relationships in which they occur are broad. The damage intended by curses (the infliction of diseases, God's wrath, great shame) is much broader and the relationships much more limited. Badtalk and reproach deal with a target in a way that leaves the user-target relationship more or less intact albeit with the target diminished in evaluation and damaged in status classification. Curses deal with the target in a way that seems intended to end the relationship by crushing the target with holy terror. Perhaps curses occur in such relationships in societies where relationships of broad scope are being brought to an end (for instance, when a child is being renounced), but in this society where (excluding marriage) broad relationships are understood as both ideally and usually interminable, curses occur only in narrow-scope relationships.

We saw that badtalk and reproach elevate the user by implying that the user does not suffer from the undesirable qualities or traits attributed to the target, but this is not as clearly true for curses. Perhaps a curse suggests that its user is in a better relationship with God, but equally possibly, it suggests only that the target is in a bad relationship (that is, one where God should be willing to harm him) and says nothing at all about the relationship of the user.

Similarly, if curses attack status membership and evaluation as badtalk and reproach do, the attacks are much less obvious. Wishing a divinely sent disease or God's wrath on a target may imply that he does not fit in the status of those who please God (or something similar), but it is not clear that this is a category of any social consequence in Swahili society. As long as required religious activity is carried out, being the object of God's wrath does not preclude the individual from equal standing with those who are otherwise peers, or at least I have never heard of a person being put at a social disadvantage on this ground.[6] The same is not true, for example, of being understood to be of illegitimate birth or of having a mother with a reputation for wanton behavior.

The failure of curses to entail an attack on the target's status and to elevate the user on the same grounds on which the target is diminished is what would be expected, given the narrow scope of the relationship between the user of curses and his target and given the avowed aim of the curse. If the relationship is strictly limited in scope, and if the aim of the curse is to terminate even that relationship by removing the target, there is no advantage in undermining the target's standing by denying him an important status and/or by attributing to him an unfavorable evaluation on a dimension that is understood to be important. The statuses of participants are crucial to relationships in that they give the parties to the relationships a basis for understandings about their own behavior and that of others and about how it will be evaluated, but when the relationship itself is under attack, as it is when curses are used, attacking the statuses accomplishes less than attacking the existence of the relationship itself by calling for the removal of the other participant.

CONCLUSIONS

The general thesis of this chapter has been that the use of different kinds of aggressive speech among the Swahili of Mombasa can be understood in the light of the central role played by culture as distributed according to statuses. "Status" is defined here as composed of three distinguishable sets of understandings: those that indicate who is and who is not a member of the category in question; those that indicate the importance of the status, vis-à-vis other statuses, as a guide for behavior in different situations; and those that stipulate the type and content of behavior that members of the status category will (and should) or will not (or should not) manifest in various situations and contexts.

The type of aggressive speech characteristically used by category members has been seen to be closely related to the shared understandings associated with both the understandings concerning membership in a status category and the understandings concerning how status members should and should not act and/or be as concerns Swahili mothers, boys and young men, and mature men. The fact that one can see a shift from one kind of aggressive speech to another as individuals pass from one status to another provides still further support for status' central role.

We saw that young men use badtalk as their characteristic form of aggressive speech but that, as they marry, get jobs, and become substantial members of the group, they cease using badtalk and use reproach instead. This shift occurs rather uniformly for everyone who moves from the young man category to the mature man category, which indicates that status has an influence quite apart from individual differences and that in fact statuses serve to distribute culture among actors and in different relationships.

The idea that differences within populations can be understood according to differences in status is hardly new; it is the foundation of Linton's model. Here I emphasize the elaboration and application of the view that culture is distributed by the cultural constitution of different categories of actors and the assignment to these categories of additional cultural elements concerned with how they should and do act. As Spiro noted in the passage that I quoted at the start of this chapter, statuses are at the heart of social systems, and by a detailed investigation of these statuses it is possible to gain a basis for understanding the diversity of behavior found within these systems as well as the foundation for the systems themselves. Here the concern was with aggressive speech among the Swahili, but the same issues focusing on statuses and their three sorts of qualities can usefully be raised for a very wide range of behaviors in all human societies.

N O T E S

The research for this chapter was made possible by generous grants from the Wenner-Gren Foundation for Anthropological Research and the Biomedical Research Fund of the University of California, San Diego. F. G. Bailey, Daivd K. Jordan, Fitz John Porter Poole, and Donald F. Tuzin were kind enough to read earlier drafts, and their comments have been of major importance in my revisions. Sh. Yahya Ali Omar here, as elsewhere, has been my linguistic informant and mentor; his help is of inestimable value.

1. The possibility that the phrases examined here have no literal meaning—are "unetymological," as one reader of an early draft put it—needs to be examined briefly. The possibility that mothers are just mouthing a phrase when they tell their own children "Your mother's vulva" provides as good an issue as any for this examination.

First, the contention that the phrase "has no meaning; it is just a conventional insult" is parallel to the contention that inheritance systems are followed "because they are customary." One must have an inheritance system, and that which is part of the cultural heritage is readily available. That it is part of the heritage, however, does not ensure its continued use, any more than being part of a heritage ensures the continued use of badtalk. "Stenchard" and "Swounds" are part of the cultural heritage of English speakers, as are curses such as "Pox on you," but they are no longer heard in popular use. If meaning has nothing to do with aggressive speech, it is as difficult to explain why some of the commonest American badtalk ("motherfucker," "bastard," "sonofabitch") concerns the target's mother's improper sexuality as it is to explain the uses of Swahili badtalk without reference to the meaning of its phrases.

Second, even if we set aside the evidence that abusive phrases do actually have meaning, we must still explain why the particular phrases used are chosen. One answer might be that there are no alternatives. This, however, is far from the actual case. Such abusive phrases as "fool," (*mjinga*), "uncivilized person" (*mshenzi*), "dirty one" (*mchafu*), and "idiot" (*mpumbafu*) are common enough in the Swahili language but are not used the way "your mother's cunt" and "bastard" are in relations between mother and children. The frequency of the latter and the emotionality of the mother in using them sets them apart from other aggressive speech.

Finally, it might be argued that badtalk is best explained by conformity in its use. Every mother abuses her child with the same phrases, this argument runs, and each uses the phrases employed because the others do. This reasoning, however, does not explain why the common phrases were chosen rather than others. This argument merely shifts the issue from asking why particular phrases are used to noting that they are generally used. The latter observation does not answer the former question.

2. The possibility that they used the badtalk defensively in attacking the friend

before she could attack them for their involvement in a disapproved adventure is lessened by the fact that in my observation the usual Swahili view about misbehavior is that it is best hidden rather than emphasized, as it was by using badtalk on someone who might otherwise not have noticed what was happening across the street. Also, according to the understanding of their caste, young women do not usually judge their peers harshly, or badly at all, for activities such as these.

3. An incident remembered by an informant, however, involved an unusually forthright and uninhibited woman, who called her adult son "mwana haramu" when he particularly annoyed her on one occasion. He is reported to have replied: "Ah, now I understand what puzzled me before: how *you* could bear a legitimate child."

4. "Nobles," or *waungwana*, include all those whose forebears are both unquestionably Swahili and unquestionably free of slave ancestry. Some people who claim membership in the group are viewed by others as having slave forebears and as being, therefore, not nobles. Some of these men, though by no means all, have been heard by me to use badtalk. Similarly, some Swahili waungwana pride themselves on their rough and crude manners. These nobles do not concern themselves with wearing high-quality clothing as other waungwana do and are willing to earn their living as manual workers—usually as fishermen—as most other waungwana are not. These "tough guy" waungwana come from a particular neighborhood in Mombasa and include some mature men who use badtalk.

5. Given the differences in the aggressive speech used by mothers and by fathers, it is interesting to remember that all sons and the vast majority of daughters were seen to report loving their mothers more than their fathers. It may be that the denial of membership in a status that one obviously occupies is taken less seriously than the accusation that one has failed to meet the requirements of understandings that are, in fact, often unmet. Other explanations of the differences, such as ones based on the scope of the relationship, are also interesting.

6. *Kisirani* refers to evil omens and that which brings misfortunes, but it also refers to the condition of having misfortunes. A person in this condition seems to be pitied rather than shunned or derided even though such a person can hardly be seen as enjoying God's favor.

PART TWO
Culture and Personality,
Gender Roles, the
Oedipus Complex, and Dreams

6

Culture and Personality

A False Dichotomy

ROY G. D'ANDRADE ⟡

The nature of the relation between culture and personality remains a contested issue. Some anthropologists and social scientists argue that culture is independent of personality and its operation. Many who take this position find any claim of a relation between culture and personality to be reductionistic, indicative of a failure to appreciate that culture is an emergent phenomenon existing on a different level from personality.

On the other side of this issue, a number of anthropologists and social scientists claim that there are significant connections between culture and personality. Melford Spiro has been a major protagonist of this position. In articles and monographs beginning with his 1951 paper "Culture and Personality: The Natural History of a False Dichotomy," Spiro has presented a comprehensive theory about the nature of the relationship between culture and personality. While Spiro's theoretical position has evolved considerably since 1951, this early paper is still a landmark in the debate about the relationship between culture and personality.

In 1951 Spiro presented a carefully reasoned argument about what, given certain premises, must necessarily be the case about the relation between culture and personality. Although most anthropologists did not accept the most sweeping claim of this article—that culture and personality are basically the same thing—the paper has been widely read and cited. Read today, it remains informative. While Spiro's more recent papers take a different position with respect to the relation between culture and personality, treating them as distinct but related entities, many of the issues raised in the 1951 paper are still significant problems. To understand these long-standing problems better, it is worth returning to this article to see how the issues were originally posed and to compare the solutions available at the time with the possible solutions available now.

The article begins with a discussion of the historical background of the concept of culture.

> With the American Historical School, anthropology took a new turn. Rejecting all prior conceptions of cultural evolution, and insisting on firsthand empirical knowledge of primitive peoples, American anthropologists began their intensive studies of specific primitive societies, guided, at least implicitly, by Tylor's definition. . . . A culture, as that complex whole, was conceived as an objective entity, which was acquired by the members of a society. And if a given culture could be acquired by the members of a society, the anthropologist could learn it from one of the members who has already acquired it. Hence arose the crucial role of the informant in anthropological research.
>
> Gradually, however, the report of the informant and the behavior of the people became fused in the ethnographic reports. The culture was not only something that could be acquired—a social heritage—but it was also the behavior of the people that acquired it. The published ethnography of a given society was not only a description of the way that the members of a society did behave, but it was, at the same time, a statement of the way they were supposed to behave; and the descriptive and the normative became blurred. Within these two confusions is implicit the concept of cultural determinism. In effect it is argued as follows: Since culture is something to be acquired, and since everyone who acquires it behaves in the same way, it follows that they behave that way because of their culture. [Pp. 21–22]

The problem raised by field research and ethnographic reports was that of the ontological status of culture—what was it, really, something inside people or something outside people? Something that made people behave as they do or something produced by their behavior? Spiro outlines three different formulations developed by anthropologists in the 1930s and 1940s which attempted to answer these questions. One formulation, which Spiro calls "cultural realism," holds that culture is a superorganic entity, with its own laws and processes, not affected by human will or passion. A second position, which Spiro calls "cultural idealism," holds that culture is primarily "ideational," consisting of ideas about how one should behave held by the members of a society. The third position, which Spiro calls "cultural nominalism" and which he describes as holding the dominant position within anthropology in the 1950s, held that culture has no special ontological reality; it is simply an abstraction from human behavior, made by the anthropologist.

Spiro observes that the position of the cultural nominalist has the great drawback of making it impossible to argue that culture influences behavior. If culture is just an abstraction in the minds of anthropologists, it obviously cannot be the cause of the behavior of the people whom the anthropologists have studied. The superorganic position, Spiro argues, is hardly an improvement, since it separates humans from culture so completely that no specific set of causal mechanisms has ever been proposed by those who hold this position to explain how culture affects behavior. According to the superorganic view of culture, culture floats so far above the individual, and is so separated from human functioning, that one must imagine that it influences behavior, like gravity, by force at a distance.

The cultural idealist position Spiro also finds unsatisfactory with respect to this issue of the effect of culture on behavior. In some cases, according to the cultural idealists, people follow their ideas about how things should be done. However, in other cases—as the cultural idealists admit—people do not do what they understand to be right. The relation, then, between behavior and ideas is an indeterminate one. Cultural idealism, in claiming that culture consists of ideas, has the problem that any understanding about the means by which culture affects behavior depends on having a reasonable theory of how ideas affect behavior—how cognition is related to action— something which was noticeably absent from American psychology and social science in 1950.

Thus anthropology found itself with three different solutions—cultural idealism, cultural nominalism, and cultural realism—to the problem of the relation between culture and behavior. None was satisfactory. To develop a more adequate statement of the relationship, Spiro examined the basic nature of the relationship between humans and culture. The term "culture" itself, Spiro notes, has two meanings, one referring to what particular individuals have learned, the other referring to all the learning of the people of a society. Spiro uses the analogy of gene flow to illustrate the different senses of the term "culture" and to show how they are interrelated.

> Just as the gene pool of any society is the sum total of genes in that society, so the cultural heritage is the sum total of ideas, knowledge, beliefs, techniques, and so on, in that society. And just as the biological inheritance of any one individual (genotype) does not include the entire gene pool, . . . so the social inheritance of any individual is that portion of the cultural heritage which he inherits from his parents. And just as the gene pool is not a superorganic because it is greater than the number of genes found in any one person, so the cultural heritage is not a superorganic because it is more than any one person can know. And just as the biological inheritance of an individual is not a superorganic because it exists before he was born, and continues to live on

after he dies, so his cultural inheritance is not a superorganic because it exists before he was born and continues to live on after he dies.

However, Spiro argues that the process of genetic transmission cannot be an exact model of the process of cultural transmission because of the considerable distortion which occurs in the learning process.

The cultural heritage is inherited by learning, and learning is not a uniform process, but one which varies considerably from individual to individual. Much of what is taught by the parent (the cultural heritage) meets with tremendous resistance on the part of the child, for much of the teaching constitutes a thwarting of some of the child's strongest drives. . . . The imperious nature of the child's mammalian drives renders forever impossible a conception of social learning as a simple conditioning process and the conception of the individual as an inert object which is "moulded" by the cultural heritage. . . . Not only do different children assign different meanings to the cultural heritage, resulting in qualitatively different cultural heredities, but the degree of acceptance or resistance differs, as well, so that some children may accept the cultural heritage in its entirety, whereas others may refuse to learn certain aspects of it. Thus, when these children become adults the cultural heritages which they will pass on to their children will be different. Furthermore, individuals may and do discard certain aspects of their cultural heritage, which they had once learned. [P. 38]

One result of the "distortions" which occur in learning one's cultural heritage is that there is considerable variability in cultural behavior across individuals, since each has learned different things. Detailed field observation has, in fact, shown that the naïve expectation that all the members of a culture will exhibit the same practices even with respect to such standard cultural systems as the use of kin terms is doomed to disappointment (Roberts 1951). This variability in cultural practices and beliefs makes it even more important to distinguish sharply between personal culture and the cultural heritage.

The traditional ethnography is a description of the cultural heritage of a society, and one of the major sources of confusion arising from attempts to relate cultural norms and cultural behavior is the failure to distinguish between the cultural heritage of society and the culture of an individual. Einstein's relativity theory, the social democracy of Jefferson, the teachings of the Prophets—all these are part of the cultural heritage of American society. But they have little effect on any given individual until they become part of his culture. Until they are learned by him, they have little influence on his behavior, though they may exist in the cultural heritage of the society, as part of the culture of other individuals. [P. 41]

In Spiro's view, the individual's learning of his or her own personal culture is an important part of the process by which culture affects behavior but is not the entire story. While some social and psychological theorists have assumed that learning is a sufficient cause of behavior, Spiro does not. For Spiro, learning is a necessary but not sufficient cause of behavior.

Once a particular behavior pattern is learned, why does it persist? We know that many things which are learned are quickly forgotten. We know that all molar behavior is motivated, or goal directed, involving the satisfaction of a need or the reduction of drive intensity. We know that behavior which accomplishes this end—rewarding behavior—is reinforced, whereas punishing behavior—behavior which does not result in drive reduction—is extinguished. But we also know that much of that learned behavior, which we call culture, persists despite its unrewarding character. It often happens that what a person wants to do and what he thinks he ought to do are in conflict, and we find his choice is made in favor of the ought. [P. 32]

Where does this "ought"—the sense of compulsion—which motivates so much of cultural behavior, come from? From whence comes the moral imperative of culture?

The point I have been trying to make, therefore, is that what the anthropologist observes in the field is people behaving in certain ways—ways which may be objectively described in terms of predictable regularities and may be termed their culture. But the person who is behaving experiences, among other things, the feeling that the way he behaves is the way he ought to behave—or ought not to behave. Any field worker knows that the members of a society, when asked why they do behave in a certain way, almost always reply it is because they ought to behave that way. The statement, "This is the way we do things," is not merely a descriptive statement, but contains a moral imperative as well; the implication being that "the way we do things" is the right way of doing things, because it is the only way of doing things—at least, the only human way. [P. 34]

If some behavior has the compelling dimension which I have been stressing, and if the compulsion is not exerted by some entity outside the organism, as the realists seem to think, one must look inside the organism to discover this compelling power. The moral imperative in behavior, it is my thesis, is a function of a psychodynamic process within the organism. [P. 34]

149

Spiro goes on to describe the situation of the infant, with its intense dependency on its parents, as it creates for the infant the experience that "goodness" consists of doing as the parents request, while "badness" consists of doing what they have prohibited. Eventually the child develops a superego based on the child's identification with its parents and its representation of parental admonitions.

> Thus the problem that evoked this discussion—the compelling nature of behavior—may be answered. The child learns what his parents teach him and what they allow him to retain of what he may have learned by himself or from others. But their teachings—beliefs, cognitions, attitudes, emotions, behavior—do not remain models outside himself, which he continues to imitate. They are incorporated within himself to become his beliefs, his cognitions, his attitudes, his emotions, his behaviors. Thus, though the behavior to be learned is determined by powers external to the organism—his parents—the persistence of behavior is determined by a dynamic within the organism—the superego which is a symbolic representation of the external parents. . . . The behavior of their parents constitutes, for the children, a cultural heritage. But once this cultural heritage is learned, it is no longer external to them, existing in the past; it is within them, part of them. Thus in terms of the superego concept, the cultural heritage does not remain in the past, determining behavior from afar. It is, rather, incorporated as an integral function of the psychodynamics of the organism.

In later papers and monographs Spiro analyzes a variety of other motivational systems besides the superego which underline cultural behavior, pointing out that rewards and punishments outside the moral dimension motivate cultural and social behavior, such as the desire to conform to whatever it is that other people do, the external sanctions of money, approval, disapproval, prison, and the direct satisfaction of needs through the performance of cultural roles (Spiro 1965a).

The overall thrust of Spiro's argument is that culture, in being learned, becomes a part of the individual. Furthermore, what is internalized is not just a set of simple responses, or behaviors, or habits, because much of cultural learning is not simple conditioning but involves complex psychological processes involving identification and internalization. And as a result of such complex processes, some parts of the cultural heritage come to have special psychological characteristics, such as the special moral and valuational character that pervades much of the cultural heritage.

The final part of Spiro's argument is that "personal culture" is learned through the same process and in the same way that "personality" is learned. Both are learned primarily from parents, and both are modified by later interactions with people outside the family. Of course, one's personality includes various idiosyncratic learnings which were never part of the cultural heritage and which will not be transmitted to later generations. However, the core of both is the same—they consist of learned behaviors. Hence, Spiro argues, culture and personality are basically the same thing, and the separation of the two concepts, one as it applies to individuals, the other as it applies to a society, is the construction of a false dichotomy.

The argument is logically sound, yet the conclusion seems odd. For example, my usage of kin terms and my knowledge of arithmetic are both part of my "personal culture," but most social scientists would not call these things part of my "personality" unless I had an unusual way of using kin terms or bizarre ideas about numbers, in which case these distortions of the "cultural heritage" might be said to reflect something about my personality.

But if both "personality" and "personal culture" are learned behavior systems, wherein lies the difference? One solution might be to treat "culture" as one kind of learned behavior and "personality" as a different kind of learned behavior. This would account for the oddness of considering my knowledge of arithmetic to be part of my personality but would swiftly lead to other problems. What about the high value I place on science? This value has been noted as a generally shared part of American "culture." Can we say that, because it is part of my "culture," it cannot be part of my "personality"? The Japanese are noted for their strong assumption that hierarchy is a necessary part of social relationships (Benedict 1946). Is this part of their "personality" or part of their "culture"?

Resolution of the issue depends upon clarifying the notions of culture and personality. Spiro's 1951 argument indicates undeniable similarities in the way both culture and personality are acquired. However, similarity in acquisition does not entail similarity in function: one can acquire both a reputation as a fierce tennis player and a sore elbow through the same events, but a sore elbow and a reputation as a fierce tennis player are not the same kind of thing, because each is part of different systems of functioning. I believe the analogy holds for the problem of defining what is culture and what is personality: in general, neither personality nor culture can be defined by behavioral *content*. Rather, both must be defined with respect to some system of functioning. Thus personality is not just a set of behaviors (LeVine 1973). Personality consists of affective, motivational, and cognitive systems which enable human beings to maintain and regulate themselves as individual organisms. Loosely speaking, something is part of one's personality because it fits into a system which works to keep one running as a behaving organism.

In the 1950s, when Spiro's "False Dichotomy" article was written, the dominant psychological theory was behaviorism, which defined personality as *responses* characteristic of an individual. And indeed, if personality is taken to consist of just those responses which are characteristic of an individual, and if culture is taken to consist of just those responses which *are* characteristic of a group, then one's personal culture and one's personality are basically the same kind of thing.

In later observations on kibbutz culture and personality, Spiro shifts to a nonbehavioristic and "inner-process"-oriented definition of personality:

> The findings of the kibbutz study had a strong . . . impact on my image of man and my conception of anthropology. Although the kibbutz children were raised in a totally communal and cooperative system; although their socialization had as its primary aim the inculcation of a cooperative, non-competitive ethic; although the techniques of socialization were mild, loving, and permissive; although the target responses were reinforced; although, in a word, almost all of the culture conditions were designed to exclusively promote cooperation and sharing, the data clearly indicated that the kibbutz children, like other children, do not wish to share scarce and valued goods—they want them for themselves and they resist the attempts of adults to get them to share them. They view as rivals those with whom they are obliged to share, and they aggress against those who frustrate their desires. . . .
>
> This does not mean, I hasten to point out, that the kibbutz has been unsuccessful in transmitting its ethic of sharing, equality, mutual aid, and cooperation to its children. It has, on the contrary, been surprisingly successful, if "success" is defined as the perpetuation, by successive generations of adults, of the social and cultural systems for which they were socialized. . . . The real mark of the kibbutz success is that although its children have developed competitive and acquisitive, as well as cooperative and sharing dispositions, when, as adults, they experience conflict between them, they usually resolve the conflict in favor of the latter dispositions. In short, the kibbutz values have penetrated to that part of the personality which is the true measure of the internalization of cultural values—the superego. [Spiro 1978b, p. 345]

If one were to limit one's observations to the behavioral level, the predominant behavior one would see would be that which reflects the ethic of cooperation, and one might suppose that kibbutz culture and personality were isomorphic. But distinguishing between culture as a system of meanings through which human groups adjust and adapt to their environment and to each other (D'Andrade 1984) and personality as a system of cognitive, affective, and motivational processes through which individuals regulate and maintain themselves, one can see that there are real differences between the culture of the kibbutz and the commonalities found in the kibbutz personality. Culturally, there is a very strong ethic of cooperation and non-acquisitiveness. At the personality level, there is conflict, with tendencies toward cooperation and sharing in conflict with tendencies toward competition and acquisition.

What, then, does this distinction do with respect to our understandings of the relation between culture and personality? If they are different systems of functioning, are they unconnected? And if they are connected, in what specific ways are they connected?

One kind of connection between culture and personality involves causal/functional relationships. Causal/functional relations typically involve the satisfaction or frustration of some motivational condition. Thus cultural beliefs in an omnipotent and benevolent supernatural have been hypothesized to satisfy dependency needs (Spiro and D'Andrade 1958), male initiation rites to help resolve problems for males who have disruptive feminine identifications (Whiting 1961), monastery life to protect men who have problems coping with disruptive sexual needs (Spiro 1982a), and so forth. Such connections postulate a functional relation between personality and culture (in that something in the culture serves to make individual personalities function better) and a causal relation between culture and personality (in that something present in the culture directly affects the personalities of individuals). The directions of causality is also thought to flow the other way; given especially salient needs on the personality level within a cultural group, one can expect the culture to develop the appropriate institutions to satisfy these needs. Cultural groups with unusually high levels of the need for achievement, for example, are likely to have vigorous, expanding economies (McClelland 1951). In general, as Spiro has argued, one can expect to find a considerable degree of "fit" between the cultural system and the personality system in most human societies—although at some times and in some places this degree of correspondence may diminish to the point where social anomie and personality disintegration become common (Spiro 1961b). LeVine has treated this type of causal/functional relationship between culture and personality within an evolutionary framework at length, arguing that over time both systems accommodate to each other across various feedback pathways (LeVine 1973).

Another important kind of relation between culture and personality is theoretically and empirically less well understood than the type of causal/functional relation described above. This is the relation of "overlap," which Spiro describes in his "Dichotomy" article. That is, putting aside the final definitional conclusion, the major argument of the "Dichotomy" article is that at least part of what people "learn" in learning their culture becomes part of their personality. *That is, although culture and personality are different systems of functioning, there is "overlap in content" between the two systems in that certain learned items have functions in both systems.* For example, the kibbutz ethic of cooperation and sharing is both a part of kibbutz culture and a part of the personality of most members of the kibbutz. These cultural values have become part of both the moral order that regulates the group and the moral order through which individuals regulate themselves.

Although some "learnings" play a role in both the cultural system and the personality system of many of a society's members, most cultural items do not become a significant part of the personality systems of most individuals. That is, human cultures contain huge arrays of information, techniques, norms, and representations. A reasonable estimate is that the culture of even a simple hunting and gathering society contains at least enough information to fill several hundred encyclopedia volumes. Just the description of the construction and use of items of material culture in such a culture, if presented with the same degree of detail that the information is held by informants, would run to dozens of volumes (D'Andrade 1981). Given such enormous repertoires of information, *it is unlikely that all of any culture is integrated into the personality of any individual in any society.* Furthermore, given suitable conditions, individuals appear able to exchange large amounts of their cultural repertoire without its affecting their personalities to any significant degree, as indicated by Margaret Mead's study of change in Manus (Mead 1956). This is not to say that there is no discomfort or sense of strangeness when such shifts are made. But a large amount of cultural change can apparently be made without massive disorganization to the individual's personality system.

I stress the point that only *part* of culture is directly incorporated into individual personalities here because of the extensive and justifiable criticism directed toward the Mead-Benedict "configurational" approach. LeVine (1973) has summarized the three major criticisms of the configurationist position: first, this position exaggerates the internal consistency of culture by selecting a central "pattern" and then relating everything in the culture to this pattern. Second, when culture and personality are assumed to be equivalent, the degree of adjustment between the individual and his or her culture cannot be assessed; one must assume a perfect fit. Third, there is no way of assessing what causes what; the isolation of cause and effect in the relation between culture and personality becomes impossible.

The criticisms of the configurationalist approach have been telling, and anthropology has generally moved away from this position. However, I am not proposing here that we return to the configurationalist approach. Since only a small part of any culture is being postulated as integrated into individual personalities, problems of consistency, adjustment, and causality can still be directly addressed. For example, although Spiro treats the kibbutz ethic of cooperation and sharing as something which has become integrated into the superego system of most individuals in the kibbutz, he is still able to consider in detail the problems of psychological adjustment which individuals encounter in living in the kibbutz (Spiro 1978b).

While there has been considerable theoretical development with respect to the kinds of causal and functional relations to be found between culture and personality, as exemplified in Spiro's discussions of the relationship between need satisfaction and the functioning of social systems (Spiro 1961b), Whiting's discussion of the relations between "maintenance," "child rearing," and "expressive" culture systems to personality systems (Whiting 1961), LeVine's Darwinian model, and so forth, much less has been done with respect to the relation of "overlap"—perhaps because of its association with the configurational approach. To date, the most valuable theoretical constructs we have for understanding the relation of "overlap" involve the notions of *internalization* and the *superego*, as Spiro shows in the "Dichotomy" article.

A somewhat different type of overlap has been proposed by Obeyesekere, who has written about the way in which certain symbols and symbolic actions, like the cutting of hair when a person enters a monastery or the cultivation of matted locks by possessed Sri Lankan devotees, reflect unconscious symbolic meanings (1981). In Obeyesekere's theory, cultures contain a number of public symbols with strong unconscious meaning. For some individuals, these symbols become central aspects of their identity, and the possession of these symbols acts as a symptomatic resolution of personality conflicts. (See also Poole 1987.) For such individuals, these symbols are both part of their personality and part of their culture and represent another type of overlap between culture and personality.

Recent work in cognitive anthropology may prove valuable in adding to the stock of useful ideas about the relation of "overlap" between culture and personality. A central construct in modern cognitive science is the *schema* concept, although the term is, in fact, not at all new (Kant 1929; Bartlett 1932; Piaget 1953). (See McClelland 1951:240–280 for an individual case history analysis using the concepts of schema, trait, and motive.) A schema is a mental representation of an object or event. Schemata vary from highly specific representations, such as the representation of someone's face, to very general and abstract representations, such as the schema by which one recognizes that "reciprocity" has taken place. Schemata are hierarchically organized, so that, for example, a representation of the event in which somebody "buys" something from someone else contains subschemata by which "money," "price," "exchange," and so forth are represented (Fillmore 1977; Rumelhart, McClelland, and the PDP Research Group 1986; D'Andrade 1987). Schemata are not carbon copies of objects and events but rather "prototypic" representations of these events and objects which "fill in" the unobserved aspects of the event or object in accordance with what is expected. Humans comprehend events through the schemata that these events activate, and the schematic analysis of events proceeds interactively, with new input triggering various "hypotheses" about potential schematic applications until the highest and most general or abstract schema has been activated. An important thing to stress about schemata is that they are active mechanisms for the interpretation of events and objects—they are processing units, not pictures in the mind (Mandler 1984; Rumelhart et al. 1986).

A *cultural* schema is learned, communicated, and intersubjectively shared by a social group; one expects others to know the schema, and one expects others to expect others to know the schema (D'Andrade 1987, n.d.). Cultural schemata, also called "cultural models" and "folk models" (Quinn and Holland 1987), are generally learned through informal tuition and typically depend on the power of language for symbolic representation. Individuals can rarely describe the cultural schemata they use fully and explicitly, although they can usually do so partially. Most cultural schemata appear both propositional and imagistic in content; this conclusion reflects the observation that people's talk when using cultural schemata contains both propositional statements and imagistic terms (Lakoff 1987; Quinn and Holland 1987).

Schema theory marks an advance over previous theoretical constructs used in the study of cultural ideational systems. Taxonomic and paradigmatic relations, while of major importance in understanding the structure of the lexicon, do not adequately capture the complexity of cultural "understandings," to use Swartz and Jordan's good term (1976). The development of semantic networks, in which the semantic relationships between sets of terms are traced out, developed by Frake (1964), Metzger and Williams (1966), and Werner (1985), improved upon purely taxonomic and paradigmatic models in that it gave the analyst much greater flexibility and modeling power, but it had the disadvantage of swamping the analyst in the combinatorial explosion which occurs when we try to trace the many possible ways of linking terms together (D'Andrade n.d.). Schema theory, in focusing on the way elements are linked together to form prototypic representations of things and events, appears to be a more effective method for the analysis of the basic units of a culture.

Since its first application in anthropology in an unpublished paper by H. Gladwin in 1972, the schema concept has become relatively common in cognitive anthropology. A review by R. Casson (1983) covers the major applications since Gladwin's paper. A recent collection of papers by Quinn and Holland (1987) contains work on a wide variety of cultural schemata—

termed there "cultural models"—ranging from American schemata for gender (Holland and Skinner 1987) to Trobriand ghost schemata (Hutchins 1987).

With respect to the "overlap" relationship, a basic question is "what is the relation between cultural schemata and individual functioning?" One basic function of schemata is to define the situation in which the individual finds himself or herself. The importance of the "situation-defining" function of cultural schemata for an understanding of human behavior is generally recognized; a dream about a dead parent may be a life-threatening experience in one culture, while in another culture the same kind of dream may be an auspicious occasion. That cultural schemata are involved in the way individuals define their situation is obvious in the case of superstitious beliefs, but the degree to which the ordinary and so-called realistic assessments which people make are based on cultural schemata should not be underestimated. The schema-guided recognition that one's soul is in danger and the schema-guided recognition that now is the time to harvest the corn are likely to be equally cultural.

As part of defining the situation, schemata play an important role in the arousal of "affect." It is generally agreed that the arousal of feelings and emotions requires a preliminary cognitive appraisal of the situation. Such an appraisal is typically accompanied by a set of expectations about the kinds of feelings there are and which feelings should appropriately be aroused by which situations (Gerber 1985). These expectations can vary significantly across cultures and may play an important role in how affect is displayed and in how it is experienced. As Levy (1984) has argued, even such "normal" reactions as the sadness and grief aroused by the death of a close companion may not be experienced in anything but a fragmentary way in cultures which downplay the expectation that sadness and grief follow personal loss.

Perhaps the most significant personality function of schemata involves the structuring of goals. One way in which schemata structure goals is by defining means-ends relationships; that is, certain high-level goals are schematically linked to other, lower-level goals. For example, among Buddhist peoples, the earning of merit is a subgoal which must be achieved in order for the individual to qualify for reincarnation into a better life. The linkage here depends on the law of *karma*, a complex schema linking the degree of merit achieved in one life to the advantageousness of position into which one is born in the next life (Spiro 1967, 1982a). For such means-ends linkage to be effective, the higher-level goal must, of course, be sufficiently motivated.

If some schemata create goals by linking certain conditions to already existing goals, what creates the already existing goals? One explanation is that, as a result of drives being satisfied when the certain conditions were reached, these conditions became "cathected" as goals (Spiro 1961b). In some simple cases the connection between the condition and the satisfaction is obvious; for example, the eating of ice cream. Unfortunately, drives and goals are rarely so obviously connected. Not only do personality theorists fail to agree on the nature and number of the various human drives, but more important, the relation between the goal and the drives being satisfied is often very complex. For example, goals are said to be cathected because they have been incorporated into the superego or because they reduce anxieties caused by unconscious fantasies. In such examples it is unclear exactly which drives are involved. A general trend in personality theory has been to consider all the drives as an undifferentiated "energy" source and to concentrate on what has been "cathected" rather than on what has done the cathecting.

While it is often impossible to determine exactly which drives create the impetus to pursue any particular goal, the determination that a particular individual is impelled by whatever drives to pursue a particular goal is much less difficult. In general, people who are motivated to reach a particular goal say that they want to achieve that goal, do the effortful things necessary to reach that goal, frequently describe situations with respect to how they fit into reaching that goal, have fantasies about achieving that goal, display positive affect when they reach that goal, and show frustration and aggression when they are blocked from reaching that goal. Of course, people may "say" they want to achieve a certain goal because that goal is considered the right thing to achieve, not because they are motivated to achieve it, making observations about effort, fantasy, and affect crucial. In general, determining whether or not a particular individual is motivated to reach some goal, such as getting high grades, buying a car, or obtaining merit, is a skill that is taught as part of normal socialization—a skill in which many people, ranging from mothers to used car salesmen, appear to attain a high level of expertise.

A general hypothesis which has emerged from study is that most so-called upper-level cultural schemata are, in themselves, important goals for most people. It appears that the more general cultural schemata are not just "maps" of the world which tell one what is where. Rather, *upper-level schemata tend to be complex representations of highly general conditions which people want to bring about or avoid*. That is, in the normal course of events, a major function of schemata is to "guide," "orient," and "direct" behavior— schemata are systems of interpretation, and humans generally interpret what is out there in order to get where they are trying to go. Thus, lower-level schemata act as goals only when they are linked to some upper-level schema which is currently functioning to "guide," "orient," and "direct" the flow of action. Thus some lower-level schemata are temporary goals—goals of the moment—whose activation depends on their "recruitment" by some higher-level schema which has been cathected. Sometimes one wants to "go home," and sometimes one does not, depending on the more general goal that one has. But the schemata which are at the very top of the interpretive system, since they are the most general source of "guidance," "orientation," and "direction" in the system, form the most general, permanent, and stable goals in the system.

Although the highest-level schemata tend to constitute the most general goals for the individual, the highest-level *cultural* schemata may not necessarily serve as the most general goals for the individual, since it is always possible for any high-level cultural schema to be linked to an even more general idiosyncratic schema. One could imagine a world where all the cultural schemata that each person learned were at a relatively low level within that person's total hierarchy of schemata, while each person's upper-level schemata were composed entirely of personal and idiosyncratic material. In such a world the goal status of any cultural schema would depend on which upper-level schemata were recruiting it at that moment. As a result, in this world none of the cultural schemata would be likely to have much stability over situations or permanence over time as goals; they would function "locally" rather than "globally." The extent to which cultural schemata are to be found at the top level of individual hierarchies is a matter for empirical investigation.

Psychologists who have studied human motivation in natural contexts, such as Henry Murray (1938) and David McClelland (1951), have generally postulated the existence of a top level of goals composed of needs for things such as achievement, recognition, acquisition, affiliation, power, and so forth and fears of things such as rejection, failure, aggression, and so on. While the definitions given for these motives are relatively abstract, there seems to be a high level of similarity between the cognitive content of the various needs and fears and the very general American and European cultural schemata of achievement, recognition, acquisition, affiliation, and so on. Unfortunately, while such a similarity may plausibly exist, work done on the specific content of the relevant American and European cultural schemata has been insufficient to demonstrate such a congruence. The hypothesis that the top-level goals of most individuals are, in large part, culturally formed remains at this time little more than a hypothesis often commented upon. A large amount of work on the identification and description of cultural schemata and on the assessment of human motives remains to be done before this type of overlap between culture and personality is really understood.

In summary, several kinds of overlap between culture and personality have been hypothesized. Some cultural values appear to be incorporated into the individual's superego—to become a part of the individual's deepest sense of what is right. Some cultural symbols appear to have unconscious meaning and under certain conditions apparently become an important part of an individual's identity. And some upper-level cultural schemata appear to be internalized by most individuals and to function as general goal systems or motives. While much about the nature of the various kinds of overlap remains to be worked out, with respect to both theory and method, a core of observational fact does seem to demonstrate that certain "learnings" function in both the cultural system and the personality system.

Given such a conclusion, Spiro's assertion that the terms "culture" and "personality" are a false dichotomy can be seen to be correct. That is, to say that two things form a *dichotomy* means not just that the two things are in some sense distinct but that they are *mutually exclusive:* nothing can be both. With regard to the relation between culture and personality, such an assertion is false. Not only do we know about some things which are both, but we also have some idea of how such things fit into the functioning of both systems. The belief that culture and personality are dichotomous domains, which in my experience is still the majority position in anthropology, sociology, political science, and psychology, preserves disciplinary boundaries but keeps even dedicated observers of the human condition from seeing much that could be seen.

7

On the "Petticoat Government" of the Eighteenth-Century Cherokee

RAYMOND D. FOGELSON ᖇᗩᗯᖇ

I

Melford Spiro's scholarly agenda is broad, subject to periodic revision, and colored by productive controversy as he tilts against various anthropological windmills. Yet his approach to anthropology shows continuity of several kinds. Primary among them is his unwavering insistence that an anthropology which lacks or denies a psychological dimension is incomplete. He has survived the vicissitudes leading to modern psychological anthropology, whose emerging synthesis can largely be measured as a series of footnotes to his influential work. But even if he had never explored psychological issues, Spiro would still be reckoned an important anthropologist, as evidenced by his contributions to theoretical issues in the study of kinship and social organization, to political anthropology, and to comparative religion.

A central theme in a large part of Spiro's scholarly corpus is the relationship between culture and human nature. Spiro's mature view of culture encompasses both its generic aspects ("Culture with a capital C") and its more specific, individuated contents and organizations ("culture with a small c"). The generic concept of culture not only looks to universal design features that are characteristic of a human level of existence but also seeks their rudimentary protocultural foundations in human evolutionary history. Contemporary cultural determinist and relativist views see culture as a semi-autonomous emergent level, heuristically independent of biology and purged of inherent psychological drives. Culture, from this standpoint, is considered highly malleable in its specific manifestations. Spiro has recently taken issue with those extreme forms of cultural relativism and cultural determinism which, if followed to their logical conclusions, would make cultural comparison impossible (1978b, 1986). He continues to believe that anthropology can be scientific, that it can test hypotheses, and that rigorous comparison can produce, if not laws, at least probabilistic generalization.

Spiro has been critical of extreme cultural relativism and of dehumanized, sterile symbolic analyses. However, a close reading of his publications reveals a keen sensitivity to ethnographic particularity, to anomalous findings, and to the imponderables of daily existence. Moreover, Spiro has amply displayed his skills as a cultural analyst in decoding multiplex symbolic meanings embedded in myths and cultural performances (1979c, 1982c). Not only does he succeed in exposing underlying cognitive structures, but he also reveals affective psychodynamic dispositions that can be functionally interpreted as "culturally constituted defense mechanisms" (1965a).

Spiro's larger project is thus not a simplistic form of psychological reductionism, nor is it a retreat into the suffocating arms of sociobiology. It is an attempt to reconcile, where possible, the richness of cultural diversity with more encompassing universal dimensions of a human cultural level of existence. It is ironic that a too often forgotten father of modern cultural analysis, Clyde Kluckhohn, not only espoused an elaborated and coherent philosophy of cultural relativism but also maintained a lively interest in the problem of cultural universals.[1] The same inclusiveness is exemplified in the significant lifework of Spiro's major mentor, A. Irving Hallowell.[2]

Spiro's *Oedipus in the Trobriands* (1982c) sets in sharp relief many of the issues raised above. This monograph is a closely argued refutation of Malinowski's claim that the classic Oedipus complex, as formulated by Freud, did not occur in the Trobriand Islands but was replaced by a different type of nuclear complex more consonant with the Trobriand islanders' matrilineal descent system, residence pattern, exercise of jural authority, and denial of male paternity. In a carefully rendered analysis of the primary source material, Spiro demonstrates that Malinowski's data and interpretations are neither necessary nor sufficient to rule out the Oedipus complex. The fact that the mother is the first love object of the male child, the inference that a boy's sexual rivalry with the father seems indicated on a repressed, unconscious level, and the fact that the authority of the mother's brother becomes salient only after the normal Oedipal period is passed—all conspire to demolish Malinowski's thesis. Spiro goes so far as to offer empirical evidence and theoretical arguments to assert that the classical Oedipus complex may be even *stronger* in the Trobriands than in the West.

Trobriand specialists and others may dispute evidential details, their use, and inferences made from them, but such critics will have a difficult time dismissing Spiro's intricately constructed case. Only new or previously uncited primary data directly bearing on the issues raised would be sufficient to invalidate Spiro's conclusions. He leaves open the possibility that somewhere, sometime, an alternate nuclear complex may emerge that differs structurally from the classical Oedipus complex, but thus far he finds no comparative evidence to support the claim that one will. For Spiro, the Oedipus complex is, indeed, a cultural universal. Nevertheless, it is important to recognize that he does adopt a relativist position regarding secondary features of the Oedipus complex. Cultural factors may thus exert a decisive influence on the intensity of the complex and on its outcome in terms of a complete resolution or a partial one.

Spiro's underappreciated book *Gender and Culture: Kibbutz Women Revisited* (1979a) also emphasizes the tension between cultural influences and human universals. This study analyzes changes in gender patterning after an initial study (Spiro 1956) and a restudy twenty-four years later. The utopian kibbutz ideology advocated "the total emancipation of women from the 'shackles—sexual, social, economic, and intellectual—imposed on them by traditional society" (Spiro 1979a:5); reforms intended to achieve this goal were implemented, especially with regard to the socialization of children (Spiro 1958). Here was a case where cultural beliefs were acted upon in an effort not only to induce purposive social change but to contravene accepted wisdom about presumed "human nature."

This utopian experiment succeeded briefly, but by the time of Spiro's revisit, gender patterning had dramatically reverted toward the traditional norms. Cultural and historical factors may be adduced to account for the reversion to traditional marriage patterns, family structure, child-rearing practices, and sexual division of labor, but Spiro opts for more basic psychobiological explanations—reassertions of nature over culture. Spiro essentially concludes that biological constraints cannot be eliminated by cultural fiat and that sexual equality might better be realized by complementarity than by identity in gender behavior and expectations.

II

This essay considers the role of women, and of gender, more generally, among the eighteenth- and early nineteenth-century Cherokees of southeastern North America. Traditional Cherokee society invites comparison with the Trobriand situation. With a Crow-type kinship system, a dominant rule of matrilocal residence, and the presence of matrilineages and matrilineal clans, the Cherokees in many ways embraced a more thoroughly matrilineal system than did the Trobriand Islanders. Moreover Cherokee women of this period enjoyed a considerable degree of freedom and autonomy in their relationships with men. They possessed an unusual amount of political and economic authority and, as I will try to demonstrate, were repositories of magico-religious power.

The materials to be cited are mainly ethnohistorical. As such they are subject to expectable observer bias and incompleteness. These documents are tempered by personal ethnographic observations and reconstructive ethnology conducted with Cherokee traditionalists in the late 1950s and early 1960s. The data, particularly those on child rearing, are insufficient to "test" the presence of the Oedipus complex in Cherokee society. Nevertheless, I shall try to make qualified inferences about issues that bear upon Oedipal matters in this matrilineal system.

My major focus, however, will be the role of women. The historical Cherokee case affords a naturally occurring instance that can be compared with the more temporally condensed, experimentally induced "Venture in Utopia" studies by Spiro in Israel.

III

The History of the American Indian by the Scots-Irish trader James Adair (1775) remains a principal source for southeastern ethnology. The essential thesis of Adair's book, set forth in a series of twenty-three arguments, was that the Indians were descendants of the lost tribes of Israel. Rather than rendering his descriptions worthless, the Hebrew hypothesis forced Adair to explore certain domains of Indian culture that he might otherwise have neglected (Hudson 1977; Fogelson 1978:12). Charles Hudson and I agree about Adair's qualities as an ethnologist, but while Hudson tends to emphasize Adair's dour Scottish practicality, I stress his Irish sense of humor and irony.

One particular passage from Adair has long piqued my curiosity. He wrote:

> The Cheerake are an exception to all civilized or savage nations in having no laws against adultery; they have been a considerable while under a petticoat-government, and allow their women full liberty to plant their brows with horns as oft they please, without fear of punishment. On this account their marriages are ill observed, and of short continuance; like the Amazons, they divorce their fighting bed-fellows at their pleasure, and fail not to execute their authority, when their fancy directs them to a more agreeable choice. [1775:145–146]

The context of these remarks is a discussion of Indian marriage customs, divorce, and punishments for adultery as compared with ancient Hebraic law and custom. Adair reported the severity of punishment for adultery among the Illinois, the Chickasaws, the Creeks, and the Choctaws, all of whom practiced a double standard in which punishment for the adulteress ranged from death to permanent disfigurement by cropping the ears, removing the nose, or cutting off a portion of the upper lip. In this comparative context, then, the Cherokees are exceptional, although Adair went on to mention one promiscuous adulteress who was gang-raped by fifty of her husband's outraged kinsmen (1775:146).

But the quoted passage indicates more than the absence of Cherokee laws against adultery. It suggests that women possessed unusual authority and power in eighteenth-century Cherokee society. In one satirical anecdote, Adair described the conversion to Christianity of a Cherokee woman named Dark-lanthorn and her immediate marriage to a white man.[3]

> There was a gentleman who married her according to the manner of the Cheerake; but discovering that marriages were commonly of short duration in that wanton female government, he flattered himself of ingrossing her affections, could he be so happy as to get her sanctified by one of our beloved men with a large quantity of holy water in baptism—and be taught the conjugal duty, by virtue of her new christian name, when they were married anew. [Adair 1775:126–127]

There follows a humorous account of Dark-lanthorn's "conversion" and her particular difficulties in grasping the logic of the unity in the trinity and the trinity in the unity. Finally the marriage ceremony is performed. Adair continues:

> This [ceremony] being over, she proceeded to go to bed with her partner, while the beloved man sang a psalm at the door, concerning the fruitful vine. Her name he soon entered in capital letters, to grace the first title-page of his Church book of converts; which he often shewed to his English sheep, and with much satisfaction would inform them how, by the cooperation of the Deity, his earnest endeavors changed an Indian Dark-lanthorn into a lamp of Christian light. However, afterward to his great grief he was obliged on account of her adulteries to erase her name from thence, and enter it anew in some crowded page of female delinquents. [1775:129]

Adair's comments inspired me to review more systematically the status of women in traditional Cherokee society. First, I will survey other ethnohistorical sources chronologically to confirm, question, qualify, and amplify Adair's statements. Next I will briefly examine traditional Cherokee social and political structure with particular reference to the status of women. Finally, I will pursue a deeper understanding of the situation of Cherokee women by analyzing some important symbolic associations.

Alexander Longe, a trader who had a firsthand acquaintance with the

Cherokees during the first decades of the eighteenth century, left the earliest English ethnographic account. He anticipates Adair's later observation of the casualness of the marriage bond and the inordinate power of Cherokee women. After describing a minimal marriage ceremony in which wild game is exchanged for horticultural products, Longe noted:

> Yet for all these ceremonies that they use, I have seen them leave on the other in 8 or 10 days with as little concern as if they never had known one the other, the men gone and takes another wife and the woman another husband, the priest giving reasons that they had better be asunder than together if they do not love one another but live for strife and confusions. Sometimes they will live together till they have 5 or 6 children and then part as unconcernedly as if they had never known one another, the men taking the male children and the women the female and so each marry with contrary parties. I have this to say that the women rules the roost and wears the breeches and sometimes will beat their husbands within an inch of their lives. The man will not resist their power if the woman was to beat his brains out; for when she has beat one side like a stolk [?] fish,[4] he will turn the other side to her and beat till she is weary. Sometimes they beat their husbands to that height that they kill them outright; but then the husband's parents assemble and kill the woman. [1969:30]

Apparently there was a limit to husband beating!

Longe also recognized a bilateral pattern in naming customs. Daughters were named by their maternal grandmothers, while sons were named by the senior man in the father's lineage. If a woman died in childbirth, the infant was adopted by a wet nurse. The husband of the wet nurse was expected to treat the adopted child even better than his own children. He was also prevented from sleeping with his wife while she was nursing. Long mentioned that, in such cases, "yet the woman sometimes gives them leave to get a mistress to serve them. But they lose their husbands sometimes by it for the mistress keeps the husband for good and all. Yet this is small grief to either parties" (1969:34). Longe's observations suggest that the mother-child bond was stronger than the tie between wife and husband and that the mother or the surrogate was the first love object of the child.

In 1730 Sir Alexander Cuming, a roughish adventurer and diplomat, first noted that Cherokees "regard only the Descent from the mother's side" (Williams 1928:124). This statement occurs in a discussion of chiefly succession.

During the French and Indian War the Cherokees laid siege to the recently built Fort Loudoun. Apparently many soldiers had Indian "wives" and mistresses who smuggled small amounts of daily provisions to their besieged lovers. When the Cherokee war chief Willanaweh threatened the women with death, "they, laughing at his threats, boldly told him, they would succour their husbands every day, and were sure, that, if he killed them, their relations would make his death atone for theirs" (Timberlake 1948:189–190). Although the smuggling was insufficient to forestall the fall of the fort, the very notion that they could defy military authority and disrupt war operations with impunity underscores the power of Cherokee women. This power seems premised on retaliatory action by matrilineally related men.

William Fyffe, a Scottish physician and South Carolina planter, wrote a letter to his brother on February 1, 1761, in which he noted that "Squas" were being used to convey information and victuals during wartime. Indeed, in several recorded instances white settlers were given advance warning of Indian raids through intelligence provided by Cherokee women. Fyffe also mentioned in his letter enthusiastic female participation in war dances and in the torture of captives. Fyffe described the militant spirit and manipulative power of Cherokee women in the following statement: "The women (as among the whites know how to persuade by praises or Ridicule the young men to what they please) employ their Art to make them warlike, even their women have some of it in their disposition, nor do they affect the contrary, as we do."

Lieutenant Henry Timberlake, who undertook a diplomatic embassy to the Cherokees in 1761 and subsequently conducted two delegations of Cherokee leaders to England before his death in 1765, commented on marriage customs:

> There is no kind of rites or ceremonies at marriage, courtship and all being . . . concluded in half an hour, without any other celebration, and it is as little binding as ceremonious; for though many last till death, especially when there are children, it is common for a person to change three or four times a-year. Notwithstanding this, the Indian women gave lately a proof of fidelity, not to be equalled by politer ladies, bound by all the sacred ties of marriage. [1948:89]

Timberlake felt it necessary to qualify his statement regarding the marital fidelity of Cherokee women with the adverb "lately," suggesting a recent change from previous practice. Although children helped cement some marriages, he also observes that, upon separation, "the children go with, and are provided for, by the mother" (1948:90). Finally, Timberlake mentions that senior "war women" who no longer accompany warriors to the field were invested with the title "Beloved Woman" (sometimes translated "Pretty Woman") and that they possessed the power to redeem captives: "they can, by the wave of a swan's wing, deliver a wretch condemned by the council, and already tied to the stake" (1948:94).

With regard to the status and prerogatives of "war women," William G. De Brahm, a German surveyor-cartographer who maintained intermittent contact with the Cherokees from the 1750s through the 1770s, reports that

> a Gang or Troop take only one Woman to War with them. She is to take care of the Camp, Fire, Provisions etc. This Woman, after some Campaigns is raised to the Dignity of War Woman, to which all Prisoners must be delivered alive (without any Punishment) as her Slave, if she requires it, which is a Privilege no Man can enjoy, not even their Emperor, Kings, or Warriors; there are but few Towns in which is a War Woman; and if she can come near enough to the Prisoner as to put her hand upon him, and say, this is my Slave, the Warriors (tho' with the greatest Reluctancy) must deliver him up to Her, which to prevent they in a great hurry drive a Hatchet in the Prisoner's Head, before the War-Woman can reach him; therefore the War Women use that Stratagem to disguise themselves as Traders, and come in Company with them, as if out of Curiosity to see the Spectacle of the cruel War-dance. [DeVorsey 1971:109]

Some of the structural implications of "War Woman" and "Beloved Woman" in the context of problems of Cherokee dual organization have been discussed elsewhere (Fogelson 1977:192–193).

The celebrated Philadelphian naturalist and traveler William Bartram briefly visited the Cherokees on the eve of the Revolutionary War. Bartram judged the condition of Indian women to be happy, modest, loving, and faithful:

> there is no people anywhere who love their women more than these Indians do. . . . They are courteous and polite to the women. . . . An Indian never attempts, nay, he cannot use towards a woman amongst them any indelicacy or indecency, either in action or language. . . . I never saw nor heard of an instance of an Indian beating his wife or other female or reproving them in anger or in harsh language. And the women make a suitable and grateful return; for they are discreet, modest, loving, faithful, and affectionate to their husbands. [1853:39]

Bartram also reported that he "neither knew nor heard of any instances of the females bearing rule, or presiding either in council or the field" (1853:32). He did record a local tradition that a particular war-woman was once elevated to the position of queen or chief of the nation.[5] While Bartram does emphasize the complementary equality of men and women in Cherokee society, in general tenor his remarks sharply differ from other accounts cited here.

It should be realized that Bartram's outlook manifested Quaker idealism and optimism. He endorsed the ideology of the Noble Savage and helped perpetuate it as a literary convention through his strong influence on such English romantic poets as Wordsworth and Coleridge.

The most distinguished traveler to the Cherokee country in the eighteenth century was the Duke of Orleans, later to be crowned King Louis-Philippe of France, who visited in the spring of 1797. His personal diary, the accounts of his companions, and paintings and drawings inspired by the journey contain useful ethnological material. In considering moral issues involving chastity and sexual jealousy, the Duke contended that "the Cherokees . . . are exceedingly casual. If a Cherokee woman sleeps with another man, all he does is send her away without a word to the man, considering it beneath his dignity to quarrel over a woman. And all Cherokee are public women in the full meaning of the phrase: dollars never fail to melt their hearts" (1977:72). He goes on to moralize about a similar degradation occasioned by liberalization of divorce laws among contemporary French women. The Duke continues, "The Indians have all the work done by women. They are assigned not only household tasks; even the corn, peas, beans, and potatoes are planted and preserved by the women. The man smokes peacefully, while the woman grinds corn in a mortar" (1977:73). The future king also noted the prevalence of white men with Indian wives living in the Cherokee area, and he acutely perceives, "Among the Cherokees and, I believe all Indians, the family is reckoned around women rather than around men as in our society. They claim that only motherhood is sure. In consequence, the children of white men and Indian women are Indians like the others" (1977:76). And he offered an erotic "firsthand" observation. "Our guide entered every house, and when the husband or fathers were distracted, he made no effort to disguise his little *games* with the wives or daughters: and they were so little embarrassed that one of them who was lying on a bed put her hand on his trousers before my very eyes and said scornfully, *Ah sick*.[6] Some of these Indian women are quite lovely, and I was struck by their flirtatious ways; they are very different from their neighbors, and no French woman could teach them a thing" (1977:84–85). The Duke of Orleans's impressions accord rather well with those of Adair a generation or so earlier.

Major John Norton's report of his trip to the Cherokees in 1807 contains little information on the status of women. However, after mentioning the severity of punishment for adultery among the Creeks, he contrasted the situation among the Cherokee. "The Cherokees have no such punishment for adultery; the husband is even disgraced in the opinion of his friends, if he seeks to take satisfaction in any other way, than that of getting another wife" (Klinck and Talman 1970:78).

Raymond D. Fogelson

A document in the Georgetown University Library,[7] in the hand-writing of C. C. Trowbridge, the assistant to Lewis Cass, contains useful commentary for present purposes. The document probably responds to a standard questionnaire and seems to date from the mid-1820s. Once more we learn of the fragility of Cherokee marriages:

> The husband or the wife was at liberty for any cause which appeared to justify the course, to separate from the partner and to procure another companion. But such separations were most frequently the consequence of the husband's displeasure, which was sometimes excited by jealously, sometimes by the friendship or ill temper of his wife, and sometimes without any cause at all. There was no general law on this subject, but every man followed the dictates of his own judgement or of his passions. [Trowbridge n.d.]

Certain patterns emerge from these ethnohistorical accounts. First it seems clear that Cherokee women enjoyed notable freedom from, and with, men. They possessed considerable power, which they exercised within the household and in other selected domains. Many observers reiterate that the Cherokees had no laws regarding the punishment of female adultery, and in this they contrasted sharply with neighboring tribes who otherwise have similar cultures and social structures. Marriage ceremonies among the Cherokees involved symbolic rather than substantial exchanges of wealth, and marital unions were highly unstable.

Second we can note subtle changes in the status of women occurring through the chronologically arranged commentaries. In the earlier sources women seem to have much authority; they seem to be the initiators of sexual activity; and the women often humble the men. Gradually power appears to shift toward men; the men are increasingly reported to be unfaithful and initiate separation from their wives. Perhaps as a reaction formation, women become so dishonored in male eyes that their misbehaviors are not considered worth fighting about. Underlying these dimly reflected changes in relative gender status are, I submit, some very significant transformations in local ecology and in economics, social structure, and political organization that cannot be fully analyzed here.

In the early eighteenth century, the Cherokees lived in small, relatively self-contained village communities. Maize horticulture constituted the basis of subsistence, supplemented by hunting, fishing, and the gathering of wild plants. Farming and the fields were the province of women, and men assisted only in clearing the fields and in the harvest. Hunting, warfare, and the extravillage world were male domains, and into these activities and areas women seldom ventured. Cherokees traced descent matrilineally, although names and military titles might be bestowed through and by patrilineal kin.

Matrilocal postmarital residence usually entailed movement to another village for a newly married man. The resultant core of any household thus became a group of matrilineally related kinswomen, usually extending to three generations. Men, especially younger in-married husbands, occupied a marginal position within the local household and village, and some of this marginality was expressed in the fact that they spent a good part of the year afield on long-distance hunting, military, and trading expeditions and in visits to their natal villages. Much of the apparent power of Cherokee women, the fragility of marriage, and the absence of punishment for adultery seem ultimately to stem from this type of domestic situation.

Certain other secondary structural sequelae are consequent upon strong matricentered households. The levirate, a widespread custom according to which a man marries the wife of his deceased brother, would *not* fit the Cherokee situation, in which women stay put and where a man would thus have difficulty in maintaining relations in two different, often geographically distant, households. The sororate, an institution according to which a man marries his dead wife's sister, or sororal polygyny, in which a man weds two or more sisters, would both fit the Cherokee structural situation, but neither is reported to any significant degree. One interesting, overlooked marriage type, however, is mentioned independently in two sources. This is the marriage of a man to a woman and her daughter. Adair disdainfully reported, "The corrupt Cherokee marry both mother and daughter at once" (1775:199). Trowbridge about fifty years later observed, "It was very common for a man to marry a mother and her daughter at the same time and to raise a numerous family from them both" (n.d.).

Mother-daughter marriage would seem structurally to stand in a relationship of vertical complementarity to the lateral institutions of the sororate or sororal polygyny. As such, it would seem consonant with the Cherokee household pattern. One wonders how such a marriage type developed. Most probably this is an example of what Kroeber (1948:399–400) has labeled stepdaughter marriage, whereby a man marries a woman and later takes on her daughter by a previous union as his second wife. Kroeber shows that mother-daughter marriage was sporadically present among the tribes of western North America, including the matrilineal Navajo (1948:399). It is interesting to speculate about the internal family dynamics occasioned by such a marriage type. Although the mother-daughter bond was strong in Cherokee society, it was a relationship characterized by superordination and subordination. Obvious structural strains could ensue from having mother and daughter sharing the same husband under a common roof. One might also imagine why long absences from the household, while on various expeditions, might be attractive to a husband caught in the cross fire between mother and daughter cum senior and junior wife. Spiro might regard such a strategic retreat as a "culturally constituted defense mechanism"!

These speculations and structural concomitants aside, one can begin to appreciate how the local household constituted both the source of and locus for female power in traditional Cherokee society. Some of that power diffused outward into other domains, but in general, authority outside the domestic household was vested in men. Men held political offices; men were the formal decision makers. Women participated in making political decisions through informal channels, however, especially through their influence on brothers, sons, and other male members of their matrilineage. The office of war woman and other titles encountered in the literature, such as beloved woman or pretty woman, hint at the existence of a formal authority system partly replicating male political organization. Any power the women's offices may have had did not persist, however, and the titles became largely honorific and inoperative (cf. Fogelson 1977).

In reviewing the traditional status of women in Cherokee society, it is tempting to invoke the much abused and frequently misunderstood concept of matriarchy. Indeed, the Cherokees are linguistically related to the Five Nation Iroquois, who, at least since the breakthrough researches of Lewis Henry Morgan, seemed as likely as any group in native North America to qualify for classification as a matriarchy. Matriarchy, however, remains an unfortunate concept subject to serious misconstrual. Certainly traditional Cherokee society cannot technically be regarded as a matriarchy, since women did not hold formal office in the wider political-religious system. Nevertheless, if we restrict our consideration to the domestic sphere, in which women controlled the means of both production and reproduction, then it could be argued that Cherokee women exercised sufficient authority for us to regard at least this microcosm as matriarchal. Pure matriarchy, in which women wield absolute power on a societywide basis, can scarcely be envisioned outside mythical constructions and the psychologically regressive wish fulfillment of Utopian philosophers. We seem instead to encounter societies with relative degrees of male and female power, with various intersecting checks and balances. Rather than seeing manifestations of these powers as inherently antagonistic, we can better understand the relations as complementary. Thus the household and surrounding fields represented legitimate sectors of female authority in traditional Cherokee society; the male domain included not only the world external to the local town but also such central areas in the local village as the semisubterranean temple-council house and adjacent ceremonial grounds. These latter arenas were normally off limits to women.

An ideology of pollution was fundamental in maintaining boundaries in these gender-segregated zones. Spiro (1968c:391–392) has argued that pollution, at least as conceived by Mary Douglas in her influential book *Purity and Danger* (1966), is vaguely defined and admits a multitude of meanings, including "dirt, defilement, danger, power, taboo, the beliefs pertaining to them, the rituals concerning them, the (magical)-punitive consequences attendant upon contact with, or violation of, them" (cf. De Vos 1975b for another psychologically informed critique of Douglas's sociologically reified theory of pollution). Rather than associating pollution with dirt, impurity, or the disgust or discomfort elicited by violation of social categories, I prefer to consider the more basic meaning of pollution as premised on culturally constituted conceptions of negative or dangerous power. The functions of taboo, then, are to restrain, control, and restrict this dangerous power.

The central symbol of feminine pollution among Cherokees is blood, particularly menstrual blood and secondarily the blood associated with childbirth. In Cherokee belief the taboos surrounding menstruating women were not predicated on a view of menstrual discharge as dirty or disgusting; rather, menstrual blood was regarded as a potent force possessing rare destructive capacity. In Cherokee myth the blood of the seven menstruating virgins overcame the monstrous cannibalistic ogre Stoneclad (Fogelson 1980). This power could also be unleashed against enemies in sorcery procedures and in war and ball game rituals. Women were isolated in menstrual huts far removed from the household during their menstrual periods. This practice was considered not a rite of degradation but a means of containing and limiting contact with a dangerous substance. Unlike Athabascan-speaking groups and many tribes in California, the Cherokees did not celebrate elaborate public girls' puberty ceremonies as a symbolic effort to "domesticate" this "natural" power and direct it to productive channels. A young girl at first menses was taken aside by adult women in the household and instructed in proper behavior. A highly charged fear of menstrual blood persists among many male Cherokees today; I know of one successful Cherokee man who finds air travel excruciatingly painful because he is afraid to use the sexually desegregated toilets in modern aircraft.

In the indigenous Cherokee system of physiology, blood is considered an unstable substance that can easily become "spoiled" or "exhausted."[8] Periodic bloodletting by means of a specialized scratching instrument, called a *ga.nú.ga*, was a prophylactic measure to maintain health. It was also felt that a skillful medicine man could examine the blood of his patient to divine symptoms and sources of illness. Fresh, healthy blood is semantically associated with the color lexeme *gi.ga.gé*—a bright crimson, whereas "spoiled" or "tired" blood would be described as *wo.di*—a dull brownish red. The last category includes not only menstrual blood but also red hematite, an iron oxide widely used for body painting.

For the Cherokees, kinship is literally defined as a relationship of blood. Blood is not, as it is for us, the metaphor for kinship that is indicated by such terms as "consanguineal" or such phrases as "blood is thicker than water." The Cherokee theory of procreation holds, in common with the beliefs of other Iroquoians, that the female contributes blood and flesh to the fetus, while the father provides the skeleton through the agency of sperm, which can be considered a form of uncongealed bone. The blood tie of an individual to a mother is thus regarded as a bond of living, procreative substance, not a metaphoric figure of speech.

I realize that a full Cherokee ethnohematology has yet to be written. I will not attempt one here. However, one small bit of evidence collected in the field bears importantly on the present discussion. Twenty-four years ago I had the privilege of numbering among my teachers in Cherokee ethnology Mollie Sequoyah. Mollie died several years ago at more than ninety years of age, and an inestimable amount of knowledge about traditional Cherokee culture accompanied her to the grave. I recall once walking with Mollie in the cornfields and asking her about the traditional Cherokee male disinclination to engage in day-to-day agricultural labor. I already knew that according to the conventional wisdom cultivation was women's work and that in the past warriors discovered working the fields were considered effeminate and shamed by their peers. However, Mollie gave me an unexpected response. She confided that women did not *want* men in the fields, that the growing of maize was a sacred activity involving specialized magical and practical knowledge, that men were unclean—"bloody" was how she expressed it—and that the presence of "bloody young men" in the cornfields could endanger the growing crops. I duly filed this information away and promptly forgot it, as it seemed to run counter to received opinion reflecting male-centered interpretation.

Only recently did I remember Mollie's comments and begin to rethink their implications. Maize horticulture was, indeed, a calling imbued with sacred religious significance. Maize (and beans and squash) were gifts of Selu, the Corn Mother in Cherokee myth, who was slain by her sons. At the time of first creation, Selu magically produced corn autogenously from her body. Before the primal matricide, she instructed her sons to drag her decapitated body over the fields seven times. Where drops of her blood fell, corn would instantly grow, reaching full maturity the next morning, if only the boys stayed awake with her corpse. The major Cherokee calendrical rite, the Green Corn Ceremony, can be interpreted as an annual commemoration of the death and resurrection of the Corn Mother, since *se.lú* is also the generic Cherokee name for maize.

However, more interestingly, Mollie's remark implied that there was an intrinsic relationship between bloody warriors and menstruating women.

Both were charged with powerful destructive energy. Indeed, the condition achieved by young men only after elaborate ritual preparation for warfare or the ball game (*da.na.wá us.dí*, "little war") was regarded as a red structural pose (Gearing 1962; Fogelson 1971). Warriors in this change of state were empowered to spill the blood of their enemies, as well as being ritually prepared to ward off the possible dangers of their own spilt blood. An important component of ritual preparation for warfare was raking the skin with the aforementioned ga.nú.ga to draw blood; and the warriors' bodies and weapons were also decorated with mnemonic designs marked in red hematite.

I am arguing, in other words, that warriors became the symbolic equivalent of menstruating women. Whereas menstruation was a natural event for women, men achieved this condition only through culturally constituted ritual means. One is tempted to see in this process something analogous to ritual nosebleeding or subincision, as practiced in many parts of the world. Bettelheim (1962) has interpreted subincisions as "symbolic wounds" through which men express fascination with, and jealousy of, female sexual organs and function and attempt to assume metaphorically the procreative powers of women. However, what seems to be occurring in the Cherokee case is a male effort to expropriate the presumed destructive power of menstruating women.

The "red" condition of the warriors was periodic, like that of the women, and this state could not be sustained indefinitely. Warriors regularly underwent purification rituals in fast-flowing streams and took sweat baths to "wash away the blood" before reentering the domestic village or resuming normal civil life. Sometimes the "red" condition might be maintained for extended periods, as with warriors kept in a state of ready alert or with players in training for ball games over the course of a summer. Some early accounts mention that returning warriors took refuge in the council house, which doubled as a kind of men's house, where rituals of purification were conducted. Other accounts report that returning warriors had to camp outside the limits of the local village for a fixed number of days for purposes of purification.

Still more interesting for the argument being advanced here is the observation recorded by Adair (1775:124–125) that wounded warriors, particularly those with open wounds, were compelled to remain in specially constructed small huts outside the settlements for a lengthy period, where they were treated by medicine men and were attended by postmenopausal women. Adair sees the striking parallel between these recovery stations and menstrual hut, since his remarks appear in the context of a general discussion of laws of uncleanness and the "lunar retreats of women."

Time and acculturation have neutralized the special power of women among the Cherokees. Menstrual huts are now but a memory, and war paint is faded history.

IV

The secondary theme of this essay concerns the Oedipus complex and its controversial status in matrilineal societies. Although relevant documentation is insufficient to make a definitive statement, it seems likely, as Spiro has persuasively argued for the Trobriands, that the Oedipus complex was also present in traditional Cherokee society. I shall limit myself mainly to some brief comments on key, normative, dyadic relationships in Cherokee family structure that reveal important similarities with and differences from the Trobriand situation. Inferences about Oedipal matters can also be drawn from Cherokee myths, particularly from the sociogenic narrative of Selu and Kanati (Mooney 1900:242–249, 431–439), but a full analysis of these rich materials would require a separate paper, if not a small monograph.

The mother-child bond was primary in Cherokee life. The mother was the first love object of the male infant, and the affectual attachment to the mother, though not without conflict, remained strong throughout the life cycle. The breast was, as Holzinger (1960:233) suggests, the omnipresent pacifier. It is tempting to speculate that with frequent, and often permanent, absence of the father from the household, the nursing baby became the exclusive beneficiary of the libidinous energy of the mother. However, Holzinger reports that culturally conservative mothers in the big Cove community of the late 1950s "do not seem to enjoy the nursing experience particularly. Moreover, they often display real ambivalence toward their children. There are occasions during the nursing period when the mother seems to be seductively warm and affectionate; but more frequently her handling seems, rather, dictated by a desire to keep to a minimum the child's intrusions on her attention" (1960:233). There is, of course, serious danger in generalizing Holzinger's observations to describe the scene two hundred years ago. Nevertheless, inconsistent mothering seems to accord well with what can be deduced from the Cherokee projective system, as inferred through myth, other customs, and the prevalent male suspicion and distrust of women. Surely the primal matricide in the Selu and Kanati myth, which is motivated by the boys' perception that the mother's magical production of food from her body makes her a dangerous witch, is consonant with the lack of affection in nursing and the often abrupt weaning reported by Holzinger (1960:233). Breast feeding usually continued until the arrival of another baby, and the Cherokee ideal was to space children at two-year intervals (Olbrechts 1931).

176

Let us return to the killing of Selu, the Corn Mother. The drops of blood from her severed body became seed that ultimately blossomed into milk corn—the early form of "roasting ears" or, as translated by the Cherokee term, "they have bulging foreheads" (Witthoft 1949:34), suggesting the globular forehead of a newborn baby.[9] But this gratification is not instantaneous; the corn does not ripen overnight, as Selu prophesied, because her sons fell asleep before dawn, and as a result, it now takes several months for the corn to mature. Thus it may not be too farfetched to suggest that the Green Corn Ceremony represents not only the death and resurrection of Selu but a return of the repressed to the blissful period of infancy.

Cherokee families tend to be large, and the growing child normally had a number of real or classificatory siblings with whom to interact. Older siblings, particularly girls, at an early age were entrusted with caretaking responsibilities for their younger brothers and sisters. The extended family included a number of adults with whom the child could form partial identifications. Mother's sisters often served as surrogate mothers; grandparents played important roles as socializing agents. Cherokee boys, unlike their sisters, enjoyed great freedom and were given few responsibilities.

The father-son relationship, when the father was available, tended to involve mutuality and was characterized by considerable sharing. As mentioned previously, there was no denial of physiological paternity, and paternity often continued to be acknowledged even when bonds of marriage were not recognized. A father normally took pride in the accomplishment of his son. Some degree of patrifiliation was manifest in naming customs: father's sister sometimes named the newborn infant, and later war titles were conferred by members of the father's descent group. As in the Trobriands, the Cherokee father did not discipline his children. The withdrawal of affection and invocation of a third party to frighten children or punish misbehavior seem to have been the principal mechanisms for expressing paternal displeasure.

The tie between brother and sister among the Cherokees was close and enduring. Here, though not in the Trobriands, this relationship was not unmarked by strong taboos or special avoidance patterns. A brother was expected to defend his sister, and she could call upon him for assistance in times of need. A sister was expected, in turn, to honor her brother, especially before her children. The situation also contrasts with that in the Trobriands in that there is little evidence to suggest the pressure of repressed incestuous desires between brothers and sisters, except perhaps for an aggressively laden joking relationship that obtained between an unmarried man and his brother-in-law.

The Cherokee relationship between mother's brother and sister's son at least superficially resembled that of the Trobriand Islands. The mother's brother was an authoritarian figure for the young boy, and indeed the kinship term applied to mother's brother could also refer to war chief or, more generally, "boss." Besides serving as an instructor in practical learning and a transmitter of ceremonial knowledge, the mother's brother was also responsible for the health of his sister's children. If a child became ill, the mother's brother either attempted a cure himself or selected an appropriate medicine man. This nurturant side of the mother's brother's role can also be seen in the responsibilities of the war chief. This man, besides being an inspirational leader with little coercive authority, had the duty of making sure that his warriors returned safely or of being subject to the wrath of their maternal kin. Thus, in addition to serving, from a Western viewpoint, as something of a father surrogate, the mother's brother role can also be conceptualized as a kind of "male mother." As in the Trobriands, the mother's brother did not become a significant figure in a boy's life until later childhood.

Given Cherokee postmarital residence tendencies, there was a high probability that the mother's brother lived some distance away in another village. While the Cherokees had no formal pattern of avunculocal residence, many male teenagers would reside temporarily with their mother's brothers to break ties with the natal household and to facilitate socialization into adulthood.

A strong libidinal feeling often developed between a boy and his mother's brother's wife. Sometimes a young man's first sexual experience was with the mother's brother's wife or her equivalent (for example, one of her sisters or parallel cousins). An undercurrent theme in Cherokee myth and fantasy involves elopement with the mother's brother's wife and sometimes the slaying, or other displacement and replacement, of the mother's brother. Much of the attraction of mother's brother's wife seems psychodynamically related to a rebellion against the authority of mother's brother. At a more unconscious level, it may reflect a delayed reaction against previous rejection by the mother.

The Cherokee kinship system entails a structural equivalence between a young man and his mother's brother not only in terms of women with whom it was permissible to have sexual relations but also in the fact that the children of the mother's brother and the mother's brother's wife are terminologically classified by a male ego as sons and daughters. From a female point of view, sexual liaison with one's husband's sister's son might stand as an incompletely developed structural analog to the mother-daughter marriage that I discussed previously. In both cases lineal equivalence would appear to override generational difference.

To summarize briefly, the primary Oedipal love for the mother seems abundantly clear. Strong evidence for sexual rivalry with the father is less obvious, although such feelings may be repressed. The authoritarian role of the mother's brother generates hostility, and some of this hostility may be expressed in sexual rivalry over the mother's brother's wife. I am suggesting that traditional Cherokee society was characterized by a primary Oedipus complex with strong love for the mother and muted sexual rivalry with the father. The father might be interpreted as an instrumental obstacle to the exclusive affection of the mother, but fathers lacked sufficient authority to become strong objects of hatred and identification. A secondary, or delayed, Oedipal reaction, stemming from incomplete resolution of the first, developed in the relationship between a boy and his mother's brother. Here hostility and ambivalence seem to be the basic emotions, as the boy attempts both to rebel against the authority of the mother's brother and to identify with him and replace him. In this secondary aspect of the Oedipal conflict, the mother's brother's wife plays an instrumental role.

V

This chapter must perforce remain inconclusive with regard to major issues concerning human universals and cultural relativism. Spiro's antirelativist position is neither vindicated nor disqualified by the data and interpretations offered here. However, his stimulating influence looms large in formulating and shaping the issues raised in this chapter.

The status and power of Cherokee women in the eighteenth century appear unusual when viewed from either a wide or a more restricted comparative perspective. Despite deep recurrent social tensions, a fair degree of individual psychological stability, institutional synergy, and cultural integration seems to have characterized Cherokee society before white contact drastically altered the situation. The high status of women in traditional Cherokee society does not seem to have represented an unstable or transitory phenomenon, despite the dramatic changes in gender-role patterning occasioned by rapid social and cultural change. Yet it is important to emphasize that traditional Cherokee society, while strongly matrilineal, never constituted a matriarchy, since various checks, balances, and separations served to limit full or absolute expression of female authority. Neither culture nor human nature, if the two can ever be operationally divorced, seems infinitely flexible.

The Oedipus complex among the matrilineal Cherokees seems clearly indicated from a structural standpoint, to use Spiro's terminology. It is difficult to gauge its intensity from available evidence. Some displacements of Oedipal feelings are postulated, and these appear to differ in degree and kind from those found both in the Trobriand Islands and in the West. The outcome of the Oedipus complex seems delayed or incompletely resolved

Raymond D. Fogelson

in traditional Cherokee society. In offering these generalizations, we must recognize that normative patterns and expectations undoubtedly mask a high degree of contingent variability.

From a symbolic perspective, the polysemic referents of "blood" seem significant. Blood linked traditional Cherokees together in ramifying bonds of kinship; blood epitomized female power; warriors attempted to appropriate the bloody condition of women when they took to the field to avenge slain kin; and in the primordial matricidal narrative, the blood of Selu, the Corn Mother, provided seed for maize, the economic mainstay of traditional Cherokee society and life.

NOTES

1. In this regard, see especially Kluckhohn and Kelly (1945) for an encompassing view of culture and Kluckhohn (1952) for a discussion of "Universal Values and Anthropological Relativism." See also Kluckhohn's attack on ethical relativity (1955), his overview of cultural universals (1953), and his essay on recurrent themes in mythology (1960).

2. Hallowell's efforts to unite universalistic and culturally specific perspectives are probably best exemplified in his influential essay "The Self and Its Behavioral Environment" (1955d) and in his wide-ranging survey of behavioral evolution (1959–1963). Spiro's assessment of Hallowell's significance can be found in the obituary appearing in the *American Anthropologist* (Spiro 1976) and in an entry on Hallowell in the supplementary volume of the *International Encyclopedia of the Social Sciences* (Spiro 1980).

3. "Dark-lanthorn," as is obvious from the context and as I have been informed by Richard Randolph, is an earlier English form for "Dark Lantern."

4. "Stolk fish" is probably a reference to stock fish, which included herrings, shad, cod, and other species that were frequently pounded into a flattened shape to facilitate transportation and preservation during colonial times.

5. Queens or female regents were frequently reported in the early contact period of the Southeast, particularly by the Spanish chroniclers of De Soto's expedition in 1539–1540. However, none of these references can as yet be taken as definitely meaning the Cherokees.

6. I have been unable to ascertain the meaning of this term. William Sturtevant (personal communication 1980), who has examined the original French documents, informs me that "Ah sick" appears there also. Perhaps the expression represents frontier English and refers to a penis in repose.

7. I am indebted to Ives Goddard for discovering this source and to the Georgetown library and Leigh Coen for obtaining a copy of the manuscript.

8. Ideas of "tired" or deteriorating blood are widely distributed around the world. Such ideas are well developed in part of Melanesia. For instance, John Whiting in

his pioneering monograph *Becoming a Kwoma* (1941) reports that the Kwoma believe that blood which circulates too long in the body becomes poisonous and must be removed. He also notes that the word for milk is cognate with "blood" and is glossed as "breast blood." Whiting fails to follow up this association to suggest that weaning occurs when the child attains sufficient linguistic competence to realize that he or she is drinking potential poison. Bloodletting ordeals are also important in highland New Guinea male initiation rituals, and Hogbin has discussed the symbolism of male menstruation in Wogeo (1970).

9. Witthoft (1947:40), citing Frank Speck, suggests that "big foreheads in motion" or "big foreheads projecting out" may refer to the former practice of artificial cranial deformation. He also suggests possible connection with Seneca social dances, one of which dramatizes "a young man's infatuation with an older woman who has bumps on her head" (Witthoft 1947:40). My late Cherokee teacher Lloyd Runningwolf Sequoyah associated bulging foreheads with milk corn.

8

Male and Female in Four Changing Cultures

GEORGE AND LOUISE SPINDLER ❧

GENDER AND CULTURE

In *Kibbutz: Venture in Utopia* (1956), Melford Spiro analyzed the social and political dimensions of life in a single kibbutz. In *Children of the Kibbutz* (1958), he investigated the unique system of collective child rearing ("lina meshutefet"), describing some of the problems and dilemmas of the system as well as its successes. In *Gender and Culture: Kibbutz Women Revisited* (1979a), he deals at length with what kibbutz people themselves have called "the problem of the women"—the complexities of gender relationships in the milieu of the Israeli kibbutz. We too will deal with the "problem" of women in four changing cultures, but we will first briefly discuss *Gender and Culture* and its reception.

In his analysis of Kiryat Yedidim in *Gender and Culture*, Spiro showed us that the initial parity in sex roles, the *identity of* roles in the pioneering kibbutz movement, had declined and that women had left the arena of political decision making and high-prestige production largely to men in favor of more domestic and service-oriented activities. Though others, before and after the publication of this book, have noted the same trend (e.g., Tiger and Shepher 1975; Bowes 1978; Borish 1982), probably no recent publication in the social sciences, particularly a sober, empirical study of one small human community, has stimulated more controversy, much of it acerbic.

Spiro's critics persistently miscast him in the role of the sociobiologist who claims that biological factors take precedence over cultural determinants. This, as any careful reader knows, is not Spiro's position. He is careful to make plain that any system of sex-role differentiation is a culturally constituted system; that is, it consists of a set of rules and norms which, viewed as cognitive messages, inform social actors of the appropriate behavioral means by which precultural needs may be gratified (Spiro 1979a:108). The problems come with the definition of "precultural." Careless readers, or readers blinded by preconceptions, prejudice, and politics, have ignored or misinterpreted Spiro's struggle to define what he infers is there (in "human nature") but that he has trouble (understandably) defining in trouble-free operational terms. In many places in *Gender and Culture*, however, Spiro clearly states his position, and it is certainly not simplistic biogrammatic determinism.

As Spiro states, it is impossible at present to disentangle biological and sociocultural determinants.

> . . . the difficulty is compounded in this case because evidence can be marshalled to plausibly support the claims of both polar types of determinism—biological and cultural; and inasmuch as the polemical context in which contemporary discussions of women are embedded arouses strong affect, a dispassionate assessment of either type is difficult to achieve. [Spiro 1979a:61]

> On the basis of these data, however, there is no way of deciding whether the sex differences in precultural needs that are reflected in the counter-revolution are genetically or experientially acquired. [Spiro 1979a:101]

These cautions did not deter one commentator (Mednick 1981) from calling *Gender and Culture* a "political tract" and claiming that Spiro labeled the search for equality between the sexes "pernicious liberal dogma"— literally a misquotation. What Spiro actually did was to mention the "liberal dogma" that "individuals must be identical in order to be equal" (1979a:109).

In an editorial in the *Jerusalem Post Magazine*, another commentator (Yongerman 1981) aligns Spiro with the new Jewish right in the United States, and with Midge Dector, whom the editorialist labels "the scourge of feminists, free lovers, and homosexuals" (p. 26).

There were, of course, thoughtful and supportive reviews. Among them, one by Edwin Cook in the *American Anthropologist* (1982) concludes with the following statement: "any further interpretive attempts must address the problems that he has tackled. The uncompromising cultural determinist should pay particular heed to this book. Spiro is no precultural militant, nevertheless he has provided countervailing theorists with a case history that cannot and should not be ignored" (p. 424).

George and Louise Spindler

The Kibbutz: A Special Case?

It is at best difficult to make generalizations in anthropology, and the area of gender and culture is no exception. Our reading of the literature suggests that others also find this area difficult. One cross-cultural generalization seems safe: males dominate the areas of public life that carry the greatest prestige. A second generalization seems almost as safe: female activities center upon domestic life, and these activities constitute a supportive infrastructure necessary for the maintenance of social life. A third generalization seems safer than either of the first: it is difficult to make any generalizations that cannot be challenged by ethnographic observations from somewhere, and words such as "dominate" are exceedingly difficult to operationalize without getting into serious trouble.

The kibbutzim reported on by Spiro, Tiger and Shepher, Bowes, Borish, and others, where Sabra women have moved or retreated, as the case may be, into domesticity and service roles, are not exceptional in cross-cultural perspective. Males usually dominate overt, public, political decision making, military operations in their direct combat aspect, and those sectors of production with the highest prestige. Females are usually primarily engaged in support and service functions, including birthing, child care, mothering, nursing, schooling, kin relations, and the manifold service functions necessary to the maintenance of society. These regularities may be considered "precultural," though for reasons we will set forth later the term troubles us. In this perspective the kibbutz movement in its early, pioneering phases was a departure from the cross-cultural norm—a bold experiment. Spiro makes a similar point (Spiro 1979a:106). The "prekibbutz" forces became preponderant as the initial impetus of the movement subsided.

WOMEN IN FOUR CHANGING CULTURES

Our presentation of data on women in four changing cultures, and its analysis, is not directed at all of the questions raised by and about *Gender and Culture*. Nor does it try to settle the unresolved, and perhaps unresolvable, question of biological against sociocultural determinants of gender-linked behavior and social position. We do extend the analysis of women's adaptations to culture change into some settings quite unlike those of the kibbutzim. Our analysis will raise some new questions but will also support the generalization of Spiro's findings.

We think of "culture change" in the broadest possible sense. We are concerned with changes in the conditions of life, including processes such as privatization, urbanization, modernization, shifts in hegemony, confrontation with alien values and norms, and ideological changes. We focus on people's adaptations to the changes in the conditions of their lives and their perceptions of these changes. We have worked on these problems for some years among four culturally distinctive peoples: the Menomini Indians of Wisconsin; the Blood, or Kanai, of Alberta, Canada; the Mistassini Cree of Quebec, Canada; and the inhabitants of a certain part of the Rems Valley (Remstal) in southern Germany, not far from Stuttgart. The first three are native American communities; the last is European. The Remstäler are more unlike the Menomini, Blood, and Cree than is mainstream America, in their culture, their history, and the contemporary conditions of existence. And yet the people in these four different contexts exhibit some similarities in their adaptations to culture change, and particularly in sex roles and sex-linked behaviors, our focus in this discussion.

We will center our discussion on the Remstäler. They, like the kib-butzniks described by Spiro, are Europeans, so the cultural baseline is roughly controlled. Furthermore, certain data we have collected from a sample of several hundred men, women, and children in a field study in 1968 and in a restudy in 1977 exhibit some trends that seem quite related to Spiro's observations of the kibbutz women and their "recidivism."

Notes on Methodology

Unlike most of our colleagues, we have chosen to elicit responses to instruments as a way of producing statistically treatable data as a measure of adaptation. It is not that we have neglected ethnographic data or indices of social and economic change. Rather, we have used easily quantified and statistically treatable data to establish some parameters of adaptation. Our research designs have all been focused on intracommunity comparison—between traditional and "acculturated," transitional and adapted, urbanized and village-land oriented, high income and low income, Protestant and Catholic, native and migrant, older and younger, and so forth, and between male and female.

We have applied hundreds of statistical tests of difference and association to the distribution of responses to our eliciting devices in these four populations to determine whether these distributions are divided along economic, social, cultural, political, and age/sex lines.

We can make one firm generalization on the basis of our extensive testing, irrespective of the population involved or the type of eliciting device used: *sex is a more influential antecedent variable than any other single variable in our data matrix.* It is important to note that we are talking about *intracommunity* differences. Our statements apply to comparisons within the Menomini community, within the Blood and Cree communities and within the Remstal as represented by two rapidly urbanizing villages, Burgbach and Schönhausen, particularly the latter.

What are our "eliciting devices"? At this point many of our colleagues will disengage. Our devices are the Rorschach, the infamous "inkblot test," and the Instrumental Activities Inventory (IAI), a tool devised by us in response to research needs. There is a large and convoluted literature about the Rorschach, and we do not feel it necessary either to support or condemn its cross-cultural use. We have discussed elsewhere how and why we used it. (See particularly L. Spindler 1975, 1978.) We find that our Rorschach data correlate strongly with our ethnographic, socioeconomic, and autobiographical data and that the instrument allows us to discriminate in certain ways that our other data do not. For the purposes of our discussion here, we will say only that, whatever the Rorschach is or is not, and whatever it does or does not do, it does elicit perceptions of new, problematic stimuli from informants who have never seen it before and are willing to tell us what they see—and our informants were all more than willing to tell us.

We used the Rorschach with the Menomini and the Blood. We used the Instrumental Activities Inventory with the Blood, with the Cree, and in Germany. It is designed to allow us to approach more closely (than the Rorschach) the social realities with which our informants are coping and from which they are choosing. It consists of line drawings of activities in which people can engage to attain their goals. These drawings are based on ethnographic work and photographs from the field. The range of possibilities in any one human community, even a relatively isolated homogeneous one, is considerable. The range of possibilities in a complex, heterogeneous, changing community is much greater, and we are interested in this range. We designed the IAI in response to our felt need for an eliciting device standardized *within* each research population.

Interested readers can find our rationale for the IAI in our publications (G. Spindler and L. Spindler 1965a, b, 1982; G. Spindler 1974a, b; L. Spindler 1978). The instrument and its model have been attacked recently (Funnel and Smith 1981) with a brief rejoinder by us (G. Spindler and L. Spindler 1981). The issue was less the instrument than the model, the critics opining that we were using psychological constructs such as "identity" that lay outside the mainstream of current anthropology.

The essence of our position on the IAI is that the native informant is a social actor who must constantly choose from an array of possible activities (working, traveling, recreating, owning, and so forth) that are instrumental to his or her survival and satisfaction. In a culture change situation the choices become conflictful and sometimes very painful (G. Spindler 1974a, b) and often require choosing from instrumental possibilities about which one knows little. We have tried to encapsulate and present in easily managed visual pictorial form a representation of certain critical choices possible within each given changing community. Respondents choose drawings of activities in which they would like to engage, or in which they would not, and explain why they made these choices. For the Blood there are drawings of medicine men with their patients, nurses and doctors with theirs, traditional chiefs, modern political leaders, mixed marriages, house building, going to school, painting pictures, breaking broncs, ranch work, storekeeping, haying, clerking, and white-collar work—thirty-four such drawings that sample the range of instrumental alternatives from the most traditional to the most modern within the Blood Indian Reservation community and its immediate surroundings. For the Mistassini Cree the range was similar, but the drawings themselves were adapted to the cultural context. For the Remstäler more drastic changes in cultural content had to be made, but the *categories* of culture (dwellings, varieties of work, ceremony, recreation, for example) remained much the same. No Blood or Cree could choose to live in a *Reihehaus* (row house) or in a traditional *Fachwerk* (traditional external beam construction) house or to work in a vineyard. The drawings are as close to life as possible. They are drawn from photos and monitored by native informants. They are emically constructed for etic purposes (we vulgarize a bit). They must be ethnographically accurate in every detail and must be perceived as real choices by informants.

It would be all too easy for us to let ourselves be carried away by methodological considerations. Our greatest pleasure has been to do fieldwork and devise ways of eliciting information from informants. Like many of our colleagues, we have collected much more information in our twenty-eight field trips than we could analyze or write up in the available time.

The Menomini

The Menomini were our first culture case—we began fieldwork with them in 1948—and we found it imperative from the start to consider males and females as two distinct populations. Others working with American Indians had noted that females tended to be both more conservative, in that they could and did preserve more cultural continuity in the circumstances created by white domination, and at the same time made better adjustments to white cultural expectations (Joffe 1940; Hallowell 1942, 1955c; Caudill 1949). Similar observations have been made more recently (Murphy and Murphy 1974; McElroy 1979; Maynard 1979).

Our analysis of male/female differences for the Menomini centered on Rorschach data (L. Spindler 1962; L. Spindler and G. Spindler 1958) and appears to represent the first systematic analysis of this or any other kind data with direct intracommunity male/female comparisons. Despite the early appearance of this analysis, it has had relatively little influence on the development of anthropological thinking about sex differences, probably because it used Rorschach data. Nevertheless, the differences are impressive and presage the kinds of differences that we, and others, were able to delineate later.

Our sample included sixty-eight males and sixty-one females, divided into five sociocultural categories relating to identifiable indices of Menomini traditional culture (participation in ceremonials, language, subsistence, etc.) as against adaptation to mainstream United States culture (same indices plus culture-specific ones). We established the categories as significantly different by applying exact probability tests. We administered the Rorschach to each person in these socioculturally defined categories. We also collected Rorschach responses from a control group of white men married to Menomini women and resident on the reservation (Spindler and Goldschmidt 1952; G. Spindler 1955).

From the intrafemale and intramale analysis of both Rorschach and sociocultural data, we knew that men and women were not differentiating in the same way in their responses to culture change and apparently were constrained differently by the norms of their various groups. We tested to see whether males and females, when compared as a bloc on Rorschach responses, would show differences. They did. Women were significantly different from men in reaction time (they were quicker). Women were less emotionally constricted. Women were closer to their own emotional and "biological" drives. They were less tense. They were not as conflict-ridden. They exhibited better reality control (L. Spindler and G. Spindler 1958).

These consistent differences suggest the Menomini women were more flexible, more open to change, less committed to the norms and restraints imposed by their group affiliations, and therefore less anxious about identities and about departures from these norms. Certain social and political events of the past two decades suggest that their psychological attributes had behavioral consequences. These inferences fit with observations made by newer generations of workers in gender and culture, although the language used and the types of data employed are so different as to obscure the fit. Some of these inferential generalizations were anticipated by Mead (1932) and Hallowell (1942), though again translations are required.

The Blood

Though we have a comparable Rorschach sample for the Blood, we will bypass further analysis of these data in favor of the IAI. We do not have IAI data for the Menomini, though related research by Robert Edgerton employed line drawings of value choices using our Menomini sample (Gold-schmidt and Edgerton 1961). Edgerton's results related well with discriminations made by the Rorschach.

The Blood informants, forty-eight males and thirty-four females, ranging in age from eighteen to eighty-seven and representing all known socioeconomic, religious, and other groupings on the reservation, were presented with choices of twenty-four line drawings depicting an equal number of instrumental activities. They represent instrumentalities from within the traditional framework, from the contemporary reservation community, and those stemming clearly from modern Western culture.

The results were tested for differentiation with respect to sex, age, socioeconomic status, formal schooling, ceremonial affiliation, and religious affiliation. We will deal only with differences in responses by sex. Sex provided more differentiation than any other variable. Eleven out of twenty-four possible choices of instrumental activities were significantly different for males and females. The highest-ranked female choices were mechanic, artist, doctor, nurse, white-collar office worker, and barber. The highest-ranked male choices were ranch work, carpentry, farming, haying, and rodeo. Female respondents chose marriage with whites more frequently.

The Blood female orientation is more toward the outside world and less toward the reservation community and not at all toward its traditional aspects. Blood females aspire to a style of life that was scarcely represented on the reserve at all at the time the responses were elicited (for example, artist, medical doctor, nurse, white-collar desk worker, mixed marriage). Males are oriented more toward instrumentalities that are current within the reservation community. They are pragmatic and choose what a man can actually do within the reservation. The activities they choose also tend to be ones that require outdoor, often risk-taking, activity that is culturally defined as masculine. Health, vigorous activity, and risk were specifically given as supporting values by respondents. Males appear to be relatively satisfied with the actual range of instrumental activities available. Blood females tend to be dissatisfied, to want something different, something that is not available and is "out there" (G. Spindler and L. Spindler 1965a, b).

The Mistassini Cree

We worked on Mistassini (Hudson Bay) Post, in Quebec, in the summer of 1966, to initiate a longer-range study of Cree enculturation and particularly the effect of the off-Post school. We devised an IAI before we actually saw the Post or a Cree person there, from photographs in books and from private collections. Our fieldwork in part attempted to test just such a potential effect. Our target group was teenagers who had been away at a distant residential school for at least one year. Though we made reports to the Economic Development Program then under way, sponsored by the Indian Service at Ottawa, we never published anything on the work. The experiment was a success, but our sample was relatively small, and we felt that a broader context must be furnished than our modest enterprise made possible. We administered the Cree IAI to twenty-two young people ranging in age from ten to twenty-two years, with ten males and twelve females. The line drawings depicted twenty-one instrumentalities divided by occupation, schooling, events and activities at Mistassini Post, and housing.

Top-ranked choices by males included carpenter, hunter, fisherman, and beaver trapper. The log cabin and framed tent were the most frequently chosen habitations. White-collar work was most frequently rejected. Top-ranked choices by females included auto mechanic, pulp cutter, and white-collar worker. Beaver trapper and hunter were most frequently rejected. Tents and log cabins were disdained, and wooden frame houses preferred.

Again the males and females came out differently in the kinds of instrumental choices made. Like the Blood, Cree males chose from instrumentalities extant within the Post culture and its environs. Hunting and trapping are the traditional activities for the Mistassini Cree. Carpentry is one of the instrumentalities available on the Post itself. Hunting and trapping take one out into the traditional hunting grounds, as does fishing. The same principle holds true for choice of habitation. The males chose the more traditional structures—the ones at the time actually available on the Post and in the bush. And the males rejected white-collar work at a desk as too confining. They said they would grow restless, and they did not like figuring and writing. The females were oriented to quite a different lifestyle. Hunting and trapping were too lonely and cold, and the work too hard. Their choices, if acted upon, would bring them much further into the modern, white-dominated world than the choices of the males.

The trap line is a hard way of life for both men and women. But men experience more satisfactions in the hunt and on the line, out on their own, in country that can be dazzling for its beauty as well as for the threat it poses. The women must stay much closer to home, and they have to clean and prepare all of the skins. Inconvenience and hardship are a way of life they do not choose when alternatives appear.

Das Remstal

The 1968 Sample The 1968 IAI sample from Schönhausen in the Remstal consisted of 278 children aged eight years and eight months to fifteen years and nine months, distributed throughout grades three through nine, of whom 122 were male; thirty-one parents, age range twenty-six to forty-eight, of whom six were male (those attending a PTA meeting where the

IAI was administered); and to the nine teachers of the *Grundschule* (elementary school), one of whom was male.

A preliminary run with thirty-seven line drawings was made with thirty-one individuals not included in the final sample; the seventeen of the original thirty-seven were selected for administration, and slides were made of them. They were shown, using two 35 mm projectors, so that paired drawings could be shown simultaneously to a group of children (usually about thirty at a time), their parents, and the teachers. Some were shown singly. The choices included such instrumentalities as living in a traditional *Fachwerk* (open beam) house or a modern house, being a *Weingärtner* (a farmer primarily occupied with wine grape production) or a white-collar worker, working in a factory or as an independent shop owner (*Selbständiger*), a small farmer versus a machine worker, old and new churches, big-time farmer (*Grossbauer*) versus technical draftsman, living in a *Bauernhaus* (a "great house" sheltering humans and livestock), a quiet dinner at home versus a lively party at a tavern, going to school, and the grape harvest (*Weinlese*).

We also included two statements to which we asked everyone to respond: "City life is better than life in a small village" and "The life of a *Weingärtner* is better than the life of a factory worker."

Respondents were asked to choose instrumentalities depicted in the line drawings, and to explain their choice. Our analysis permitted us to make statements about supporting values as well as the priorities assigned to the various instrumentalities and their organization. The responses were tested for differentiation with respect to age, sex, regional origin in Germany, degree of urbanization, religious affiliation, and father's occupation.

Again, sex is the most powerful variable. Girls prefer city life more often than do boys. For the girls in 1968, the life of the factory worker was better than that of the Weingärtner, the modern house was preferable to the traditional Fachwerk house, the white-collar worker was preferred to the Weingärtner, the factory to the independent small shop, the new over the old (traditional) church, and the party outside the home over the quiet party inside the home. Girls also rejected living in a *Bauernhaus* more frequently than boys did, and they were more often neutral to negative about the time-honored *Weinlese*.

Girls and older children were more frequently urban oriented than were boys and younger children, teachers, and parents. Of course, all these statements must be regarded as relative. Many girls chose village and tradition-oriented instrumentalities but proportionately (and significantly) less frequently than boys, parents, and teachers did (G. Spindler 1974b).

A Decade of Change In the spring of 1977 we returned to Germany to collect a new sample or responses to the IAI and continue our ethnographic work in the Schönhausener Grundschule and the local community (G. Spindler and L. Spindler 1978a, 1982, 1987).[1] During the nearly ten years since our first intensive study of the school and the collection of our first IAI sample, much had happened. A sweeping educational reform had been implemented at both federal and provincial administrative levels. The effects of this reform had just begun to surface at the Grundschule during our 1968 field study. New reading books for the third and fourth grades had just appeared that stressed modern life, high technology, and the realism of contemporary urban life. They were in sharp contrast to the romanticized stories about life in the country and village that children had been reading for several generations.

This initial surfacing of reform soon extended to every sector of school life. The curriculum for all grades was completely revised, new textbooks, readings, and work manuals were supplied; a stream of directives to school personnel clarifying the new objectives issued from the ministries of education; and new teachers fresh from the teacher training institutions appeared in numbers.

The *Bildung Reform* (educational reform) was only a part of a vast effort to modernize and urbanize. Though West Germany had experienced the *Wirtschaftwunder* (economic miracle) and, thanks to the need to rebuild bomb-shattered industrial plants, had an essentially new production technology and industrial plant, the administrative structure of nonurban areas, the methods of agricultural production, transportation facilities, and residential construction had lagged. The great increase in the population of West Germany due to the tidal wave of migrants and escapees from the Soviet zone created problems of accommodation that had never been entirely resolved.

The population of the Remstal had increased threefold overnight, and rural areas and idyllic *Weinorten* (wine-producing villages, such as Burgbach and Schönhausen) had been inundated, tripling and quadrupling in size. The final phase of accommodation to these dramatic changes took place during the near-decade between our 1968 and 1977 studies.

The decade between our first study and restudy was therefore one of great change and sweeping intentional modernization. The purpose of our restudy was to try to pin down the consequences of these changes in the functioning of the school as a mediator of change. The school is mandated to serve as such a mediator. Its purpose is to prepare children for the conditions of life that they will experience in an urbanizing and modernizing environment.

In 1977 we again administered the IAI and carried out an intensive ethnographic study of the school and its immediate community context (G. Spindler and L. Spindler 1978a, 1982). Our assumption was that the changes, particularly the intentional educational reform, would affect the perceptions of instrumental alternatives in the intended direction—toward a more modern outlook. The Remstal IAI had been designed with this point in mind. The choices that respondents can make all lie between traditional-village and modern urbanized instrumentalities, as they are construed in the Remstal. We were jolted by the results, which showed the opposite to be true, though we did not appreciate their full significance until we had thoroughly computerized the data upon our return to Stanford.

These data and their significance extend well beyond the focus of this chapter on sex roles and adaptations to culture change. Our discussion will be highly selective and will keep to that focus.

The 1977 Sample We have described the 1968 sample. In 1977 we collected responses to the IAI from 233 children (grades three-nine), age range nine-sixteen years, of whom 122 were again male(!), sixty-five parents, of whom thirteen were male, and nine teachers of whom one was male. Innovations included the use of a control sample of sixty-five additional respondents from a nearby urban elementary school. In the sample all occupational, educational, cultural, and region-of-origin categories and degrees of urbanization present in the Schönhausen community were represented.

Again the responses were sifted for associations and differences between these background factors and IAI choices. Again age and sex (and other variables) produced statistically significant results, with sex producing the most consistent differentiations. The differences within the new sample by sex were fewer than in 1968, for reasons we will clarify. The new (1977) sample was also tested against the old (1968) sample. And here were the surprises.

The 1968 and 1977 Samples Compared by Sex The first surprise revealed by our data analysis was that the 1977 sample as a whole, excluding the teachers, produced choices of instrumental alternatives that were more traditional land-village oriented than those produced by the 1968 sample. The overall sample trend toward more traditional choices (e.g., village residence, traditional dwelling, or Fachwerk Haus, old church, Weingärtner) was significant. It would be interesting to make many comparisons between the old and new sample and within the new sample between age groups. We will concentrate on the 102 children in the Grundschule, who are our core group, and their mothers.

First, let us take a look at the old (1968) sample of Schönhausen girls. Within the 1968 sample there were statistically significant differences in the distributions of choices for boys and girls ranging from .01 to .0007 (using chi-square) for instrumental choices of village versus city; Fachwerk versus modern row house; Weingärtner versus white-collar work; factory versus independent small shop; technical draftsman versus small farmer; traditional versus modern church; party at home versus party in a tavern (*Gasthaus*); participation in the Weinlese; and living in a *Bauernhaus*. In each instance the girls chose the modern, urban instrumentaliities more frequently than boys did. We had anticipated this finding from our work with the Menomini, Blood, and Cree, and it fit our hypothesis for the 1977 sample.

When we computerized our results from the 1977 field trip, we were shocked when we compared boys and girls within the new sample (1977) from Schönhausen. We again find differences, but their direction is *reversed*. Girls make the more tradition-oriented choices; boys make the more urban-oriented choices. The differences between sexes are statistically weaker than within the 1968 sample, for the sample as a whole is more traditional. Nevertheless, it is startling that the direction of choices is reversed for the two sexes.

The most interesting differences, however, appear when we examine the distribution of IAI responses for new (1977) girls as against old (1968) girls. The new (1977) girls chose the village over the city, the Fachwerk over the modern house, Weingärtner over working in an office, independent shop owner over factory worker, small farmer over machinist, large-scale farmer over technical draftsman, traditional over modern church, a party at home over one in a tavern, and participation (as against nonparticipation) in the harvest. The girls in 1977 unquestionably made an abrupt swing toward traditional instrumentalities.

When we examine the differences in distributions of responses for new (1977) as against old (1968) boys, we find a pattern that is statistically much weaker than for the girls but that is in the opposite direction. The new boys more frequently chose modern instrumentalities than the old boys did.

Particularly startling to us is the fact that, in three instrumental choices, the new (1977) girls almost totally reversed the distribution of responses as compared with the old girls. The three instances are the Fachwerk house, Weingärtner, and party at home. Nearly 100 percent of all new girls responding to the IAI made traditional choices in these areas, where a slight to heavy majority had made modern choices before (in 1968). These traditional/modern reversals are particularly significant because they are at the core of the village-land domestic complex. They are a statement of apparently near-universal agreement within the 1977 sample of girls that the traditional instrumentalities, particularly as they relate to domesticity and village-land lifestyle, are more desirable than modern instrumentalities.

Comparisons of the distributions of IAI responses for older students (through the ninth grade and including several kinds of schools) show the same general trend toward more traditional choices for the 1977 sample, but the responses are less consistent, and the differences less marked. The realities of instrumental choices in an urbanizing environment have forced themselves upon the consciousness of these young people. In contrast, the Grundschule children in the third and fourth grade can express "pure" sentiments, largely unaffected by practical considerations, that in muted form are distributed throughout the sample as a whole.

The same statement can be made about the parents. Again, the 1977 sample tends toward more traditional instrumental choices than the 1968 sample of parents. New mothers are more traditional as a group. We also compared the sixteen working mothers with those who did not work and found no significant differences between the two groups.

Summary of Statistical Differentiations We chose a prose style to report the results of statistical tests because we wanted to avoid pages of charts and columns of figures. To clarify the relationships we discovered, we summarize the main findings for the Remstal data.

1. A major mandated reform effort to modernize the agricultural, residential, administrative sectors in West Germany reached its major phase of implementation in the Remstal in the period between our first study of Schönhausen in 1968 and our restudy in 1977.
2. The Schönhausen sample as a whole in 1977 made more traditional instrumental choices than in 1968—the opposite effect from the one we had predicted.
3. Sex differences for the 1968 sample were highly significant, with females choosing modern instrumentalities more frequently than males.
4. Sex differences for the 1977 sample were still significant but less so than in 1968. Males chose more modern instrumentalities, and females made more traditional choices, in the 1977 sample than in 1968, thus reversing the distribution of choices by sex.
5. Females in the 1977 sample chose traditional instrumentalities much more frequently than females did in 1968.
6. Particularly significant, in both a statistical and interpretive sense, is the fact that three "reversals" occurred in distributions of instrumental choices for the females that relate most directly to the traditional land-village domestic complex.

DISCUSSION

The males and females in our samples from four quite unlike contexts clearly responded differently to the stimuli we presented to them with our instruments. The Rorschach stimuli are entirely unrelated to any specific environmental or symbolic context. The IAI stimuli are context specific. Neither of these instruments will satisfy critics who reject all instrumentation of this kind. To us the results suggest that the two sexes constitute distinctive populations in their perceptions of and responses to a broad range of environmental stimuli, that "culture change" is a dimension of those stimuli, and that we have encapsulated related phenomena in our instruments. The argument is, of course, easier to make for the IAI than the Rorschach, for it is not only context specific but culture change specific. The discriminations made by the Rorschach suggest to us, however, that sex differences go deeper into psychic organization than differences in highly specific instrumental choices. This point is contestable, but we cannot pursue the matter further here (see L. Spindler 1978).

The discussion can take many directions from this point. The Menomini case becomes dramatic when we consider that, in the crisis created by termination of federal support and services in 1961, the women displayed the most productive behavior. After affairs had deteriorated to near collapse, the women proselytized and politicized at home and in Washington, D.C., for restoration of reservation status—which they finally obtained in 1974 (L. Spindler 1976, 1979; G. Spindler and L. Spindler 1978b, 1984). We think that the "conducive base" provided by traditional Menomini sexual parity and by the qualities of flexibility and low anxiety that we have described as criterial differences between men and women under the duress of rapid and disjunctive culture change helped make this movement to power possible (L. Spindler and G. Spindler 1979). Interestingly, a recently formed "Warriors' Society" takes as one of its aims the destruction of the "dictatorship" of women in the Menomini community. There has been a reassembling of male-dominated coalitions. At present women retain important political and economic positions in the community, but a shift is taking place toward the old status quo.

Various developments have occurred among the Blood as they have turned back land leases held by non-Indians, taken control of their sociopolitical and economic life, and, more recently, built an entirely new industry (named "Kanai Industries") to construct mobile homes. The traditional Blood culture was more male dominated than the Menomini. Women could compete with men for honor or recognition in few situations. There were culturally defined "manly-hearted" women who assumed some stances and symbols of masculinity and were rich, but even the prerogatives that they exercised were limited. One of the problems with which the Blood had to cope when Kanai Industries began operation was the dissatisfaction of the women, who, clearly more oriented to "outside" instrumentalities than were men, now found themselves isolated from both their men and the new occupational roles. Programs were devised to co-opt the women into activity groups of various kinds. The employment of women in industry is increasing, but the industry remains male dominated. Unless further accommodations are made, more trouble is to be expected.

We know little about developments in the Mistassini Cree area. Much of the hunting and residential territory is being flooded as the vast Quebec hydroelectric project is implemented. Traditional male roles are increasingly difficult to carry on. We expect some of the same adaptations to be made as in the case of the Inuit (McElroy 1979), where women, less tied to traditional roles than men and more oriented to change, make relatively viable adaptations to the new situation.

In the Remstal a later phase of adaptation to change has begun. Again, sex differences are apparent and for the 1968 sample in the same directions among the Menomini, Blood, and Cree, as unlike as they are culturally. But by 1977 there had been a significant reorientation in the traditional direction, as we have demonstrated. There has been a recent shift in sentiment toward traditional land-village-family relationships and away from more urbanized and modernized alternatives—all the more striking because this shift in sentiment is taking place in the context of rapid urbanization.

There are parallels between the Remstäler and the kibbutzniks studied by Melford Spiro. In both instances there was a dramatic movement toward a new articulation of political and economic life and new alignments of domestic life and the public domain. Granted, the movements are quite different, but they had in common at least the dislocation of traditional male-female relationships. In both cases the apparent response, after a significant pause, has been to reorient toward traditional roles and relationships.

Generalization tends to obscure critically important specifics. Nevertheless in both cases some point in change was apparently reached that became threatening—possibly for quite different reasons. The reorientation to traditional relationships can be seen as a response to that threat. Paradoxically, in all the cases we know directly, and in many that our colleagues have observed (see particularly McElroy and Mathiason 1979), women wanted change and perceived and valued instrumental opportunities available outside their immediate communities. When the changes actually occurred in the Remstal case, they eventually triggered a reorientation to a more traditional position. And our Remstal data do not make it seem that reorientation of sentiment was forced on women by men, though it is true that, as women actually experienced the new alternatives created by change, they encountered role structures that had not been transformed and that can be interpreted as disadvantageous to women.

Modernization and development are often disadvantageous for women. They tend to suffer significant role loss as technological development and rationalization occur, and their special orientations, needs, and capacities are rarely taken into account (Dauber and Cain 1981; D'Onofrio-Fores and Pfafflin 1982; Meon et al. 1981; Rogers 1981; Jacobs 1982). In the Remstal, the woman in the traditional Bauer or Weingarten family was a pivotal factor in survival and success. Women kept house, took care of children, fed livestock, prepared meals, and worked in the vineyard and fields. Male roles were extendable into female domains to some degree, but female roles extended into male domains much further. In public life, at formal church affairs, or in politics, males represented the family, but at home the picture of the all-dominating paterfamilias that seems widely shared by everybody but the natives themselves is laughably off the mark. Women worked very hard and long, but their lives were not dull. They were important and knew it. When the traditional land-village-family pattern is broken up, this importance declines. Some women become wage earners, like men, but generally not in equally permanent or prestigeful positions, or they become mistresses of small apartments or houses devoid of livestock and economically productive activity, and unrelated to either the community or the land around it. Interestingly, the one single anxiety explicitly voiced most frequently in the IAI protocols by female respondents of all ages in the Remstal was the fear of being socially isolated. Women and girls often supported their choices of Weingärtner, independent shop owner, farmer, traditional residence, participation in the harvest, and hosting at home with expressions to the effect that these settings would make it possible for them to work and be with their husbands and with their families and neighbors. No male respondent expressed any similar sentiment.

CONCLUSIONS

One can argue that precultural, cultural, biogrammatic, socioeconomic, or political determinants influence males and females and their relationships in the directions we have discussed. It is difficult to explain with the same paradigm *both* the return to traditional sex-role relationships *and* the consistent tendency for females to want something different from what they have. The best explanation available seems to be the lower public prestige accorded women's roles in most, perhaps all, social systems, including changing systems. If there is residual dissatisfaction with one's lot all of the time, and acute dissatisfaction some of the time, one would understandably want a change. Once the change has been experienced, if the whole prestige system does not change, women will find competition with males, especially competition in the framework of identity, an uphill battle. There may then be a reversal of priorities and a return to domesticity and service.

It is also possible to posit that domestic and service roles are intrinsically rewarding in themselves, that they afford alternative satisfaction, and that when these rewards are threatened, there is a swing back to them. Our qualitative analysis of the Remstal females' IAI protocols supports the latter explanation, but the wider literature on women and culture change, particularly in complex societies, appears to support the former.

Probably, as with most issues in our convoluted field, both explanations are right, but the valence of one may be greater than the other at any given time in a particular culture change situation. Whatever the case may be, these are sociocultural explanations, and they are the ones with which we work.

We are left without a resolution of the biology-versus-culture argument. The problem here is that there really can be no biology-versus-culture issue. Human evolution could not likely occur without selection for complementary sex-linked capacities, and these capacities probably influence adaptation to continuing changes in the conditions of existence but never in "pure," or direct, biological form. There seems to be no logical or empirical way to separate biology from culture. Males and females have different external sex organs, reproductive systems, skeletal and muscular structures, endocrine systems, oxygen-using capacities, and perhaps even brains. One sex menstruates, becomes pregnant, gives birth, and lactates. The other does not. One sex is more resistant to disease, lives longer, is born more frequently, and survives to procreate more frequently unless there is cultural interference. But these differences gain meaning, among humans, in social contexts. They become, and always have been, *cultural translations*. There is nothing "precultural" for *Homo sapiens*, nor probably for any of our ancestral species, seen from this point of view. Panhuman universals, with considerable built-in variation, can be considered as antecedent to any one culture at any given time, but these universals are cultural translations in themselves. It does not seem strange that the translations should apply cross-culturally, at least as a broad framework of similarity. It would be strange if humans in different communities did not pay attention to the biological differences (which are relatively invariant) between the sexes. Nor does it seem unreasonable to assert, as some theorists of psychodynamic inclination have, that men should compensate for their inability to reproduce. They ultimately depend upon women for survival, both for the community and for the individual. As the Papago women studied by Ruth Underhill told her when she asked them why they did not resent the male dominance of certain rituals and the exclusion of women from them: "Why should we envy men? We have the real power. We made the men!" (Underhill 1979:91–92; our paraphrase). Men dominate public affairs, including politics, religion, and warfare, for otherwise they are powerless. We need not accept this explanation, but it is an example of the way in which biological differences may influence a cultural translation that would have universal tendencies. Likewise, the conditions of survival for human communities through evolutionary time have doubtless influenced cultural translations of biological differences. Necessary specializations in food procurement and defense are alone enough to account for many similarities in cultural translation cross-culturally.

We can and do work with the cultural translations, both as men and women and as anthropologists. Women respond differently to culture change and the images of change not because of some direct biogrammatic determinant(s) but because their social experience has molded them. And though our language and emphases are different, we and Mel Spiro are saying much the same thing.

We do know that women respond differently from men to culture change, and there is evidence in at least the Remstal and kibbutz cases that traditional sex-role orientations tend to reassert themselves after some level of significant disruption in these relationships has occurred. We think we see supporting evidence in many situations other than the ones we have cited in this discussion, including our own in the United States of the 1980s. We think there is a swing back to certain features of the traditional sex roles and relationships wherever change in these relationships has gone far enough and long enough. Our research task in this area as a discipline, we think, should be devoted in part to discovering what "far enough" and "long enough" mean under varying conditions and to what features of the traditional arrangements there is a return. Certainly there is never a whole recreation of the traditional system.

Whether or not one accepts the tasks as defined, one thing seems sure: studies of adaptation to the changing conditions of life that fail to take into account male/female differences in perspective and response must be considered inadequate and potentially misleading.

NOTES

Steven Borish regards the recent privatization of the kibbutz and the low prestige accorded service roles as pivotal; he develops his position both in his dissertation (Borish 1982) and in an as yet unpublished paper on the "problem" of women in the kibbutz. He contributed much to our thinking in prolonged discussions and criticized an earlier draft of this chapter. We are also indebted to our colleagues at Madison—Herbert Lewis, Arnold Strichon, and Susan Millar—and to Bernard Siegel at Stanford for careful readings and useful critiques of the first draft.

1. We returned again in 1981 and 1985 to examine the role of the school in the transmission of culture under conditions of culture change and urbanization (G. Spindler and L. Spindler 1987).

9

Cloths of Heaven
Freud, Language, and the Negation
in Pitjantjatjara Dreams

ARAM YENGOYAN ᖇᐧᕋ

The study of dreams and the dream life of individuals in particular societies, either by anthropologists or psychologists, has been dominated by two major issues concerning the ways in which dreams are understood and interpreted. One issue is the degree of convergence between the manifest expression of dreams (dream elements and content) and the underlying structure or the basic representations which exist at a deeper level. Deep or covert representations may also derive from fundamental psychic processes which are unique to each society, as Boas would have it, or they may reveal certain universal principles or at least universal tendencies which underwrite our humanity. The interpretation of universals in dreams may be Freudian or Jungian, may be embedded in universal grammatical structures, as established by Chomsky, or may exist as logical structures which comprise unconscious systems that give rise to cultural features such as myth, kinship, and the nature/culture dichotomy. As Lévi-Straussian structuralism would have it, it is not that humans created the structure of myth, but rather that the logic of myth governs the minds of humans.

A second issue in the interpretation of dreams is the kind of continuity or coherence which exists between the logic of a dream or dreams, on one side, and the structure of the culture which embeds that set of dreams on the other. As Spiro (1965a) has correctly stressed, dreams cannot be interpreted out of context and will frequently express culturally specific ways of dealing with problems and issues. Thus we are committed to demonstrating how dreams relate to a particular cultural ethos and, at the same time, how these dreams might express and partly resolve cultural and psychological conflicts between the individual and the social milieu. To stress the relationship between dreams and the cultural basis of existence, one need not argue that we are seeking isomorphic connections between the two or that one will be a mirror reflection of the other. At best, anthropologists can show how, in particular cases, culture and/or language may constrain the structure and content of particular dreams and, in turn, how dreams would focus on those features of a culture which are critical to the dreamer or those aspects of social life which culminate in internal conflict and tension.

It is my conviction that this type of minute cultural analysis of dreams and their cultural basis is not only revealing of particular cultural representations but may also contribute ideas and interconnections which would be of theoretical interest and concern in other social contexts. Others feel that this type of particularism is limited and incapable of producing useful generalizations (e.g., Kilborne 1981:179). But virtually all of our anthropological generalizations have emerged from the minute study of particular cases, or from the comparison of such cases, and even Freud worked within a particular context from which generalizations emerged as the basis of his interpretation of dreams.

Our ability to develop generalizations has been limited not by the particularistic orientation of anthropological inquiry but by the common tendency of anthropologists to adhere to one theoretical framework to the neglect of others. Thus a purely functional theory of society and culture yields generalizations which are interesting but are also lacking in other dimensions. At the same time, symbolic perspectives generate a portrait of human interaction and cultural existence which conveys only one aspect of human society.

The polemic conflict among symbolists, structuralists, and functionalists has been one of many factors limiting the anthropological ability to generalize. Furthermore, to stress one type of explanation over others not only limits our generalizations and comparisons, but also distorts our primary end, which is to portray, understand, and explain particular expressions of humanity. If the generalizations are limited, or if they are so broad to be meaningless, or if the explanations and generalizations are irrelevant, the problem is basically how anthropologists have spent and misspent their intellectual energies by pushing for one theoretical position and attempting to dismiss or at least to dismantle rival expressions of theory construction.

In a recent work, Spiro (1979b:323) recognizes and refutes this unfortunate polemical debate by insisting that "functionalism without symbolism is blind, and symbolism without functionalism is lame." Actions of individuals and groups are cognitively constituted as well as symbolically formed, while the existence of symbolic structures is expressed as private acts and also as public statements. Not only has Spiro demonstrated how this dual approach relates to the study of religious thought, but in another important analysis he has shown that many aspects of culture, including ritual and myth, are created through processes of human socialization with respect to aggressions and sexuality. In a recent work on the *Id*, Spiro (1979c) clearly shows how Lévi-Strauss bankrupts certain lowland South American myths in order to avoid questions relating to aggression. While Freud concluded that aggression was as much a part of nature as it was of culture, for Lévi-Strauss the acute distinction between nature and culture means that aggression as a psychological phenomenon is limited only to nature. Although the animation of Bororo myths is posited on the expression of aggression, Lévi-Strauss concludes that aggression is behaviorally based and thus couched in ritual, which in turn is systematically divorced from myth. By focusing on the forces of aggression and sexuality in Bororo myths, Spiro has creatively demonstrated how these myths could be more fully and meaningfully interpreted.

My concern, then, is to address these issues through analyzing dreams which I collected while working among the Pitjantjatjara of central Australia. Rather than attempt a complete content analysis of these dreams, however, I will discuss only a few of those features which relate both to Freud and to language. The inclusion of language is essential to understanding how the manifest expression of dreams relates to deeper and more abstract issues of psychic development; language itself is also of primary importance in comprehending what is cognitively critical to the dreamer. Hence language reveals the life situation and the social milieu which embeds the dreamer. As such, language is the common thread which ties the deepest emotions in the dream to the manifest content of the dream and to the dreamer and eventually to everyday realities which embrace the dreamer.

My analysis of the use of language in Pitjantjatjara dreams is inspired by Freud's conception of language and negation. Recently, critical evaluation of the interconnections between language and psychoanalysis has been undertaken by both Lacan and Benveniste. I examine the latter's theoretical conceptions in some detail in this chapter. I am interested in eventually demonstrating some potential and actual connections between the logic of language and the structuring of Pitjantjatjara dreams.

ON THE LANGUAGE OF NEGATION AND PERSPECTIVE STRUCTURES

What is the language of dreams, or is some form of language linked to dreams? An analytical language of dreams and dream interpretation probably emerged only in those societies where dreams and dreaming were isolated from their social and cultural context. Thus, in the West, the rise of psychoanalysis, through either Freud or Jung, created a special language of concepts, terms, interrelationships, and oppositions which are now a metalanguage understood only by the analyst. In such cases, the analytic language has become powerful enough to appropriate the reproduction of the dream structure and content in most or all of their manifestations. However, as Benveniste (1971:72) astutely maintains, in most "primitive" societies there is no language of dreams; rather "it is the dream which is brought to the categories of the language. The dream is interpreted in connection with actual situations and by means of a set of equivalences that submit it to a real linguistic rationalization." It is also valid, then, to explore the idea that dreams do not create their own language; rather the primacy of language in particular societies shapes the contours that dreams take. This approach will also permit us to investigate the manifest content of dreams in a way by which we might determine patterns of coherence between culture structure on one side and dreams on the other.

Freud also realized the power of language in explaining certain structural features in dreams. In two brilliant and concise essays, Freud (1910a, 1925) explored the positive and the negative in language and the ways in which they were related to dreams. Even earlier, in *The Interpretation of Dreams,* he noted that "the way in which dreams treat the category of contraries and contradictories is highly remarkable. It is simply disregarded. 'No' seems not to exist so far as dreams are concerned. They show a particular preference for combining contraries into a unity or for representing them as one and the same thing. Dreams feel themselves at liberty, moreover, to represent any element by its wishful contrary; so that there is no way of deciding at a first glance whether any element that admits of a contrary is present in the dream-thoughts as a positive or as a negative" (Freud 1900:318). In his essay on negation, Freud went on to argue this point in a more precise way: "Thus the content of a repressed image or idea can make its way into consciousness, on condition that it is *negated.* Negation is a way of taking cognizance of what is repressed; indeed it is already a lifting of the repression, though not, of course, an acceptance of what is repressed. We can see how in this the intellectual function is separated from the affective process. With the help of the negation only one consequence of the process of repression is undone—the fact, namely, of the ideational content of what is repressed not reaching consciousness" (Freud 1925:235–236). Freud (1925:239) concluded that "this view of negation fits in very well with the fact that in analysis we never discover a 'no' in the unconscious and that recognition of the unconscious on the part of the ego is expressed in a negative formula."

Without the negation, then, dreams in one sense become a realm of almost total freedom, in which particular linguistic and cultural constraints are held in abeyance. Yet even though dreams and the act of dreaming might be one of the least culturally and linguistically bound characteristics that humans possess, the language of the dreamer and the speaker still shapes the structure and content of dreams. Benveniste (1971:71) succinctly summarizes this position as follows: "The claim that the distinction exists but that it is not verbalized would demonstrate the insensitivity to contradiction not in the language but in the researcher, for it is indeed contradictoriness to impute to a language both a knowledge of two notions as opposite and the expression of these notions as identical. . . . It is the same with the logic of dreams. If we characterize the unfolding of a dream by the total freedom of its associations and by the impossibility of acknowledging an impossibility, it is primarily because we retrace and analyze it within the framework of language, and the quality of language is to express only what it is possible to express."

Language and dreams are both unconscious and symbolic, but language, at least a particular language, is learned, and in the process there is created a world of different lexical, syntactic, and phonological elements on which discourse is based. In contrast, the symbolism of the dream is universal in Freud's view, since the vocabulary of dream translation (the analytic language in this case) is universal to all societies regardless of differences in language. However, Freud goes further by claiming that the symbolism of the dream is also generalizable to other aspects of culture, and so " . . . this symbolism is not peculiar to dreams, but is characteristic of unconscious ideation, in particular among the people, and it is to be found in folklore, and in popular myths, legends, linguistic idioms, proverbial wisdom and current jokes, to a more complete extent than in dreams" (Freud 1900:351).

Although one might conclude that Freud's position is here almost Lévi-Straussian in claiming that a certain logic underwrites different facets of culture, in reality the only common feature in both approaches is the appeal to the structure of the unconscious. Furthermore, the only property that dreams have in common with the other cultural dimensions which Freud listed is that they are all expressions of an unconscious symbolism. Dreams and myth depart in that dreams show an absence of negation, a situation in which any form of ultimate freedom of thought, associations, representations, and repressions can occur in a most vivid way. Myths, legends, folklore, and folk wisdom cannot be so constituted. In fact, most anthropological inquiries have insisted that mythic and folkloric accounts function to propel individuals and groups into socially sanctioned behavior.

For Freud, the absence of negation in dreams could be used primarily as a means for establishing what the patient was unconsciously repressing. He argued that, by focusing on what a patient verbally denied during therapy, the analyst could make a methodological breakthrough in the analysis if he could generate discourse in the patient which directed the subject to tabooed areas indicated by the use of negation. Thus dreams were characterized by their unlimited freedom of representations, especially since negation is not a grammatical fixture of the dream language.

From Freud's perspective, there results a disjunction in individuals between the nearly complete freedom with which dreams are constituted and the reality world that is culturally formed and expressed in ways which prohibit what an individual may do. Just as Freud understood dream representations to be an approximation of total freedom, he also assumed that the social milieu of individuals was highly restricted in terms of norms and institutional features which curtailed what individuals could do. Although Freud does not spell out this point, I think we may fairly assume that the ancestral home of psychoanalysis in late nineteenth-century urban Jewish culture in Vienna was highly restricted by cultural norms and values which limited the individual. However, on an even broader scale, most West European culture at that time (and more so now) was dominated by a social structure based on an absence of positive or prescriptive rules. The proscriptive basis of Western culture did not come about through a recent change over the past few hundred years; its roots appear in biblical times. The Ten Commandments constitute virtually one proscription after another, and from the early Greeks to modern-state cultures, rule and law are fundamentally based on the assumption that the individual is innately anarchic and the function of the state is to create a structure which limits what individuals and groups can do, thus making all members of society safe. Acts that the state and modern cultures deem to be forbidden and harmful are eventually imposed on individuals as legal and normative restrictions. The violation of these restrictions results in punishment.

What then propels individuals into action? Since prescriptive rules and laws are limited and highly confined only to domestic/familial behavior, most expressions of institutional behavior (economic, political, religious, etc.) are an enactment of negative restrictions. Here the assumption is that, if an act or an event is not forbidden, it can be performed; however, if such behavior becomes destructive of the social fabric, it must be curtailed through political and legal mechanisms which are the underpinnings of the modern nation-state as we know it.

Thus negation, which is so basic and dominant in discourse, is also a fundamental principle in the state (or any modern Western society) as it is constituted. In turn, proscriptive laws and norms are internalized in the life situation of individuals and even in the dream experience. Freud was correct in assuming that, when his patient said no or denied a particular affect, the denial indicated what had been repressed. Furthermore, the heavy emphasis on the negation is reinforced in discourse and socialization. Surely a day never goes by when parents do not use negatives in discourse with children.

In fact, most socialization of children in America culture is virtually one negation after another. The assumption is that what is not negated is what a child or an adult can do until even that act or event is also proscribed.

What might we expect in societies that are fundamentally based on prescriptive rules and structures which dictate what must be done or ought to be done as opposed to societies that rely on negative rules which demarcate only prohibitions? To what extent is this type of cultural given expressed in dreams, in language, and in social behavior? One of the major contributions of ethnographic reporting has been the presentation of the ways in which societies differ, not only in content, but in very fundamental structural and cultural givens which cannot be equated or reduced to those of more complex societies.

At the extreme end of this range of structural difference and "otherness," we find aboriginal Australian cultures, societies which are solidly based on prescriptive rules which establish the realm of law as a continuation of the most ancient past (the Dreaming) into the present. As directives for conduct, behavior, and practice, these ordained rules are cultural laws as well as representations of the moral foundations of society. The moral underpinning of the law is coded in myth and legend, and as a given in society, the moral dimension of life is seldom debated, argued, or negotiated. The inheritance of the past as custom and tradition is an everyday reality, and thus the realm of law and rule is dominant, since this moral force not only binds everyone to one another but also dictates what kinds of behavior are socially sanctioned. In theory all individuals are propelled into action through rules and laws. Even where options of choice may be possible, such choices and options are culturally based with respect to such rules.

THE ETHNOGRAPHY OF PITJANTJATJARA DREAMS
IN THE CONTEXT OF LANGUAGE AND STRUCTURAL PRESCRIPTION

The analysis of dreams among nonliterate societies has long been of interest to anthropologists, and in most cases there has been a concern to show the interconnections—either causal or associational—between the manifest content of dreams and everyday realities. The basic issues, in terms of both empirical linkage and theoretical concerns, were elaborated by D'Andrade (1961) and Eggan (1961), and their analysis of the critical problems is still essential to our understanding of how dream life relates to cultural and social imperatives which embed individuals in a social milieu.

I am concerned to show how Pitjantjatjara dreams relate to certain aspects of everyday life: that which is based on established marriage rules determining marital events and also that point at which conflict and structural tension might occur. Roheim, who worked in central Australia in the late 1920s, also collected dreams, but he was generally concerned to show how dreams mirrored universal human psychic conditions. The analysis of Aboriginal dreams by Roheim nearly always stresses that the dream as a particular event is cast back onto the Dreaming. In fact, dreams and the Dreaming differ not only in content and structure but also in the language by which each is portrayed. At least among the Pitjantjatjara, when individuals talk about their Dreaming, they commonly use the imperfect (either the tense or the aspect), which indicates the continuity of action and thought, while dreams are conveyed in the present tense, on the assumption that they are neither connected with the Dreaming nor founded in Pitjantjatjara cosmology and mythology.

Thus the Aboriginal approach to dreams in a way separates it from the Dreaming. The best study of the dream life of an aboriginal society as it relates to social regularities is Schneider and Sharp's (1969) analysis and interpretation of Yir Yoront dreams. Their joint analysis provided the inspiration for my collection of dreams, although the focus of my field studies among the Pitjantjatjara has changed over time.

The Pitjantjatjara have been described extensively in the anthropological literature on the aboriginal Australian; thus I will present only that ethnographic material which is relevant to the issues. I will focus on the nature of dreams which were collected since 1966, when I first worked among the Pitjantjatjara. Today the Pitjantjatjara inhabit the areas of central Australia to the west and southwest of Alice Springs, an area ranging from Ernabella Mission on the east, west to the Rawlinsons and Ayers Rock, and south toward the northern fringes of the Great Victorian Desert. Throughout this area, deserts are interspersed with a series of mountain ranges which run east and west. The soaks and rock holes of these ranges provide an almost permanent source of water, although in prolonged periods of extreme drought even these sources will evaporate.

Culturally, the Pitjantjatjara are similar to the Walbiri, Aranda, and Luritja; however, the richness of cultural elaboration in myth, ritual, and social structure which characterizes the latter groups is in many respects absent among the Pitjantjatjara. Most myths are similar in terms of motif and structure, but the extreme variation and intricacy of detail are not present in Pitjantjatjara myth and cosmology. The reasons for these differences are another matter; however, it should be noted that the direction of cultural borrowing among all these groups is such that the Pitjantjatjara regard Walbiri and Aranda as groups from which they borrow cultural content only if it is more elaborate and complex than that which they themselves already possess.

208

SEXUALITY IN DREAMS

Given the relatively small number of collected dreams and the incompleteness of each dream, I will focus on two subjects, dreams which pertain to sexual intercourse and those which deal with matters of aggression. A total of sixty-six dreams are analyzed, all from male informants, fifty-one of whom were fully initiated and the majority of whom were married. I had some difficulty in eliciting dream information, because males do not pay much attention to dreams, nor do they regard the content of dreams as exceptional, with regard either to their own individual behavior or to anything that is collective. As a result they make little attempt to interpret them. Dreams become critical only when a particular dream or an event in a dream may be related to the individual's Dreaming, whereby an aspect of the Dreaming is vividly enacted in his dream consciousness. If this does occur, the dreamer will usually draw together with other men to discuss the dream in terms of possible future events. How often such dreams occur is difficult to determine, but in most cases the dream events are discussed in the early morning hours, a time which allows for a vast amount of discussion before the men move off for their daily tasks. Of further interest is the belief that certain individuals, and relatively few at that, have had dreams which are more germane to the Dreaming than those of others. These individuals possess a quality for assessing future events through their own dreams.

Two guiding principles govern the nature of Pitjantjatjara marriages. One is the existence of alternate-generation-level endogamous moieties that are not only categorized with names but are also egocentrically linked to particular individuals. One's own group is named *nganantarka*, which means "our bone" or "we bone," while the opposite category, to which ego does not belong, is named *tjananmiltja*, which means "their flesh" or "they flesh." As merged alternate-generation moieties, one's own generation is merged with one's grandparents and grandchildren as the "we bone," while the "they flesh" opposition would include the generation of one's father(s), mother(s), mother's brothers, father's sisters, sons, daughters, nephews, and nieces. Marriage is always with one's nganantarka but only with individuals who are spatially and genealogically distant, though they might have some totemic affinity. In theory, a male could marry in an alternate generation, especially those which contain classificatory grandchildren or others such as ego's sister's son's daughter.

The second principle is the existence of matrilineal first- and second-degree cross-cousin marriage. In terms of a male ego, one in theory would marry only a MoBrDa or a MoMoBrDaDa; however, in some cases terminological differences between the two were absent. Both types of marriage form the basis of a four-section system which is now common among the western Pitjantjatjara, although the system appears to have come from the northwest. Thus the ideal marriage was with the daughter of one's mother's brother (*kulpirrpa*). Since the kulpirrpa was the circumcisor and subincisor of ego, it was his moral obligation to bestow a "daughter" on ego as a future spouse.

Marriage with ego's sister's son's daughter was permissible within the rules of alternate-generation-level endogamous moieties as well as in the four-section system. However, there was a wide divergence of opinion on this matter. Elder males claimed that it was the "law," while younger men, who were on the verge of marriage, claimed that it was allowable but was only done to enhance one's polygynous state, a feeling which is supported empirically. Optional marriages consist of arrangements which run through the patrilineal line or with "sisters" who are very distantly related. In terms of these prescriptions, more than 80 percent of all marriages conform to the rule (Yengoyan 1970:87–88, 1979).

Of the sixty-six recorded dreams, forty-five dealt with sexual intercourse; however, many of these dreams also contained material on other subjects. Table 9.1 summarizes incidences of sexual intercourse in dreams and the kinds of unions which are prescribed, prohibited, or unknown.

Of the forty-five cases, thirty-four (75.5 percent) conform to various

Table 9.1. Incidences of sexual intercourse in dreams according to type of marriage relationship

Marriage Relationship	Number of Cases
Prescribed	
(MoBrDa, MMBDD)	29
(SiSoDa)	5
Prohibited	
(Da-Untalpa)	0
(SiDa-Ukari)	1
(SiDaDa)	2
(Ygr.Si-Malanypa)	2
(MoMoBrSoDa)	3
(Elder Si-Kangkuru)	1
(Distant MoSi-Ngunytju)	1
Unknown	1
Total	45

prescriptive marriage restrictions. The remaining dreams involve prohibited unions, although the dreamers themselves see reasons to downplay the seriousness of the violation. On occasion Pitjantjatjara males claim that the illicit unions are initiated by seductive women who are prohibited for marriage in terms of the structure. Still other attributes may minimize the violation. For example, in the one case of the genealogically "distant" mother's sister, the age of that particular person was close to ego; the liaison was interpreted as not really correct but also not very offensive.

When the prohibitive union is clearly wrong and the degree of violation would induce strong negative sanctions in the waking life, the dreamed act of intercourse is without pleasure and, in many cases, damages the male organ. Thus in three cases which involved relatively close and clearly prohibited kinsmen, each male claimed that following intercourse his penis shrank or became knotted in a way that kept it from becoming either flaccid or turgid. The result was a condition which in waking life they felt prevented urination. Thus the pain brought about by illicit sexual intercourse was thought to last beyond the dream itself. Intercourse is committed in dreams, but the dire consequences evoke a painful condition which temporarily debilitates men.

However, the obvious interpretation of these data is that the system of marriage based on prescriptive marriage rules not only propels individuals into correct unions and marriages, both in reality and in the dream life, but also acts in a way that sanctions illicit unions in dreams severely. The consequences of such acts are not just private matters but ones which males have discussed among themselves. Males feel that in their waking life certain females belonging to prohibited marriage categories have enticed them toward a sexual liaison, and even if this liaison did not materialize, the temptation was enough to provoke intercourse in a dream. Thus blame for the violation in such cases is attributed to the females, while males suffer the ill effects of the act committed in their dreams. This change of sex roles in dreams is interesting, since most myths among the Pitjantjatjara have as their premise that men always deceive women and that men are seldom punished for their deceitful behavior.

In dreams of sexual acts, men seldom reported having contact with a biological mother, sister(s), or daughter(s). When I mentioned this possibility, the act not only was dismissed as perversion of the worst type but also prompted great laughter; the men felt that such experiences, even in dreams, were a waste, since they would provide virtually no pleasure. This feature was also indicated in the Yir Yoront data (Schneider and Sharp 1969:24); Roheim's findings, however, indicate that dreams did involve fornication with biological family members.

Aram Yengoyan

AGGRESSION IN DREAMS

I use "aggression," to mean only conflict that is structurally established, as opposed to forms of physical or verbal abuse that are of a personal or random character. Acts of aggression involve the aggressor (the individual who initiated the verbal or physical attack) and the aggressed (the individual who was the target of the attack). In many cases the aggressed soon becomes the aggressor, and that also is an event of aggression.

Of the sixty-six recorded dreams, only twenty-nine had material which involved structurally based aggression. Others contained aggressive acts toward particular individuals, but these were commonly related to personal animosity in the waking life. In the twenty-nine dreams, four categories of aggressive acts are essential in trying to explain what happens in the waking life and in dream reality. There are structured relationships between ego and his mother's brother (kulpirrpa), between ego and his brother-in-law (*marutju*), between an unmarried male and elder married men, and between a man and his wife (*kuri*). The cases of aggression between ego and each of the four kin categories are enumerated in table 9.2.

In the eleven dreams of aggression between ego and his mother's brother, nine of them indicated that ego was the aggressor. Acts of aggression involved physical attacks, sneaking up on his mother's brother and stealing his goods or eating his food, putting water in the gasoline tank of the mother's brother's vehicle, and so forth. In one case, aggression was limited to verbal abuse only. There was also an isolated case in which a male dreamer copulated with his MoBrWi as an expression of revenge. In this instance, the dreamer indicated that the act of copulation was painful and most unpleasant, but it had to be done to show the kulpirrpa that he should mend his ways.

The role of the mother's brother in regard to ego expresses virtually all of the essential social attributes connected to the way in which ego obtains a spouse. The kulpirrpa is the circumcisor and subincisor of ego; he assists ego in the rites of passage prior to full initiation as an adult male, and furthermore the kulpirrpa has the moral responsibility to bestow a "daugh-

Table 9.2. Cases of aggression between ego and the four kin categories

Kinship relationship	Number of cases
Ego versus mother's brother (kulpirrpa)	11
Ego versus brother-in-law (marutju)	8
Ego versus elder married men	7
Ego versus wife (kuri)	3
Total	29

ter" on ego as a future wife. Thus, ego is structurally in debt to his kulpirrpa. Since ego realizes this state of liminality with his kulpirrpa, why the aggressive dream acts in which ego is the aggressor and not the aggressed? In each particular dream, ego's aggressiveness was based on the fact that the kulpirrpa had not completely fulfilled his moral obligation to ego. Since ego cannot openly abuse his mother's brother, the dream is consequently based on what he would desire to accomplish if social norms permitted such behavior. In most cases, the kulpirrpa is concerned, committed, and even affectionate to ego. Unfortunately I do not have material from dreamers in such situations and hence do not know whether aggression is present or absent in their dreams. Nonetheless it seems that the expression of dream aggression occurs only in specific cases in which a kulpirrpa has abused his relationship with ego or in which his paternallike nurturing of ego was not satisfactory. From these cases and the context in which they occur, it would seem that such aggression on the part of the dreamer almost covaries with the fact that the mother's brother has been amiss in his obligations to ego. Normally the kulpirrpa is not an aggressive figure, and I would not expect dreams of aggression to be directed toward such individuals. But when aggression in particular cases occurs from the mother's brother to ego, such aggressive dream responses do occur. In structural terms, this bond is loaded, if not overloaded, with moral obligations between both individuals, and thus a denial on one side would result in fractured social ties, ambivalence, and, of course, aggression.

If inherent structural conflict with the kulpirrpa generates anxiety and tension, both in waking life and in dreams, the interaction between ego and his brother-in-law (marutju) also revolves on how this social bond is structurally expressed. Of the eight dreams which had data on this interaction, six of them indicated that ego was the aggressor, and in the other two the marutju initiated the aggression. Structurally, ego has a vested interest in his sister's life and marriage, since he is concerned that she be adequately cared for, that she not be physically attacked by her husband, and that her children be tended carefully. The marutju, on the other hand, realizes that his wife's brother will come to her rescue if maltreatment and violent aggression become common in the marriage. He also realizes that his brother-in-law does exert control and influence over his wife and thus is fully aware that he does not have open license to abuse his wife or wives physically or verbally over prolonged periods of time. This is a peculiar social bond, since the interaction exists as a triangulation of three individuals and assumes a fragile quality that can lead to aggressive responses and counterattacks if any one person feels that he has been abused by another.

Usually a man does not exhibit paternal behavior toward a sister; however, he is always in touch with her or others who know what is happening.

Therefore, if any kind of normal daily abuse from the husband becomes excessive and openly displayed in the camps, a man will physically and/or verbally assault a brother-in-law, thus hoping to shame him for excessively abusing his spouse. However, such behavior on ego's part toward a brother-in-law does not occur if that man is taking another wife as part of a polygynous union. Yet if one takes a second wife and gradually drops the first wife, a brother will be provoked enough to reprimand the husband.

In cases in which ego was the aggressor in dreams (six out of eight), the aggression resulted from having a sister abused by the marutju, and thus the dreamer either had already reprimanded the marutju in real life or was "planning" how to do it through dreams. In the two cases of aggression on the part of marutju, the husband felt that he had publicly been ostracized in an unbecoming way by his wife's brother and hence the dream aggression. In the other case, the wife, who was a woman of formidable stature, would have none of his wimpishness, and his aggression toward her could only be repressed and redirected toward the brother-in-law. The dynamics are socially heavy, especially when the abuse is overt, and I suspect that what is repressed in public expresses itself in dreams.

The third category of dreamlike aggression consists of seven cases in which an unmarried ego was either the aggressor or the aggressed in relating to elder married men. The common property among these married men was their polygynous behavior, and in three cases, the men had three or more spouses. Elder men, especially those who are partly feeble, become most defensive in protecting spouses and younger wives from single men who desire a spouse. Thus camp fights between the two generations of men usually occur over the possession of wives who are customarily controlled by men over age thirty-five. Men in their late twenties must meanwhile wait. Violence between polygynous men and young initiated men can be treacherous physically, since both sides resort to clubs and sticks to assault one another, with the full intention of drawing blood, bruising scalps, and scarring tissue. Of these seven dream cases, five involved polygynous men who virtually assaulted young men. The aggression of these five men toward young men in waking life was even more graphically portrayed in dreams. In the two other cases, single men had attacked the elders, one nearly breaking an elder's forearm.

Of the four categories, this one displayed the most noticeable hostility and open physical aggression. Very seldom was aggression shown verbally; moreover, if one could display aggression only verbally, this limitation would usually be taken as a sign of weakness. For the Pitjantjatjara, words have greater than normal impact only if they are physically supported through some expression of physical violence.

Dreams of aggression toward wives occurred in cases in which a man thought that his spouse was having an adulterous affair with another person; however, the key source of familial aggression was males who seemingly used their waking hours to berate their wives both in public and in private. This type of bullylike behavior was rare and curtailed, but in two of the cases, the dreams were from men who were openly hostile and belligerent toward their wives. The dream reflected such behavior in a way that seemed to support their view of themselves within the domestic context.

By and large, most aggressive acts in Pitjantjatjara dreams expressed a consistency with everyday realities. Where structural prescriptions created aggressive behavior, the dreams also reflected this pattern. However, the quality of the aggression was not simply one way. The target of aggression in waking life would commonly appear in dream aggression, especially if no prescribed social norms sanctioned overt aggressive expression. To a certain extent, Pitjantjatjara dreams do subvert aggression but only where social and structural constraints occur that prevent the aggressed individual from retaliating through normal channels.

DISCUSSION

The analysis of selected Pitjantjatjara dreams indicates that the content of dreams and how they are interpreted strongly reflects both the structure of Pitjantjatjara rules of marriage and the expressions of aggression which are structurally established in the network of social norms. Continuity from the waking life and its prevailing structure is expressed in dreams where individuals convey the beliefs and sentiments which establish the arena of social action. Acts of dream aggression are a response to conflict generated from the built-in existence of contradiction and tension within the social structure. In the introductory section, I argued that societies which stress or even overstress the domination of prescriptive rules as the basis of conduct and practice would have a high degree of consistency between the realm of an incarnate set of structural prescriptions, understood as moral givens, and the actions of individuals who are propelled into action. Thus we would not expect a disjunction between structure and behavior, since the structure generates the behavioral event which in turn verifies the rule.

Pitjantjatjara dreams also work in the same direction. Random and highly personalized dream experiences might be pitted against the structure or might be liminal in their focus; however, the overwhelming tendency in dreams is to understand and interpret such experiences in terms of the dreamer's place within the nexus of society. In showing how the individual's role and status change with increasing age, one would expect to find different though overlapping constraints occurring which channel the force and focus of aggression. To a certain extent, we are able to predict what will occur in

Pitjantjatjara dream life, just as we can predict marital and ritual behavior from social structural principles as well as cosmological structures. A common and dominant thread combines the dream and its content, the dreamer, with the everyday realities of Pitjantjatjara social life. The encoded set of structural prescriptions and their moral force are the foundations providing the waking life and the dream life with coherent historical continuity. There is no discontinuity from one to the other, of the sort that Freud would postulate for Western societies.

The question still remains unanswered regarding the role of language, in particular the role of negation. Freud's contention that the logic of dreams is based on total freedom in associations and symbols is in part predicated on the notion that the language of dreams is not limited by negation. In theory, almost anything can emerge in dreams; there are no restrictions on content. The repression occurs when free-floating associations, symbols, and meanings are suppressed in the individual, in part because of the nature of the social reality.

From Pitjantjatjara dreams, it appears that freedom is not very extensive, since individuals dream about sexual and aggressive acts which are neatly confined and confirmed by the social structure of the waking life. There is a very strong tendency toward coordination between social realities and dreams, although in dreams many acts of aggression are an inversion of the structure. What have been described as prescriptive and positive sanctions, so dominant within the social fabric as an inducement to maintain behavior and action within socially designated rules, function as a way of limiting and curtailing actions in dreams which are either antisocial or asocial.

Linguistically, Pitjantjatjara is similar to many other aboriginal languages in central Australia. In the use of negation, however, Pitjantjatjara, along with a few other desert languages, manifests certain features which are peculiar both at the level of structure and at the level of discourse. The term for "no," "not," or "never" in Pitjantjatjara is *wiya*, but *wiya* is seldom, if ever, used as a single lexical item. Usually *wiya* is combined with *palya* as "wiya palya," which literally means, "No, but of course you can." This response is used only when one asks a question about something which is absurd because it is self-evident. Thus, if a child asks his/her mother, "Are you going to feed me tonight?" a mother will respond "wiya palya," glossed as, "No, but of course I am." Here, the "no" indicates that the question or request is foolish or nonsensical—of course you can do it or of course I am doing that. *Wiya* alone is seldom used, especially among elders. Over the past twenty years, however, the younger generations have begun to use it alone as a single expression. This is a response to Europeans who have picked up the use of *wiya* as simply "no" and used it as "no" when they want to deny a request made by an aboriginal, for example for a cigarette. Younger people may use *wiya* among themselves but never with older people. Thus "wiya palya," as it stands, affirms a request and indicates only that the request or question or demand is so absurd that it is funny to ask it.

On the grammatical level, the Pitjantjatjara can use expressions that possess a negative, but they seldom do so. For while such expressions might be grammatically correct, they are culturally unacceptable. For the sake of brevity, I will give but one example of this contrast. In the following construction, both forms are grammatically acceptable; a Pitjantjatjara, however, would use only the latter.

1. "Ngunhu ngaarta yimpaarna ngaarnrtu mayayi, mirta karringu."
   That   man   passed   my   house   not   stopping.
   That man went past my house and did not stop.

2. "Ngunhu ngaarta yimpaarna ngaarnrtu mayayi karringuwarrimarta."
   That   man   passed   my   house   stopping-without.
   That man went past my house without stopping.

Of these two forms, number two is nearly always used, and is preferred, while number one would be stated only if it was elicited in that form. In fact, it was claimed that number one would be used only by a non-Pitjantjatjara, one who knew the language but did not know the culture as a determinant of what was socially acceptable or unacceptable.

Even in commands, what is wanted is stated in a manner which carries information that will lead to positive prescriptive behavior. An example here might suffice to clarify this point. If a person is walking toward you and your hat is on the chair to your right, how do you indicate that you do not want the approaching individual to sit on your hat? In English, one would say "Don't sit on my hat," which means only that and carries no other information. Thus a person can sit anywhere and is free to choose. In Pitjantjatjara, to convey "Don't sit on my hat," one will always use a construction which is positive in that the message tells the hearer what he/she should do—for example, "Sit to my left," or "Sit on that chair there." The resulting action occurs as an affirmation of the statement or the request. Not only do positive requests and statements carry more information which propels action, but they restrict and cut off any other response that the hearer might desire.

At present, the absence or minimal development of negation in central Australian aboriginal cultures and languages is difficult to determine. However, Hale (1971:472–482) notes that in the structure and use of *tjiliwiri*, a secret male language among the Walbiri, lexical opposition from Walbiri to tjiliwiri is never created through the use of negation. All oppositions are based on positive rules, of which the contrast between pairs of minimal opposition is the most fundamental. The same principle also seems to occur in Lardil and their secret language (*dam:en*).

If the semiabsence of negation in discourse and/or grammar reinforces the cultural preference for prescriptive rules, it also minimizes choice, variation, and freedom. The analysis of Pitjantjatjara dreams indicates a strong propensity toward coherence, consistency, and continuity between the dream world and the waking world. This finding also supports similar conclusions from the Yir Yoront (Schneider and Sharp 1969). However, since I am unaware of how negation is used in Yir Yoront, in terms of language or culture, my discussion of this aspect of the problem is limited to the Pitjantjatjara data.

Of more importance is Freud's analysis of the conjunction and disjunction between the dreamer, the dream, and the reality world. The existence of the prescriptive social structure supported by the semiabsence of negation in grammatical structure and in discourse indicates that Freud's development of the issue is still critical in understanding how particular cultural expressions relate to the dream life. In both Freud's analysis and the Pitjantjatjara data, we do not discover a no in the language of the dream consciousness. It is absent in the dream life of both cases but for different reasons. Freud interprets the absence of negation as the complete approximation of freedom in the unconscious, and thus the no (when it emerges to consciousness in psychoanalysis) is an indicator of the patient's repression. In Pitjantjatjara, the absence of "no" in unconscious expression, such as dreams, is not the patient's repression but an extreme affirmation of structural prescriptions which dominate and underwrite both language use and cultural norms.

What the Pitjantjatjara are repressing and whether they are repressing at all remain problematic. On the one hand, repression might not be a problem. The sexuality of cultural life, as indicated in numerous ethnographic accounts, is literally as well as metaphorically overt, arising openly in conversation and finding expression in myth, ritual, and cosmology. My own belief is that repression in our Western psychoanalytic sense is not an issue; however, it might be expressed in different forms which have escaped our ethnographic scrutiny. The hidden id as an abstract, deep, and covert psychic state might not in fact be very hidden. In everyday conversation among Aborigines, the issue of deep structure and repression is, of course, difficult to detect.

The absence of negation in verbal discourse thus reinforces the absence of negation in dreams. In Pitjantjatjara dream life, the absence of negation promotes and maintains an approximation of freedom; however, to an extent, this freedom is limited by the prescriptive structure of society and the moral givens which are expressed in cosmology. Dreams are controlled and structured by prescription found in myth and in the unfolding of the ever-present Dreaming.

When Freud postulates a hiatus between the dream life and the waking life which creates repression, the degree of discrepancy is connected to the contradiction and conflict of marked freedom in the dream life and the existence of a proscriptive social structure. For the Pitjantjatjara, either the gap between the dreamer/actor on the one side and structural prescription on the other does not exist, or its development is minimal; thus contradictions and disjunctions do not create psychological dilemmas. However, the degree of freedom in individuals' dream life is still limited, and it would be fair to conclude that the freedom Freud and Benveniste proposed might not even exist in such an extreme version. The parallelism which runs from social structure to language strongly curbs variation in dreams; however, the variation that does exist cannot always be explained by or traced back to the structure. I am sure that dreams in the realm of sexual fantasy and aggression exist as an escape from structural constraints. However, it is difficult to assess the frequency of such dreams, the background and the personality of the dreamer, and the extent to which these dreams qualitatively depart from structural constraints.

Since Pitjantjatjara dreams are closely linked to structural rules and constraints, and since the structure is anterior to the dream as well as to other kinds of collective behavior, what do these dreams mean with regard to the dreamer's own perception? It was noted earlier that dreams have little importance to the dreamer unless they relate to something in the Dreaming. Although the essential demarcation in language and culture between the Dreaming and the dream is quite different, they do work together to form a unity of expression. As Stanner (1956) has brilliantly observed, the Dreaming is as real to the individual as any other form of social expression. The Dreaming is not only maintained from the most ancient past into the present by myth and legend but is organically connected with the physical environment too. Virtually everything sacred has a physical referent. The two are closely intertwined, and at times, the use of language with reference to the physical and the sacred tends to blur any potential distinction. The Dreaming has a pictorial accompaniment which enhances its impact as a sign system that is real, overt, and highly visual.

However, dreams are different. Dreams, as a form of imagery, are not buttressed by the visual supports found in the Dreaming. Since dream imagery is not bound or limited by visual and auditory referents, the ability to evoke and create images is far greater in dreams and more powerful in elaborating new and unique associations. The medium of fairy tale imagery as discussed by Bettelheim (1975) would fit very well with the expansive, unframed imagery which exists in Pitjantjatjara dreams, although the only constraints on dreams are structural regulation. In many ways, the dream not only is free floating but also provides different means of comprehending one's experiences, permitting the dreamer a more acute understanding of his/her Dreaming. Images evoked in dreams are thus primarily linked to structural rules, but at the same time, the quality of freedom from these constraints allows the dreamer to take his creative imagery far beyond every-day life. Dream representations can manifest a complex of ideas only because auditory, visual, and tactile constraints are not impinging on the dreamer. Dreams and dreamlike behavior provide new vistas which permit the ex-trapolation of meaning from one frame of experience to another as a means of understanding the total expression and implication of one's Dreaming. Yet the content and meaning of dreams are not simply a playing out of structural constraints within the individual. Melford Spiro and his intellec-tual efforts have always directed us back to the dominant theme of sexual aggression in the formation of the id, which provides the essential features in which the social animation of individual desire and cultural form takes place.

Thus the analysis of Pitjantjatjara dreams reveals a number of possible generalizations about dreams. By demonstrating that the absence of negation in dreams relates to different societal contexts (prescriptive-rule-structured societies in contrast to proscriptively structured societies), we are able to assess the expression and degree of conjunction and disjunction between the waking life and the dream life in particular societies. In theory, we should be able to predict how different social structures are congruent with different dream motifs. Furthermore, what is critical is not the language of dreams but the manner in which language shapes the structure and expres-sion of dream life. Again, we might predict within limits how languages which possess grammatical similarities affect dreams in their respective con-texts.

Freud's brilliance in understanding negation as a key to the repression of experiences means that dreams not only are powerful statements about the workings of the human psyche but also are essential to understanding the depths of our humanity as social collectivities. A complete translation of dreams might be an impossibility even in their own cultural context, but dreams still give us clues about the ways in which cultures are structured as ontological givens. Whether we can or cannot translate dreams, whether dreams relate to particular descriptions or to global theory, dreams are events which require utmost caution in their collecting and interpretation. Our caution for understanding and appreciating dream events, events which are so peculiarly human, can best be conveyed by Yeats's (1956:70) injunction: "Tread softly because you tread on my dreams."

NOTE

I thank Les Adler, Alton L. Becker, David B. Edwards, Kenneth George, Fran Markowitz, and Sherry B. Ortner for their assistance and perceptive critique of the various ethnographic and theoretical issues presented in this chapter. Much of my inspiration for working on dreams comes from the reading of David M. Schneider's analysis of Yir Yoront dreams, which is the singly most important ethnographic work on the subject. My reading of Yeats added a vital perspective which I would never have obtained if I had mastered only the anthropological work on dreams. I wrote this chapter while I was a Fellow at the Center for Advanced Study in the Behavioral Sciences, Stanford, California. I am grateful for financial support provided by the National Science Foundation, grant number BNS-8011494, and by the University of Michigan, Ann Arbor. The final rewriting of this paper was done during the 1987–1988 year as part of a fellowship from the John Simon Guggenheim Memorial Foundation. I express my appreciation to the Guggenheim Foundation for their continued support.

10

From Empathy to Alienation
Problems in Human Belonging

GEORGE DE VOS

THE KINESTHETIC CONUNDRUM AND SELF-CONSCIOUSNESS

To explore personality patterns cross-culturally, I have worked with Mel Spiro in analyzing samples of Rorschach responses he gathered in Ifaluk, Burma, and Israel. In these cases as in many others, I have been struck by the fact that members of practically every society tested produce kinesthetically influenced "projection"; that is, they perceive in the blots human figures in motion. Why in motion?

As I have thought about this problem over the years, it has seemed to me that perhaps human motion deserves a more important place than we have given it in our understanding of self and of psychosexual development. Grossly stated, the knowledge of how we ourselves feel when we move may be central to our understanding of how other people feel when we see them moving. If so, then the perception and imitation of body motion could turn out to be a critical aspect of the development and maintenance of human empathy and identification. And empathy and identification, of course, are central to the experience of human belonging. (I have begun to suspect that we have also tended to give theoretical short shrift to empathy and belonging.)

Briefly, then, I have come to see attention to motion as important to identification and to see identification as a central coping mechanism in the structuring of personality and in the maturation and social development of one's sense of belonging in society. It is not enough to say simply that we "internalize" our environment, which is pretty much all that either Durkheimian sociology and psychoanalytic psychology have to tell us about it.

222

It is time to pay more attention to the details of how this internalization works. This essay discusses some aspects of the basic ego mechanisms that seem to me to govern the processes through which stimuli enter and become part of an experiential "self" (or fail to do so). Kinesthetic perceptions of Rorschach inkblots are of course one window on this subject, but they are minor compared with the larger issues that turn out to be involved. There are, naturally, differences both among individuals and among groups, and the differences are important.[1] But in this essay I shall attend rather to the general underlying coping mechanisms at work in various forms of human behavioral expression and their relation to the general issue of motion, empathy, and belonging. Here, then, are my adventurous contentions . . . so far!

INTROJECTION, IMITATION, AND IDENTIFICATION: VICISSITUDES IN THE DEVELOPMENT OF HUMAN EMPATHY

I remember in my youth being much amused by the singular imitative genius of Danny Kaye and the chameleon capacities of Sid Caesar, individuals who could quickly communicate to an audience caricatures of national character, whether Russian, German, or English. By gestural as well as verbal imitation, they could "become" a variety of types in their outrageous exaggerations, causing humorous recognition in their audience. More recently Woody Allen as "Zelig" has created for us the picture of the perfect chameleon, who in the presence of "significant others" changes bodily contours to those of an underworld figure, a major league baseball player, or a Nazi storm trooper. Allen presents us most graphically with the inner experience as well as the pathological problem faced by an individual who is uncontrollably imitative and cannot find a resolute developing core around which to define his "self." More seriously, we read news reports periodically of "frauds" who may be naturally gifted but cannot take a role in which they are really themselves. Instead they seem compelled to play at being somebody rather than actually becoming somebody. In psychoanalysis recently there has been further exploration of these so-called borderline problems (Kernberg), formerly considered "narcissistic character disorders" related to problems of identification in adulthood.[2]

Resonance

Without succumbing to simplistic analogies between animal social behavior and human social behavior, we may nevertheless begin with some assumptions of how our animal inheritance of sociability has afforded us innate biological capacities of relevance to our problem. Paul Ekman (1970) has been conducting research in an attempt to establish the universals in facial gesture. He considers these basic gestures to be biological capacities for giving to emotional states an outer expression that is roughly communicable across humanity. It is implied, of course, that there is an ability to read the gestures, not merely to produce them. The smile, the frown, and the expression of disgust are all immediately readable cross-culturally. But how do we spontaneously kinesically "read" these gestures by a responding resonance, and how do we then come to understand kinesthetically or consciously what we are reading?

First, let me postulate biological inheritance of a spontaneous muscular expression and resonance triggered from our extraceptors, visual, tactile, auditory, and olfactory. At first we automatically read and respond; later, humans develop various degrees of controlled or conscious mediation which allows us on the one hand to manipulate our expressive gestures instrumentally and on the other hand to control overt response while attempting conscious monitoring of the interactive situation. We come to monitor both the reading and the response, albeit imperfectly, since no one achieves total consciousness of all that is interchanged. We nevertheless learn to induce desired reactions by our more or less consciously guided gestural behavior.

One must postulate two alternative forms of biologically given response: one that imitates and one that is complementary. Biology is not the whole story. In humans our social definitions help us selectively to resonate in equivalent or contrastive ways, depending in part upon the definitions of self that are learned from infancy on, and our responses come to be progressively governed by status and role considerations. And even in animal social groups the appropriateness of these responses comes to some degree to be governed by role specificities and expectancies. But the responses start, in all mammals, from the biological givens of relative helplessness by relative size and relative age and from the biological facts of hormonal balances and engrammed sexual selectivity. Let us briefly consider some examples.

It has been the genius of psychoanalytic thought to recognize the pervasiveness of libidinal interaction in all social behavior. It may also be the shortcoming of psychoanalytic thought to assume that all social bonding is thereby necessarily "sexual" in nature. While some primates "present" nonaggression by a receptive sexual posture, it is never mistaken as having sexual intent (Phyllis Dolhinow, personal communication). This "presentation of self" in everyday social groups among primates, while derivative from a posture assumed in the sexual situation, does not cause sexual arousal when there is presentation, but rather causes a diminution of the alternative potential for antagonism. One must consider nonsexual sociability as part of mammalian interaction, whether it is presenting, grooming, or stroking. In

Birdwhistell's films he amply demonstrated in slow motion that a heterosexual conversation was full of unconscious signaling suggestive of an undercurrent of sexual communication. It is important to know that the
individuals involved in conversation were totally oblivious to this signaling
but that it probably created an undercurrent of interest and gave a positive
"tone" to the ongoing social interaction (Birdwhistell 1970, 1983).

It has also been integral to psychoanalysis to assume the innate aggressiveness of the human animal and the need for this aggressiveness to
be canalized and socialized. Socialization minimized destructive potential
within the human group, the argument runs, as well as directing such potential externally. Since the human animal is continuously driven from
within, his aggressiveness, like his sexuality, must be adaptively transmuted
into various social and environmental forms. But humans also continuously
resonate positively or negatively to the sexual, sociable, and aggressive postures taken by others. It is always problematic to determine how much inner
tension and readiness to respond occurs between or among actors in given
interaction situations. Within many social species, such as wolves, patterns
of relative dominance are adaptive such that combative potentials are minimized within the group and possible destructive mirrored antagonistic interaction is prevented. A fascinating mechanism involved with this
phenomenon is play. Wolf puppies play, as do other social species of mammals. In play, because of its nature, forms of reciprocal and mirrored responsiveness are assumed in a transitory way. Gradually the relative status
of the individual is established. Males particularly learn to maintain a socialized pattern in modulating their competitiveness.

Evident from birth onward is the inherited capacity for what comes
to be defined as "emotional" responsiveness, an interactiveness related to
facial and postural gesture. Studies of neonates demonstrate that this social
interaction begins with the intimate care of parent for child. On the child's
part there may be a relatively rapid particularization of individual features.
There is also a rapid generalization of facial gestures. The child gradually
comes to "know" kinesthetically by his or her own response the feeling
related to the kinesic pattern of facial muscles.

In going from animal analogues to human interaction, we continually
look for the transcendent intervention of consciousness and the development
of a "self." Here we are concerned with coping mechanisms that transmute
more direct kinesthetic messages into socialized forms. For the most part,
however, these activities remain totally unconscious. Gestural undercurrents
may lead us toward emotional states vis-á-vis others, but their entrance into
consciousness is governed by a defensive maintenance of self-consistency,
and individuals remain close to their social roles. It would be highly disruptive for most individuals to attend consciously to undercurrents that are

going on in postural interchange. We are constrained to pay attention to the overt, socially constructed instrumental aspects of the relationship and to role definitions which are more important than the momentary messages of our bodies as we relate to others. Some individuals are unaware of the modes of antagonism or aggressiveness that they are communicating, modes that cause in others unconscious negative responses; so too some individuals are "popular" because their bodily communications are sought after by those with whom they come into social contact.

To understand how biologically inherited resonance is transmuted within the development of specifically human consciousness, we must return to an exploration of coping mechanisms in general and of the way in which "resonance" relates to "introjection" and "identification" within human culture. The human ego structure operates by means of a number of interactive, more or less mutually balanced coping mechanisms that govern the processing of sensations from the environment as well as the states of unresolved tension arising within. Sensory experiences gain relevant "meaning" (1) when they are selectively incorporated, integrated, and synthesized or (2) when they are selectively excluded as irrelevant or disposed of into the "unconscious" as inconsistent or threatening to continuity. The "ego" functions automatically in performing the screening and filing of experiences into proper categories tolerable to the safe continuity, if not further development, of the experiential "self." Our next consideration must therefore be the ego and its coping mechanisms.

MECHANISMS OF COPING: THREE BASIC MANEUVERS

Central to the understanding of mental functioning cross-culturally is what Freud and, later, Anna Freud (1937) termed "mechanisms of defense." These basic maneuvers have also more recently been termed "coping mechanisms" by Haan (1977) and others. In my own work (1980, 1982, 1983a, 1983b, 1985), I have paid attention to these coping mechanisms as they operate in the establishment of social identity, especially in situations of minority status. I have attempted to organize my understanding of these psychoanalytic mechanisms around three basic maneuvers: (1) exclusion (that is, boundary protection), (2) contrast or expulsion, and (3) intake or introception. During the earliest phase of ego development, we find these three basic mechanisms defined as "denial," "projection," and "introjection," respectively, names which have gained broad currency in the psychoanalytic literature. Among the three, the third is of greatest interest in the present connection, and I place it last to simplify discussion, but all three must be considered together before they make sense.

The earlier modes—denial, projection, and introjection—taken by

226

these mechanisms become prevalently transmuted through maturing processes, so that finer differentiation becomes possible. They remain throughout in some form of interactive balance, although one or another of the mechanisms by its relative proneness to be used may become more dominant. Such dominance may come to produce what is recognized as a characteristic personality pattern.[3]

When the three basic mechanisms exhibit an imbalance toward exclusion, it prevents adequate differentiation and growth of complexity in thinking. Its absence prevents concentration, focus, and the efficient exclusion of disruptive irrelevancies, or "noise." Imbalance toward the contrastiveness leads to empty, bloodless abstraction in the understanding of human events or, in the world of science, a lack of inventiveness or creative innovation. The relative absence of a developed ability for contrastive thought leads to a lack of controlled, dispassionate examination and verification of experiences by objective criteria. An imbalance toward receptivity without the balance of exclusion and contrast is an inability to judge or order experiences and an inability to focus or to attain any satisfactory closure—in short, an identity diffusion. Lack of introceptive, gestalt thought leads to an inability to generalize, to bridge gaps in knowledge by deduction, or to reach any synthesis of meaning or events. It is to lack the experience of how either things or people "belong" together.[4]

Mauneuver A: Protective or Exclusionary Functions ("Denial")

The first basic maneuver initially operates by totally excluding external stimuli from inner experience. In its most early rigidified operations, it appears in childhood "autism," later in some form of massive "denial" or reality. As an experiential self develops, unwanted or dangerous perceptions can also be rejected or deflected by an expulsive discriminatory mechanism into what becomes the "unconscious," a residue of "repressed," inconsistent, affect-laden experiences which are kept out of consciousness by the operation of the exclusionary mechanism, which now serves to seal off these expelled materials in a separate compartment. As "repression" the exclusionary mechanism continues to interact with the discriminatory "contrastive" mechanism in an increasingly complex series of self-protective ego functions.[5]

When the exclusion mechanism is used too rigidly to avoid some new experience, cognitive growth is sacrificed to defend one's self against the conscious experience of potentially disruptive thought. Affect-laden, ego-alien, dissonant experiences are automatically avoided or are prevented from entering consciousness.

Exclusionary protective functioning sometimes appears as "dissociation" and is sometimes manifested culturally in socially acceptable guise in religious rites or institutions using trance or mind-altering drugs (De Vos 1986). It may also appear in what are perceived by some to be "psycho-pathological" states in the form of so-called culture-bound syndromes. Individuals, in the context of their social groups, can learn to use altered states of consciousness in order to gain some indirect expression (either in ritual or in a socially recognized mental disorder) of those social inconsistencies which are not appropriate to their stable, rigidly defined social roles. Dissociation of this kind is very widely expressed in religious ceremonies such as the Peyote Cult or southern snake-handling groups in the United States (La Barre 1938, 1962). In most societies, some members, particularly those of lower status, often women, use some form of trance or "possession" experience.

Maneuver B: Contrastiveness and Control ("Projection")

The "contrastive" discriminatory mechanism appears in its earliest form as "projection." As such it is at first related to the maintenance of a sense of omnipotence which occurs before self and nonself become well separated. In some instances a defensive continuance of a sense of omnipotence or grandiosity is used to protect the individual against an alternative experience of utter helplessness. Throughout its progressive development, this contrastive mechanism is intimately related to the dynamic human experience of power and control. In its progressive transmutations, when subject to some degree of socialized transformation, this basic mechanism can be observed to be operative in such so-called neurotic conditions as "displacement" or "reaction formation." These defensive maneuvers demonstrate how contrastive thought throws out the affectively less desirable of two dissonant perceptions and keeps what is more useful in maintaining control and more self-enhancing. What is judged "good" is kept; what is "bad" is rejected. Eventually the three mental mechanisms conjointly come to maintain a more or less effective, permeable boundary between an experience of the inside and that of the outside. Before this happens, unwanted experiences are "projected" out. In a later stage of development they are instead extruded beyond conscious availability into the "id," which is kept separate by an internal barrier now maintained by the exclusionary mechanism. The unconscious serves as a repository, from which what is expelled may then be diverted to appear in negative judgments directed externally as a "displacement."

Mastery: The Control of Causality What is kept "within" by the discriminatory functions of a contrastive mechanism is the sense of force or power.

The psychoanalytic approach to projection has aptly pointed up features of grandiosity and omnipotence found in paranoid conditions. In later forms, contrastiveness becomes related to defensive maneuvers termed "intellectualization" or "isolation." The individual is self-distanced from internally disruptive affectivity, which is disparaged and rejected as causing loss of control.[6]

Projection, from the very beginning, as it expels what threatens from within, helps develop a sense of self in which the experiential locus of control is at all costs kept within. The experience of power and the initial process of thinking itself are not separated. Indeed, much thought can remain inherently "magical." Mastery through thought is an instrumental intentionality experienced within, and early thought is experienced as causing things to happen. In its more mature transformations, the distancing aspect of this mechanism can finally lead to the attainment of objective, analytic, logical thought as a basic mode of coping with, and ultimately of controlling the environment through the understanding of causal dynamics.

The primary adjustive psychosocial progression of the contrastive-expulsive mechanism through inherent maturation evolves in a growing capacity to use conceptual problem solving as a means of maintaining internal control as well as assuring an internal locus of control over the external environment.[7]

Some Anthropological Considerations about Projection The early maturational phases of thought processes, guided by expulsive defenses related to control, are involved in various forms of prelogical, magical thinking (Piaget 1927, 1932). Institutionalized forms of magical thought are prevalent in every society, including so-called modern ones, and expulsive defenses and the "contrastive" maneuver are an important link in the psychodynamically informed interpretation of many "exotic" practices.[8]

Maneuver C: Intake: Introceptive Mechanisms ("Introjection")

"Introception" refers to the process of "taking in" perceptually organized experiences. Introception helps selectively define consciousness of self in any society. In given operations this mechanism, as it differentiates in the course of physiological maturation, is transmuted progessively into processes of identification, and it culminates in more mature forms of social group involvement and social belonging. Obviously, it is the maneuver of most significance to our consideration of belonging and empathy. Consciously experienced "empathic" sensibility is also related to the regulation of this "inclusive" developmental mechanism first found operative as introjection. My contention in this respect takes issue with some discussions of coping mechanisms (e.g., Haan 1977), where "empathy" is regarded as a developmental capacity arising from the early mechanism of projection. I differ with this view. For example, projected hostility may be misperceived or distorted because of the manner in which two basic mechanisms are defensively interrelated. Projection interferes with empathic receptivity rather than becoming receptivity at a later stage of development.

I believe introception as a basic mechanism has become the common heritage of mammals generally. Just as we resonate adaptively to facial and postural gestures, we come to "identify" with given external objects because our body automatically responds kinesically to visual, auditory, or olfactory stimuli (De Vos 1986).

Following psychoanalytic formulations of basic psychosexual stages, one can distinguish three progressive phases that transform the coping mechanism governing the "taking in" of experiences as part of the self. Interestingly, "introjection" is given less attention in the social science literature on the development of group inclusiveness than is "projection" in the literature on the formation of prejudice, out-group derogation, and social distancing. Even in the psychoanalytic literature itself, there is almost no discussion of how introjection sequentially relates to normal forms of personal and social identification. In some cultural traditions it has been usual to consider oneself part of, or inseparable from, others. In psychoanalysis, however, theoretical attention has been given to the disorders of the introceptive mechanism.[9] *Mature* forms of empathy or even adhesion or attachment in "social belonging" have not been systematically explored in a positive sense due to what I consider an individualistic bias in all Western social science, including psychoanalysis. Western psychology in general considers personal autonomy and distinctiveness the ultimate goal of self-realization. In contrast, civilizations such as the Chinese and Japanese have developed and maintained a more interactive concept of personal maturity (Tu 1984; De Vos 1985; Hsu 1985).

Psychoanalytic theory does not usually concern itself systematically with the cognitive structuring that uses introjective processes. Introjective functioning is, however, a central feature of Piaget's developmental theory of norm cognition. He describes the progressive differentiation of cognitive schemata as due to processes of internalizing experience by means of "accommodative" and "assimilative" processes. I would suggest that the process of "accommodation" as delineated by Piaget is basic to the development of schemata of social "belonging" generally. These schemata are central to definition of the social self. (They are further altered only in accordance with the selective permeability of the exclusionary mechanism functioning as "repression," screening subsequent experiences, as we have seen.) The "exclusionary" mechanism, functioning as concentration, however, is necessary to proper cognitive functioning. In mature thought, it is continually interactive with both "introceptive" synthesis and "contrastive" analysis. In assisting the process of introception, exclusion functions to screen out "noise," allowing for perceptual clarity. It helps in organizing experiences toward previously patterned consistencies.

Let us now return, briefly, to the Rorschach human movement responses, which, after all, prompted this discussion. In attempting to understand this kinesthetic projection of human movement into inkblots, one is attempting to measure the relatively controlled introceptive capacity of individuals and groups, an introceptive capacity which takes place in a consciousness of both one's own feelings and the feelings of others. Through just such consciousness there arises a capacity for self-control in social responses. "M" on the Rorschach, whether given by an Arab, a Japanese, an Athabascan, or an Apache, is a symbolic indicator of some relative maturation and adult control in human empathic kinesthetic responsiveness within the social environment.[10]

Imitation, Play, and Field Dependency: Processes Prior to Identification
What causes lasting personal identification, as the term is used in psychoanalytic theory? What is the difference between such identification and mere behavioral imitation? What prevents such identification? Do "diseases" prevent these permanent forms of accommodation? What prevents the type of internalization necessary for adult self-consistency? What is identity diffusion really? Why do some individuals exhibit the defensive maintenance of some form of immaturity which prevents them from becoming the people they would like to be? What prevents the individual from reaching his "ego ideal"?

It is not coincidental that an extreme capacity for Protean imitation—the quick assumption of the gestural patterns of others—indicates both some inner emptiness and an incapacity to experience satisfactorily some sense of permanence in self-definition. In effect, one can characterize individuals according to their balance between a sense of inner consistency and a need for definition from the outside. Witkin (1967, 1969, 1978), in his definitions of field independence and field dependence in children, measures some form of ability at self-definition. Witkin demonstrates that this capacity is developmental—that field dependence invariably precedes a capacity for field independence.

Some relative degree of field independence facilitates controlled learning. Witkins and others (e.g., De Vos 1980) have demonstrated how the positive relationship between cognitively structured field independence and learning in school is relatively more advantageous for groups of children from one culture or subculture than for others. I contend that school learning is indirectly related to the type of socialization experiences that resolve problems of identification. Satisfactory resolution of identity (at least vis-á-vis one's parents) increases one's capacity for self-modulated learning experiences. Learning becomes more subject to conscious control and can therefore be used instrumentally in coping with the external environment.

There are costs. To cure the aforementioned Zelig is to delimit his potentials of "becoming." To become someone is to be able no longer to take on other identities. To take on some form of adult commitment is to relinquish other imaginative potentials with which we play. Adult definition ends the agony of diffusion but also diminishes the potential for alternatives. For some, this cost is unacceptable, and empathic incapacity results.

Empathic incapacities, in fact, are found in many spheres. The unresolved problems of the narcissistic personality, for example, include an incapacity to empathize without momentarily "becoming" or, conversely, a capacity to empathize only with those who are like oneself, having a selective incapacity to comprehend similar processes in dissimilar individuals. This inability may also be found in the sexual realm as a defensive incapacity to empathize with members of the opposite sex. Empathic incapacity can also be seen as a within-groups defense. As such it is an inability to empathize with the out-group. Malfunctioning, or a defensive use of the introceptive mechanism, may be caused by hypertrophy or on the contrary by an inability to use the mechanism on a level of mature adaptation.

Introceptiveness, as Piaget envisioned it, has two aspects: first, the taking in, and second, the retention within by an act of accommodation occurring within a schema. A capacity for imitativeness does not necessarily lead to permanent identification or to social identity. What is introjected, even when repetitive, for some can be only temporarily experienced "inside," never becoming a permanent part of the self. One may become facile at imitation, like Danny Kaye "becoming" a Dane or a Russian, without any stable identification of thought, feeling, or behavior considered a permanent attribute of the self. This temporary experience "inside" is the very nature of "play."

Similarly, one may "feel" an ethnic role without permanently becoming it. Only progressively in a balanced progression of coping mechanisms do experiences lead to permanent accommodations and limitations in ego boundaries. For example, one may imitate another, more desired ethnic identity without assuming it permanently for oneself. "Passing" may become a chronic social condition, and yet one may never become the outer facade of one's position, occupation, or competence, however it may be accepted by one's peers.

What, then, might be the process by which an identification is fixed? There is inherent difficulty in growing into a more powerful but always vulnerable state from the relative helplessness of childhood. That is, as Freud saw, an inevitable circumstance of human maturation. And, indeed, we find psychologically that satisfactory maturation remains an ideal rather than an accomplishment for the majority in every society. It is always a matter of "more or less." One "identifies" as a means of contending psychologically, if not physically, with a competitive situation where power is perceived in the stronger other. The defensive use of identification permits the individual to sense power through taking in and "being." It is then possible to respond to a competitive contention or a competitive confrontation girded with new strength. One becomes capable of a certain amount of confidence in an inner sense of mastery in such circumstances.

How does the imitative experience of playful dominance held temporarily become accommodated so that it becomes a permanent experiential part of the self? Or conversely, what prevents the individual under some circumstances from assuming some form of self-assurance about personal prowess? Power cannot be assumed to be part of the self or recognized as nondestructive in others when a person feels overwhelmed by it or when its exercise would destroy others. No easy internalization can take place when either intensive intrusion of destruction from the outside or impulses of a sexual and/or destructive nature must be experienced as part of the conscious self by internalization. The inability to "become" what one fears and hates occurs in humans regardless of the cultural setting. (One also hesitates to become a victim or to assume a subordinate role.) Rituals of transition are socially practiced by societies to ensure such eventuality.

More or less satisfactory forms of adult identification do occur, of course, even if residues of difficulty are found in many symbolic representations. (The tensions and problems of childhood past are to be found in the myths and legends of various societies, whether they are the Trobriands as recently reexamined by Spiro [1982c] or the Victorian Europeans studied by Freud.) One clue to the way in which the process works itself out appears in Freud's understanding of identification with the aggressor. One gains release from anxiety by maintaining internally as best one can some inner sense of mastery using any available symbolic means to bolster one's sense of inner capacity. These are often symbols of being in a dominant position or of adhering to some dominant group. Those destined to be socially subordinate may find restitutive tricks to maintain a sense of ultimate, if not immediate, triumph.

However, in order to be able to maintain the assertive role, the individual must also seek social support in the attitudes of others. Should this social support be lacking (or should the assumption of aggressiveness be considered inappropriate), social sanctioning will work against self-assertion, whatever the sense of inner capacity. Conversely, when assertiveness is expected, sanctioning conduces toward a permanent accomplishment of the expected identification. It becomes more difficult to sustain one's real self in the face of continuous social attitudes to the contrary.

At least in the case of early childhood, a labeling theory approach may be applied. Early social expectations are highly inductive of one's self-concept. A child observes how role expectations are directed toward those he is supposed (or destined) to emulate. Later social attitudes are influential only if they reinforce what has been set up in early childhood expectancies.

Formation of a Social Self

Cultural Emphases in Coping Patterns In thinking of the social "self" as a series of interactive-composite schemata characterized by internal consistency, we must distinguish among the socialization patterns found to be relatively operative in various cultures. Some culture patterns develop toward a relatively ready receptivity; others use exclusion defensively in a manner which narrows down receptivity to new experience. In an unmodulated use of introception there may occur too ready resonance, so that the individual experiences an incapacity to empathize without at least momentarily becoming the other individual. The maturation of the empathic capacity of a human being depends ultimately on the ability to experience empathy without losing a sense of inner consistency in maintaining separation and self-definition.

Identification in Personality versus Identification in Social Sex Roles Identification of character traits and sexual identification per se must not be confused. For example, in a patriarchal society, if a woman identifies with the aggressive behavior of a father, this aggressiveness can be sustained only if it becomes redefined behaviorally as part of being a daughter/woman. As a result, in its external presentation it may be expressed quite differently from the way it would be as part of a pattern of identification assumed by a son. When we consider patterns of character formation of specific individuals, then, we find that sex identification and character identification are fairly independent of one another. The mother in her own identification with her destined role may maintain a positive idealization of the male, but sometimes this positive ideal is directed toward the son's future realization rather than being viewed as actualized in her spouse. Under such circumstances the son is freer, perhaps, to identify with an idealized dominant male role—not directly with the father as a flawed "aggressor." If the mother turns to the son vicariously, as in Japan (De Vos 1975a), to act out male prowess, the son may even avoid direct identification with a "weaker" father. In effect, the Oedipal rivalry is deflected into dealings with an idealized image held by the mother. A child can identify with the *character* traits of either parent, regardless of sexual orientation. Indeed, Dolhinow (personal communication), it is interesting to note, has found that very often the male offspring of dominant females among primates in turn assume relative dominance in a primate society when they reach adulthood. It comes as no surprise, then, to find that the same phenomenon occurs among humans (De Vos 1978).

Should there be too threatening or dangerous a subjective implication attached to permanent accommodation of schemata or "identification," the individual may be able only to imitate or "play" at the assumption of a dominant posture. Indeed, the essence of comedy is very often the subordinate or small figure ultimately triumphing over the large, oppressive, higher-status individual through guile, cleverness, or happy circumstance. In enjoying comic drama, we all still identify with the difficulty of the small child who needs to cope with the more dominant adult, but in the happy optimism of a comic posture, we see its eternal possibility.

The Development of Social Sensitivity Sensitivity to social feelings allows one to "identify" with another without needing to become the other. There is a progressive maturation of "taking in" toward mature self-control in the experience of empathy and compassion. The adult individual who becomes part of a specific ethnic group, for example, progressively develops a relative sensitivity in the taking in of social feelings. Some feelings are excluded as inappropriate, disharmonious, or threatening. Other feelings evolve progressively into an empathy and compassion that he can safely extend, without changing his own identity, to others not of his group.

The mechanism of introception from an early stage emphasizes first fusion, then identification. Later, with an adequate, mature use of the exclusion mechanism, one can experience similarity and closeness without becoming totally "identified." There can be a development of the sympathetic recognition of experiences as going on within other individuals and, in turn, knowledge of the essential similarity of experience with others without any loss or threat of loss of self.

The Experience of Belonging, Religious and Secular In the most primitive level of introceptive coping, there is as yet no complete separation of the self from the outside; external stimuli are experienced internally. A very important continuing aspect of such early introceptive experience is that "power" or the sense of causal sequence is experienced as "personalized," that is, it is related to intentional attitudes. Self-consciousness develops from an internal recognition of the continuous interrelationship between inner feelings and the "feelings" attributed to others in the social environment.

One seeks selectively for experiences of protective reassurance by adhering or remaining as close as possible to those to whom one feels attached (de Grazia 1948). The fearful and aggressive are kept as distant as possible. One remains "part of" a family, later a group, possibly an ethnic group. In Piagetian terms, certain internal conceptual or perceptual schemata are continually open to accommodate new personalized experiences that are part of oneself, while this helpless "self" is not completely separated from immediate, but exterior, beings of power. A well-balanced, socialized self is continually experiencing the ways in which it is related to the immediate social environment. Hence the mechanism of inclusion at each stage has to do with the social development of this sense of belonging. There is a continual, progressively differentiated taking in and permeability to in-group social attitudes (Sarbin and Scheibe 1983). Protective social identity can become very complex in a modern society. In seeking to assuage "belonging" in a multiethnic situation, one must contend with a richness or even confusion of potential alternatives.

On a strictly cognitive level, processes constituting internalization can be related to perception of categorical similarity and, ultimately, to emphasis on forms of "synthetic" or "creative" thought. These processes govern all social representations and are involved centrally in religious experiences and the recognition of poetic relationships. Conversely, representations of social difference arise from the "contrastive" projective mechanisms previously discussed that come to govern inductive analysis and affectively distant or objective thought.

The mature individual therefore maintains as part of his or her self a sense of social belonging and group commitment. At the same time, he or she recognizes the interdependence of the self with other parts of a total social system. There is controlled involvement in events. Ideally one can arrive at a satisfactory balance between synthetic and analytic thought, between compassion and detachment, between moral social concerns and scientific objectivity. These concerns will be found in the way in which an ethnic identity is maintained and in the relative degree of salience with which it is maintained.

Overall, we see that the introceptive mechanisms must be in a dynamic balance with those that govern selectivity of experience and those that govern detachment and objectivity. Malfunctioning of some defensive mechanisms may cause hypertrophy or, on the contrary, the inability to use the introceptive mechanisms on a level of mature adaptation.

Moral Order and the Dangers of Anomie During Piaget's "heteronomous," or other-directed, stage of moral development (Piaget 1932), the mechanism of introjection is transmuted gradually through a number of minor disciplinary crises that occur before a stable identification takes place. When the developing ego structure has remained properly balanced, social directives are gradually internalized as a more permanent part of the self so that there is progressively less need for immediate external sanctioning to guide behavior.

Sometimes the three mechanisms are imbalanced in the direction of continually too ready acceptance of new introceptions. Then consistent self-regulating forms of identification do not take place as readily. The psychodynamic reasons are too complex to be discussed here. Suffice it to say that the problem may have to do in some instances with the limiting implications of a stable identification. When a stable type of identification defining one's relationship with others remains incomplete, there come to be problems of anomie experienced as alienation or the loss of a sense of investment in others. In contrast, other individuals seeking to attain a sense of belonging may submit themselves temporarily or permanently to a leader or belief system which gives them regulation. Erich Fromm, in his volume *Escape from Freedom* (1968), discusses such a sequence of anomie and diffusion in Germans prior to the Nazi "ethnic affirmation" of Adolf Hitler. This external submission to authority is necessary because the individual finds his sense of inner regulation insufficient in situations of social anomie.

As I have already noted, individuals suffering a sense of malaise in this respect may also seek to guide their action through "imitation." In Reisman's terms (1958), they have an "other-directed" nonstabilized superego, which necessitates continued use of an outside reference group. Peer-oriented forms of belonging become a viable solution. To extend Erikson's term, "identity diffusion" occurs as part of an experience of internal conflict over inconsistent or contrastive directives or purposes.

ALIENATION AND BELONGING: PROBLEMS OF SOCIAL ADHERENCE

Freud postulated that "separation anxiety" resulted from the sense of separateness. The individual's loss of attachment is a price paid for the establishment of independence in the realization of the self, a necessary stage in the establishment of social reality as separate from one's internal experience. Durkheim, in his description of egoistic suicide, describes what Sartre and Kierkegaard view as the existential anxiety of individuals in modern Western culture. However, this same loss of meaning is resolved in others by forms of religious conversion. (We see this resolution just as clearly in "roll narcissism" and the etiology of Japanese suicide [De Vos 1973, chap. 17].[11] It is part of the insightfulness of Durkheim that, while he understood the dangers of attenuation of beliefs as the symptoms preceding what he called "egoistic suicide," he also understood the role of communion and the experience of power in communal ritual. Sebastian de Grazia (1948) delineates "separation anxiety" well and shows that belief systems can serve as an answer to it. Through religious beliefs one symbolically maintains social attachments which replace the psychological rupture between parents and child.

In effect, the converse of problems of attachment and introjection is experienced in religious ecstasy or in a catatonic schizophrenic crisis. There is the fear of the void, the fear of total emptiness and lack of meaning, and a sense of incompleteness, but the religious ecstatics resolve this difficulty by attaching themselves again to a power, often personalized, which fills them with new meaning and social purpose.

Such investment is directly related to patterns of social cohesion on a social level and the experiential sense of social experience as part of self-development. The development of belonging starts with the early attachment to the mother. It is transmuted by socialization into other symbolic representations in every culture. These symbolic representations compose the organization of belief, which Kardiner (1939) called a "security system." Socialization of social belonging takes place in a context of available cognitively organized beliefs that relate the individual experientially to his environment as a member of a particular society. Society is not simply the people about us but a world of symbolic meaning. Any idea, whether that of God or, as Durkheim suggested, society itself, or even the ideal of the individuated self when examined in its final analysis, is a symbol that, if it works properly, is experienced subjectively as an "overriding reality" filling one with life's meaning.

Many religious thinkers have attempted to describe to others experience of a quest for ultimate meaning in those who have lost a primary attachment. A conversion may occur, or one may achieve a sudden dedication to social meaning of an ideological nature. One can thus understand the difficulties experienced by an individual who tries to break with an ideology that has proven unfulfilled. A loss of ideology necessitates a type of "secondary" separation anxiety that many cannot countenance. In Japan during the military period, for example, religious conversion of former communists took the form of a patriotic loss of self in the name of the Japanese state. Tsurumi (1970) reports that during this period it was difficult for some to comprehend how well-known radicals could rededicate themselves to the belief in the emperor and a divinely ordained imperial destiny for Japan. These men gave up their more individuated opposition to the military state by an inundating act of belonging that drowned out their own social disquietude. They found meaning again in being "Japanese."

By belonging to an entity larger than oneself, one also, to some extent, escapes the fear of death. Some theories of continuity include the personal continuity of the individual, but deep down, many people believe in the continuity of the group or of their family. The purpose of life very often for parents is to see themselves perpetuated in their children. Intellectuals who are a bit narcissistic like to think of the continuity of their ideas, their "intellectual children." It is difficult for an individual to envision total oblivion and death both from the standpoint of the self envisioning death and from the standpoint of envisioning a permanent loss of someone close is difficult to contemplate. Most often death is experienced as a form of separation. In Buddhist belief, a separate ego and self are acknowledged to be illusions. But one is assuaged by the reassurance that one's true essence partakes of the essential continuity and inclusiveness of all life. The gnawing pain of personal isolation and separation can be symbolically healed by such belief.

We should note that intensely introspective individuals do not accept the same levels of belief and belonging that satisfy the uncritical. They are explorers into the far reaches of the human psyche, and as such they become far removed from the acceptable as prosaic. They dare give idiosyncratic meaning to life, and they suffer thereby. They dangerously expose themselves to the possibility of vertigo or a sense of profound alienation through questioning beliefs that readily sustain others.

CONCLUSIONS

We have inherited an inherent capacity to resonate with other human beings. If one person sees another cry, tears are ready in one's own eyes. One knows how it feels to cry, and one is able to feel that way. Resonance, empathy, identity, and identification—all these terms describe processes of taking in experiences not only through our distant perceptive senses but also physically, through our musculature. Humans learn to act deliberately in a way that causes emotions in others. A capable actor can cry on command. The conscious use of the body to induce emotions in others is part of every cultural system. It involves conscious control of those things that we usually express only very spontaneously. In a Rorschach response, one knows how it feels in one's muscles to experience emotion, and the projection of humanity onto the inkblot, with attendant emotion, easily involves the projection of movement as well.

In concluding this exploration of human communality in honor of a beloved fellow-traveler of the same road, I am aware of many thoughts still to be pursued and many issues yet to be understood related to the timing of generational continuity and the replacement of the old by the young.

George De Vos

Some societies have a sense of grace about continuity. In others it is harshly attained. Far better a festschrift than a totemic feast.

NOTES

1. American Rorschach specialists have gained statistical evidence showing that the ability to perceive human motion becomes progressively more apparent with age in children (e.g., Exner 1982). This developmental trend is also evident in the native American and Japanese children's samples which I have personally examined (Muramatsu et al. 1962, Day, Boyer, and De Vos 1975; Boyer, De Vos, and Boyer 1983). Also clear in the cross-cultural samples is the appearance of various defenses that selectively *prevent* such perceptions in some individuals in every society. (See, e.g., Helm, De Vos, and Carterette 1960; Miner and De Vos 1960; Day, Boyer, and De Vos 1975; Boyer, De Vos, and Borders 1978; De Vos and Borders 1979.) In other contexts I have also been concerned with minority or ethnic problems involving constrictive adaptive strategies (De Vos 1978), with the maintenance of loss of identity (De Vos 1980, 1982, 1983b), and with alienation and suicide in Japan (De Vos 1973). In each instance there are clear differences in both statistical and case-history materials.

2. Erikson (1968) cogently used the term "identity diffusion" to describe a malaise of adolescence that sometimes becomes protracted and continues into adulthood. Robert Lifton (1970) discussed "Protean man," a modern malaise named after Proteus, an early expediential Zelig, who in the ancient Greek myth would take many forms, depending upon situational exigencies.

3. The persistence of less transmuted primitive functioning in imbalanced, maladjustive, and rigidified psychological structures may result in various forms of socially unwanted conduct. In some societies such unwanted conduct or concomitant aberrant thought and emotional disturbance may be diagnosed as a form of possession, "craziness," or "mental illness." One must stress the fact, that, whatever the society, such diagnoses are usually attempted only when some form of rigidified or out-of-control conduct interferes with expected social functioning (De Vos 1974).

On the other hand, very often primitive forms of coping mechanisms can be found to operate without maladaptive results within socially condoned or even socially sought-after situations (Miner and De Vos 1960). Shamans, for example, can instrumentally as well as expressively "regress in the service of the ego." In effect, shamans can use primitive mental operations "in the service of the group" (Boyer, De Vos, and Boyer 1983).

4. To illustrate the interaction of these three modes, it is provocative to consider how repression as a mechanism continually interacts with projection and introception in understanding ethnic continuities and situations of minority status (De Vos and Wagatsuma 1966; De Vos 1978).

5. In clinical psychoanalytic practice, dealing most often with "neurotically" rigidified behavior, the general exclusionary mechanism, in the form of "repression,"

From Empathy to Alienation

is most manifest in unresolved problems characterizing the so-called "phallic" or sexually differentiating stage of psychosexual development. Repression is characteristically used to ward off the sense of a threat that would prevent one from realizing the meaning of one's own unconscious impulses. It is also used to block awareness as well as to prevent the conscious learning of behavior whose meaning is not appropriate to one's allocated status and gender roles. *The awareness of meaning in particular is repressed.* Affectivity can remain available. Such individuals are "motoric," action oriented, but lack "insight" into their behavior.

When cognitive control remains dominant in character formation, the "contrastive" discriminatory mechanism appears dominant on a neurotic level in "obsessive-compulsive" forms termed "isolation" or "intellectualization." In neuroses governed by the expulsive mechanism, affect is repressed. Thought is allowed as long as feeling and motoric display remain blocked off.

6. These defensive maneuvers are apparently especially present in middle-class Western adolescents (Anna Freud 1937).

7. Note that when we examine the inner experience of power in causal sequences, the line of thought espoused here makes it unnecessary to posit any new, "internal" effectance capacities other than the functioning of the same basic ego mechanisms.

8. Discussion of these must await another paper and is omitted here in response to the editors' concern with brevity—another illustration of the same mechanism!

9. These disorders are usually related to unresolved problems encountered during the "oral" period of development. Such disturbances can result in what is clinically defined as "narcissistic" character disorders or so-called "borderline" conditions (Kernberg 1975).

10. The usual clinical assumption related to the appearance of human movement in Rorschach protocols is that it indicates a time-binding capacity so that the individual is not constrained to respond immediately to outer stimuli of an emotional nature. In Rorschach analysis, understanding of the perception of the human content is counterpoised to the perception of color as a determinant. We assume that a reaction to color relates to an affective responsiveness to outer environmental stimuli. This responsiveness is immediate and spontaneous. However, given the balancing of the capacity measured by the sight of human movement, one can presume that the conscious control of kinesthetic impulses allows the individual to constrain behavior, so that there is no immediate motoric display of internal activity, attitudinal within the individual. This greater conscious control over interior processes is more evident in introversively or introceptively conscious individuals.

11. In discussing forms of suicide in Japan, I contended that most, but not all, suicide indicates some form of immature fixation or regressive withdrawal of what is termed "object cathexis." Object cathexis is an individual's investment of meaning in parts of himself as well as in the objects of his social and natural environment. The nature of this investment is an attachment of inner being with outside objects that give meaning. This bonding assuages separation anxiety. Because of the human capacity to symbolize, the object cathected or invested with meaning can include not only other persons but also inanimate objects, ideas, or even parts of one's own body. In the course of psychosexual development, an individual is usually "socialized

out of" a state of primary narcissism so as to invest meaning in objects and persons that have social as well as personal value. The process of investment in the self is always in dynamic tension with both instrumental and expressive investment in objects outside the self. In examining biographies of authors who committed suicide, I found attempts at dedication to aesthetic refinement following unsatisfactory resolution in religious belief. Interestingly, I did not find a single alienated author in the series who had been brought up by his own mother: a singular finding in a culture quite fixed on the mother as the ultimate source of comfort and refuge.

PART THREE
Religion and Personality

11

Religion beyond the Functionalist Frontier

MANNING NASH ༄

The scholarly tradition in the anthropological treatment of religion has been channeled by three constraining matrixes. First, Tylor (1958:12) fathered a long line of intellectualist interpretations. Religion was a mistaken inference from common experience, just as the notion of souls wandering in dreams gave rise to the theory of animism. The second group of theories of religion includes the correspondence hypotheses. Religion expressed social structure, or aspects of it, according to Durkheim and others. Similarly, in the third matrix religion was taken as a false reflection of the social relations and conflicts in a society in the Marxist view. This view regarded religion as a distortion in the service of the ruling class, an opiate for the oppressed, and a solace, the heart of a heartless world.

Functionalism, a product of these three lines of thought, added to them the notion that religion met some set of personal or social needs. The explanatory hypotheses generated by functionalism tended to be both tautological and teleological, and where they avoided these pitfalls, they fell into near banality or repetitive and unproductive iteration (Geertz 1966:2).

Some of the current trends in contemporary cultural anthropology are beginning to show us how to blaze theoretical and methodological paths beyond the functionalist frontier. I propose to strengthen these trends by

1. proposing a somewhat novel definition of religion. This definition aims to set forth the empirical dimensions of religious belief and practice and to differentiate religion from other domains while leaving open its mode of integration into the whole.

2. suggesting why man in society continually generates religious belief and practice and how the historical vicissitudes of the existential situation of man in society gives rise to different religious formulations.

Religious belief and the rituals and practices consequent on those beliefs have two coexisting features that mark them off from other domains. An act or symbol[1] falls in the domain of religion when it implicates another order of reality. In Firth's (1959:3) expression, "it shifts the index pointer of reality." Spiro (1966b:96) is even more definite as to where the index pointer is shifted—in the direction of "interactions with [the] culturally postulated super-human." Religious symbols suggest, implicate, define, and constitute a realm of transcendence above, beyond, more powerful than, or essentially different from the realm of empirical, naively real ordinary existence. But religion requires more than a postulated ontological realm. The realm of transcendence inevitably entails worship, which encompasses the attitudes of awe, dependence, respect, and eventual helplessness held by the actors toward those symbols. Succinctly stated, *Religion is a system of symbols and acts oriented to an order of reality transcending the observable and merely empirical world, with those symbols and acts regarded and performed in a worshipful manner implying dependence.*

This definition distinguishes religion from magic (the magician may coerce the hidden order), from the so-called secular or civic religions (the sense of dependence is absent when a Russian visits the tomb of Lenin or an American the Lincoln monument) and from deeply moving experiences (such as being stirred by a book which changes one's life). The conceptual span of the definition also stretches to include the Australian churinga rites, in the same phenomenal realm as the Old and New Testaments. The definition does three things: (1) It specifies and stipulates what is meant by the term "religion." (2) It avoids tautology and teleology. And (3) it is diagnostically useful for cross-cultural comparison.

Some ethnological examples will help clarify the terse definition. In a village in Upper Burma where I conducted fieldwork in 1960–1961, there was an outbreak of night crying and fear among many children. The village headman (*lugyi*) finally decided after consulting with the village elders that the malaise was caused by the *yokazo*, a spirit dwelling in a large tree in the village. One night the lugyi and I stood before the tree in which the yokazo resided. The lugyi addressed the tree. He called to the yokazo, and when he thought he had its attention, he lectured it. He admonished the yokazo to stop bothering the children and to behave itself. Finally he threatened to drive it from its tree residence if it did not desist from its harassment. As we returned to his compound (where I lived), he shook his head in exasperation and remarked that the yokazo ought to know better and that he and the yokazo had had this sort of confrontation several times in the past.

According to the definition earlier offered, this vignette does not belong in the domain of religion. The children's night terrors did receive a transcendental explanation; the yokazo implicates another order of reality. But the yokazo inspires no feeling or attitudes of worship or dependence. Conversely, when a Burmese jeep driver stops on the stretch of road from Mandalay to Maymyo to pick up three rocks, gives them human names, and puts them aboard the jeep so that the passenger total reaches the number nine, he is performing religious ritual. That particular stretch of road is, culturally, the territory of *nats*, the nine lords of the region. These nats can be malignantly harmful to people who insult them by ignoring their sovereignty over the territory. The jeep driver, by bringing the number of occupants up to the number of nats, recognizes their overlordship and placates them. That the other occupants of the jeep do not complain about the inconvenience of the stop or show surprise when the rocks are given human names indicates that the activity of the driver is not an idiosyncrasy but part of a religious domain of public and shared symbols and meanings.

Religion, then, is a theory of reality, even if much of that posited reality is not amenable to observation. This postulated reality has a social and cultural existence based on premises other than theories of the real as expounded in science, ethics, and aesthetics in a given cultural system. In everyday life, man in society is engaged in the social construction and validation of reality. The socially held, culturally defined reality is exhibited in human interactions in a set of social relations which are taken for granted (Berger 1970; Schutz 1970). Ideas of the real are social products.

It is fairly evident why man in society generates plausibility structures (theories) about the physical and biological world (science), about the social world (economics and sociology), and about human power relations (political science and ethics). These realms must be dealt with in everyday life. The nonhuman environment must be processed to yield the material basis of life, which must be parceled in an orderly and legitimate manner. The knowledge and codes for handling the environment and forming a set of legitimate expectations about the members of the society give rise to the physical and social sciences. In the old anthropological wisdom, in interacting with the environment and with other men, "man makes himself."

But why do people fashion religions? Why is there, in most societies, a system of symbols about an unseen order of reality, the transcendental, the totally postulated, or the extraempirical? This chapter attempts in part to indicate the recurring sources of the continual generation of religious cognitive categories in the same commonsense way that a resisting world and refractory others generate science and the social sciences.

Religion derives from ineluctable aspects of the continuing human condition. People make theories adequate to their past experience and to their continued existence. They fashion the beliefs that will serve, but not randomly or freely, for they are historically and situationally constrained. At any point in time for a given society, there is a set of beliefs already existing, to which further symbols must be accommodated. There is room for some degree of freedom but not for free play. And not only do the existing sets constrain symbolic creativity, but religious symbols must resonate in the experience of a large number of the members of the society. All religion comes from the minds of men as they condense, shape, and interpret experience. Those systems that have social viability make socially plausible symbolic statements in a manner resonating with experience and symbol sets of large numbers in a given society in definite historical circumstances.

The existential conditions for the continuity of social life include the processes of social and cultural production and reproduction. A society continues when generation replaces generation and senior generation passes on to junior generation a cultural heritage. The demographic and socialization dynamics demand that a worldview and other symbol systems must be passed on from adult to child, adjusted to the child's capacity to absorb. New members of a society, children, do not have the capacity to validate or to test what they are taught. Parents teach and train so that children may grow into well-incorporated members of a social order (no matter that nobody does so perfectly or that the best of intentions often go astray). In order to rear children, parents affirm the world. They often affirm that which is not. Small and helpless children inducted into a world fare batter when that world is presented so that order, regularity, justice, goodness, and control seem to be properties of it. Parents from experience may know better, but they cannot transmit this adult perception to children. The first and basic source of religion lies (no pun) in the situation of reproduction and the socialization of the psychically and physically nearly defenseless child.

Sometimes parents believe what they transmit, and sometimes they knowingly transmit fictions that they believe conduce to socially necessary ideas of order, trust, and regularity in the world. A Burmese Buddhist believes he is relating historical fact when he tell the Jataka tales to his children; a Hopi is aware that his telling of the sacred kachina story is only partly true and that the child will eventually see an unmasked relative in the kiva, and an American knows he is transmitting fiction when he tells children about Santa Claus at Christmas.

All symbol systems come under the dialectical attack of experience. There are tensions in the way symbols mesh with their meanings and referents. The hypotheses of trust and orderly expectation are imperfectly documented by organized social life. There is the random occurrence of affliction—

who dies when, what illness strikes whom, who prospers and multiplies, who suffers and wants—all this and more is aleatory and hence stands in opposition to an orderly, just, and trustworthy world. An adult might handle this tension by some formulation of probability theory or by adopting a generally pessimistic view or by some existential philosophy of the essential meaninglessness of things and experience, but a child can neither apprehend nor be socialized under such premises.

For the reproduction of society, these tensions are made bearable for children (and for those adults in whom early socialization systems persist) by a religious formulation. "Formulation" is used advisedly, since the symbols, meanings, action implications, and referents pass through the minds of actors at some point in real history.

The generally most widespread resolution of the tension between order and trust on the one hand and random affliction on the other is the postulation of spirits, beings, or forces in another reality but capable of manifesting themselves in the affairs of men. In this sense a belief in spirits is the basic stratum of religion. Tylor's (1871) grasp of this component in all systems of religion led him to the evolutionary conclusion that "animism" is the soil from which more complex trees in the forest of religious belief grow. But Tylor's stance that animism was an intellectual solution to a logical problem differs from the existential view of rooting beliefs in a wide cultural matrix of experience. Spirits (all those forces implicated in animism, up to and including active deities) derive their authority not only from ratiocination but from an emotionally charged human experience and specifically from the experience of trance and possession by the public exhibition of shamanistic display. Shamanistic spirit possession and control have all that is required for awe coupled with transcendence. Shamanistic possession usually begins involuntarily (though procedures for inducing a spirit to enter a medium may hasten the onset of trance). The shaman is visibly disassociated. He acts another's apparent will, and important, his state finds resonance in other members of the society (Lewis 1971). In trance possessions I have observed in Kelantan, Malaysia, members of the audience are frequently swept up into the disassociation of the medium. I recall an informant who panicked and had to flee from the audience while he was explaining to me the "main puteri" curing ritual of an eminent Malay magician. (See Firth 1974; Skeat 1967 for accounts of shaman roles.) Similarly, in Burma when the *natgadaw* is possessed by her nat spirit husband and begins to dance in trance, members of the audience (there to ask the *natgadaw* to make predictions) are frequently carried away, and they themselves begin a trancelike gyration (Nash 1965).

Shamanism is the simplest cultic religion in the ethnographic record, and as the sole, or nearly sole form of transcendence, it is found in the

249

simpler, fluid, band-organized societies. But in a peripheral role shamanism persists in all levels of social complexity as the Loa cults of Haiti, temple dances of Bali, Bomohs of Malaya, and glossolalia and Pentecostal enthusiasm in the canonical religions attest. Among the Arctic Tungus, the locus classicus of shamanism, the paradigm of the dialectic of order versus chaos is laid out. The Tungus are organized in patrilineal clans, and, depending on the size of the clans, from one to five lineages form a band, who hunt the moving game in a precarious and difficult environment. Each patrilineal clan has its own shaman, whose tasks are involved with the luck of the life-supporting hunt. The death of a shaman means unbearable vulnerability to uncontrolled and possibly malignant spirits. To make the hiatus between control and chaos as brief as possible, the Tungus make the office of shaman hereditary. Other band societies in precarious ecological niches that make shamanism their central ritual include the Chukchee, the Yahgan, the Senoi, and the Ona— and the list of similarly structured and environmentally marginal groups could be much expanded.

Religious belief and practice, I maintain, are generated from tensions in existential conditions of man in society. Another such tension is the antithesis between work and play, between the serious and the frivolous, between time which is socially important and time which is time out. Escape from work, from seriousness, from socially important passages of time, exists in all societies in the forms of play, ecstasy, frenzy, or frivolity. These escapes may be more or less spontaneous, or drugs, intoxicants, music, dance, and chanting may serve as time changers and scene shifters. The central formulator in religions based on states leaving the mundane workaday world behind is the mystic, the seer, the visionary. When the mystic's or seer's formulation can condense and name experience so that other members of the society can share or respond to those flights, religious symbols are formed. That the holder of an uncommunicated or incommunicable gnosis, however achieved, is labeled a deviant or a psychotic reflects recognition of Durkheim's insight that religious symbols must be public and shared; they are group symbols and derive their authenticity from their status as collective representations. The mushroom cults of southern Mexico where the toxic mushroom allows communicants to see vivid colors and to hear the voices of the gods, the native American church with peyote button rituals of hallucination, the Tantric rituals of Tibetan Buddhism, the Bhakti path of devotion within Hinduism, and the early Hassidic elements in Judaism are all instances of religious symbol systems built from ludic elements (Huizinga 1955) in contrapuntal interaction with the serious elements of social life. These playfully derived symbols make available to the cultural repertory socially controlled, patterned escape from the serious world into dimensions of oceanic feeling, of eternity, of complete pleasure, of the lifting out of the self. Hence it is not strange that erotic love is often a template for religious meaning, for this form of play is frequent and available to most members of a society. The human ability to laugh, to create humor from incongruity, to pun, to create metaphor, to be secretive, and to confabulate and fantasize are other ludic sources of religious symbols.

No sets of social action are ever complete and final. Social action points to a future, to a tomorrow, to a new state of affairs. The uncompleted project-like notion of social action entails the condition of futurity. Futurity can be sustained only by hope, not by the empirical world where plans misfire, where the finality of death is omnipresent, and where disappointment is rife. The human capacity for hope rather than its enemy, apathy, rests on symbols that necessarily transcend the empirical world. Hope is the vision of a friction-free world, where men in all confidence may pursue their un-completed projects and somehow merge with eternity.

Probably the most elaborate theory of hope as central to religion is that found in the Pali canon of Theravada Buddhism (Nash 1965; Spiro 1970). The idea of reincarnation, or of metempsychosis along the chain of beings until there occurs the final detachment of self from the wheel of life in the state of Nirvana, is a counsel of hope, of moral perfectibility, and of final arrival in the friction-free state. Moreover, it is available to all men by their own effort, and without great interior strain or conflict, since they can do only what their temperaments and past incarnations permit them to do about working out their salvation with diligence.

This salvation idiom had a supposed founder—the Buddha—and this case is instructive for all religions that put a doctrine of hope and salvation at their center. The Buddha was a prince in India living in luxury and shielded from the cares and blows of the world. The Buddha ventured out of his palace and saw death, disease, decay, and suffering. He renounced his princely life and sought the causes of these evils. He wandered and meditated; and under the bo tree in a flash of insight, the origin of suffering and its cure came to him. The doctrine and practice of Theravada Buddhism derives from this nuclear experience of its founder. In Burma today, when a novice is inducted into the monkhood by the ceremony of *shinbyu*, there is a symbolic, detailed reenactment of the nuclear Buddhist experience.

The central formulator of a religion of hope is the prophet. His prophe-cy solves the problem of hope in a refractory world. Prophecy arises in a socially differentiated society where there are already class and cultural differences and conflicts of some intensity. The prophecy is accepted in cir-cumstances of turmoil and uncertainty which make hope impossible. The Buddha preached his message at a time when castes were becoming more rigid in India and when princely armies went forth to battle and conquer and enserf sizable populations. All the salvation religions exhibit similar patterns in their nuclear, originating experience. Moses fleeing Egypt, wandering the wilderness, receiving the commandments, and delivering the former slaves to a land of milk and honey as a chosen people is the experience from which the central symbols and practices of Judaism are elaborated. For Christianity, the life of its prophet Jesus is the template for symbolism, and this prophecy arose in the Roman oppressed state of Israel, where the upper classes were collaborators with the conquerors and the lower classes were exploited. Similarly, Islam's prophet Mohammed came at a time of internecine warfare and moral decadence in the Arabian peninsula, and his life is central to Islam, otherwise starkly devoid of icon and symbol. The religion of the Sikhs, founded by Guru Nanak in the fifteenth century, at a time when the Muslims had established hegemony over northwestern India and were persecuting the Hindus, equally fulfills the social and historical conditions for the rise of a prophetic religion. The founding and histories of the Baha'i faith, or of the Church of Jesus Christ of Latter Day Saints, add weight to the proposed conditions giving rise to prophetic religion. And in the ethnographic record, the Ghost Dance, Handsome Lake, and a host of millenarian cults attest to the rise of prophecy in times of turmoil and conflict, when hopes are dim and many moral systems compete with each other.

One not widely distributed tension in the social life of some societies gives rise to a distinctive religious formulation. This is the tension between a small ruling elite and a large peasant mass, when the hierarchy does not reflect transcendental warrant and symbol. This is the tension of unwarranted hierarchy. The central figure in this religion is the priest, and the priest's power rests on control of esoteric knowledge, not available to the laity, nor are laymen able to perform the required ritual. The priest probably develops from the shaman or the magician. He had special knowledge useful for the control and continuity of the food supply. When there is a relatively sudden explosion in the quantity and reliability of the food supply, the magician may develop into the priest and collectively become a member of the literati, an elite entrusted with maintaining and renewing the world. The most notable examples of priestly, world-maintenance religions are found in civilizations that arise from the Neolithic revolutions in the New World, along the Nile, between the Tigris and the Euphrates rivers, and in the Indus valley or along the Yellow River. The Aztec and Maya religions were certainly led by priestly elites, as were the pharaonic and the others named above. The elaborate calendrical calculations, like the monumental architecture, were consciously or unconsciously devised so that the priestly elite could stage religious dramas for the lay masses.

This chapter has offered a somewhat novel definition of religion. Using that definition, it has enumerated four areas of dialectical tension stemming from what I have called the existential tensions of man in society and has postulated four different dominant modes (since the tensions and various modes of resolution may continue to coexist, whatever religious form is dominant) of handling these tensions that give rise to four different sorts of religious symbols and rituals. In these pages I have also sketched some of the historical circumstances under which the shamanistic, the mystic, the prophetic, and the priestly religious are likely to arise. In the limited space of an article, these assertions must remain nearly bare, but they have structural and empirical relevance and will, I believe, direct further stimulating work beyond the functionalist frontier of meeting social and individual needs.

Surely the urgency in the anthropological study of religion does not relate, and has not done so for a long time, to the testing of empirical generalization; the challenge is, and has been, not to formulate answers, but to deepen the questions.

N O T E S

Readers familiar with Peter L. Berger's incisive and charming essay "A Rumor of Angels" will appreciate my debt to it. I write as an anthropologist and not as he did, seeking a grounded theology. By "functional frontier" I mean the explanation of religious act and symbol by imputing to belief and ritual functional consequences in meeting some postulated set of social system or personal "needs" or "requisites." This chapter focuses on existential "tensions" or "dilemmas" to which religion may be one solution, possibly one among many.

1. The problem of "the stuff" from which symbols are forged and how they become public property is tangled and mooted. In *Natural Symbols* (1973), Mary Douglas shows the power of the human body as a source of metaphor. But in a wider sense, all symbols are "natural" because they are created from aspects of shared social experience. In a second sense, all symbols are natural in that they form a system and make sense only in the extended discourse. Within the social and historical experience of the users, the intersubjective meanings are not arbitrary but tied to the system in which they are embedded. Symbols have a logic and a vitality not fully reducible to the human organism and social groups. This is but another way of arguing for the analytical separation of culture, society, and personality as systems.

12

Recruitment to Monasticism among the Sherpas

R O B E R T A. P A U L 🙠

In his major work on problems of psychological anthropology, religion, and Buddhism, *Buddhism and Society* (1982a), as well as in other works too numerous to mention here, Spiro addresses himself to the complex relationship of personal character and individual motivation to social and cultural systems by examining the austere doctrines of Theravada Buddhism as these are understood and lived by real Burmans. His psychologically sophisticated depiction of the personality of Burmese Buddhists, particularly monks, combined with his Weberian approach to sociological and cultural aspects of religion, stands as a model of how the social sciences, or the humane studies generally, are to combine the study of individual lived experience with the larger patterns which social and cultural theory have made plain to our view.

Encouraged by Spiro, I have taken an interest in the writings of Freud, convinced of the inescapable power of his analyses. But committed also, like Spiro, to the traditions and insights of cultural anthropology (especially as these were so well represented at Chicago), I saw the need for a comprehensive approach and finally reached a position not far from the one described by Spiro in his recent autobiographical study (1978b). Recognizing the need for a theory which preserves both the unity and the diversity of human experience, I espoused a "generative" model of psyche and culture which I put to use in my own analysis of Tibetan culture (1982). In that work, I employed a system which used Freudian premises, stated formally as core or deep structural "axioms," from which, through a set of transformations derived from my study of symbolic anthropology and structuralism, could be derived in demonstrably regular ways the manifold universe of intracultural and even intercultural diversity.

In that study I deliberately concentrated my attention on cultural symbolism alone and even concluded with the remark that my cultural analysis could well be valid even in the absence of supporting data concerning individuals—indeed, even in the presence of contradictory data from that arena. I intended to defend the independence of cultural analysis, fending off any attempt to make its validity rest on material external to it.

In fact, however, the evidence from the study of individual psychodynamics is neither absent nor contradictory, and therefore I wish in this chapter to present a review of my essential findings concerning an important aspect of individual action, namely the choice of religious roles in Sherpa society and, more particularly, the decision to take monastic vows.

As I argued in my book, there are in contemporary Sherpa society four possible religious roles open to men, in addition of course to the role of the layman. (For a variety of reasons, my remarks here pertain only to Sherpa males. I am unable to speak with comparable authority on the matter of female religious roles.) Though of very unequal status, these four roles—those of the monk, shaman, married lama, and reincarnate lama—do form what I regard as a reasonably coherent conceptual system, as I demonstrated elsewhere (1982). In this chapter I wish to concentrate primarily on the role of monks, since both from my own theoretical perspective and from the Sherpas' point of view this is the most marked and in some ways the most salient category. From my psychodynamic viewpoint, the lifelong commitment to sexual abstinence demands some investigation into its underlying psychology and motivation. For the Sherpas, at the time of the ethnographic present from which I speak, monasticism is considered the most orthodox and appropriate outlet for authentic religious expression.

That the world is divided into monks and nonmonks in Sherpa consciousness is indicated by the fact that the common expression for the decision to become a monk is "not to take a wife" or "not to have a wedding." The monastic vow is thus equal to but opposite from marriage in status: on taking his vow, a man receives the fair share of his inheritance from his father which would otherwise be his on the completion of his marriage. This culturally given conceptual clarity—a true binary opposition existing in ethnographic reality—together with the equally clear distinction with respect to sexual behavior—yes or no—presents an advantageous research opportunity for the investigation of possible correlations between significant life history events, their presumed psychodynamic consequences, and subsequent adult behavior as reflected in career choice.

Of particular advantage is the fact that we are relieved of the necessity of having to perform our own evaluation and classification along some scale or other of observable adult actions: these have already been nicely sorted out for us by the informants themselves, who will have voted with their feet, as it were, through their choice of an adult career. If we can link certain childhood or developmentally important events with subsequent role choices, then our argument will have a certain inherent plausibility as long as we grant the fundamental premise that something of some significance must be causing decisions of such diametrically opposed import for the sexual life.

In order to understand fully what it means for a Sherpa man to choose to become a monk, it is necessary to survey some features of the monastic institutions in socioeconomic and cultural terms. Indeed, one aspect of the motivation to enter the monastery—the economic one—demands immediate attention. Unlike their counterparts in much of pre-1959 Tibet, Sherpa monasteries provide no financial support for their inmates, or if they do, it is only to buy them tea or to sustain them during the performance of a particular ritual. Sherpa monks must buy their own living quarters at the monastery, purchase their own books and equipment, pay for their own instruction, and support themselves in all other ways. The monasteries by and large possess no communal lands, herds, vineyards, or whatever else may be conjured up by the contemplation of their Western equivalents; or if they do have a communal business, largely limited to trading and money-lending, this is supposed to be done by officials using monastery funds alone, which are not for group distribution. (There is one exception: the monastery called Spyi-dbang, near the town of Phaphlu in the Solu Valley, does provide all its inmates with a stipend.)

It follows from what I have just said that Sherpa monasticism is not normally open as an option to anyone who does not inherit a reasonable amount of property. In the normal, case, what happens is that a monk, who is supposed to be prohibited from agricultural and manual labor except in the service of the monastery itself, lets out his portion of his share of the family estate to tenant farmers or else has it worked by his brothers or other relatives, who then support him financially with profits from the sale of his crops. In practice, many monks do work their own lands, as well as trade, lend money, and so forth, to make ends meet.

Monks are also paid for the services they render to the public, which consist principally in presiding over the very extensive funeral ceremonies which punctuate village life. These are frequent, given the number of communities served by a local monastery, and according to a general Sherpa value, the more monks chanting at a funeral, the better. The sponsors of these events provide the monks with sustenance while they are engaged and also with some cash payment. While this income is not very high, neither, it must be recalled, are the monk's expenses.

Frugal living is widely considered by Sherpas to be the great attraction of being a monk (apart from the spiritual benefits); one has no family to support and hence virtually no major expenses beyond the purchase of a house at the monastery. Often enough, too, monastic living quarters are passed on by inheritance within a family, for instance from paternal uncle to nephew. Having no family, furthermore, the monk has the freedom to come and go as he pleases, liberty that most Sherpa laymen envy.

In summary, then, there is indeed a perceived economic motivation to joining a monastery, insofar as it liberates one from the burdens and debts of family life. On the other hand, though, it is by no means a free lunch, nor is it a viable option for someone from a poor family, except in the rare case where he might be supported by some charitable benefactor, as occasionally happens. Sherpa monasticism thus differs from the monasticism of traditional Tibet in that it cannot serve as an avenue of career advancement for upwardly mobile, talented, but poor or low-born men.

Another major economic difference between Sherpa and Tibetan monasticism is that Sherpa monks do not beg for alms—they are too smart for that, knowing that begging would not be well received. As one monk put it to me, Sherpa monks refrain from begging so as not to impose on the laity the sin of refusing to give. Some rich families regularly make voluntary charitable donations to monastaries, but these amounts do not constitute a major source of support in comparison with the state support and general almsgiving which characterized Tibetan monasticism in its florescence.

A family can also make a major contribution to a monastery by giving it a son. Sherpa cultural wisdom says that a family with three or more sons ought to send one of them to a monastery. All other things being equal, the middle son is customarily expected to be the first candidate to take the vows. By sending a son to the monastery his parents enjoy the economic advantage of reducing the amount by which the family estate needs to be subdivided, since the remaining sons can in effect use the monk's land. Having, as I said, relatively low expenses, a monastic son or brother is not a serious burden on a family with land and brothers. And of course, in addition to its economic return, the commitment of a son to the monastery rewards the father in terms of merit which will be credited to his own account in the reckonings of karma.

Obviously, in cases where the decision to send a son to the monastery originates with a father with several sons, the father's rather than the son's motivation needs to be explained (though the son need not bow to his father's wishes; nor, having taken the vow, will he remain if it does not suit him). Often such a decision on a father's part is clearly influenced by karmic considerations, for example in the case of a deathbed wish through which he hopes to achieve a favorable rebirth. Similarly a father may send a son to a monastery after some major setback or misfortune in his own life. Fathers of several sons will often choose whichever of their sons they deem to have the least prospects of success, by reason of personality or intelligence, in the outside world. They calculate that such sons will be better off earning merit for everybody concerned than trying to make a go of enterprise in the real world.

It should be mentioned, apropos of the force of paternal wishes, that no one can force a man to take a monastic vow against his will and that monasteries are supposed to accept only those recruits whose decision is voluntarily taken and endorsed by significant relatives (including not only the father and mother but even the wife or former wife if he happens to have one).

Sherpa monasteries are relatively unstructured institutions. They do have bureaucratic offices which supervise their religious and institutional functioning (for descriptions, see Fürer-Haimendorf 1964 and Paul 1970). But on the whole, monks are left alone to mind their own business except during the performance of a monasterywide ritual or during group confessionals, which occur every fifteen days. Monks are not expected to take meals communally. Each monk arranges for his own instruction and practice in religion, sometimes from a teacher who is not even an inmate of the monastery. Monks accept commissions to perform funerals as need or interest dictates, though the monastery administration makes some effort to arrange for commissions.

Monks are encouraged to have as little to do with ordinary village life as possible and especially to avoid unnecessary contact with women. Some monks are great scholars; some are pious hermits. Most are rather ordinary people, as one might expect, and some are worldly, as can be imagined. A few notorious ones have used the red robe as a cloak behind which to engage in indiscretions, from incest and fornication to armed robbery.

In general, Sherpas take an ambivalent attitude toward the monastic role. On the one hand, official doctrine grants monks high spiritual status. In addition, monks are the object of envy by laymen, since the comparative ease and freedom in which they live is perceived to outweigh the rigors of their celibate regime. On the other hand, the public finds something uncanny about monks, having to do with their liminal status and their close association, both symbolic and real (through funerals), with death. Nor do the Sherpas lack skepticism and realism about the extent to which sanctity is prevalent in the monasteries. As one proverb has it, "if living high up were meritorious, birds would go to heaven" (Sherpa monasteries are located at higher altitudes than villages); "if wearing red were meritorious, cows would go to heaven." (In other words, the outward trappings of piety by no means guarantee its inner presence.)

As for the strictness with which celibacy is actually observed, I cannot speak with certainty on the subject. Opportunities for liaisons exist, both

258

with village women and with nuns in nearby nunneries. Monasteries with nunneries nearby regularly lose inmates through elopement. Being found out would be quite a scandal, and anything other than the most furtive affair will usually mean that a monk must leave the region. But, informants noted, if a monk wanted to have sexual adventures without marrying or leaving the monastery, the obvious course of action would be for him to direct his attentions to his brother's wife. (This suggestion indicates that monasticism and fraternal polyandry are closely related conceptually and in practice.)

The courses of study available to monks are divided into three main branches: the practice of ascetic discipline, embodied in the various vows of abstinence; the academic study of theological and philosophical texts and commentaries; and the mastery of mystical power through initiation. These are called, respectively, 'dul-ba (Sanskrit *vinaya*); *mdo* (Sanskrit *sutra*); and *rgyud* (Sanskrit *tantra*). The first, the 'dul-ba, or "subduing," is considered by Sherpas to be the essential and defining feature of monasticism. The other two paths may be pursued or not, but one cannot pursue them and still be a monk without also practicing 'dul-ba. (It is just this that monks hold against married lamas.) Sherpas also generally value ascetic discipline most highly. Great scholarship and mystical power in themselves are not valued as much if saintly practice does not accompany them.

The initiated novice takes a vow consisting of 10 abstentions; higher grades call for 36 and finally 250 or so. A fully ordained monk is called a *dge-slong* (Sanskreit *bhikku*) and is entitled to wear a distinctive yellow sash. Ordinary monks are called *grwa-pa*, or "student."

Such then, briefly, is the institution of Sherpa monasticism. What kind of people find it congenial? Spiro, in his characterization of the psychology of Burmese monks, suggests that narcissism plays a major role. Certainly, given my description of the Sherpa monastery as an institution in which men live isolated not only from the world but even to a degree from each other, narcissism seems at least initially plausible. Particularly in recent years, however, the term "narcissism" has become freighted with a great number of meanings and has inspired arguments within numerous different spheres of discourse; limitations of space preclude any attempt to sort them out here.

I will therefore simplify the issue by noting the explicit ways in which the cultural expectations and values surrounding the role of monk emphasize isolation and self-sufficiency in opposition to participation in larger wholes of any kind. In my view individual humans, like everything else in the universe, constitute themselves both as discrete, autonomous, self-contained entities and as parts which together with other parts join together in some kind of patterned, systemic relationship to form a more encompassing discrete unit—itself subject to the same dichotomous view. Human life involves balancing the claims of these sometimes contradictory imperatives. I list here some of the larger wholes in which human organisms participate and show how the practices of the Sherpa monk attempt to minimize, deny, or offset their influence, so that the monk may, as they say, "fare lonely as rhinoceros."

1. The food chain. Any organism, including a person, is simply one node in an endless metabolic process of intake and output of organic matter-energy as it transforms itself in a boundless self-devouring and self-sustaining process. But Sherpa monks are expected to eat only one small meal a day, and fasting is a major element in all meditation practices. In popular Sherpa opinion, the ability to fast and subsist on little is the most often mentioned praiseworthy characteristic of monks—especially given the enormous importance placed on the intake of large quantities of food in normal social life (for more on this subject, see Ortner 1970, 1978, 1981). A layman speaking well of a monk whose piety he admires will typically hold up the tip of his little finger and say "he only eats this much food a day; but we lay people are always greedy, always wanting more food."

At the other end of the alimentary cycle, monks symbolically try to minimize the need to eliminate waste; it is said that the dge-slongs defecate little or not at all or that their waste is so pure that it is not polluting. They carry flasks of holy water with which they ritually purify themselves after defecation. Some great religious virtuosos of legend and lore are described as having been so holy that, if they drank beer, they would urinate the same beer, fit to drink. In any event, it is being asserted that digestion does not occur: the person and the beer or food have no influence on each other—in other words, the monk is not really part of the food chain at all.

A similar point can be made about breathing, one of the most basic forms of interaction with the external world as "not-self." As is well known, most meditative systems rely on the effort to control breathing.

2. The DNA. Each individual is the phenotypic realization of a possibility inherent in the genotype, carried in the DNA and existing across countless generations in time. But the distinctive feature of the monastic role from this standpoint is the vow of celibacy—in other words, the choice not to pass on the DNA which one has inherited. At the same time, in taking a new name, identity, and clothing, and upon monastic initiation, one goes as far as possible toward symbolically denying biological descent from one's parents. The doctrine of karma, likewise, places responsibility for one's past, present, and future destiny in one's own hands rather than on descent or lineage, as in the lay Sherpa world. The monk, in emphasizing karma over descent, thereby asserts self-authorship.

Abstention from any form of sexual relation with others is also clearly a denial or avoidance of relation and an assertion of self-containedness. Masturbation and involuntary ejaculation are also polluting because of the violation of body boundaries. (The Sherpas are by no means as concerned as are Indians about the loss of vital power through ejaculation, but the idea is nonetheless present.) In short, one should contain and control one's semen, not be controlled and transcended by it.

3. Social exchange. A person is a member of a community, which, as we know, is held together by, and expresses and realizes itself through, mutual rights, obligations, duties, expectations, and of course the exchange and continuous flow of goods, services, symbols, and partners in marriage.

Monks live in the most isolated communities possible and do not participate in the social life of the village (at least in theory) except to officiate at funerals. This fact is itself significant, since funerals may be seen as rituals of separation of the deceased from the lay world and initiation into the world of death—the void or intermediate state, from which, if they are lucky, they will not return.

Monks do not participate in marriage or in any other form of exchange (except trade for business), nor do they have obligations or expectations with respect to the laity. They may accept gifts freely given to them, but as a token of their nonreciprocity they are not supposed to say "thank you."

Among themselves, monks try to live out an idea based on antistructure, communitas, and mechanical solidarity, in which sociality rests on the identity of atomic parts, bound by "narcissistic" bonds of like to like, but not on exchange, obligation, or organic solidarity. Like most such "antistructural" men's groups, they rather paradoxically pursue at least the trappings of bureaucracy and hierarchy (see Turner 1969).

I have observed elsewhere (1982) that being a monk is a little like being stuck in the middle of an initiation ceremony; it is a liminal life. The rebirth which in the lay world occurs vicariously through the birth of children (with whom, in Sherpa society, one in fact identifies through the practice of teknonymy) for monks occurs only after death, passage into the next life. The great symbolic importance of reincarnate lamas has to with their ability to act out the ideal scenario of being reborn into the same identity.

4. History. Temporal flow and the mutability of all things is denied by the notion that one could, ideally, be born and die only superficially, while some essential identity remains unchanged. Over against the changeable flow of history, monasticism asserts a stable, unchanging truth which endures and in which, in some sense, nothing ever really happens. The recitation of texts and the performance of rituals are actions in which innovation, change, and creativity are discouraged in favor of the exact and perfect replication of an enduring archetype. In short, this is the attempt to live life as much as possible in illo tempore, to use Eliade's evocative phrase.

5. Karma. The doctrine of nonaction is the ultimate statement that it

is desirable not to interact with the world in any way. The cost of such a posture might seem to be a great one: the whole world. But the gain is the affirmation of one's narcissism, grandiosity, or call it what you will: the myth that one has generated oneself and is responsible to no one else, in the most literal sense.

The opposition which I described earlier as existing in Sherpa society between becoming a monk and marrying may thus be reinterpreted in the light of the foregoing discussion as an opposition between the ideal of autonomy and the idea of relationship and participation in larger wholes. Marriage, which establishes the domestic sphere within which eating, copulating, reproducing, exchanging, earning, paying, living, and dying will all take place, is clearly the opposite of monasticism on all these scores. Given this very clear choice, how are we to understand why a man opts for one or the other?

To grasp this point, we must bear in mind that such choices are made not on the basis of theories and abstract ideals and principles but in a field of powerfully lived dynamics within which the opposing tendencies to reproduce, eat, exchange, and so forth and not to do these things are felt not as theoretically alternative possibilities but as pressing imperative and self-evident realities. The economics of these two opposing vectors in the field of force within which life is lived is the province of the psychoanalytic conflict model of the psyche, which uses metaphoric concepts such as instincts and the agencies of id, ego, and superego to try to characterize the inner conflicts. (It is fashionable in some circles these days to regard Freud's "energy" model of the mind as crude and outdated. I cannot understand this attitude, since contemporary physics teaches us that everything, including matter itself, is a transformation of energy, the stuff of which the universe is made. Why the same should not also be so in human life, as indeed it is so clearly felt to be in any but the most willfully perverse act of self-observation, continues to elude me. See Spiro's lively remarks on this subject [1979c].)

One of the most eloquent and useful descriptions of the struggle between the conflicting imperatives, using the language of ego psychology, was made by Anna Freud (1937). According to her, the ego strives for integrity in the face of the onslaught of instinctual demands which present themselves with renewed force at adolescence, threatening to undo the still fragile ego which has only recently been laboriously constructed. She describes the variable mood characteristic of adolescents, their often exaggerated asceticism, their idealism, and their intellectualism, together with their rapid swings to the other ends of the spectrum, as the symptoms of this fierce contest.

So the question then becomes: which impulse will prevail in the psychic economy of any given individual? My strategy in answering begins with my choice as paradigm, from all the ways in which individuals can be linked to others in large wholes, of the act of sexual intercourse. I justify this choice first and foremost because, as I have said, the Sherpas themselves provide us with the model according to which the world is divided on just this basis between lay and monastic. While it is true that a monk vows to abstain from some activities other than the sexual, undoubtedly the sexual area is culturally and psychodynamically the central and crucial one. A monk may fast or not and study or meditate or not, but he is still a monk. A monk who engages in sexual intercourse, however, is by that token no longer a monk. The cultural expression of this view has it that breaking any of the other vows is like cutting the branches of a tree: the branches may grow back, and in any case the tree itself will survive. But breaking the vow of celibacy is like cutting the trunk of a tree: the whole tree is thereby destroyed.

To specify further the terms of the problem as I understand it, monastic versus nonmonastic choice results when the imperative of object-directed sexual libido does or does not overcome the opposing imperative toward self-sufficiency and isolation, what I have loosely been calling narcissism. This issue comes to a head in what I called, in my study of Tibetan and Sherpa symbolism (1982), the succession crisis, when, in adolescence and young maturity, a boy passes from junior male to senior male, the distinguishing marks of senior status being legitimate access to females for the purpose of reproduction and political authority, that is, decision-making influence. Junior male status is, of course, defined by the absence of these features. The succession crisis requires that the junior male must symbolically kill and be killed by a senior male or males but that both be equally swayed by the contradictory command not to kill, spare, or unite with each other in identification and union. In this core paradox I saw the generating force of much cultural symbolism, including religious symbolism.

According to my analysis, only a magical hero can solve this insoluble puzzle, and so such heroes are posited by religion to enable the ordinary man to weather the crisis under the hero's tutelage. In Sherpa culture, the victorious hero is epitomized by one of the two great gods of the religion, the tantric master Guru Rimpoche, who is thought to have brought the Nying-ma-pa doctrine to Tibet in the eighth century and who now has divine status. The other great god of the pantheon, the bodhisattva Spyan-ras-gzigs, epitomizes what I take to be the ideal model of the opposite choice, the monastic one.

The monk, I argue, instead of passing through the succession crisis by becoming a disciple of Guru Rin-po-che, turns away from the struggle and, turning around, as it were, introjects as his "ego ideal" not a senior male but an idealized image of himself as asexual youth, physically embodied in the childlike and asexual reincarnate lamas and in the benign god of ambiguous sexuality, Spyan-ras-gzigs. If the monk and the layman (identified for present purposes with the tantrist, or married lama) represent the division of Sherpa society, then the reincarnate lama and the shaman represent another binary pair. The shaman is forever locked in the midst of the succession struggle itself, in a role characterized by violent and self-assertive conflict with malign supernatural beings. The reincarnate lama, in contrast, represents, in his benign, asexual tranquillity, the union of opposites, including those of junior and senior male. If the shaman is frozen permanently at the succession crisis, the moment when junior males turn into senior males, the reincarnate lama straddles the opposite moment—the moment of rebirth when dying senior males are reborn as junior males.

The married lama and his client the layman then represent senior males in this scheme, while the monks are those who never achieve senior status but live out a career which symbolically transforms the status of "junior" male into a valued role.

It follows from this model that the factor which determines whether one undergoes the succession crisis or avoids it is the strength of the fear which the psychic and symbolic conflicts of the crisis engender; in other words, just how much one is afraid of being killed and/or castrated. If one has the audacity to act on one's heterosexual libidinal impulses, one encounters the retribution of death and/or castration at the hands of senior males. At the same time, and from a different direction, one also risks death and dismemberment by undergoing the dissolution of the solid scaffolding of ego-boundedness and separation built up throughout the youthful process of separation-individuation and culminating in adolescence. In short, then, the central contest is between the impulse toward achieving senior status, powered by sexual energy, and a fear of psychic, spiritual, and physical disaster if one makes the attempt.

Women as objects of desire tempt one out of isolation and into the succession crisis. But because this psychic experience is frightening, a woman is perceived as a dangerous being who can take on a tempting guise but who is malevolent and dangerous in that she can lure one into a position fraught with peril and dread. The act of sex with women is therefore connected with the anxiety and nausea associated with castration and death.

And so, to return to our still unanswered question, what predisposes a man either to overcome this fear and go through the ordeal or else to solve the problem by fleeing from temptation, a temptation rendered resistible because of the strong negative feelings surrounding it?

Having thus clarified the question sufficiently, I can without further ado proceed to the answer. The single most strongly correlated life event differentiating monks from nonmonks is the experience of the death of one or both parents at some time prior to the time when a decision for either monasticism or marriage must be made—that is, before the succession crisis.

This correlation is so strong that I may state it as a general rule: a young man at least one of whose parents has died prior to his career decision will choose to become a monk except in clearly specifiable cases where clearly specifiable counterrules must be invoked. Without the presence of one or more of the conditions specified in these counterrules, there are *no* exceptions to this rule of which I was aware in my (limited) field experience. (The *ns* are so small, however, that I see no point in statistical analysis.)

Four conditions can offset the weight of parental death in monastic career choice.

1. If a young man's parent or parents have died, but he is too poor to become a monk, then he obviously cannot and will not do so. Since in most cases monks must be self-supporting, some otherwise likely candidates must, however much they may wish to enter a monastery, work at agriculture, herding, wage labor, or some other trade either for themselves or for other family members, such as, for example, a widowed mother.

2. In cases where a man's parent or parents have died, but he himself is physically ill or deformed, he may not become a monk because the rules of monastic life strictly specify that candidates must be in sound physical condition. The rules are enforced to exclude the physically handicapped, the mentally handicapped, chronic tuberculars, and others.

In these two situations, I was acquainted with a number of people fitting my descriptions who made it clear to me that, but for poverty or infirmity, they would have chosen to be monks. In one case, a handicapped man lived his life at home exactly like a monk. He dressed like a monk, obeyed monastic rules, and would have become a monk in two seconds except that no monastery would have him.

3. If a man has lost one or both parents but is the only surviving son, or the only surviving son who is not already a monk, then he will, in many cases, not become a monk, since the result would be the dying out of the line and the passage of the patrimonial estate into alien hands. But even in some cases of this kind, I knew of men who chose to become monks rather than heed considerations of lineage and property. In every case I knew of in which a set of brothers had lost parents, all but one of the brothers, or in some cases all the brothers, became monks.

4. In a few cases, a young man who has experienced parental death becomes a shaman rather than a monk. I will briefly discuss this case shortly.

I should note that, while my central rule and its four counterrules are, to the best of my knowledge, iron-clad, the converse does not follow. One cannot be sure that a man who has not lost a parent will not become a monk, nor is it the case that a man who is a monk has necessarily lost a parent.

After all, people do or do not become monks for other reasons, and as I shall argue, parental death is in any event only the most extreme and clear-cut situation in which the kind of psychodynamics I describe may be expected to develop.

How are we to interpret this empirical regularity in the data? In the first place, the death of a parent in youth, especially in early youth, is obviously a form of failed object relations, a lesson in the danger of investing libido in external objects, and a bitter experience of the loss of love from the superego. Freud argued that the ultimate fear with respect to death and castration has to do with the loss of love by the superego or the parent upon whom it is modeled, because only this love defends one against the expression of the other, wrathful aspect of the superego.

The result, then, is a sense that attachment of any kind is futile, dangerous, and untrustworthy; association of experience of loss, grief, and rage with the idea of relationship in general; absence of "basic trust"; and a strong sense of isolation and fear stemming from the experience of the loss of love of the most highly valued other. The connection between these feelings and attitudes and the monastic role as I have described it should be clear enough.

The absence of a loving parent also deprives the young child of the atmosphere of total support, security, and protection which allows for the necessary illusions of independence and self-sufficiency upon which the faith that permits the growth of the fragile ego rests. The ego therefore requires extra protection and is unable to withstand the blows awaiting it in the conflicts of adolescence, with its instinctual assaults on the ego and the threat of ego dissolution.

Furthermore, the absence of a real parent deprives the child of a figure against whom to test his initial grandiose ideas of self and object and thereby reduce the exaggerated images of infancy to human scale. Parental absence denies the child the opportunity for reality testing and thus allows fantasies, including those of separation and castration from infancy, to flourish unchecked. A child who has lost a parent does not usually simply ignore the absence but, on the contrary, preserves in the psychic space reserved for that person a caricature, often split into extremes of good and bad such as characterize infantile mentation.

This statement is all the more true since, in my experience, step-relationships among the Sherpas are not particularly well designed to re-assure stepchildren and provide them with alternative sources of love and assurance. Stepchildren I knew were not made to feel on an equal footing with their half-siblings or were induced to forget that they and their step-parents were in some sense strangers, even adversaries. Therefore, my rule about parental death goes so far as to discriminate among half-siblings. For example, there was a man with three grown sons, two by his first wife who had died early, the third by his second wife, who was still alive. As the rule demands, the two older sons both became monks, while the youngest brother became not only a layman but the proprietor of a tea and beer shop. It is hard to imagine a more striking contrast than that between the genial tavern host and his two gloomy half-brothers, who were among his best customers.

Next, the death of a parent is generally experienced by a child as a rejection or an abandonment (no matter that this charge is of course usually not justified by reality) and, more particularly, as a rejection caused by some fault or crime of the child's. The anger turns inward, and the feelings of guilt and unworthiness which result seem perfectly designed to produce a personality which will feel at home in the monastic role.

The situation is exacerbated by the fact that children may regularly be expected to harbor strong death wishes against their parents, so that the death of a parent may, in a child's imagination, be understood as the ful-fillment of the child's own wish, thus making the child a guilty parricide and the author of his or her own loss. Once again, such a dynamic would be consistent with a self-punitive and melancholy attitude, a fear of and fascination with "magical powers," and an association of love with death in an uncommonly strong way.

Finally, in the case of the death of a father, it would be the case not only that the death wishes would have Oedipal components—this point follows by definition—but also that the boy would be deprived of a positive figure with whom to identify and upon which to construct his own ego, ego ideal, and controlling superego in a balanced way. In the case of the death of the mother, it would be more likely that the psychic traumata would involve complications in the realm associated more specifically with the formation of object relations and separation-individuation. But both these instances would produce the outcome whereby the adolescent ego lacked sufficient strength to risk its integrity in the upcoming succession crisis. These observations are further complicated by the fact that, in the reverse Oedipus complex, which every boy experiences as a matter of course, the roles are reversed so that the father is the object of desire and the mother the hated rival. It thus emerges that the death of either the father or the mother complies with Oedipal wishes and fears.

In summary, then, the psychodynamics involved would seem to in-clude distrust of libidinal relations, absence of realistic parental role models to modify infantile images and provide positive objects of identification, grandiosity, aggression turned against the self, and self-punitive ideas un-tempered by ready resources of love. This picture is clearly appropriate for those in whose psychic balance the fear of death and punishment outweighs the threat to self which seems to be entailed by the succession crisis.

It is relevant to repeat here a point I have made elsewhere (1982), namely, that the fear of death which I have been discussing is, as it is experienced in the psyche, less a fear of death as nonbeing than it is of death followed by a punitive afterlife. Indeed, Buddhism regards the inability of all souls simply to die as the source of endless sorrow and proposes to heal this sorrow by teaching the way to nirvana, that is, genuine death as nonbeing. The fear of death which motivates an overriding concern with one's behavior in this life as a preparation for death and judgment is the fear of dying into a nightmarish state of separation, guilt, and suffering, not of cessation.

I trust I need hardly observe that my interpretation concerns dynamics which are for the most part unconscious, and the ability or inability of respondents to confirm them is neither here nor there. There is, nonetheless, what I consider to be quite strong evidence in the life history reports of Sherpa monks and others of Oedipal conflicts centering on the passage into maturity. In addition to the death of parents, the other most striking feature of monastic lives as reported to me is the presence in them of an episode so common and so distinctive as to be considered a social fact rather than a chance historical event. This is the unsuccessful early marriage of the boy at the behest of his father, mother, or guardian—though it is most often the father.

This story as it is usually told occurs when the boy is somewhere between ten and fourteen years old. His father (or whoever is responsible for him) arranges a marriage with a woman, a stranger to the boy and usually considerably older. Almost invariably, the informant claims that the motive was not pure solicitude for the boy's happiness but a more selfish concern on the part of the elders: the wish to add an extra hand to the work force of the households. (I should mention that Sherpa women do not only domestic work but almost all varieties of garden, pastoral, and field labor except plowing.) A more covert implication of the situation may be that, since the boy is really too young to be a husband, the woman is to be a potential or real sexual partner for the father as well.

As the story goes, the woman, being older and either more developed or more experienced or both, makes sexual advances to the young husband, who responds with fear and humiliation. Several outcomes are possible: the son may insist on having the wife "sent back," as the saying goes; or the father may prevail, and the marriage may become permanent; or the boy, in desperation, may run away from home, perhaps to a monastery, perhaps to some Sherpa settlement far from Solu-Khumbu, in Tibet, India, or the Kathmandu Valley.

In cases where the girl is sent back or the boy runs away, he very often turns to monasticism. In cases where the marriage holds, in most instances the boy becomes either a married lama, by way of a compromise between his religious inclinations and his married state, or a shaman. (I describe such a case at length elsewhere, in Paul 1988.)

Several elements of this story highlight the specifically Oedipal components. The first is that the boy is young, sexually immature and inexperienced, and psychologically unequipped to respond successfully to a sexual opportunity. He therefore suffers a blow to his narcissism.

Second, the women are typically older than the boy and serve an equivocal function between the boy and his father. This situation repeats the earlier childhood Oedipal situation, just as the boy's inability to perform is a replay of earlier Oedipal failure.

While this episode was by no means universally reported to me by every Sherpa cleric I interviewed, it was told to me almost exclusively by those who had become monks, shamans, or married lamas. Although Sherpa marriages are in fact typically arranged by parents and often do involve young boys and older women, no adult man who had chosen a lay career related the story to me as having any serious importance. The religious professionals, on the other hand, not only related the episode but assigned it decisive influence on the course of their lives.

It is not possible on the basis of the information available to judge whether these episodes should be understood as causal or symptomatic with respect to the personality dynamics leading to a religious role choice, nor indeed is it ever possible to ascertain the extent to which they are historical events and the extent to which they form an embellishment or fantasy added to his narrative by the informant, with the benefit of hindsight. In any event, however, they do serve the methodological purpose of demonstrating that Oedipal dynamics of the kind I have suggested ought to be present are indeed there to be elicited from Sherpa informants and do have psychic and social reality of some kind or other, perhaps better to be determined by subsequent research.

A number of other considerations support my present contention that the choice between being a monk and a nonmonk in Sherpa society may be understood as a binary opposition, presented to every maturing male at the moment of succession to senior male status, and that the succession crisis requires the boy to challenge the authority of existing senior males, most usually his own father, for the purpose of winning for himself legitimate heterosexual relations but at the cost of reactivating earlier Oedipal dynamics, as well as generating new ones, in which the threats of death, castration, ego dissolution, and guilt are inevitable; and that, given this choice, the outcome will be determined by the predominance of the drives either of object libido or of fear of punishment and narcissistic concern with ego survival, the final outcome being dictated by unresolved Oedipal conflicts most typically resulting from the experience of parental death.

First, this analysis is entirely consistent with the detailed explication of Sherpa and Tibetan cultural productions which I undertook in *The Tibetan Symbolic World* (1982). That study left little room for doubt that the succession scenario as I have described it is indeed vitally operative in generating the symbolic forms of Tibetan culture. The method by which I arrived at this conclusion—a structural symbolic analysis carried out entirely on the level of cultural symbolism, with no reference to individuals or actual personality dynamics—complements the present study, in which the same result is reached through the examination of individual psychodynamics revealed in patterns of actual behavior in a clear-cut situation. Taken together, and with the added perspective on the matter provided by Paul (1988), which considers the psychology of a single Sherpa shaman in detail and further corroborates the present analysis, I lay before the public a case which, while still only circumstantial, it is true, strikes me as being persuasive.

Second, since in anthropology, as elsewhere, prediction is often proclaimed to be the hallmark of science, I will simply mention that the various considerations discussed here have enabled me to predict with a high degree of accuracy which boys among those whom I first knew in the field many years ago would subsequently become monks and to say why on the basis of my direct knowledge of the circumstances of the various childhoods.

Third, thanks very much to the efforts of Spiro (1982c), among others, it is every day becoming clearer that the old standard anthropological objections to the idea of the importance and universality of the Oedipus complex are being overcome, and a more realistic picture, consistent both with ethnographic data, on the one hand, and with our rapidly improving knowledge of primate behavior and the biological bases of behavior, on the other, is developing in the discipline.

Fourth, my contention is based, obviously, on direct knowledge of a number of actual cases. While it has not been possible to cite them here as corroboration, I may refer the reader to the account I have given elsewhere of the actual people and situation upon which I base my thinking (Paul 1970).

Fifth, it may help matters if I clarify the status of parental death as I see it in relation to Oedipal dynamics, since while not all monks have experienced parental death, yet I would argue that the institution is still "about" the struggle between junior and senior males, which in any individual life we experience as the Oedipus complex. I view the death of a parent as simply the most extreme and clearly observable instance in which a family constellation results in intergenerational relations of anger, distance,

coldness, or hostility not equally offset by a flow of love, support, and identification. This development can occur in plenty of other circumstances; for
example, when the personality features of the parents and/or their actions
have the same results. In many cases it was perfectly clear to me from
observation of father and son that a monk had entered a monastery in part
to escape an authoritarian father, whose personality and behavior inspired
fear and resentment. While it might appear that the difference between a
parent who dies and one who is too present as an overbearing, controlling
force is very great, the underlying problem is the same: the forces stressing
conflict and distance outweigh those leading to love, identification, and a
realistic human-scale relationship.

The main reason for omitting parental personality from my examination
of the factors leading to monastic role choice is that including it would involve
the very problem of scaling, diagnosis, or clinical assessment of hard-to-
determine personality factors, which is just what the feature of parental death
avoids by being so clearly observable and so unambiguous. I therefore use
parental death as a prime indicator of unresolved intergenerational conflicts
because it is the clearest; but my broader argument is that the family constellation itself, not parental death per se, is the essential determining factor.

But while I have been stressing the personality dynamics of potential
monks mainly with an eye toward the ascetic and isolating aspects of Sherpa
monasticism, the institution has other features as well which require mention. These have to do with the fact that, at least until the advent of the
mountaineering and tourist trade, the serious study of religion was by far
the most interesting thing for a Sherpa to do if he had any interest in or
talent for intellectual or artistic matters. People who, on the basis of their
psychic dynamics, are attracted to the ascetic narcissism of the monastic life
are seemingly like people who find it rewarding to live in a world of books
and who appreciate the rich symbolism of religious iconography and ceremonial—rather than, say, a world monopolized by concerns of business, agriculture, labor, and debt.

There is a paradox here, however, since, in the explicit view of most
Sherpas, high intelligence is actually regarded as a distinct drawback for a
successful monastic career. The Sherpa word for intelligence, which is rendered in English as "cleverness," carries with it the connotation of "calcu-
lating, good at business and worldly affairs, but not particularly virtuous."
Intelligence in this sense is thus antithetical to a religious career. The quality
of character the Sherpas value in a monk is a good *sems* or, loosely, "soul";
and this is an ethical faculty rather than one of mind. There is, then, a good
reason why fathers prefer to send to the monastery boys who are decent
and earnest but intellectually slow and short on imagination. Since such boys
are not likely to make a great worldly success in any event, both they and

their parents perceive that the monastery gives them an opportunity to achieve something in life which they might not otherwise have.

On the other hand, unusually intelligent or artistic boys will often want to become monks, as I have just shown, while their fathers will have chosen them to succeed in the wider world because of precisely the same talents. Thus it is that the inmates of Sherpa monasteries may be characterized as both the most and the least enterprising and intelligent members of society. Those who are self-selecting, however, will tend to be in the former group, whereas those who have been selected by their fathers are more likely to fall into the latter category. This pattern explains, too, why there are monks who are successful and happy in their monastic lives but whose life shows no evidence of conflict with the father or the family.

I will very briefly summarize what I perceive to be the important patterns involved in the selection of the other religious roles available to Sherpa men. The role of the married lama has, as I have said, lost something of its charisma in Sherpa society. Traditionally it was passed from fathers to sons, most often in certain lineages known for this characteristic. This remains the case today, though the institution is less prevalent than it once was. In the cases I knew of in which a man from a nonlama lineage had taken on the role or had not inherited it from a senior patrilineal relative, there had invariably been a compromise between a son who wanted to become a monk and a father who had insisted on arranging a marriage for him and making it stick. In these cases too, as in monastic cases, the son's motivation included both ascetic personality factors and a fascination with the intellectual and symbolic aspects of religion, and of course, conflict with the father's will was a central feature in the situation.

The three male shamans I knew had all suffered parental death in their youth and had had unsuccessful arranged first marriages which ended in divorce but, taken as a group, had eventually had twelve wives among them: one, still in his twenties, had married twice, one had married three times, and one had had seven wives in all. It is not entirely clear to me why these men became shamans rather than monks, as my analysis of monastic choice suggests they should have done. But it is interesting that both shamans and monks deviate from the norm of marrying a single wife, the monks by not marrying at all, the shamans by marrying many times in succession. I have argued elsewhere (Paul 1988) that shamanism and monasticism may be seen as standing in the same relationship as a perversion and a neurosis; the one is based on acting out, the other on repressing the same conflict-producing impulse.

The shamanistic call is, in any event, not a voluntary choice, since the seizure signaling the onset of a shamanistic career is sent by the gods and is described by the informants themselves as a fit of insanity. The choice is, therefore, certainly an unconscious one. Perhaps we may say that it befalls those who *ought* to have become monks but who for some reason have not done so.

Like shamans, reincarnate lamas do not choose their role but are chosen at a very young age. Sherpas say that a reincarnate lama announces his true nature when he first begins to talk: instead of saying "mama" and "papa" like a typical child, he makes some reference in his speech to his past life, or quotes a sacred book, or makes some other unusual utterance. Such boys are, ideally, raised by their parents for another few years and then at about age eight are taken to the monastery, where they are trained in religion and are groomed for their future leadership role by the monks. (It is said that they learn very quickly, since they are being taught what they already knew in a past life.)

The reincarnate lama is a crucial personage in the symbolic configuration of monasticism. The institution coheres around his charismatic center, and he himself expresses many of the key symbols of the religion in his very nature. Standing at the opposite pole to the active figure of the tantric master, as well as to the wrathful and punitive male deities in which the Tibetan religion abounds, he is a completely self-contained, benign, asexual person who realizes the monastic goal of personal immortality by his ability to survive death and retain his personality. Whereas the symbolic figure of the tantric master expresses the idea of one who elects to participate in the wider world, with its limitations and complexities, and who triumphs there, the reincarnate lama epitomizes the monastic value of self-fulfillment through isolation from the world, and the generating of one's own satisfaction and salvation from one's own resources.

The reincarnate lama is regarded as a being filled with sacred power, or *dbang;* thanks to the boundless spiritual properties of this force, it overflows from him and becomes a source of sacred strength for the community as well. Monastic initiation is the transmission of dbang to the initiate, and originally, in theory, dbang erupts into the mortal realm mainly through the agency of reincarnate lamas.

It follows, then, that, to be effective in the role of reincarnate lama, a person ought to possess the character of a monk carried to a higher degree. He should be self-contained, "narcissistic" in the loose sense, and concerned about what Becker calls his *causa sui* project (Becker 1973). But he differs from the ordinary monk in that his self-absorption and grandiosity should make him not a bottomless pit of dependence and ego neediness but rather a person so utterly secure in his own superiority as to inspire confidence and respect in those around him.

Sherpa practice actually uses the techniques I would predict it ought to in producing such persons through socialization. That is, the socialization

Robert A. Paul

of reincarnate lamas forces upon the chosen candidate precisely the traumatic experience I have posited, loss of love and failure of parental relations, by taking the boy from the bosom of his family and the love of his mother and father at an early age. I have shown elsewhere (1982) that Buddhism as a salvation religion is fundamentally concerned with healing the wound of primary separation from the mother, and so the process of taking a monk from his family and raising him (sometimes over the family's objections) in a monastery ensures that he will experience in the core of his being the problematic which he is supposed to resolve.

At the same time, the socialization of reincarnate lamas gives back with the other hand what it has taken away with the first: whereas normal children suffer fatal narcissistic blows during their passage through the Oedipus complex and into middle childhood, in the course of which they accept, however reluctantly, their relatively powerless status and the destined failure of their most deeply cherished wishes and illusions, the reincarnate lama receives reinforcements for all his narcissistic and grandiose fantasies, delivered to him by no less an authority than the reality principle itself.

Even before he leaves home permanently, from the moment he is recognized, he begins to participate in religious ceremonial as the head of a congregation of monks. Few sights are more dramatic in all ethnography, I am sure, than that of a monastery full of grown men prostrating themselves before a two-year-old boy dressed in full ceremonial regalia and wielding the bell and thunderbolt weapon he owned in his previous life. Even his own mother and father pay homage to him, and he is treated in every way like a sovereign whose wish is someone's command.

One has but to imagine the effect this experience, repeated from the time he is two years old, will have on the lama's own conception of his place in the scheme of things to see how his narcissistic project differs from that of the ordinary mortal monk. He carries into adult life the unrepressed charisma that goes with the self-assured possession of psychic and spiritual omnipotence, born of the real fulfillment of the wishes to be center of the universe, and, indeed, to succeed in the dream of being author of one's own being.

The symbolism of the reincarnate lama thus expresses *in nuce* the profound wisdom of Buddhism: all worldly projects, all social ties, are ephemeral and will end in disappointment, pain, and sorrow, but it is possible to overcome these through the self-sufficiency that comes from nonaction and nonattachment. The reincarnate lama, in his person, exemplifies the hero who not only conquers death but survives the experience of the traumatic severance of family ties and nonetheless achieves tranquillity, self-sufficiency, and victory over the world with its temptations and sorrows.

274

13

Ritual Trance and Catharsis
A Psychobiological and Evolutionary Perspective

WILLIAM WEDENOJA

Ritual trance as a subject is not simply colorful and dramatic but also theoretically interesting. It is an outstanding example of an intersection between human psychology and culture, which makes it a very appropriate and illuminating subject for psychological anthropology. It is a panhuman phenomenon; therefore it may shed some light on the relationship between biology and culture.

The vast literature on ritual trance includes many descriptions and interpretations of it in particular cultures, some cross-cultural comparisons, and several overviews and theories which emphasize social and psychological functions. This essay explores the psychobiology and evolution of ritual trance. It seeks to develop a more holistic and biocultural approach by drawing on some recent advances in the neurosciences, which a few anthropologists have begun to use.

The main argument of this essay is that the capacity for trance is a byproduct of the evolution of the brain and a psychobiological universal, which has been "domesticated"—manipulated by rituals and shaped and interpreted by cultural expectations—by many societies because it meets some fundamental human needs.

My approach to the subject is stimulated by Melford E. Spiro's views on human nature and the relationship between religion and personality, which seem to offer an excellent framework for the development of a holistic, evolutionary, and panhuman understanding of ritual trance.

SPIRO'S APPROACH TO HUMAN NATURE, CULTURE, AND RELIGION

Melford Spiro's work has attracted the attention of a wide audience. One reason for his influence is suggested by his statement that "my intellectual interests have always been more philosophical than scientific, and . . . for me anthropology has been the handmaiden of philosophy, a tool for the empirical investigation of some central issues concerning the nature of man" (Spiro 1978b:332). Spiro always addresses fundamental questions and never shies away from taking controversial positions. Perhaps the most important issue he has dealt with is the nature/nurture problem.

For most of its history, American anthropology has taken an extreme environmental or cultural determinist position, emphasizing a great degree of human plasticity, a broad range of cultural diversity, and the uniqueness of every society. Human universals and biological foundations of behavior were ignored, and the subject of human nature was virtually taboo. However, in "Buddhism and Society," Spiro made a startling remark: "Human nature, no doubt, *is* a product of culture, at least to some extent, but . . . there are limits to its plasticity, beyond which culture is impotent to mold it. Indeed . . . I would argue that these limits are dramatically narrower than we have traditionally conceded them to be" (Spiro 1970:13).

While the mainstream of cultural anthropology was moving toward an increasingly relativistic and idiographic approach with a "new ethnography" that focused on the "native viewpoint" and a humanistic "interpretation of cultures," Spiro was moving in the opposite direction, toward a more nomothetic and scientific approach. In *Burmese Supernaturalism* (1978a:5–6), he characterized the "emic" approach as "intellectually trivial" and outlined an "unabashedly etic" approach in which "a *narrow* range of common psychobiological needs" (human nature) is satisfied by a "*wide* range of diverse forms" (Spiro 1978a:6). Spiro has borrowed several terms from other disciplines to conceptualize this relationship between human nature and cultural variations. In "Culture and Personality" (1968a:559), for example, he spoke of a "search for the psychologically 'genotypic' bases of . . . 'phenotypic' cultural constructs"; later, it had become "a narrow range of deep-structure variability . . . underlying [a] broad range of surface-structure variability" (1978a:xviii).

Cultural determinism led to an increasingly cerebral bias in anthropology, which is apparent in the recent schools of structuralism, symbolic anthropology, and ethnosemantics, but Spiro's psychology is much broader and encompasses "needs (id), values (superego), and executive-response processes (ego)" (1954:28). While not denying the importance of cognitive processes, he has always emphasized panhuman needs or drives such as sex and dependency, which often conflict with societal values and must be repressed and canalized into institutionalized roles and settings such as shamanism and ritual.

Spiro's career began at the height in popularity of culture and personality studies and psychoanalytic theory, and he steadfastly followed them even after they had come under serious attack and had been abandoned by many colleagues. The application to anthropology of a Freudian model leads quite naturally to a psychobiological view of human nature because it has a biological foundation and deals with universal stages and processes. Sigmund Freud's structural model of personality (id, ego, and superego) encourages a holistic integration of the biological, psychological, social, and cultural dimensions of behavior. His topographical theory provides us with a model for studying relationships between unconscious, individual, and primary-process thought, on the one hand, and conscious, collective, and secondary-process thought, on the other. Furthermore, Freud's emphasis on conflict between components of personality alerts us to common problems that all humans face because of their makeup, including conflicts between personal drives and cultural norms, which all societies must find ways to accommodate or resolve.

Spiro's approach to the study of religion is largely psychological, and one of his interests has been the relationship between the conscious and public knowledge of religious tradition and the private and unconscious aspects of individual faith. He argues that religious systems must be interpreted, like dreams, at two levels of meaning: the "surface" level, which is cultural and based on secondary-process thought, and the "deep" or personality level with primary-process thought, where he finds the motivational basis for religious belief and involvement (Spiro 1982b:64–65). For example, his explanation for the ontogeny of religious belief, which is based on the Freudian model, is that prolonged helplessness, extended dependency, and a relatively late acquisition of language in the human species lead children to develop reified images of parents as powerful beings, and displacement of these images to the gods establishes an isomorphism between personal experience and religious beliefs, giving credibility to the latter (Spiro 1978a).

Spiro is "an unregenerate functionalist" (1978a:7) who regards religion and other cultural institutions as "institutionalized means for the satisfaction of needs" (1966b:96). He has said that religions seek to satisfy a universal human need "to know, to understand, to find meaning . . . for otherwise meaningless and inexplicable phenomena" (Spiro 1966b:109–110), which is emotional as well as intellectual: "Religious beliefs comprise answers to questions that derive, at least in part, from deep-seated emotionally based questions, concerning which the believer is troubled, concerned, anxious— not merely curious" (Spiro 1964:105).

Like Max Weber, Spiro identifies suffering as the main concern of religion. It is an inevitable facet of human life, and every religion provides an explanation for its existence and inequitable distribution. However, Spiro notes that religions not only explain but also attempt to reduce or overcome suffering. He makes a distinction between "religion-in-belief" and "religion-in-use" (Spiro 1978a:xxviii) and often emphasizes the instrumental aspect of religion: "Religious ideas are not so much used to think about or classify with, as to live by. That is, they are used to resolve conflict, to cope with tragedy, to rationalize failure, to find meaning in suffering" (Spiro 1970:6).

In order to reduce suffering, a supplicant may engage in ritual transactions with superhuman beings. He can, for example, blame misfortune or illness on a malevolent spirit and have it pacified, warded off, or exorcised, sometimes by appealing to more powerful and benevolent spirits. At the psychological level, religious beliefs and rituals often serve to reduce anxieties and fears about threatening events beyond human control. They can also be used to resolve inner conflicts between personal desires and cultural norms by permitting the disguised expression of repressed drives. Kindly and benevolent gods can satisfy longings for dependency and nurturance, and aggressive and malevolent gods can serve as objects for the projection or displacement of hatred and fear (Spiro 1978a:xxviii). These "culturally constituted defense mechanisms" simultaneously provide approved channels for the expression of potentially disturbing and disruptive drives, resolve personal conflicts, motivate religious participation, and prevent deviance (Spiro 1965a).

RITUAL TRANCE

The discussion that follows will draw heavily on my study of a ritual trance cult in Jamaica called Revival (Wedenoja 1978). However, my purpose is theoretical rather than descriptive, and I will heed Spiro's admonition that "The practitioner of anthropology as 'science,' placing the local setting in a theoretical context, is concerned with the local as a variant of—and therefore a means for understanding—the universal" (Spiro 1978a:xvi–xvii).

Revival is a unique amalgam of African religious traditions, slave religion, and missionary Protestantism. It is similar to Voodou in Haiti, to Batuque and Candomble in Brazil, to Santeria in Cuba and Puerto Rico, to Shango in Trinidad, and, most closely, to the "Spiritual Baptists" of Trinidad.

"The Great Revival," a major religious movement in Jamaica in 1860, led to a massive defection from missionary churches and the emergence of Revival cults, which became the popular religion of the island (Wedenoja 1988). In recent decades, however, American sects—first the Adventists, then several Pentecostal groups—have grown rapidly, and Revival is now on the wane (Wedenoja 1980). In an area of sixty square miles in the central highlands of Jamaica, I located thirty-three Orthodox, thirty-three Pentecostal, eleven Evangelical, two Jehovah's Witnesses, and thirty-one Revival churches.

Revival cults are close-knit groups based on personal devotion to the leader that range in size from about eleven to sixty members. Ideologically, they are Christian and rely principally on the Old Testament, but their form of worship is very spiritual and fundamentally African in nature. There is a great deal of singing and dancing to the beat of goatskin drums at Revival services, which include healing ceremonies, feast "Tables," fastings, and communions. Revivalists believe in a host of spirits, largely derived from the Bible: benevolent ones such as Jesus, God, "angels" (including Old Testament prophets and New Testament disciples), and the Holy Ghost; and malevolent ones such as Satan, demons, fallen angles, and duppies (spirits of the dead). Illness and misfortune are generally attributed to duppies and Obeah (sorcery), and these malevolent forces are combated by securing the assistance of angels, who send "messages" and "warnings" in visions and dreams and become manifest in ritual trance.

The Surface Structure

According to Spiro, religion "is first of all a cognitive system" in which beliefs "serve to explain, i.e., to account for, give meaning to, and structure, otherwise inexplicable, meaningless, and unstructured phenomena" (Spiro 1964:105). Revivalists carry on intimate relationships with spirits, and they have an impressively complex lexicon and set of beliefs to describe, explain, and give meaning to this experience.

The following phenomenological description of ritual trance is primarily cultural, although it may appear to be psychological. Subjects' accounts of their trance experiences are inevitably colored by folk taxonomies and cultural beliefs and expectations. However, their cultural categories and beliefs very probably result from genuine attempts to relate real experiences, and the fact that there are significant differences among the reports of individuals seems to indicate that they have some psychological validity.

In Revival ethnopsychology, normal consciousness and personality are called the "temporal" or "natural self," and the religious altered state is called the "spiritual self." Everything associated with the latter is known as the "spiritual work," including: (1) the process of transformation between temporal and spiritual selves, (2) ritual means for effecting this transformation, (3) expected forms of behavior while in the spiritual self, and (4) the "gifts" and obligations of spiritual participation.

Revivalists conceive of ritual trance as a cyclical process of self-transformation that includes phases of segregation, liminality, and reaggregation (Table 13.1). Ritual trance is a highly valued "blessing" in Revivalism. Normally, individuals must have a "conviction of sin" that leads to "spiritual rebirth" and must live according to the rather stringent expectations associated with "being a Christian" before they can "get in the Spirit." Indi-

Table 13.1. Stages of spiritual transformation.

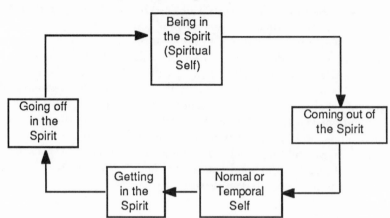

viduals are sometimes spontaneously "taken away by the Spirit," but the normal route is to follow some prescribed rituals for "getting in the Spirit" (table 13.2).

Revivalists decorate their churches and perform rituals to "entertain the spirits" and "invite the Holy Ghost." Flags are flown on poles outside Revival churches to attract spirits and guide "pilgrims" and healing patients. Banners are hung on the interior walls, candles are lit, offerings of food are displayed, and chalk symbols or "seals" (resembling the Haitian vever) are drawn on the floor. Every ceremony includes a great deal of singing and dancing, which is often accompanied by drums and punctuated by prayers, readings from the Bible, and preaching. The most dramatic technique for spiritual transformation is a hyperventilative ring dance called "shouting" or "laboring," which is regularly performed at quarterly feast "Tables" and occasionally at communions and healing services.

When someone "gets off in the Spirit," he is said to be "taken out of his natural self by the Spirit [Holy Ghost], which tells or shows him things." "Going off in the Spirit" can make a woman very "emotional" (histrionic), so she should wrap her head in a turban "to keep her nerve" and prevent "madness." Many informants say the Spirit is a "thrill" that "passes through the body," "comes and goes like the wind," and makes them feel "chilled" or "nervylike," but a few describe it as a "hot, terrible feeling."

"Receiving the Spirit"—that is, "going off in the Spirit" for the first time—is often said to be painful, uncontrollable, and dramatic. After this experience, however, they "have the Spirit" and can reexperience it with less effort and more control. In addition, they may acquire a guardian angel

Table 13.2. Taxonomy of ways of getting in the Spirit.

Ways of Getting in the Spirit												
Inviting the Holy Ghost					Entertaining the Spirits					Shouting	Fasting	To live (according to Christian precepts)
Reading the Bible	Dancing	Singing	Preaching	Prayer	Seals	Candles	Fruit, soda, rice	Perfume	Banners			

to guide and instruct them and warn of impending dangers. Revivalists say they have no conscious awareness when they are "high in the Spirit" and usually cannot recall the experience afterward. However, they have some awareness when they are "low in the Spirit" and retain some memory of it. A person feels "light" or "tireless" "in the Spirit" and has no pain or weariness because "it is no longer him but the power of God in him" that is doing the "moving," but pain or exhaustion is often felt after "coming out of the Spirit." Many informants say it is a pleasurable experience, and some say they "love" the Spirit, but a few feel "fire and pain," as if they are "going to die." Perception is altered by the Spirit, so that everything looks "marvellous" and "different." The meaning of ritual symbols—for example, flowers, banners, painted conches and rocks, "spirit writing," the design of altars and seals— is revealed in the Spirit and sometimes understood in the temporal self, but it cannot be expressed in words.

The altered state—"being in the Spirit"—has many recognized forms or "manifestations" in Revivalism (table 13.3). Sometimes people are simply entranced—unaware, unresponsive, and with a glazed, unblinking stare— or they may have minor convulsions—a "touch of the Spirit." "Moving in

Table 13.3. Taxonomy of ways of being in the Spirit.

Manifestations of the Spirit														
Talking in tongues	Laboring in the Spirit			Preaching in the Spirit	Being led by the Spirit	Moving in the Spirit			Touch of the Spirit			Trances	Dreams	Visions		
	Receiving the Message	Drilling				Jumping	Stand up and twirl	Wheel and turn (spiritual dancing)	Rock you (jerk from side to side)	(pelvis/spine jerk)	(head and neck jerk)			Spiritual commissions	Warnings	Prophecies

the Spirit" refers to dancing with a spirit. Someone may be "led by the Spirit" to discover sorcery objects or identify those who are ill or in distress. These "manifestations" are clearly defined in the minds of believers, who notice slight deviations. Newcomers often unknowingly violate these guidelines, but their behavior is soon shaped by observation, imitation, and verbal or nonverbal reinforcement. Someone who regularly deviates, either in the form of his behavior or by displaying it in the wrong setting, is said to be "queer in the Spirit" and "getting off," that is, "mad" rather than in divine contact.

Revivalists believe that God guides and protects them by sending angels to deliver prophetic messages, on which they rely very heavily. "Visions" are visual or auditory "warnings" of future events, events occurring in a distant place, or "spiritual commissions," and they can occur in any "manifestation of the Spirit," especially dreams, as well as in a normal state of consciousness. "Spiritual commissions" are "orders" from God, for example, to "warn" others about Judgment Day, to "journey" on a pilgrimage, to wear a certain uniform, or to follow certain guidelines to regain health and well-being. Ceremonies enable people to "work for" and "receive" a message. During a shouting ritual, the dancers get in the Spirit and "work off the messengers," who "drill" them in new rituals or reveal new knowledge, sometimes in "tongues" (glossolalia).

Revivalists believe that supernatural powers—including the "gifts" of healing, prophecy, discerning of spirits, "reading a person," and "seeing through the Spirit"—are bestowed on some of them by God. If a person abuses this "gift" ("mixes the Spirit") or fails to follow a "commission," then he or she will "take a sword" from God, that is, be punished by a grave illness or misfortune.

Revivalists use this cultural system to differentiate, account for, evaluate, communicate, and give meaning to ritual trance experiences. These idioms are also role expectations that limit and shape ritual trance behavior, making it normative rather than idiosyncratic. However, ritual trance is not simply a matter of behaving in accordance with cultural expectations. It is literally a "spine-tingling" experience. There is an underlying structure to the behavior and experience that is not cultural but psychobiological.

The Deep Structure

The first task of an ethnographic study is to identify and describe the cultural construction of reality of the subjects, although, as Spiro sometimes stresses, this "emic" analysis should not be an end in itself: "The interpretation of cultures consists in part in the translation of surface-structure cultural symbols into deep-structure meanings" (Spiro 1978a:xviii). The cultural construction of ritual trance in Jamaican Revivalism is unique, but there is no reason to think that the underlying psychobiology differs significantly from that in other societies.

Ritual trance and other forms of religious ecstasy are common and have a worldwide distribution. A cross-cultural study by Erika Bourguignon (1973) identified institutionalized states of "trance" or "possession trance" in at least 90 percent of a sample of 488 societies. Ritual trance is not practiced by Christian denominations, but surveys indicate that 20 percent to 50 percent of all Americans have had a "mystical" or "religious" experience. In England, 36 percent of the respondents in a national sample and 65 percent of a sample of postgraduate students admitted to having been "aware of or influenced by a presence or power . . . different from their everyday selves" (Hay and Morisy 1978; Hay 1979). Three important conclusions can be drawn from these data: (1) a distinction should be made between religious ecstasy as a psychological state and as a cultural practice, since the former can occur in the absence of the latter, (2) religious ecstacy is virtually a cultural universal, and (3) religious ecstasy is probably a panhuman psychological experience.

Anthropologists have come to regard ritual trance as an altered state of consciousness (ASC) that has been modified by culture for religious purposes. Psychological research indicates that the human brain has the potential for ASCs, which most anyone can experience under the proper conditions, but they are influenced significantly by the set and setting of the experience. In other words, the potential for ritual trance is inborn or part of the "hardware" of the species, but the form, function, and meaning of ritual trance are determined by culture or the "software" programs of societies.

Almost every culture has a unique set of terms, classifications, values, expectations, induction techniques, beliefs, and social uses for ASCs, which shape the "surface structure" of ritual trance and imbue it with moral and cosmic meaning and purpose. These cultural constructions may be necessary to control ASCs and prevent them from leading to psychological disorder. As Spiro (1978a:7) has noted: "Since . . . man is not only a rational animal, but also a biological and social animal, culture is the means *par excellence* for controlling the nonrational and irrational forces inherent in biology and society." There is great variation in the surface structure of ritual trance throughout the world, but a scientific approach should attempt to reduce it to a few underlying processes. The deep structure is probably based on various combinations of a few psychobiological factors, which have been identified in several different—but not necessarily exclusive—theories of ritual trance.

One of the more widely held theories is that ritual trance is a culturally elaborated form of the hypnotic state (e.g., Walker 1972). The ceremonial context in general and the leader or preacher in particular may serve as a functional equivalent for the timing and sanctioning roles of the hypnotist, while religious beliefs provide expectations or "suggestions" for behavior. Hypnotic trance seems to be "an inherent capacity in the individual" (Spiegel and Spiegel 1978:30) that is "as natural as, say, sleep" (Hilgard 1968:308). Most people—about 90 percent—can be hypnotized, but there are individual differences in susceptibility (Hilgard and Hilgard 1975).

One difference between ordinary hypnosis and ritual trance is that the latter is generally associated with a state of often intense arousal. "Driving stimuli" such as singing, drumming, dancing, and preaching are common elements of ceremonies that can produce an "ergotropic" syndrome characterized by cortical excitation; increased muscle tone; sympathetic nervous system discharges, such as an increase in cardiac rate, blood pressure, and perspiration; and an elevation in hormones such as adrenaline and noradrenaline. Excessive ergotropic stimulation can lead to a "trophotropic rebound," including cortical inactivity; relaxation of muscles; parasympathetic nervous system discharges such as reduced cardiac rate, blood pressure, and perspiration; and the release of acetylcholine and serotonin (Gellhorn and Kiely 1972).

It is helpful to view rituals as techniques that alter the brain and nervous system and induce ASCs. Several elements in the Revival taxonomy of "Ways of Getting in the Spirit," as well as drumming and clapping, can produce the ergotropic syndrome, which may be the neurophysiological substrate for "going off in the Spirit," and push some Revivalists through the "doors of perception" to "being in the Spirit." In Haiti, for example, Alfred Metraux (1972:178) remarked that "the drummer . . . [is] the linchpin of every Voodoo ceremony. . . . A talented drummer can induce or terminate possessions at will."

Only a few Revivalists seem to pass beyond a state of ergotropic excitation. Some report a feeling of peace or relaxation and the absence of tension, pain, and anxiety after "coming out of the Spirit," but a service is largely an exhilarating experience for most of them. We should be wary of attributing too much importance to the attainment of a trance state and give more consideration to the psychosocial effects of ritual stimulation. Exposure of a group of people to common driving stimuli may serve to synchronize their cortical, emotional, and physiological states, fostering "communitas" or a sense of group identity and fellow-feeling. In addition, exhilaration is reinforcing and could encourage greater commitment to the group and its belief system.

Recent research on the bilateral asymmetry of the human neocortex has established that the left hemisphere is almost totally dominant in the area of language, while the right hemisphere is, to a lesser degree, dominant in visuospatial functions. Otherwise stated, the left specializes in "symbolic-conceptual" and the right in "nonsymbolic directly perceived" strategies of cognitive processing (Restak 1984:250–252). Research on epileptic patients who received an operation to sever the main connection between the hemispheres led Michael Gazzaniga to postulate that each hemisphere comprises a "separate mental system" or self (cited in Restak 1984:255). This research has given rise to rampant speculations on many subjects, including ritual trance, which are intriguing but often go far beyond the present state of knowledge.

Several theories have associated ritual trance with the right hemisphere. Julian Jaynes (1976), for example, argued that possession states are vestiges of an ancient "bicameral mind" and that ritual trance induction techniques temporarily suppress the "man-side," or "analog 'I'," of the left hemisphere, leaving the "god-side," or right hemisphere, in control of speech. He also suggested that hypnosis and schizophrenia are modern residues of this archaic mentality that have lost their religious context and meaning in secular societies. Similarly, Raymond Prince (1974) proposed that ritual trance involves a shift in dominance from the "everyday ego" of the left hemisphere to the normally "submissive" right, where an alternative personality or possessing spirit is formed by religious enculturation. According to Barbara Lex (1975/76), ritual driving stimuli and ergotropic arousal facilitate a shift to right hemisphere dominance and produce a timeless, nonverbal state of mind, a trophotropic rebound, abreaction, and feelings of pleasure, relief, and well-being. Eugene d'Aquili and Charles Laughlin (1979), associating the ergotropic syndrome with the left hemisphere and the trophotropic with the right, posited a simultaneous stimulation of both syndromes and activation of both hemispheres, accompanied by limbic discharges of a cathartic nature, in ecstatic states.

Some facets of ritual trance in Jamaica suggest that it involves the "minor" hemisphere. Revivalists say that "going off in the Spirit" involves a transformation from the "temporal" to the "spiritual" self, which could be a cultural recognition of a shift in hemispheric dominance. They also say they experience a sense of wholeness; lack of conscious awareness, a sense of self and will; heightened sensory awareness; altered perceptions and significance; and timelessness "in the Spirit." These are common elements of ecstatic and meditative states everywhere, which Robert Ornstein (1972) attributed to the right hemisphere. Revivalists also say that it is extremely difficult to describe trance experiences in words, perhaps because there is little or no verbal encoding in the right hemisphere.

Nonverbal symbolism, primary-process thought, and creativity are sometimes said to be predominantly functions of the right hemisphere, and there is supporting evidence in Revivalism. Apparently idiosyncratic and impulsive acts such as tearing the leaves of healing plants, cutting fruits, and rubbing a person with flowers are performed in ritual trance, and many innovations in ritual and symbolism are attributed to the "teaching" of angels.

I was struck by the odd but uncannily adept balance of trance dancers, who often spin rapidly around the church, between the pews and among the congregation, frequently swinging a wooden sword or making chopping motions with their hands. They have a peculiar tendency to stagger and fall backward as they move, always twirling and regaining their balance at the last split second, but I never saw anyone actually fall, stumble into an object or person, or hit someone with a sword. This unusual coordination may be due to the right hemisphere, since it "appears to innervate nonpyramidal motor systems responsible for axial movements" (Lex 1978:292).

Parallels between epilepsy and religious experience are often noted but seldom pursued. Epilepsy is an abnormal excitation and spontaneous discharge of brain cells. The ictus, or seizure, includes a brief lapse of consciousness (called an absence), depressed awareness, or a complete loss of consciousness. It may also involve muscular spasms or jerks, rhythmic twitching of arms and legs, and acts or automatisms such as chewing, swallowing, licking, grimacing, blinking, muttering, walking, and picking at or rearranging objects.

Complex partial seizures are characteristically preceded by an "aura" or premonitory sensation, which is often intense and difficult to put into words. The aura may include autonomic symptoms such as sweating and incontinence; somatosensory symptoms such as "butterflies" in the stomach or feelings of numbness, deadness, or "pins and needles"; perceptual symptoms such as visual distortions, odors, tastes, and auditory hypersensitivities; cognitive symptoms such as déjà vu, jamais vu, flashbacks, forced thinking, and feelings of floating or depersonalization; and emotions such as fear, sadness, or elation. The postictal phase may involve localized paralysis or weakness and often confusion and amnesia. Seizures can have lasting effects on personality, and an interictal behavior syndrome of hyposexuality, aggressivity, and an intense concern with moral and religious issues has been identified.

In many ages and societies, epileptics have been said to be touched by God or possessed by demons. Freud (1923) diagnosed the seventeenth-century possession of Christoph Haizmann as a case of neurotic regression, but it was recently identified as "probably the first very well documented case of schizophrenia-like psychosis occurring in epilepsy" (Glaser 1978:273). Many symptoms of epilepsy are strikingly similar to ritual trance experiences, and either syndrome can be induced by drowsiness, fatigue, hyperventilation, and sensory stimulation. I observed a seizure at a Revival ceremony in an adolescent who had a history of the disease, and it may have been triggered by the ceremony. However, the participants clearly regarded her behavior as pathological rather than ecstatic.

Ritual trance is generally too purposeful and culturally patterned to be epileptic, although it may be somewhat pathomimetic; that is, modeled on symptoms of epilepsy. In addition, hysterical symptoms can be very difficult to distinguish from epilepsy. The existence of hysteroepilepsy indicates that epileptiform behaviors can be induced in normal (neurologically intact) individuals, possibly by ritual stimulation.

Arnold Mandell (1980) has, in fact, proposed "a biogenic amine-temporal-lobe neurology" for "transcendent states," involving a neurophysiological process akin to temporal lobe epilepsy but occurring in normal individuals. He suggested that driving stimuli could decrease the synthesis or release of serotonin, which normally inhibits hippocampal CA^3 cells, resulting in a "runaway" excitation of the mesolimbic temporal lobe structure. A left hemisphere focus might result in paranoia, fear, and rage followed by lethargy and depression, while a right hemisphere focus could be a "neurobiological substrate for transcendent consciousness" or ecstasy: hysterical, optimistic, visually symbolic, intuitive, impulsive, relaxing or euphoric experiences with an afterdischarge of positive feelings and optimal brain function lasting for days or weeks. As in grand mal, this could be accompanied by autonomic discharge, including erections and ejaculations, followed by a reduced interest in sex. In fact, I have observed pelvic contractions, increasing in intensity sometimes to a seemingly orgasmic climax, in several ritual trance states.

Endogenous morphinelike substances may play a significant role in the psychobiology of ritual trance. Enkephalin and beta-endorphin are neurotransmitters that exercise an analgesic effect by blocking the transmission of pain impulses. They are natural ligands or equivalents of morphine, which sometimes also produce euphoria, alterations of perception and the sense of time and space, and vivid visual imagery (Prince 1982a). Endorphin production is activated by extraordinary pain, proprioceptive stimulation, and probably stress. Vigorous exercise, emotional distress or excitement, psychological threat, and suggestion are all possible—but not proven—means of producing endorphins (Henry 1982; Prince 1982a and 1982b).

Rituals are often stressful experiences. Lengthy services with constant singing, dancing, and loud music can be physically exhausting and emotionally draining, and pain-inducing measures such as fire walking and wounds deliberately inflicted on the flesh are common in ecstatic religions. In addition, the content and delivery of sermons can be very threatening, particularly in "hellfire" sects of Western Christendom that encourage fear of sin and damnation.

Prince (1982b) has suggested that some rituals act as "endorphin pumps." A good example is the Revival ritual of "shouting," which involves a hyperventilative dance called "laboring." Five or six participants form a circle and dance in a counterclockwise direction, audibly inhaling with a deep, guttural sound called "groaning" as they raise their arms and straighten from a bent position to an upright one on the left foot, then exhaling loudly and forcefully in another groan as they bow forward and thrust their arms into the circle in unison and slap their right feet on the floor. As the tempo increases, they stamp their feet with greater force and the church resounds with the percussive force of this rhythmic exhalation and stamping, which is occasionally broken by an exclamation from a "shouter." Their cheeks flap like bellows and their faces stream with perspiration. Laboring often lasts more than an hour, and toward the end, when the tempo is very quick, it is so intense that the sound of overbreathing turns to a growl. Sometimes a dancer will fall back as if in a faint, to be caught and held as she speaks in "language" or tongues.

Perhaps the simplest and most comprehensive approach involves viewing the ritual trance as a ceremonially induced form of the stress response. Rhetorical threats, sensory bombardment, deliberate inflictions of pain and other driving stimuli, and the anticipation or even fear of becoming possessed may stimulate the production of stress hormones with euphoric, analgesic, mood-altering, hypnotic, ennervating, and perhaps tranquillizing and antidepressive effects equivalent to the ingestion of morphine, amphetamine, Adrenalin, diazepam, and tricyclics. If this is the case, then ecstatic rituals can be medically effective and physiologically addictive. Ritual trance cults may have a hedonistic purpose—the attainment of a euphoric high—and therapeutic purposes such as relief from anxiety, depression, pain, and other forms of distress. It is tempting to propose that ecstatic rituals evolved in order to provide people with temporary and periodic relief from chronic stress.

Catharsis

Endogenous drugs may account for some of the relief that cultists experience from ritual participation, but they do not deal with the specific personal problems of cultists. Rituals are often said to be abreactive and cathartic experiences, which evoke memories of painful events and facilitate emotional discharge. For example, in his analysis of an exorcistic séance in Burma, Spiro noted:

> In every seance that I observed, the patient . . . shouted obscenities, uttered heresies, insulted the exorcist, became physically violent, and engaged in other forms of "acting-out" behavior. . . . The patient's bottled-up resentment is now out of his system; his violence ends in physical exhaustion; recriminations end in bitter sobbing, the patient's body is wracked with trembling. . . . The abreactive aspect of the seance enables him, so I am suggesting, to achieve (in some measure) the resolution of conflict. [Spiro 1978a:202–203]

Catharsis has been a subject of much debate in psychotherapy, and psychological experiments on its effectiveness have been inconclusive. However, T. J. Scheff (1979) has developed a new and very promising approach to catharsis that is highly applicable to the study of ritual. His theory is based on the assumption that emotional discharge is a natural reflex and that inhibition of it, often because of cultural expectations, leads to repressed emotions, bodily tension, and impairments in thought and perception. In order to gain relief and improve performance, an emotionally repressed person must relive a traumatic event and experience spontaneous, convulsive, and involuntary "weeping (for [repressed] grief), shivering and cold perspiration (for fear), spontaneous laughter (for embarrassment or anger), and 'storming' (rapid, forceful movement and vocalization) with hot perspiration, also for anger" (Scheff 1979:49). Catharsis occurs when the distressful event is reexperienced at an "aesthetic distance," in which one becomes an emotional participant without relinquishing the security of being an observer. An individual will be emotionally overwhelmed, and his tension and distress will increase, if the situation is "underdistanced." He will feel too secure and be unmoved if it is "overdistanced."

According to Scheff, rituals develop around, and are reenactments of, common and recurring situations of emotional distress such as death, illness, separation, marriage, greeting, and injustice. They include effective distancing devices and provide regular and socially acceptable occasions for collective catharsis. He seems to think that rituals in traditional and tribal societies are more cathartic than modern rites, which are generally overdistanced, and he identifies the belief in possession, which holds a spirit responsible for one's verbalizations and behavior, as an effective distancing device. Similarly, Spiro (1978a) suggested that exorcistic séances in Burma are therapeutically effective when a patient has confidence in the ability of the exorcist and can abreact in a supportive and nurturing environment.

Revival ceremonies definitely deal with distressful experiences, and they are often emotional events. Cults perform funerals, elaborate wakes, and sometimes marriages, and many of them have a weekly service devoted entirely to healing. Quarterly feasts are held to honor, extol, and encourage the leader and her followers and patients. Virtually every service includes personal testimonies of hardship and suffering and long-winded sermons on deprivation and injustice. Feelings of anxiety, fear, mistrust, frustration, hostility, anger, and shame are freely expressed in phrases such as "we are the despised and rejected," and they are also dealt with ideologically, for example, by the promise that there will be "no more sorrow, pain or tears" after death. One of the stated purposes of services is to make people happy by allowing the Holy Ghost to enter into their lives.

Relief from suffering through emotional discharge seems to be a very important function of Revival ceremonies, and it is probably a strong reason for participation in services and commitment to the cult. In addition, catharsis in a group context probably serves an important social function. According to Scheff, repression interferes with interpersonal relationships and isolates individuals, because a repressed individual cannot tolerate emotional discharge in others. Collective catharsis in a ritual context should therefore enhance fellow-feeling and promote cooperation and social cohesion.

One of the main purposes of ritual trance may be to facilitate catharsis by removing normal inhibitions to emotional discharge. In *Burmese Supernaturalism* (1978a:203), for example, Spiro wrote that "in the seance-induced trance [of an exorcism] . . . [the] ego is rendered unconscious, the superego is dissolved, and the usually repressed id emerges triumphant." The ritual context of trance cults is a socially approved arena for acting out, which can psychologically disinhibit an individual, and the psychobiological state of trance seems to permit a freer and more direct access to feelings.

Paul MacLean's (1978) "triune brain" theory provides a good basis for understanding the psychobiology of repression and catharsis. He has identified three basic "drivers" of the "neural chassis": (1) the reptilian driver, or R-complex, which governs the performance of species-typical behaviors such as homing, territoriality, defense, feeding, courtship, mating, nurturing, flocking, and the establishment of social hierarchies; (2) the limbic system, which guides behavior according to feelings; and (3) the neocortex, which is responsible for language and for rational and abstract thought.

This tripartite organization can lead to intrapsychic conflicts among drives, feeling, and thoughts. In general, repression may be understood as the cortical suppression of drives and feelings from lower levels of the brain. In his evolutionary analysis of psychosomatic disorders, A. T. W. Simeons (1962:49) provided a vivid description of this process:

> In modern man all the instincts are still there as they were millions of years ago, but they have become imprisoned in the diencephalon in the sense that they no longer have a free outlet into consciousness. Before they can become conscious they must undergo a process of cortical refining, grooming and bridling which turns them into emotions. Finally, they have to pass another censorship at the conscious threshold where all those emotions that are conventionally or ethically unacceptable are screened off.

Communication in nonhuman animals is largely emotional and based on the limbic system, whereas human language is a function of the neocortex (Fisher 1982:186), and the link between the neocortex and the limbic system is weaker and more indirect in humans than in monkeys, giving us the ability to communicate dispassionately (Pfeiffer 1985:377–379). In addition, each hemisphere of our neocortex seems to be associated with particular emotions: positive affect (happiness, joking, and laughing) with the left hemisphere and negative affect (fear, pessimism, crying, and sadness) with the right (Davidson 1984).

It has been proposed that the use of masks in ceremonies is a "symbolic penetration technique" which opens up channels between the cortex and lower levels of the brain (Webber, Stephens, and Laughlin 1983). Ritual trance should have a similar effect, since belief in possession has the same distancing function as masks. This effect could be facilitated by using driving stimuli—particularly music and dance—to shift dominance temporarily from the left to the right hemisphere in order to reduce cortical inhibition, evoke negative feelings, and release repressed drives.

There are definite signs of limbic discharge in Revival cultism, where ritual trance behavior is apparently spontaneous, usually accompanied by convulsive movements and heavy perspiration, and often involves exclamations of pain, joy, laughter, and sometimes weeping. In addition, the subjective experiences of ritual trance closely resemble symptoms of limbic discharge which, according to MacLean (1978), include depersonalization, distortions of perception, hallucinations, and oceanic and eurekalike feelings.

While Scheff's theory of catharsis emphasizes the periodic discharge of repressed emotions in ritual, Spiro has focused on the gratification of repressed needs or drives: "Shamanistic possession . . . is motivated by the desire to satisfy frustrated sexual, dependency, and prestige needs" (1978a:228). Needs of this sort are openly expressed, both verbally and behaviorally, in Revival ceremonies. In fact, a Revival leader opened a service by saying, "I'm sure everyone has a need, and that is the reason why we are here."

The sanctioned expression of aggression is very prominent in Jamaican Revival cultism. Histrionic preaching—often "in the Spirit"—commonly includes vehement attacks on the government, the well-to-do, and nonbelievers. The behavioral environment of Revivalists is replete with hostile projections in the form of malevolent spirits. Every major ceremony begins with elaborate measures to "cut destruction," that is, to clear the church of bad feelings and evil spirits. Someone in trance may use a wooden sword to duel with spirits and chase them outside, vigorously swing a banner attached to a pole for the same reason, or hurl soda bottles against the concrete corners of the church to destroy forces of evil with a carbonated explosion.

Sexuality is more subtly expressed in Revival ceremonies: dancing around a seal pole, penetration of swords into circles of "shouters," and a banana laid over two oranges on the table at feasts. There is a very significant increase in physical contact between the sexes during ritual trance, especially between married men and single women, and sexual excitement is sometimes apparent. The ecstatic behavior of men is frequently associated with female performances (for example, solo songs and testimonies), and women are more ecstatic when men preach or sing. Pelvic contractions, sometimes reaching a climax in orgasmiclike behavior, are occasionally associated with ritual trance. In one follower these were regularly accompanied by verbalizations suggesting fantasized intercourse with Jesus.

Need for prestige is a very prevalent theme in the testimonies of followers, who commonly make such statements as: "We are not the people that people honor. We are not the people that people adore. We are not the people that people looked upon. . . . They doesn't notice us, they doesn't value us. We are nothing but, bless God, we are something in the sight of God. . . . And I am not ashamed . . . because Christ . . . liveth in me."

Ritual trance is a coercive, rather hysterical way of gaining attention from others but, unlike ordinary hysteric behavior, it also brings respect, since it is an honor to be chosen as the "holy vessel" of an angel or "the Spirit."

Ritual trance behavior is sometimes childish or "regressive" and may satisfy needs for dependency. For example, Melville Herskovits (1948:9) noted that the possessed sometimes "sing children's songs or play children's games or engage in mischievous pranks" in the Shango cults of Brazil and Trinidad. In Jamaican Revival, the relationship between a cult leader, who is called a "Mother," and her followers, who are called her "Children," is definitely maternal and sometimes regressive, and ritual trance may allow them to relive childhood experiences and gratify dependency needs. The organization of Revival cults seems to be unconsciously patterned on the matrifocal extended family, allowing adults to regain the sense of security and the nurturance and affiliations they had as children. Thus Revivalists gather at quarterly "Tables" to eat together and they are also regularly bathed by the Mother and her assistants to maintain their purity and health. The high point of any service, and the criterion by which it is judged, is a state of euphoric fellowship or brotherly love which often includes mutual embracing.

The cathartic element of ritual trance can make it a psychotherapeutic experience that promotes mental health and well-being. Scheff's theory of catharsis is based on the premise that repressed feelings create tension and give rise to neurotic behavior, which can be reduced or eliminated only by emotional discharge. Similarly, Spiro seems to think that repressed needs create intrapsychic conflicts, and occasional, preferably disguised, gratification of them is necessary to avoid psychological breakdown: "I would interpret both hallucinatory and dissociational behavior as defense mechanisms, by which inner conflict is expressed and/or resolved. . . . Trance . . . permits direct, albeit unconscious, satisfaction of internal stimuli (needs)" (Spiro 1978a:169).

Spiro (1978a:229) has argued that "the shamanistic role . . . functions as a culturally constituted defense, which . . . serves to avert the outbreak of psychopathology," and this seems to be the case with ritual trance, too. It is a socially approved and psychologically effective way to vent feelings periodically and relieve tension.

The cathartic release of repressed needs and emotions is generally regarded as a psychological process, but there is reason to believe—as

Scheff's theory in fact assumes—that it is physiological too. Catharsis involves a limbic discharge, and the limbic system seems to be the key to an understanding of mental illness. Many, if not most, of the psychotherapeutic drugs act selectively on it, and there should be endogenous analogues to these drugs. Cathartic experiences such as ritual trance may stimulate their release and restore, at least temporarily, a normal chemical balance.

The body has built-in defenses against physical disease, so it is not really farfetched to think that a common experience such as catharsis can have a similar effect on mental disorders. In fact, Prince (1979/80) and Julian Silverman (1975/76) have proposed that psychoses and religious experiences are endogenous, psychophysiological problem-solving mechanisms that can heal the psyche and resolve personal crises. They note that problems of identity, a sense of failure, loss of self-esteem, depression, and despair of moral or self-worth are common antecedents to spontaneous religious experiences. According to Prince, the results of these experiences include "a flood of life," a feeling of joy, loss of chronic anxiety, and greater assertiveness, independence, and interpersonal warmth. Is this not what Paul said almost 2000 years ago, that "the fruits of the Spirit are love, joy, peace, longsuffering, gentleness, goodness, and faith"? (Galations 5:22).

I have stressed the psychobiological basis of ritual trance in this discussion because it is a new avenue of research, but psychocultural factors, which have been more thoroughly studied, have roughly equal, if not greater, importance. Ritual trance and catharsis without the beliefs, values, and social support of a cult would be like a psychotherapeutic drug used without counseling. A cultural system helps an individual conceptualize and interpret his experiences, and it gives them meaning and value. In the case of ritual trance, a cult provides ritual means for evoking such states. It gives structure and purpose to them, and it shapes and guides them in beneficial directions. In some cases, ritual trance leads to identity reconstruction or what Anthony Wallace (1956) has called "mazeway resynthesis"—a dramatic change in worldview, self, and personality. Ecstatic religion is not only a widespread practice and an expression of human nature but also an important cultural adaptation to our inner or psychological and social or interpersonal environments.

Personality Variables

Spiro has steadfastly insisted on the importance of personality variables in the study of social institutions because "institutions provide culturally approved and/or prescribed means for the satisfaction of personality needs, and these, in turn, provide the motivational bases for the performance of the roles which comprise these institutions" (Spiro 1961a:471).

Ritual trance is found in most societies, but it is not experienced by everyone. About 45 percent of the adult population in my research area in Jamaica went to church on Sundays in 1975–1976, but only 37 percent of the churchgoers attended "spiritual" or charismatic churches, including 27 percent at Pentecostal churches and 10 percent at Revival cults. Fifty-nine percent of the members of a Revival cult engaged in ritual trance during a sixteen-month period of observation, but some had a "manifestation of the Spirit" at almost every meeting and others had it only occasionally. A general theory of ritual trance should explain why some individuals experience it, while others do not, and should also indicate why some do so more often than others. In order to answer these questions, we need to examine personality factors and life situations.

A study of southern fundamentalists found a significant relationship between the conversion experience and hypnotic trance and concluded that religious experience is essentially a hypnotic trance which "may be limited to that minority of the population which is capable of experiencing 'deep trance' " (Gibbons and De Jarnette 1972:155). According to Ernest Hilgard (1968), everyone is born with a potential for hypnotic trance, but developmental experiences between the acquisition of language and the onset of adolescence can prevent that potential from being realized. Herbert and David Spiegel (1978:32) suggested that the capacity for experiencing a hypnotic trance reflects the ability to regress "to an early foundation-experience type of learning, to a logic of experiences and sensation rather than thought," and noted that some individuals can even "relive parts of their lives as though they were at that age."

Spiegel and Spiegel identified a personality profile for individuals who are highly susceptible to trance, which they called "Dionysian." It includes a "bright" mood, a naive and trusting approach to people, uncritical and imaginative thought, creativity, extratension, present-orientation, the need for dependency and affiliation, compliance, a high capacity for cognitive absorption, and the use of isolation of affect and identification to cope with stress. They characterized Dionysians as "right-brained" and noted that they are "especially prone to abreact even under fairly mild stress" (1978:302). Individuals with low susceptibility to trance were said to be "left-brained," with "Apollonian" personalities: noncompliant, future-oriented, cerebral, unemotional, reserved, critical, suspicious, less outgoing or cheerful, and rationalizing.

Ritual trance seems to be associated with some of the personality traits of individuals who are highly susceptible to hypnosis. It involves a dramatic performance, passive fantasy, loss of identity, dependency, and manipulation of situations by identification with spirits (Bourguignon 1979:262) and is commonly found in agricultural societies (Bourguignon 1974), which socialize for compliance (obedience, nurturance, and responsibility) rather than for independence and self-reliance (Barry, Child, and Bacon 1959). Bourguignon (1979:258) has suggested that ritual trance is typically a female phenomenon because girls receive more socialization for compliance than boys. However, Jamaican men are often passive, dependent, and compliant, too. Although 63 percent of the followers in a Revival cult that I studied are women, statistical data on fifty-one members of this cult show no relationship between gender and ritual trance behavior (chi-square = 0).

There is strong pressure for compliance in Jamaican child rearing, and according to a "basic personality" study by Madeline Kerr (1963), Jamaicans tend to be anxious, insecure, passive, gregarious, emotionally labile, dependent, and extrapunitive. The Rorschach and Thematic Apperception Test protocols of a Revival leader and one of her key assistants, both of whom regularly engage in ritual trance, reveal many "Dionysian" traits and a characterological predisposition for trance. The leader's responses indicate extratension, emotional lability and constriction, a holistic mode of perception, dissociative tendencies, dysphoria, isolation of affect, and empathy. Her assistant's responses show an even more "Dionysian" personality: imagination and creativity, dissociative tendencies, naiveté, affective lability, impulsivity, submissiveness, dependency, uncritical perception, immaturity, a need for affection, dysphoria, lack of assertiveness, and passivity. In contrast, the responses of a Revival preacher, who never experienced ritual trance and in fact frowned on it, reveal a personality that is very matter-of-fact and unimaginative, dominant or assertive, unemotional, inattentive to others and his surroundings, cautious and conforming, excessively rational or critical, guarded or defensive, intellectualizing, intratensive, dysphoric, and anxious.

Many studies have attributed involvement in cultism to needs arising from situations of oppression and social or economic deprivation rather than personality traits; for example, a need for identity support in the context of cultural dissonance or collapse, a need for self-respect or prestige and a feeling of power in the lower classes or in subjugated populations, and a need for means by which subordinated women can manipulate men. The social circumstances of Jamaican peasants—who are politically powerless, endure chronic economic deprivation and uncertainty, suffer from lack of self-esteem due to racial bias and lower-class status, and have frequent marital, sexual, and family conflicts—can generate strong affects that may find release in ecstatic cultism.

Cults and churches are often said to meet needs for self-respect and prestige by providing leadership roles which compensate for role deprivation. However, I know many Revival leaders who hold prestigious positions, including a parish councillor, a public health inspector, a surveyor, and several teachers, clerks, and nurses. Moreover, Revival is generally regarded with disdain by the middle and upper classes, so these people have actually sacrificed some prestige to participate. Other motives evidently lie behind their involvement.

I collected a wide range of information on fifty-four members of a Revival cult and used cross-tabulations to test several hypotheses on motives for ritual trance behavior. The following variables were not significantly related to ritual trance: gender (chi-square = 0), recruitment due to illness ($p < .70$), conjugal problems ($p < .50$), number of children ($p < .50$), marital status ($p < .30$), age ($p < .30$), color ($p < .20$), length of membership ($p < .20$), and frequency of attendance ($p < .10$). Although these results indicate that no one problem in living can sufficiently explain ritual trance behavior, we should not conclude that these variables are unimportant. Ritual trance is probably motivated by a wide variety of needs and stresses rather than one or a few. The only significant finding was a relationship between ritual trance and a position of leadership in the cult ($p < .001$): 88 percent of the officers but only 35 percent of the followers engaged in ritual trance during sixteen months of observation. The implication is that leaders may have a greater predisposition for trance than followers, and it strongly indicates that ritual trance is an important role of leaders. The success of a ceremony depends heavily on the ritual trance of leaders, and this behavior also enhances their authority.

Spiro (1965a) has noted that religious roles can serve as "culturally constituted defense mechanisms," which contain psychological conflicts and prevent mental disorder by providing approved outlets for the expression of frustrated or repressed needs, and this is definitely the case in Revival cultism. The Revival leader whom I discussed earlier was sickly and suffered from typhoid fever and malaria as a child, and she had several spontaneous visionary experiences during her twenties, including disorientation, unconsciousness, and paralysis, that led her to become a healer and to start a cult. One of her assistants was also sickly as a child and saw things that others could not see. In fact, 27 percent of the members of this cult said they joined it because of a serious illness.

Psychological case studies of four Revival leaders (Wedenoja 1978), which included life histories, observations, and projective tests, showed that they led difficult lives prior to attaining their positions, with symptoms that could have led to mental disorder, but the religious roles of three of them seemed to satisfy many of their personal needs and to promote adjustment and well-being. Both the leader and her assistant used ritual trance to express and contain dissociative tendencies. The leader used her healing role as a defense mechanism, undoing, to deal with characterological hostility toward others, and she also indirectly satisfied a need for nurturance by identifying with and nurturing others. The assistant met a dominant need for dependency and gained a sense of security through intense devotion to the leader. Her almost daily engagement in ritual trance provided an approved and valued outlet for her impulsivity, and it also met her need for attention. Although she was a timid and fearful person, she often behaved in a confident and even assertive manner because of the highly structured, well-defined nature of her roles in the cult. On the other hand, the roles of a deacon, while clearly sustaining, were not sufficient. He was usually anxious and sad, he often used vague illnesses as an excuse for not farming, and he was quite fearful of the death of the leader, upon whom he was highly dependent. Although he had been a Revivalist for most of his life, he never engaged in ritual trance, and this may be a reason for his chronic distress.

Some Revivalists certainly have psychological problems, and their religious roles, including ritual trance, are often therapeutic, but the cult does not consist of abnormal personalities, and psychotherapy is not its main purpose. I have several years of clinical experience with psychiatric patients in Jamaica and the United States, and I know many Revivalists well. Most of them are at least as normal and well adjusted as non-Revivalists, if not more so. Nevertheless, they are committed to the cult, attending services regularly and having ritual trance experiences. What is the basis for their involvement?

Ritual trance is a public performance that is guided by role expectations, and in most cases it is a culturally appropriate and psychologically normal behavior. Moreover, it is a vital part of a service because it is the means by which the gods become immanent or real, present and close at hand. It is motivated, in part, by the expectations of a service, and it is also a means by which individuals can dramatically demonstrate the depth of their faith and commitment; that is, it is a sign of conformity to cultural values. The psychological effects of ritual participation and ritual trance are, for most, the simple pleasures of conforming, gaining the attention, respect, and approval of others, and the discharge of normal drives and emotional tensions. Psychological conflict may be a sufficient reason for involvement in cultism, but it is not necessary or usual. In addition, some extraordinary pleasures of ritual participation may be enhanced by ritual trance, including a sense of fellowship, or communitas, and the opportunity for creative and aesthetic expression.

Spiro (1970:14) has said that religion is "a symbolic expression of a restricted set of needs, fantasies, wishes, conflicts, aspirations, and so on which are deeply rooted in a universal human nature." His emphasis on the expression of pancultural—rather than idiosyncratic or modal personality—needs in religion allows us to broaden our perspective on the psychology of religion from therapy for a few to normal behavior for most every human being. It is normal to have needs for dependency, sex, and prestige; inevitable that we experience grief, fear, anxiety, frustration, anger, boredom, guilt, and shame; natural that we use defense mechanisms to cope with threat and pain; and important that we have regular means for expressing and satisfying or reducing our needs and emotions. Spiro has commented insightfully on this point: "Were [the shaman] deprived of this culturally constituted defense, his conflicts would again overpower him. But, on this score, I see little difference between the shaman and the rest of mankind. Without culture and the defenses which it provides we would all be conflict-ridden" (Spiro 1978a:229n).

Religion, including ecstatic cultism and ritual trance, is a response to our psychobiological nature and social condition, and almost everyone— anyone who carries the normal load of needs, drives, and feelings and not simply the distressed, abused, or downtrodden—would probably find it personally fulfilling. Studies of individuals in Britain and the United States who have experienced ecstatic states indicate that they have a high degree of psychological well-being, higher education and social class, greater optimism, less authoritarianism and racism, a greater sense of meaningfulness and purpose in life, more self-assurance, less materialism and status consciousness, and a greater degree of social responsibility (Hay and Morisy 1978). One study found that only 34 percent of all spontaneous religious experiences occurred in the context of severe distress or decision, and they were followed in most cases by feelings of immediate relief, a sense of peace, and a long-term reduction of alienation and anxiety (Hay and Morisy 1978; Hay 1979). According to Spiegel and Spiegel (1978:154), "hypnotizability . . . is a function of relative mental health . . . , and . . . impairment or collapse in hypnotizability . . . indicates a high probability of the presence of serious psychopathology." Likewise, Ralph Hood (1974:69) has said that "the ability to have an intense experience that is labelled 'mystical,' 'peak,' or 'ecstatic' [is] most likely to be characteristic of a strongly developed ego, or of a psychologically healthy person."

TOWARDS A NATURAL HISTORY OF TRANCE

Ritual trance is an ancient phenomenon as well as a common one. Footprints at Tuc d'Audoubert cave, paintings of dancers at Cogul and La Vieja caves, the "dancing sorcerer" of Les Trois-Frères, and the "dead man" of Lascaux suggest that Cro-Magnon peoples practiced ecstatic, shamanistic rites about 20,000 years ago. Theories of the psychobiological substrates of ritual trance, however, deal only with proximal causes. Since these substrates are the products of organic evolution, an anthropological approach should include an evolutionary inquiry into the distal causes or origins of the phenomenon too.

The capacity for trance is apparently innate and universal, so it must be a product of evolution, and it is often adaptive and sometimes life saving. Possession by a god served to anesthetize a Haitian undergoing surgery and another who was injured in a traffic accident, and it also allowed shipwrecked Haitian sailors to overcome fatigue and swim a great distance to shore (Metraux 1972:131). It is tempting to regard trance as a biological adaptation, but it probably is not.

Ritual trance is a biocultural phenomenon, with a deep structure that is psychobiological and a surface structure that is psychocultural. The deep structure is not a unitary phenomenon but a complex that includes some, if not all, of the following components: the ergotropic and trophotropic systems, cerebral lateralization, the triune structure of the brain, the stress response, endogenous opiates and other neurotransmitters, and limbic discharge. Each of these components has a specific evolutionary purpose, and the capacity for trance is probably a by-product or side effect of them rather than a biological adaptation.

Evolution of the Capacity for Trance

Endorphins are apparently an adjunct to the fight-or-flight response. Produced in response to proprioceptive stimulation, such as violent muscular activity, they result in anesthesia and euphoria, which are advantageous to a wounded animal engaged in a life-or-death struggle (Prince 1982b).

The ergotropic and trophotropic systems maintain a balance between energy expenditure and conservation, which is a basic need of all organisms. The ergotropic system creates a state of arousal and awareness for survival activities such as foraging, whereas the trophotropic system forces an organism to rest and conserve or restore energy (Ellison 1979).

The limbic system receives information from the internal and external environments and generates emotions, which guide behavior toward survival and procreation (MacLean 1978). Some of the "numinous" emotions evoked by religion—feelings of dependence, surrender, and love—are limbic and were probably present before the development of language and religion (Rappaport 1971).

The most extraordinary aspect of organic evolution in the human line was the rapid growth of the neocortex, the basis for language, ideas, and abstract thought. According to Harry Jerison (1975), the neocortex serves mainly to integrate information from different senses and to construct cognitive images or models of the environment, which leads to a greater degree of behavioral plasticity and quicker, more flexible adaptation. In human beings, this cortical process also involves language. We use concepts, categories, and classificatory systems to impose order on our experiences and the environment. The surface structure of ritual trance, for example, is not only a cognitive model of certain psychobiologically based experiences but also a linguistic and cultural one.

A large neocortex is undoubtedly an asset in the process of adaptation to a physical environment, but it may be even more important for interpersonal adjustment (Oakley 1979). It gives us the ability to control drives and emotions; it enables us to predict the reactions of others and mentally to try out social strategies before risking action; and it allows us to make rules for behavior. It is thus possible "to have a society based on self-discipline, conscience and custom, rather than simply on threat and display" (Fox 1979:147).

A large neocortex creates some unique problems, though. Cognitive models enable us to anticipate the future, but they cause us to be anxious and fearful about it, too. Cognitive control enables us to regulate our behavior in accordance with social rules, but such regulation often leads to frustration. Societies must develop ways to reduce conflicts and anxieties and relieve frustrations and tension in order to maintain the health, well-being, and effectiveness of their members, and this is one of the main functions of religion.

Bilateral symmetry, including cerebral symmetry, is a fundamental characteristic of life. Many cognitive functions, however, have become lateralized or asymmetrical in the human cortex, particularly language and praxic, or motor-sequencing behavior, which are largely controlled by the left hemisphere. The earliest biological evidence for laterality is the possible existence of Broca's area, which is necessary for speech, in a 1.6-million-year-old endocast of *Homo habilis.*

There are several theories regarding the evolution of laterality, but William Calvin's (1983) is particularly comprehensive and persuasive. Calvin has proposed that the use of the right hand and arm to throw stones at prey favored the development of a rapid and precision motor sequencer in the left hemisphere, which was later used for language sequencing, too. This theory suggests that lateralization may have begun with *Homo habilis,* the first hominid to make and use tools, and it was certainly established in *Homo erectus,* an accomplished hunter and tool maker.

In animals with cerebral symmetry, one hemisphere is apparently a "spare" that can take over in the event of an injury to the other hemisphere, but this redundancy is an enormous waste of neurons if an animal's adaptation is based on intelligence. Jerre Levy (1977) has argued that the asymmetry of the human brain developed to use more brain mass and almost doubled cognitive capacity. In addition, it led to two different modes of information processing, the logical-analytical and the analogical-wholistic, which "increases mightily the likelihood of a creative solution to a novel problem" (Bogen, quoted in Galin 1976:40). On the other hand, the potential for intrapsychic conflict may be a price we pay for dual modes of processing (Galin 1977). Some, if not many, tasks are more effectively performed by one hemisphere than the other, and simultaneous employment of both hemispheres can interfere with action. Normally, however, the hemisphere that is dominant for a particular task seems to inhibit or suppress the other temporarily.

The evolution of culture has put a premium on the development of the left hemisphere. For example, the throwing of stones and spears to kill game was a basic adaptation for survival during the Paleolithic age, the formative period of human psychology and society, and language was necessary to plan and coordinate hunts and other group activities. Language led to cultural constructions, including conceptions of "self," which facilitate complex social relationships, and also forms the basis for consciousness and a sense of will or volition.

The left hemisphere usually has preemptive control over speech and other forms of behavior. It can suppress the right hemisphere, preventing its contents from reaching consciousness or being expressed verbally or in action; that is, it uses repression and other defense mechanisms. However, the relatively inarticulate and unconscious right hemisphere can operate independently, without conscious awareness or will, but this dissociation sometimes results in psychosomatic disorders or conversion reactions (Galin 1977). The same process of dissociation, in which behavior is unconsciously controlled by the right hemisphere, seems to form the basis for ritual trance, but in this case there is usually a voluntary abeyance of left hemisphere control, and the results are often therapeutic rather than pathological.

The ergotropic and trophotropic systems, the stress response, endorphins, and the limbic system are mammalian characteristics, so we can assume that they were present in *Australopithecus*. Lateralization probably began with *Homo habilis* and gradually increased as hunting, tool making, and language evolved. The psychobiological bases of ritual trance could therefore have been present in *Homo erectus*. However, ritual trance also has psychological and cultural foundations, and it is a response to certain social conditions which were probably not present before the appearance of Neanderthal or Cro-Magnon.

The Domestication of Trance

The appearance of art in the Upper Paleolithic was a "creative explosion," a dramatic and spectacular revolution in culture and cognitive development. The Cro-Magnons made more than 15,000 engravings and paintings of plants, animals, and occasionally human beings in about 225 caves and rock shelters in western Europe, principally Spain and France, between 30,000 and 10,000 years ago. They carved sensuous images of women from stone and ivory and made geometric shapes and patterns, some of which may have been notations or other symbols.

Upper Paleolithic culture is much richer than its predecessors and reflects a higher stage of cognitive development. The art is not only a representation but also an objectification of nature, and it must have required self-objectification too. Percepts were made into objects, and these objects became increasingly abstract, eventually turning into symbols. Upper Paleolithic man was capable of constructing models of reality, and he must have had modern languages and conscious awareness too.

Upper Paleolithic art apparently formed an important part of a shamanic religious tradition. Caves were settings for mass gatherings and ceremonies, which included music, dance, and dramatic performances. They may have been decorated as theaters for mythic dramatizations, in order to transmit a "tribal encyclopedia" to the young, to instill and maintain a common set of beliefs, and to encourage social solidarity and obedience to social rules (Pfeiffer 1985).

The emergence of religion in part reflected intellectual developments, namely the emergence of consciousness and abstract concepts such as life, death, and a sense of self, which were made possible by the evolution of language. The most important stimulus, however, may have been a significantly more complex life. Rapid technological change in the Upper Paleolithic enabled people to congregate in larger communities, and tribal confederations of bands were probably being formed. Under these circumstances, as John Pfeiffer (1985) has noted, there would have been a marked increase in conflict, and the main purpose of ceremonies could have been to control or reduce it and to create unity within and between groups.

Ritual trance was very likely involved in Upper Paleolithic religion, although we will never find any direct evidence of it in the archaeological record. All of its psychobiological and psychocultural elements were almost certainly present by that time, and it would be hard to believe that dramatic rites involving music and dance held under the flickering light of torches in dark caves did not evoke trance states. At first, trance states and cathartic experiences must have been spontaneous, unintended, and probably awesome and mysterious occurrences, so that people sought explanations for them. Later, as they were conceptualized and given meaning, they were probably incorporated into ceremonies as an intended consequence. Through experience, some individuals may have become masters at evoking and controlling them—that is, shamans.

Ritual trance, as a facilitator of catharsis, is one of the oldest and most universal of the culturally constituted defense mechanisms. It is a response

303

to psychological burdens imposed by human nature and the human way of life, a response to fears and anxieties stimulated by a cognitive ability to transcend the present and imagine the future, a response to intrapsychic conflicts resulting from the structure of the brain, a response to repressed and unconscious memories, feelings and drives, and a response to the inevitable frustrations involved in adherence to social rules. Periodic emotional discharge is functional for an individual and adaptive for society. While relieving personal burdens and preventing or alleviating psychological and psychosomatic disorder, it can also reduce the emotional barriers that isolate individuals and lessen the tensions of social life that might otherwise lead to rule-breaking or deviance.

The ability to manipulate human psychobiology through ritual would have been a source of considerable power over others too. The simple generation of excitement or ergotropic stimulation in a group can have highly motivating and unifying effects, as in a high school "pep rally." This excitement, augmented by the euphoric effect of endorphins and the relief provided by limbic discharge, would be pleasurable and would encourage emotional commitment to a group and its culture. In addition, ecstatic states can break down previous conditioning and can facilitate the acceptance of new ideas (Sargent 1959).

Although ritual trance has a biological basis, it is essentially a cultural innovation. Some of the psychobiological components of ritual trance evolved as adaptations to the physical environment through the processes of organic evolution, and our natural capacity for trance is apparently a by-product or side effect of the evolution of the brain and consciousness. During the course of social and cultural evolution, however, as our ancestors developed an increasingly powerful ability to manipulate and control the external environment, they also found ways to alter internal states through rituals. Trance states were shaped by cultural constructions and were controlled by role expectations. They took on meaning and value, and they were used to relieve internal conflicts and distress, to promote social unity, and to gain power over others. They became a cultural adaptation to the human way of life.

BEYOND CATHARSIS

Recent advances in the neurosciences have led to some new theories of ritual trance which broaden our understanding of it by giving social, psychological, and cultural theories a psychobiological foundation. These new theories will have to be tested in the field, and this testing will be awkward and difficult, but they have already forced us to reconceptualize ritual trance.

One of the advantages of this new approach is that the use of psychobiological concepts avoids the negative connotations of psychiatric terms such as dissociation, regression, and hysteria, which can lead us to regard ritual trance as psychopathological. The psychobiological approach also focuses on pancultural rather than idiosyncratic traits, allowing us to see that the capacity for trance is a universal human potential and not an abnormality. In addition, it helps us realize that the cathartic function of ritual trance can benefit everyone, not just the downtrodden and depressed. Ritual trance is an ancient and widely practiced psychocultural adaptation to universal problems in living inherent to human nature and the human way of life.

A psychobiological approach is necessary but almost totally lacking in theories of human behavior, which have a strong cognitive or rational bias. According to Scheff (1979:3), sociological theories either ignore emotions or treat them as irrational and antisocial forces. The cerebral bias of anthropology is blatantly apparent in cognitive anthropology and structuralism, and it led Spiro (1979c), who has always emphasized emotions and drives, to ask, "Whatever Happened to the Id?" In his view, "society and culture are not only the producers . . . , but they are also the products . . . of psychobiological organisms with desires and beliefs, drives and emotions, aspirations and tensions; of creatures of flesh and blood who laugh and cry, suffer and enjoy, who have dreams and frustrations, ideals and fears; of human beings with aspirations and anxieties, depressions and elations, conflicts and goals" (Spiro 1970:28).

One of the main lessons of the psychobiological approach to ritual trance is that we are more than cerebral. The cognitive functions of the cerebral cortex evolved to enhance the capacities of lower levels of the brain and the nervous system, and all levels of the brain are interconnected and work together. Therefore, rituals excite not only the mind but also the body. Symbols not only are "good to think" but also evoke feelings and motivate us. Rituals and symbols can take an infinite variety of forms, but their effects on us are guided and constrained by our psychobiological nature. The interconnections between the cortex and other levels, rather than the cortex itself, make us unique and human.

A scientific approach, however, has some limitations even when it has a psychobiological foundation. Ritual trance is not simply a stress-reducing exercise but also a meaningful and self-enhancing experience which is often creative and aesthetic. Our growing scientific understanding of ritual trance should be tempered by a humanistic appraisal of it, too.

One of the most remarkable and puzzling occurrences in prehistory was the preoccupation of Upper Paleolithic hunter-gatherers with art and religion, perhaps the most distinctively human endeavors. John Halverson (1987) has recently proposed that the art was motivated by a natural propensity to play and find pleasure in "representation for representation's sake." A similar argument can be made for ritual and ritual trance.

Religion and the arts are inextricably intertwined in primitive religions, which use music, dance, theater, poetry, rhetoric, paintings, and sculpture extensively to dramatize myths and beliefs and to move followers. Revival churches, for example, are colorfully and symbolically decorated, and the leaders and many of their followers wear elaborate costumes. The congregation is actively involved in a Revival service, which is like a play with only a vague script, and there is much room for spontaneity and personal expression. Several people will be "moved" to preach, often in a stylized and dramatic, if not histrionic, manner, and others will stand and give personal testimonies. Virtually everyone sings and dances to the syncopated beats of a bass and a treble drum. Generally, five to ten individuals will enter an ecstatic state as they sit or stand, and three or four more will engage in active and theatrical possession states, such as "cutting and clearing" spirits from the church with a sword.

Art is a creative, imaginative, and playful endeavor that reflects our ability to symbolize. It allows us to express and communicate ideas and feelings in a concrete shape or form. However, Revival services are not simply theater or variety shows; Revivalists are making "a joyful noise unto the Lord" (Psalms 100:1). Ritual art takes place in a cosmic or sacred context. It is used to express beliefs that give meaning and purpose to existence, and it also makes existence seem beautiful. In ritual trance, for example, a god becomes incarnate in the body of a worshiper, who becomes an intimate and living symbol or representation of a belief. This is a leading role in a cosmic theater, a dance for the gods and a celebration of life.

Jamaican Revivalists are among the finest and most admirable people I have known. Sharing their religion was a very stimulating and meaningful experience. They showed me that religious experience is often, as Margaret Field (1969:13) has so felicitously stated, "wholesome and sustaining." According to Abraham Maslow (1970), ecstatic states are "perfectly natural, human peak experiences" that lead to "self-actualization" (p. 20) and evoke feelings such as truth, goodness, beauty, wholeness, a transcendence of dichotomies, aliveness, uniqueness, perfection, inevitability, fulfillment, justice, order, simplicity, richness, playfulness, effortlessness, and autonomy (pp. 92–94). Ritual trance, however, is not only a personal experience but also a transpersonal one; it can revive an individual's sense of connectedness to his community and generate feelings of love, trust, and mutual concern, too. One Revivalist exclaimed, "You are like a dead dog without it!"

Ecstatic religions are plentiful throughout the "underdeveloped" world and have been around for perhaps 20,000 years. They would therefore seem to fulfill some panhuman needs. On the other hand, the ecstatic tradition is not well established in modern Western civilization. Many Westerners have spontaneous experiences of a mystical or ecstatic nature, but as Hay and Morisy (1978:266) have observed, "20th century secular society appears intent on avoiding this area: consequently, it offers no genuinely integrative interpretation, but reduces it to something meaningless or symptomatic of illness."

There are several possible explanations for the relative absence of ecstatic traditions in modern society. One is that we are less susceptible to trance. Greater cognitive demands in work and education (particularly among the middle class) may lead to greater development of the left hemisphere and may interfere with the ability to experience trance and express emotions. Poor susceptibility to hypnosis has, in fact, been associated with more critical and cognitive thought (Spiegel and Spiegel 1978), and there is also evidence that the degree of reliance on left hemisphere thinking is related to education (Springer and Deutsch 1981).

Another possibility is that many of the functions of ecstatic cultism are now performed by other institutions. For example, states have political rituals and propaganda to encourage loyalty. Values and cultural traditions are transmitted by public education. Political leaders use the mass media to generate a following. Organizations for the arts, such as Little Theatre, offer outlets for aesthetic expression. Rock music concerts and disco dancing are ergotropically stimulating. Jogging can produce endorphins. Psychotherapy and support groups provide opportunities for catharsis and the resolution of conflicts. And drugs and alcohol are readily available for hedonistic highs.

One of the main problems with jogging, disco dancing, drugs, and the like is that they lack a meaningful—certainly a sacred or cosmic—purpose and context. This context is still offered by religions, but services in modern denominations are "overdistanced," generally lack the excitement and drama of primitive religions, and offer few opportunities for active participation. It is hard to imagine a more cathartic, meaningful, aesthetic, and motivating experience than ecstatic cultism, and the need for such an experience may be a reason for the recent growth of mystical and charismatic cults and sects such as eastern religions and Pentecostalism and for the quasi-religious nature of many psychotherapy movements in modern society.

N O T E

I am indebted to Melford E. Spiro for his ideas and tutelage and for directing my initial research in Jamaica, which was supported by predoctoral fellowships from the Organization of American States and the National Institute of Mental Health. I also thank Kathryn Guggenheim and Robert D. Tschirgi for their generous and invaluable comments on earlier drafts of this article.

14

Human Nature as "Deep Structure"
Implications for Comparative Study

ERIKA BOURGUIGNON ᘒᘒᘒ

Can the concept of a universal human nature be reconciled with the observed diversity of cultures? The question is as old as anthropology and arguably constitutes one of its central problems. At any given time, primacy has been assigned either to the universal or to diversity of behaviors and institutions. Emphasis on the latter characterized most of American cultural anthropology in the first half of this century. Its rejection is illustrated by Clifford Geertz (1973a:43–44), who speaks "of becoming lost in a whirl-wind of cultural relativism" and cites Benedict's *Patterns of Culture* "with its strange conclusion that anything one group of people is inclined toward doing is worthy of respect by another." Anyone who accepts the notion that human beings constitute a single species and that they have bodies while also rejecting a Cartesian mind/body dichotomy in fact admits to a "human nature," however defined. Edgerton (1971:xi) writes: "If we accord man a common nature, and if we also admit that all social systems have many similarities, then we must expect to find a common core in the psychological relationship of *any* population to *any* environment" (italics in original). Moreover, anyone wishing to move from descriptions and analyses of single cases to a comparative science must find ways of coming to terms with both the unity and the diversity. Yet ways of conceptualizing the "common core" and its putative relationship to cultural and social diversity remain at issue.

A debate between relativism and antirelativism risks slighting a dimension of the problem that needs serious consideration in any attempt at systematic comparative research: the well-documented observation of recurrent but nonuniversal cultural phenomena. These may be considered to constitute an area intermediate between the unique and the universal, one that may shed light on the diversity/universality issue.

SPIRO'S CONCEPT OF UNIVERSALS IN HUMAN PERSONALITY

In a number of publications M. E. Spiro has employed the contrasting concepts of "deep structure" and "surface structures," drawn from linguistics. He has used this opposition both narrowly, for the cultural subsystem of religion, and more widely, for culture as a whole. Thus he tells us (Spiro 1978b:xxiv) that to study myth and religion as culture specific and variable is to see only their surface structures, which involve conscious meanings and symbols. When their unconscious meanings are uncovered, the universal deep structure is revealed. He argues (Spiro 1978b:xxvi) that "underlying the cross-cultural diversity in the surface meanings . . . there are important cross-cultural uniformities in their deep-structure meanings: the culturally parochial external symbols constitute symbolic transformations of culturally universal internal symbols." As in grammar, the deep structure (universal) and the surface structures (culturally variable) are linked by means of transformations. And "the interpretation of cultures consists in part in the translation of surface-structure cultural symbols into deep-structure meanings" which "are grounded in the psychic unity of mankind" (Spiro 1978a:xviii–xix).

Spiro sees human nature, or personality, as "deep structure," while cultural diversity is synonymous with variable "surface structures." Thus "personality is to culture what [in language] deep structure is to surface structure, and it is to social action what competence is to performance" (Spiro 1977:xii). Elsewhere (Spiro 1978b:354) he speaks of "the fallacy of not distinguishing (. . . [in a] fashionable metaphor) surface structure from deep structure, in culture." He argues that "the much heralded plasticity of human beings is rather narrowly limited by the constraints of an underlying and universal human nature, and . . . to a large degree the variability of human cultures represents a 'surface structure' transformation of underlying and universal 'deep structural' themes" (Spiro 1982a:xvi). He then mentions "basic similarities in human nature that cut across and underlay surface structural differences in time and space" (1982a:xix).

What does this deep structure consist of? What are its source or sources? "Personality," we are told, "refers to the configuration of cognitive, motivational, affective and perceptual systems which characterize individual actors" (Spiro 1977:xii). Certain "cognitive orientations and motivational dispositions . . . are pan-human in their distribution" and constitute "basic similarities in human nature" (Spiro 1982a:xviii–xix).

The constant motivational dispositions include competitive and hostile

Erika Bourguignon

ones, and although their intensity "is culturally (and individually) variable and although culture can tame and domesticate these motives, it is culture itself (interacting with man's mammalian biology) which also, and universally, creates them" (Spiro 1978b:346). Thus created and variably tamed (or fostered), they must be expressed, and diverse avenues of expression are, theoretically, available.

As there are invariant motivational dispositions, so there are constant cognitive orientations: "some basic cognitive orientations . . . are not culturally variable (though they may be culturally determined)" (Spiro 1978b:349). Like the invariant motivational dispositions mentioned above, they are products of both culture and human biology. Examples occur in such beliefs and values as the desirability of life, of material and physical pleasures, and "belief in superhuman beings, both of good and evil, and the corollary belief that human action (religious ritual, etc.) can influence their activity by invoking the assistance of the former and repelling the harm of the latter" (Spiro 1978b:349). These "same underlying cognitive orientations . . . being culturally conditioned, take different forms" (1978b:349). And Spiro concludes (1978b:350): "These invariant dispositions stem, I believe, from pan-human biological and cultural constants and they comprise . . . universal human nature."

As ethnographic research has shown again and again, "normative values and official codes" of given cultures may not be congruent with the invariant motivational dispositions and constant cognitive orientations of human beings. Indeed, Spiro's selection of cultures for study suggests a search for what might be called "limiting cases": in Ifaluk, a cooperative social system, an ethos valuing nonaggression, and few pressures for competition for scarce resources (Spiro 1978b:339); in the kibbutz, in addition to a cooperative social system and emphasis on noncompetition, a strong stress on sharing and communal living, including communal child rearing; in Burmese Buddhism, a religion whose official and normative teachings directly oppose some of the constant cognitive orientations (Spiro 1978b:349).

How, then, can societies operate in the face of such apparent denials of human nature and such glaring contradictions of what is invariant and constant in the deep structure? How do cultures tame and domesticate hostile and competitive motives? How do they deal with the universal need for dependency? What happens when the constant cognitive orientations are officially denied?

In Ifaluk (Spiro 1978b:342), hostility created through the harsh experiences of infancy is expressed by adults symbolically through religious belief and ritual and is "tamed" through the institution of the chieftainship. Now, should both the expressive and the taming institutions be abolished (as indeed appears to have happened since Spiro's 1947 fieldwork) and "if there were no functionally equivalent structural alternatives for these institutions—hostility should be expressed in overt social aggression, or (if it is inhibited by external sanctions), in predictable clinical symptoms" (Spiro 1978b:343). (The possibility of a change in the intensity of the hostility-arousing experiences of infancy is not considered.)

The harmonious life of the people of Ifaluk, Spiro (1978b:339) tells us, particularly impressed him as it contrasted with that of the Lac du Flambeau (Wisconsin) Ojibwa, among whom he had recently conducted fieldwork. There aggression had frequently been expressed overtly. Hallowell considers this group very highly acculturated compared with related groups. Writing of the Canadian Ojibwa (Saulteaux) prior to the Lac du Flambeau research, he noted their characteristic mild-manneredness; overt aggression in face-to-face situations was notably absent. Hostility was expressed in covert ways through sorcery and fear of sorcery, while (male) ego strength was gained though power acquired from a guardian spirit, through the vision quest. Yet Hallowell (1955b:278) remarks, "If some of the basic beliefs and concepts of these people were changed their aggressive impulses would be reconstellated and the personality traits referred to [placidity, patience, and self-restraint] would no longer assume their characteristic form." Among the Lac du Flambeau people, in 1946, he concluded that there "seems to be a lack of any positive substitute for that aspect of the aboriginal value system that had its core in religious belief," so that they live "under conditions which, as yet, offer no culturally defined values and goals that have become vitally significant for them" (Hallowell 1955a:375). The old mechanisms that had held aggressive impulses in check were no longer operative.

The historical development of the Israeli kibbutz offers a different type of resolution of the conflict between "human nature" and cultural norms and values. Here, Spiro (1979a) argues, the norms of communal child rearing came into conflict, after two generations, with the "precultural" nature of motherhood. As a result of a young women's "counterrevolution," the norms were altered.

If we accept Spiro's interpretation that these changes reveal evidence of a contradiction in the original kibbutz society between an aspect of human nature (a precultural need for mothering) and the organization of the society and some of its values, then we are led to important research questions: under what circumstances do societies reorganize themselves to eliminate such contradictions or to develop improved methods for dealing with them?

It is noteworthy that there was no power structure, either within the kibbutz itself nor in the larger society of which it is a part, to enforce the values embodied in the earlier social organization of the kibbutz. Communal child rearing was not left unchanged, over the opposition of the women, by the force of the state, nor were other changes in kibbutz lifestyle suppressed by powerful sanctions. In these small, democratic communities, the people were free to make the changes they wished. Is the size of the community relevant to the apparent ease of transformation? Is its prosperity and its transformation from pioneer to social elite? What influence has the surrounding society exercised, and the larger world, including the international media? Did the cultural ideal of equality between the sexes facilitate the change? The kibbutz example suggests that political, economic, and social factors should be examined, as well as psychological ones, when we find a striking discrepancy between human constants and observable institutional forms as well as in cases where we see their dramatic transformations.

Spiro's work also deals with possible outcomes in the event of a discrepancy between official norms and values and on the one hand the cognitive orientations for which he claims invariant status on the other. In Burmese Buddhism, we are told, only a minority is able to fulfill the demands of a religion that requires detachment from human ties and earthly goods and pleasures. Yet a way of living with this discrepancy has been created and rationalized. Burmese society has done so, in fact, by offering two parallel, if contradictory, cognitive systems: Buddhism and supernaturalism. Since members of the society participate in both to a greater or lesser extent, these alternate systems of belief and ritual are not, for most people, mutually exclusive. Each offers a different set of avenues for the expression of motivational dispositions as well as different cognitive orientations. They fulfill different and complementary psychological functions, both for the individual practitioners and also for the society at large. "The world-renouncing Buddhist monk" (Spiro 1978b:xxxi) symbolized the ethical principles of that great religion. By contrast, supernaturalism (the *nat* religion), is represented by a "world embracing cult specialist" who "is the Dionysian inversion of the Buddhist monk" (ibid.). Buddhist monks embody the ego ideal; the *nat* cult reflects the "real" world, one that recognizes human attachments and strivings. The monks, we are told, represent a special group of individuals, persons who experience severe psychological conflicts which they resolve "by utilizing elements of [their] religious heritage as a culturally constituted defense" (Spiro 1965a:110). Unable to function well in the ordinary course of Burmese familial and social life, they can, in the special role of monk, express the ego ideal of the society: "The monastic system . . . serves the important social function of allowing potentially disruptive, anti-social drives to be channeled into culturally approved (institutional) behavior" (Spiro 1965a:112).

The coexistence and mutual tolerance of Buddhism and the *nat* cult seems to show how it is possible to aspire to a denial of constant cognitive orientations derived from human culture and biology and yet not impose their full realization on all. A special segment of the society "gains merit" for those too "weak" (or too human) to do so for themselves.

We may thus summarize Spiro's position: although certain motivational dispositions and cognitive orientations are constant, their intensity and forms of expression vary. Different "functionally equivalent" institutions allow for their harmless venting. However, if symbolic forms of expression and institutional "taming" of, for example, aggressive motives are not available, overt aggression or individual pathology result. Parallel outcomes may also be expected for others of the constant motivational dispositions.

The people of Ifaluk appeared to have solved their problems, under aboriginal conditions, through religious and politicoreligious institutions, the Burmese, through alternative religious systems, and the members of the kibbutz, through cultural and social transformations. Under conditions of acculturation, shifts from the successful symbolic expression and "taming" of hostile impulses in traditional societies to a breakdown of these institutions and a lack of their satisfactory replacement by functionally equivalent new structures appear, as among the Ojibwa. We may paraphrase Spiro to say that, if the constants are violated, the violation occurs at a cost both to society and to the individuals of which it is composed. An optimal society, then, is a society that accommodates the constants. Because, however, there are functionally equivalent solutions, no single sociocultural system needs to be preferred. There is still room for diversity in this scheme of things.

RECURRENT PHENOMENA: THE CASE OF POSSESSION TRANCE

As we have seen, Spiro seeks to relate the observable surface features of various societies to underlying regularities of deep structure, or human nature. Expanding the sample of societies under investigation, we note the recurrence of apparently common surface features in some of the sample but not all. Features that appear in many but by no means all societies pose a special problem. We find the same or similar solutions rather than a series of unique solutions related to a common base. Addressing these repeated methods of resolving certain problems, we operate at a level of analysis somewhere between the culturally unique and variable surface structure and the universal deep structure.

Spiro, who calls "the needs for aggression and dependency" "two especially important characteristics of the human mind" (1978a:xxx), has been particularly interested in religion. He argues that because of the "polysemic character of religious symbols, religion can be used as a culturally constituted defense mechanism for the unconscious gratification of the needs of dependency on and aggression against parents" (ibid.). And he adds: "In most traditional societies . . . , religion is the cultural system par excellence by means of which conflict resolution is achieved. In such societies . . . religion serves as a highly efficient culturally constituted defense mechanism" (Spiro 1965a:113).

Spiro's fullest exploration of religion as a culturally constituted defense mechanism is found in his extensive work on Burma and its two religious traditions. Because of the striking continuities—and some important differences—between Burmese shamanism and possession belief and possession trance religions elsewhere, a brief exercise in comparative anthropology ("is there any other kind?" Spiro [1978a:xviiin] asks), may profitably be attempted. The institutionalization, in a religious context, of dissociational or trance states is, indeed, virtually universal in traditional societies. Possession trance appears in societies of one widespread type, exhibiting distinctive structural features as well as certain geographic distributions. By contrast, visionary trance, involving psychological "absences," often conceptualized as "trips" or "journeys," is much more likely a feature of the religious systems of a different type of traditional society. The two trance forms coexist in an intermediary type (Bourguignon 1973; Bourguignon and Evascu 1977). The cases selected for comparison with Burmese supernaturalism, somewhat arbitrarily, are Haitian vodoun and Tamang shamanism, as described by Peters (1981).

Spiro calls Burmese nat religion "shamanism." This religion involves a belief in spirit possession, expressed both in illness and in trance. Shamans, for the most part, are women, so that they are the inverse of male Buddhist monks, not only in their expression of impulses which are denied or repressed by the monks, but also with reference to their gender. In emic terms, shamans are recruited to the role when a nat (spirit) falls in love with the individual and seeks marriage. Spiro proposes four types of explanations for Burmese spirit beliefs: a historical or "background" explanation and a cognitive, motivational, and perceptual one. Burmese supernaturalism has its roots in ancient animistic beliefs and also in some incorporated Buddhist influences. It coexists as a folk religion with Buddhism. Essentially the same can be said for the shamanistic beliefs of the Tamang of Nepal. In Haiti, vodoun beliefs can be traced to various West African societies, but there are also Catholic influences and some local developments. Vodoun, like shamanism in these two Asian societies, coexists with a world religion, and its participants consider themselves Catholics, as the Burmese and Tamang villagers consider themselves Buddhists. However, the Catholic church has, at various times, engaged in vigorous antivodoun campaigns, and Protestant groups, particularly the Pentecostalists, have declared open warfare against the traditional religion. In all three societies, traditional beliefs offer explanations for certain experiences, or symptoms, namely that they represent the call of the spirits. This constitutes the cognitive explanation of behavior eventuating in the assumption of the role of spirit "expert." And it offers the basis for the perception of signs and symptoms as a spirit call both by the afflicted and by experts. In all three of the societies, one does not simply "choose" to become a shaman or possession trancer but responds to a call. This response is generally at first resisted, and the resistance is followed by a variety of troubles: illness, bad dreams, harm to family members, violent dissociated behavior, and so forth. If the troubles bring the individual so afflicted to a practitioner, this expert may have several diagnostic options, one of them being the "call," and advice to accept this call, with warnings of more dire things to come. This much seems to be true for the three societies under discussion and for many others as well.

In addition to the historical, cognitive, and perceptual explanations, Spiro seeks a motivational explanation for the recruitment to the role of the Burmese shaman. He argues (Spiro 1978a:217) that nat beliefs offer extra-natural satisfaction of needs and therefore encourage individuals to seek this satisfaction. He also maintains that there is an unconscious awareness of a possible resolution to frustrations through the religious system. Need frustration and a desire for need satisfaction constitute the motivational aspect of this sequence. Finally, there are experiences resulting from the need frustration, which are interpreted as possession.

In his discussion of deep structure and surface structure in religious symbols, Spiro talks of a situation in which "the belief in the external reality of . . . supernatural beings is assured by their being identified with the reified and externalized images of the parenting figures" (Spiro 1978a:xxv). He adds as a footnote: "If, as sometimes happens, parental introjects are not relinquished, or if, having been projected, they are again introjected, the merging of parental and supernatural images in the inner world may be experienced as supernatural possession; that is, a god, spirit, or the like is experienced as having entered into and having seized control of the person" (Spiro 1978a:xxv n. 2).

Regrettably, the point is not further developed: under what circumstances is this likely to happen, in the absence of a preexisting (traditional or borrowed) cognitive system that structures the experience? A phenomenon that presents some striking similarities with that of possession trance, in the absence of a possession belief, is the multiple personality syndrome (Kenny 1986; Bourguignon 1987). Although there is dissociation and the acting out of alternate personalities, as in possession trance, the syndrome appears to be structured by a different set of cultural influences and expectations.

What is the role of shaman/possession trancer in these three societies? In Burma, the shaman is an oracle, medium, diviner, and cult officiant. The

315

activities involve impersonating a spirit's speech and behavior, including dancing, in a dissociated state (actual or feigned); the behavior is interpreted as spirit possession. The shaman is possessed by a single spirit, a single identity. Each shaman is an independent actor, and there is no active national organization or hierarchy that controls role assumption, training, or professional activities.

In Haiti, individual vodoun cult centers are internally hierarchically organized: led by a "priest" or "priestess," a center, particularly in an urban area, includes initiates at various ranks and with specialized functions. In rural areas, the cult is rooted in the family tradition and centers about family members, one of whom may hold the position of "priest." Cult centers and the societies organized around them are autonomous entities. Possession trancers may individually act as mediums, but their primary function is to dance and act out spirit roles in cult centers, under the control of the center's leader. Each individual may be possessed by numerous spirits, often arriving in sequence. There is, however, one principal spirit, the "master of the head," for whom initiation rituals are undergone.

The Tamang shaman is primarily a specialist in healing rituals. During these rituals he may become possessed by spirits, but in the classical North Asian tradition, he also engages in spirit journeys, something which distinguishes him from both the Burmese shaman and the Haitian possession trancer. Like the Burmese shaman, he is an individual practitioner and not part of either a larger organization or a local cult center, although he may have disciples.

Who are the shamans/possession trancers? In Burma, the vast majority (more than 95 percent) are women. The men who occupy the role "with few exceptions . . . seem to be either homosexual (manifest or latent), transvestite, or effeminate (and sometimes all three)" (Spiro 1978a:220). In Haiti, the majority of possession trancers (and dancers) are women. Leaders may be men or women, with men outnumbering women, particularly in rural areas. Men play various other cult roles, acting as drummers, sacrificers, or masters of ceremony. Some male possession trancers or cult leaders, like the Burmese shamans cited by Spiro, are known to be, or appear to be, homosexuals or effeminate.

Among the Tamang, only men become shamans. How does a person become a shaman/possession trancer? In all three societies, individuals are recruited to the role by a supernatural call. In Burma, a nat falls in love with the chosen person, with the intent of marrying her (or him). Women are solicited by male nats, men by female ones. Solicitation may take place in dreams or through spontaneous possession at ceremonies. The shaman candidate resists at her peril. Yet she will resist, in general, because shamans are held in low esteem. The reason is that the relationship between the woman and the spirit is a sexual one and therefore shameful. She is (therefore?) thought to be promiscuous. Punishment for not accepting the marriage or relationship with the nat ranges from financial loss to psychiatric illness to leprosy, according to Spiro's informants (Spiro 1978a:210). A full-fledged shaman goes through a complete marriage ceremony, conducted by shamans, which in effect constitutes an initiation ceremony. The admitted (conscious) motivation for accepting the relationship is the fear of reprisals for refusing. The delay between the solicitation and the acceptance is often extended, even lasting for a number of years.

In the Haitian case, one becomes a cult member—and at the lower levels of initiation this means primarily a possession trancer—as a result of having experienced a demand by a spirit. As in Burma, this call may be expressed in dreams or in spontaneous possession or in illness. In each case, the interpretation of a diviner/cult leader is likely to play a decisive role in deciding what actions the particular case calls for. Incoherent dissociated behavior or unconsciousness may be interpreted as possession by a "wild" (untamed) spirit, requiring a first-level initiation to teach the spirit to express its identity and the trancer the appropriate controlled behavior. Yet the cult specialist may diagnose not possession but disorder due to other causes (e.g., witchcraft) and may prescribe a different course of action. In the role of diviner and healer, he or she has considerable altitude to steer and manipulate the course of the disordered behavior either into cult membership or into an illness/healing episode (Bourguignon 1984).

Since affliction is likely to occur at each level of initiation, these rites may be considered healing rituals. There is resistance to undergoing them, ostensibly because of the substantial cost involved as well as fear of the proceedings. Each initiation is preceded by a period of seclusion and deprivation, symbolizing death followed by rebirth in the concluding ritual. Some women, however, liken the process to a marriage ritual, observing that the ritual establishes or strengthens a relation with a spirit personality; the seclusion involves being put to bed but also the acceptance of a spirit necklace, equivalent to a wedding ring, both following the collection of a veritable trousseau. (Marriages of humans to spirit spouses—for men and for women—do exist, but these are not part of the initiation sequence.) Each level of initiation strengthens the supernatural power of the possession trancer, who gains greater control over the spirits; in etic terms, she learns to control trance behavior to a greater extent. The possessing spirits are both male and female. They are generally acquired through family lines; some are divinized ("canonized") ancestors.

Although some shamans among the Tamang may choose the role for various practical reasons, Peters (1981:62) is primarily concerned with the type who "becomes a shaman from personal necessity and not from choice.

[He] experiences a 'calling' which is an initial affliction whose only cure is to shamanize." The Tamang believe that the initial state of "crazy possession" afflicts a young man because he is chosen by dead shamans as their patrilineal heir. When he accepts the calling he is apprenticed to a living shaman and may undergo as many as four levels of initiation, each increasing his supernatural power and control over trance behavior.

Spiro discusses the sequence of illness, resistance, and final acceptance of the calling by Burmese shamans. He suggests that the symptoms interpreted as spirit possession are largely the psychosomatic consequences of need frustrations and that the fact that the calling is accepted only after considerable resistance gives evidence of "their ambivalence about recruitment to this status. That they finally feel compelled to do so . . . indicated . . . how strong is their desire for recruitment" (Spiro 1978a:218). What is the relationship between the spirit and its human vehicle? For the Burmese, it is the love of a spirit, confirmed in marriage; though the relationship is sexual, it is said to be spiritual. The woman is known as the nat's wife. Her marriage to the spirit does not preclude ties with a human husband.

In Haiti, initiated possession trancers are known as *hunsi*, a Dahomean term meaning "spirit wife." However, no Creole equivalent of the term is used. Spirits are addressed as father or grandmother or mistress, but male spirits may address women as "my wife." One group of spirits is addressed as "cousin." In possession trance, themes of power, dominance, seniority, and kinship are expressed more directly then sexual ones. Possession is termed "mounting," and the possessed individual is called the spirit's "horse." The spirit is also said to be in the person's head or to dance on the person or on her head. Complex spirit roles are acted out, often involving personalities that develop over a period of time.

The Tamang shaman experiences visions and is possessed by a tutelary spirit, often an ancestor. In the initiatory sequence, the disciple must first learn from his human shaman guru how to go into trance for the spirit to speak through him. In the second stage he learns how to call the spirit, by whom he is said to be ridden or whom he is said to have on his shoulders. With greater control, at the third stage, the shaman "is now 'riding the guru' . . . : the shaman is now master of the spirits and thus of the affliction initially caused him" (Peters 1981:86). The final stage is reached when the shaman "can embark on magic flights . . . to soul journey to the heavens and underworlds" (Peters 1981:87).

Spiro locates the motivations of Burmese women in need frustration and a desire for the need satisfaction that spirit possession provides. He identifies several types of needs: sexual needs, dependency needs, a prestige need, and a "Dionysian" need: "the performance of the shaman's role usually . . . gratifies these needs in an undisguised and, sometimes, in a direct fashion. . . . the shaman's role explicitly permits the expression of needs which are forbidden to non-shamans" (Spiro 1978a:219).

These needs and their satisfactions, as described by Spiro for Burma, may be compared to inferences from the behaviors and associated beliefs of Haitians and Tamang. Sexual needs of prohibited kinds find satisfaction in the experience of being loved by and married to a nat: premarital, extramarital, and polyandrous needs for women, perhaps homosexual ones, and homosexual and incestuous needs for men. Marriage to spirits of the opposite sex and acting out of the roles of the possessing spirit give expression to identification with females for men and with males for women. Some male shamans call their nats "sisters" or "mothers," appellations which may involve a sexual component. Largely the same thing may be said for Haitians, who may act out opposite sex roles during possession trance; the reference to marriage is not explicit, although the sexual component of the symbolism may be transparent and that of the behavior may be quite explicit. Some spirits (i.e., possession trancers) engage in openly erotic behavior. By contrast, the sexual behavior does not appear to be present, at least overtly, in the case of the Tamang: there are no cross-sex possessions and no reference to love or marriage.

Spiro also mentions dependency needs: reference to a nat as mother may indicate the fantasy satisfaction of regressive dependency, and identification with a baby nat may express dependency. Regressive dependency, satisfied and expressed, looms by far larger in both the Haitian and the Tamang context. Haitian spirits are addressed using terms for parents and grandparents and are sometimes thought to be the spirits of ancestors. They are inherited in family lines. They are believed to be very powerful and represent higher ranks in the social hierarchy. Possession trancers identify themselves with these entities, who demand obedience. And yet, in a reversal of the dependency needs of their faithful, they must be fed. There is some indication that the spirits represent not only infantile psychological dependency needs but also physical needs. Quite strikingly, Kerboull (1973) reports for a region of northern Haiti that, as the practical situation of the peasantry has worsened, the protective and benevolent hereditary spirits have increasingly been replaced by fiercer and more insatiable ones.

For the Tamang, the shaman's tie with his titular spirit is one of kinship. This spirit, which becomes the shaman's protector and guide upon initiation, initially caused him to become mad yet provides him with a solution to his problem once he is obeyed. On further initiation, the shaman gains mastery over his ancestral spirit. Instead of being ridden, the shaman rides him.

Seemingly more important than dependency needs, for the Burmese, are prestige needs. Self-esteem and, at least temporarily, social identity are transformed by identification with and marriage to a spirit. This, Spiro suggests, may account for the attraction of the shamanistic role for women and the poor, who hold a low position in the status hierarchy.

This argument is even more significant for Haitian possession trancers, particularly for lower-class men, who are status deprived and who may be possessed by important and powerful spirits. Obeisance on the part of their community and members of their own family, if only on a temporary basis, appears to be very rewarding. Impersonating important spirits provides time out from the daily humiliations of poverty and oppression.

Because the Tamang shaman's position is quasi-hereditary, it is less clear whether and how prestige strivings contribute to role recruitment. However, as a guru to disciples, as one who has overcome the powers that made him ill, as one who can heal others and retrieve stolen souls, he exercises power and gives convincing evidence of it to others. We may assume that this demonstration of success in dealing with dangers that beset his clients, as well as himself, must be gratifying to his self-esteem and must increase the esteem in which he is held by others.

Spiro lists one final group of needs for the Burmese: Dionysian needs. He notes that, "as Buddhists, the Burmese are constrained to act in measured ways, taking their enjoyment in moderation and renouncing the orgiastic in all forms" (Spiro 1978a:222). Possession by a nat permits tabooed behavior, since it is not the shaman but the nat who is responsible for it. To an extent this fits the Haitian situation as well. Spirits challenge the social hierarchy— to a degree; nondrinkers consume alcohol; dancing is vigorous, and people engage in ordinarily inappropriate sex-role behavior.

Tamang shamans apparently neither act out spirit roles nor engage in behavior that is appropriate for spirits but not humans.

In addition to the needs that Spiro lists, two others seem relevant to both the Haitian and Tamang case, however dissimilar they may be in other respects. These are needs for mastery and for oral satisfaction.

The theme of mastery is in some ways related to dependency and sexuality; it also has a developmental dimension. Although the symbolism of mounting and riding may be seen as containing a sexual reference, the imagery of mastery and control is quite explicit. The rider controls the will and the action of the mount. The imagery exists both in Haiti and among the Tamang; in the latter case as the shaman grows in spiritual strength, he also grows in his mastery over the spirits, who are likely to be his own ancestors. The developmental aspect of both mastery and sexuality is even more striking if we consider that most first possessions—or behavior diagnosed as such—in all three of our cases apparently occur in adolescence, when conflicts over both dependency and sexuality tend to surface. Why they are more likely to do so for women in Burma and Haiti, and for men among the Tamang, is a question suggested by this comparative analysis.

The expression of dependency and the gaining of mastery appear to be linked. The trancer is dominated (or mastered) by the spirit, who takes over the individual's mind and body, speaks through the medium, and performs a variety of actions. There is an apparent abandonment of self to a greater power, one whose identity as a once powerful living person or as an ancestor or spirit ally of ancestors enhances his (or her) prestige. Yet the actions and speech of this powerful being, through an essentially passive human being, act on that individual's environment. When the Tamang shaman reaches his highest level of mastery and goes to confront spirits in their own domains—heavens and underworlds—to retrieve the soul of a patient, the drama is carried out entirely on the fantasy level: the shaman is totally immobile and unconscious. Peters (1981:125–126) says that he prepares for this undertaking by rousing his anger and calling on his helping spirits to protect him in this dangerous mission. Anger and aggression, dependency (on spirit helpers) and mastery (over evil spirits), and passivity (physically) and mastery (in fantasy) all combine in this scene.

In the Haitian case, the individual ideally grows in (esoteric) knowledge and power and in time is increasingly able to control the coming of the spirits. In older persons, possession trances appear to be rarer and lighter. Perhaps, for them, conflicts over sexuality and dependency have largely been resolved.

A final theme relates to sacrifice, feeding the spirits. An expression of oral needs and need satisfactions may be hypothesized. In Burma, offerings to the nats, including various types of foods, are a part of rituals and of the care of shrines. Haitian and Tamang spirits also require sacrifices. For the Tamang, Peters (1981:59) quotes his guru: "The spirits are hungry; if they are not fed, they will eat the people," adding, "when evil spirits attack, they are believed to cause illness by consuming their victims."

In Haiti spirits are said to be controlled by what and how they are fed; sacrifices are viewed as central to rituals, more important than possession trance. Spirit rituals are spoken of as "feasting" the gods and "feasting" the dead. When spirits and other harmful beings attack, people often speak of being "eaten." As Kakar (1982:99) writes of the Oraon of India, whose possessing spirits demand to be fed: "People who have known hunger will breed hungry spirits and must constantly struggle with the persecuting spirit of greed." The theme of hunger and hungry spirits seems to fit the Haitians and Tamang better than the Burmese.

Finally, why is it that in two of our three cases possession trancers are, in the majority, women? Among the Tamang, they are not. Spiro

(1978a:224 n. 12) tentatively suggests three possible factors: (1) systematic, sex-linked constitutional differences render Burmese females more susceptible to possession, (2) Burmese males suffer from less intense conflict than females, with respect to at least those needs which are importantly satisfied by the shamanistic role (and there is some evidence that this might indeed be the case), (3) there exist for Burmese males, but not females, institutional alternatives which serve as functional equivalents for the shamanistic role. The monastic role, for example, may satisfy at least some of the same needs that are satisfied in shamanism.

If constitutional differences do exist in Burma, either they are absent among Tamang or they are denied expression there. The second point says that Burmese women experience greater conflicts than men with regard to frustrated sexual, prestige, and Dionysian needs. (The examples given for dependency needs refer to male shamans.) Conflicts result from the inability to act on needs blocked by social norms and values. Prestige needs are of particular interest here. Spiro (1977) notes a striking structural equality of male and females in Burma, expressed in legal, economic, political, and social spheres of life. This equality is typical of Southeast Asia. Yet there is an ideology of male superiority—spiritual, moral, intellectual, and social— that is shared by women and men. Since women hold status through marriage with human mates, they can also gain special status through marriage with a spirit. And yet, Burmese women are not downtrodden.

The broader question, then, is: do women's possession trance activities reflect a suppression of women (Lewis 1971) or their freedom (Devereux 1974)? The "freedom" of Burmese women, or of the Haitian women who are economically independent or of the Theban women (Devereux 1974), means only that it is possible for them to seek alternative ways of satisfying needs in religion, not that their relative freedom and equality reduced psychic conflicts.

The case of the Tamang women may suggest an avenue for research in this regard. There some men become shamans and others Buddhist monks (lamas). For women, neither role is available. However, women do suffer from hysterical symptoms, and Peters (1981) notes that the great majority of healing rituals conducted by shamans are performed for women. In a case described by Peters, the attack by hostile spirits is diagnosed by the shaman, who induces an incoherent possession trance in the patient. The aim of the ritual is to cure her, not to turn her into a shaman candidate. As Peters puts it (1981:149), "In Tamang society, it is men who become shamans and women who are primarily beset by illness." In Nepal, as in Burma, women are believed to be spiritually inferior to men. But among the Tamang, they are also economically and politically inferior and are insecure in the marriage relationship. Nor do they have religious options: they can become neither shamans nor nuns.

Thus though Tamang women have the belief in possessing spirits (cognitive explanation) and the interpretation of psychogenic symptoms as possession (perceptual explanation), and they suffer from need frustrations and conflicts surrounding them, this sequence when they express it can be perceived and treated only as illness. Mastery of the illness through control over the spirits and long-term resolution of the conflicts in fantasy and ritual acting out is denied to them. And this denial may well be considered an expression of the unequal powers of men and women. Spiro's explanatory sequence requires a power situation that tolerates it. When it is not tolerated, the expression of conflict in the spirit possession idiom becomes subject of exorcism; it becomes, in psychological language, pathological dissociation.

In the comparison between the Burmese, the Haitians, and the Tamang, it has been possible to discuss recruitment to the role of shaman/possession trancer only at the level of belief system and institutional structures: what roles exist, who fills them, and how the recruitment process is conceptualized. We can infer needs and need satisfactions only from behavior in the ritual context and its symbolism. Information about the strength of drives and their sources in socialization practices is lacking. Yet as Spiro (1978a:223) observes, the existence of unsatisfied needs and differential drive strength among individuals is not sufficient as an explanation. There is also differential cognitive strength: people with greater exposure to spirit beliefs, and hence greater awareness of possession as a possible means of substitute need satisfaction, are more likely candidates for the shamanistic role. Note that in all three societies the role is more likely to be assumed by the kin of role incumbents.

As mentioned, individuals will be more susceptible to suggestion and psychological contagion at certain critical periods in their lives. The role of the diagnostician should not be neglected, since a choice of diagnoses may well be available. And finally, there is the matter of differential access to the shamanistic role. Becoming a shaman, or possession trancer, is one solution to need frustrations. But even where the necessary cognitive and perceptual orientations exist for spirit possession to be a possible psychological option, one in which the individual can grow and gain control indirectly over the psychological pressures at work, this role may be available only to some. People of the "wrong" social category will be treated as patients, and the development of their "faculties" will not take place. Instead, they are likely to fall ill again, at some future crisis. This is the situation of Tamang women. In some other societies the necessary cognitive and perceptual bases exist but no shamanistic role, only that of victim of demons to be exorcized, as illustrated in the long history of demonic possession in the Judeo-Christian tradition or in the case of the Jewish women in Morocco studied by Bilu (1980).

For the Burmese men, Buddhist monks and shamans alike, religious roles act as "a culturally constituted defense, which, by satisfying the shaman's frustrated needs and thereby precluding the need for idiosyncratic defenses, serves to avert the outbreak of psychopathology" (Spiro 1978a:229). This system works, by all indications, equally well for the Haitian possession trancer and the Tamang shaman. It does not work for the Tamang woman, although the healing ritual will give her relief. However different Tamang shamanism, Burmese shamanism, and Haitian vodoun may be, they function as culturally constituted defense mechanisms for their practitioners in addition to whatever other functions they fulfill. As such they are both functionally equivalent solutions to characteristically human conflicts and are expressive of locally typical stresses. Under what circumstances such culturally constituted systems of defense are constructed and to whom they are available remains to be studied. As in the case of the individual, so for the society: the existence of unsatisfied needs is not a sufficient explanation.

CONCLUSIONS

Spiro speaks of religion as a "culturally constituted defense mechanism," one that is "highly efficient" in traditional societies (1965a:113). He discusses at some length why religion serves this function less well in other types of societies. He speaks not of universal patterns of belief and behavior but of one whose efficacy is limited to certain kinds of societies, namely the "traditional" ones. Now, within the scope of such religious institutions, in some traditional societies possession trance specifically acts as a culturally constituted defense mechanism, helping both to express and to resolve conflicts. It both indicates specific stresses and serves as a safety valve. As we have seen, the Burmese example includes women possession trancers, spirit marriages, a sexual dimension to the relationship between human beings and spirits, and dissociation (trance) and illness interpreted and experienced as possession by a spirit entity. None of these is unique to Burma, however special the Burmese context framing these aspects of religious belief and behavior may be.

Since some of the needs expressed and satisfied appear to be panhuman, the question remains as to why this particular vehicle is so very widespread, a finding which suggests a special kind of effectiveness.

Our understanding of specific cultures is enhanced, I have argued, if we are able to recognize not only their uniqueness and the underlying common deep structure but also their special use of features that they share with other societies of their type. This use involves not only the special coloration of belief, practice, and experience that affects the cognitive and perceptual dimensions of their lives but also the special stresses that strengthen certain needs and thus favor particular direct and indirect ways of satisfying need. They thus provide the motivational bases for the existence of the institutions and for the behavior and experience of individual participants.

The range of solutions to shared human problems, rooted in constant needs and persistent characteristics of the human mind, though theoretically infinite, is in fact more likely to be circumscribed, and variants of recurrent solutions are more likely to occur in societies that share basic structural characteristics as well as in those that manifest geographic or historical connections.

As a result, it is useful to attend to that intermediate region between the unique and the universal, between the local elaborations of differences and the common human nature in which they are rooted—that region where societies of a similar type may be identified—and to study their varying uses of recurrent solutions in an attempt to identify the determinants of these variations. Such a focus on the middle distance will help us, it is hoped, in dealing with differences hidden behind the apparent similarities of religious institutions and their psychological functions.

PART FOUR

Aggression, Dependency, and the Skills of Social Manipulation

15

Aggression, Social Skill, and Strategy in Daily Life

A Baboon Case History

SHIRLEY C. STRUM 〰〰

A paper on baboons may seem out of place in a volume concerned with cultural anthropology and specifically with its psychological aspects. Yet although our subjects differ markedly, Melford Spiro and I share many interests. Among the earliest, in both cases, was the challenge to explain aggression in daily life and, later, a fascination with the biological universals that may apply to human behavior.

I present here not a review of animal aggression or of evolutionary theory but something different: a case history of a baboon group. Here I follow a "Spiro axiom": "single cases prove little; they are primarily useful insofar as they challenge received opinions" (Spiro 1979a:109). The baboon case history suggests startling conclusions about how we should view aggression in at least one animal society, and since models of human aggression have, for at least half a century, relied heavily on animal data, these become "facts" relevant to our understanding of humans. I will consider the manner in which these facts might be used in analyses of human evolution.

COMPETITION AND DEFENSE: SOCIAL SKILL OR BRUTE FORCE?

The first scientific animal studies of this century identified aggression as a pervasive element in daily life. Until the 1930s, however, scientists viewed aggression as both abnormal and dysfunctional, since it seemed to disrupt the basic fabric of society. The "ethologists" of the 1930s (Tinbergen 1953; Lorenz 1964; etc.) fundamentally changed our views when they attempted to understand animal behavior from an evolutionary point of view

329

(see Marler and Hamilton 1966 for a general discussion). This evolutionary approach transformed aggression into an adaptive behavior, normal instead of abnormal and central instead of dysfunctional in solutions to such animal problems as competition and defense. Conceptually, aggression soon came to be seen as an important evolutionary feature of animal society. It also became a vital structural feature, since aggression often resulted in dominance hierarchies, ordering individual interactions, and through the individuals, the group. The practical significance of aggression suggested that, everywhere and for everyone, resources are necessarily limited (e.g., food, water, sleeping and nesting places, mates) and that individual survival and success depended on obtaining these resources. (See Alcock 1975; DeVore 1965a; Lorenz 1966; Marler and Hamilton 1966.) Competition, defense, reproduction, aggression, and dominance became interrelated dimensions of animal life.

Anthropologists such as Sherwood Washburn added significantly to the developing evolutionary perspective on aggression, contributing a knowledge of functional anatomy and primate evolution to the synthesis. Washburn (Washburn and DeVore 1961; Washburn and Hamburg 1965, 1968; Washburn, Jay, and Lancaster 1965) emphasized the biological basis of aggression, noting that many physical differences between male and female nonhuman primates could be understood only in terms of the anatomy of aggression. Drawing from the field data of the time (the late 1950s and early 1960s), he concluded that "there are marked species differences in aggressive behavior and in the dominance hierarchies that result from it. Baboons and macaques are probably the most aggressive of the monkeys. . . . But interindividual conflict is important in all species described so far" (1968:471). "And in societies of nonhuman primates aggression is constantly rewarded" (1968:417). Therefore "monkeys not only have the biological basis for aggressive behavior, but also use this equipment frequently and success is highly rewarded" (1968:471).

The contrast between nonhuman and human primates allowed anthropologists to chart the evolutionary transformation of aggression in the primate order. Humans lack the anatomical structures used among the nonhuman primates in agonistic displays, and this characteristic suggested that "the evolution of language as a more efficient method of social communication including the communication of threat, changed the pressures on a wide variety of other structures that must have functioned in agonistic display" (Washburn and DeVore 1961:747) "and opened the way to the existence of a social system in which aggressive behavior is not constantly rewarded" (Washburn and Hamburg 1968:475).

In the course of human evolution, language made possible a new "complex social life" which itself modified the human body, human emotions, and the human brain. "Taken together, the new parts of the association areas and parts of the brain making language possible might be thought of as the 'social brain'—the parts of the brain that (from an evolutionary point of view) evolved in response to social pressures and the parts that today mediate appropriate social action" (Washburn and Hamburg 1968:478).

Thus aggression was seen as deeply rooted in primate anatomy and physiology and had a long and important evolutionary history, but both its biology and its function were significantly altered by the events in human evolution.

More recently, studies of animal behavior have embraced a new theoretical framework (see Wilson 1975 for a review). The classic ethologists and even the subsequent work spoke of evolutionary costs and benefits that were for the good of the "species" or the good of the "group." This formulation was at variance with modern genetics, which is based on the idea that the individual is the unit of selection. Behavioral ecologists and sociobiologists of the late 1970s shifted the focus of explanation and evolutionary interpretation from "group selection," which at best can exist only under very limited conditions (at least theoretically), to "individual selection." The units, whether genes (Dawkins 1976), individuals (Wilson 1975), kin groups sharing genes (Hamilton 1964), or pairs of unrelated individuals engaged in reciprocity (reciprocal altruism; Trivers 1971), act in such a way that they survive and enjoy greater reproductive success relative to other such units.

In these modern terms, an individual's reproductive success most often depends on the use of aggressive "strategies" of competition and defense. Strategies incorporate various tactics,[1] and they involve behaviors (of genotypic or phenotypic origin) that increase an individual's "fitness." Fitness is the relative reproductive success of a genotype as it finds expression in an individual and in his close kin.

There was an integral feedback relationship between baboon research and our modern ideas about aggression and dominance. The baboon studies of the last twenty years both fitted nicely with the new perspective on aggression and played a critical role in the elaboration of the perspective.[2] Male baboon anatomy seemed to reflect an adaptation for aggression. And males were observed to vie with each other aggressively for limited resources, organizing themselves into a stable dominance hierarchy that permitted most conflicts to be resolved on the basis of rank rather than by overt aggression. The concepts of competition, aggression, and dominance helped explain baboon behavior. Yet there were anomalous data from the beginning. Field studies of other nonhuman primates hinted that aggression and dominance might not operate as simply or as effectively as had been assumed. Even some baboon data did not fit. (See especially the works by Rowell cited in note 2.) The evidence on coalitions between individuals facing an aggressive antagonist[3] and the role of female choice in successful male reproduction[4] created an informal challenge to the traditional position.

Against this backdrop, the case study of the Pumphouse baboons that is presented here and elsewhere[5] offers even more serious objections to the traditional view. The Pumphouse baboon anomalies, in order of their historical relevance, are that (1) there is no classic male dominance hierarchy, and aggressive/agonistic rank, when it can be determined, is not positively correlated with the acquisition of limited resources; (2) there is generally little intermale aggression, yet males are superbly equipped for aggression, and a stable male dominance hierarchy is absent; and (3) friendships exist (of greatest interest are those between males and females and between males and infants). Before we can explore the significance of these anomalies, we must briefly consider a few baboon basics.

BABOON BASICS

Our subjects are a group of baboons, called a "troop," that until recently lived on 45,000 privately owned acres near the town of Gilgil, in the Central Rift Valley of Kenya. The troop, named the Pumphouse Gang, inhabited an open savannah which they shared with other animals, both wild and domestic, and with a growing human population. A baboon troop can range in size from as few as 20 animals to as many as 140 animals; the large groups result from high infant survival and the addition of adolescent and adult males who migrate between groups in a population.

Observation on Pumphouse began in 1970. My own research started in 1972 and has continued until the present. A baboon's lifetime is more that thirty years for females and slightly less for males. The current study thus represents a significant period of time from the perspective of baboon lifespan.

A baboon troop is not a random assortment of individuals; it has a basic composition and a basic structure. Adult females outnumber adult males, two or three to one, but adults are in the minority; immature animals form the troop's largest constituent part. During the last fifteen years, Pumphouse has grown in size from just over 40 animals, reaching a peak of 114 and then declining again to roughly 50 individuals as the result of the troop splitting into two daughter groups and changes in environmental conditions.

Pumphouse, like all baboon troops, is a cohesive unit with clear boundaries separating it from other troops. Individuals maintain contact with each other even when they are feeding and are dispersed over several miles. Major subgroups exist within the larger troop, the most important of them being the family group. For baboons this means a matriline (a female-centered kin group) headed by a matriarch (the mother or oldest female in the family) and including all descendant and collateral relatives. Male offspring figure prominently in these matrilines until they leave their natal group at adolescence, so that all adult members of a family are females. Paternity is difficult to assess because many males mate with a female in the cycle which she conceives. The baboons generally act as if they do not recognize biological paternity, but males become temporary members of a family group on another basis (see below). Since families can include grandmothers and grandchildren and even great-grandchildren, when aunts, nieces, and the like are added in, a matriline can be quite large.

All the troop's matrilines are ordered in a stable, linear dominance hierarchy. Each family ranks above or below other families in such a way that even the smallest infant can use its family's status to make the adults of a lower-ranking family give way. Initially the reason is the intervention of the mother or other relatives. But by the time the youngster is about two years of age, this "dependent" rank becomes independent of such intervention. The female hierarchy within the troop may in fact reflect the elaboration of the hierarchy which exists within a family. In that hierarchy, the mother ranks at the top, with the youngest offspring just below her and so on, according to increasing offspring age. This counterintuitive system reflects the mother's willingness to intercede on behalf of her youngest against any of her older children. Sons fit into the female system until adolescence, when they forcibly push their way upward through the female dominance hierarchy (aided by the fact that they are now larger than any adult female) and rise in rank not only above their mother but above all females.

The interactions among family members set the pattern for all friendly, "affiliative" relationships. Family members spend time together, feed, move, sleep, rest, play, and groom with each other. The final important activity is defense. When one individual gets into trouble and is threatened either by dangers from within the group or outside it, family members rush to give assistance.

Family groups are tied together by friendships with nonfamily members (Strum 1975a, b).[6] Friends resemble kin in that they are often in close proximity, feeding, resting, grooming, and defending each other. Friendships can develop in many ways. Young, unrelated females who grow up together as members of the same play group can form strong attachments that last into adulthood. Young males make friends in the same way, but these ties end with adolescence.

Adult males and most adolescent males in Pumphouse have come from some other troop. They begin as strangers and eventually become integral members of the troop, yet when measured in terms of a female's lifetime, they are only temporary residents. Males have friendships with females (sometimes the female initiates the friendship) and a male friend becomes one of the family, albeit temporarily. He often develops a strong tie with his female friend's youngest infant. Acting more like a mother substitute than anything approaching the formalized Western idea of "father," he stays near the baby, grooms it, and protects it. As the infant grows, he or she spends about half the day with the mother and the other half with his/her male friend(s).

The major exception to the rule of social attraction within the troop is between males. Males, by virtue of their immigrant status, are normally strangers to each other. The fear elicited by a stranger exaggerates the already large personal space of male baboons. In a few cases, males from the same troop may be in another troop together, but at least initially, they act like strangers rather than familiars.

Unlike the males in previous baboon studies, Pumphouse males cannot be ranked in a stable linear dominance hierarchy. Relationships among males are basically dynamic, fueled to a great extent by male comings and goings. The most important factor in understanding Pumphouse males appears to be the length of time each male has resided with the troop. For simple convenience I have identified four residency categories: "newcomers," whose tenure is less than one and a half years; "short-term residents," those between one and a half and three years of tenure; "long-term residents," whose tenure ranges between three and five years; and a recently created category of "longest residents" for those few males who have been with the troop longer than five years. Males in each of these categories treat each other preferentially. Males who are longer-term residents both fear newcomers and support each other against them, but that is the extent of their affiliation with each other. Newcomer males are more aggressive[7] than residents, and in the constant back and forth between males, newcomers win[8] more of their encounters with residents than vice versa, although this situation can change during one hour or one day. As a result, male behavior is less predicted by stable dominance, based on various forms of aggression, than by the history of each of the males in the troop.

All these intricate interactions and relationships exist by virtue of an elaborate communication system which is nonetheless severely restricted by comparison with humans. Baboons use sounds, gestures, and postures to convey a range of signals, primarily expressions of the emotional state of the sender. These communicate, for example, the following messages: I am upset, I am excited, I am angry, and I am in conflict (when two sets of opposing emotions find expression at the same time). External reference is limited except that others, receiving this information about an individual's emotions, assess it within the current environmental and social context. Within this system, all actions and all behaviors carry communicative potential. Crucial to our understanding of baboons is the observation that baboons communicate through "behaving" rather than by talking about behaving.

One final point will complete this brief overview. Baboons are born relatively ignorant. Although a baby baboon arrives in the world equipped to cling tenaciously to his mother, roots and sucks with little difficulty, and finds contact with another baboon both necessary and rewarding, the baby is certainly ignorant of the other basics of survival, such as what he should eat besides mother's milk or how to negotiate the social complexities of the troop. All this learning occurs by observation and imitation, through play (where the lessons of adult life can be learned without serious punishments for mistakes), and sometimes through trial and error. The mother is the first model and source of information; family members and friends, then playmates, and finally the rest of the group provide the necessary additional information and experience.

ANOMALIES

Why Are There Friendships?

A new male joins the troop. His first approach is not an aggressive takeover but rather a period of quiet watching from the sidelines, sitting as close to group members as his "stranger" status will allow. He does just what a human observer of baboons does—determines the kinship and friendship structure of the troop and monitors troop interactions until he understands what is going on. Then he acts. But even at this point his actions are not to challenge the resident males. He picks a female and begins to follow her, signaling friendly intentions while trying to approach. The female is initially too frightened to let this stranger close, but his persistence, patience, the friendly sounds, gesture, and postures may finally win her over. Her change of "heart" is signaled by their first grooming session, during which the male grooms the female. When she reciprocates, grooming him as well as letting him groom her, their friendship is truly under way. Then the female follows the male, as much or more than vice versa, while he selects another female to befriend in the same way, winning their initial acceptance into the troop through the females. And all residents have strong friendships with females.

We encounter problems when we try to interpret friendships within the traditional aggressive competition model. From that perspective they are just "noise" in the system, what we might expect when many individuals live together for a long period. But as will be seen, the Pumphouse data suggest that, rather than being superfluous socializing, friendships are an integral part of the methods that baboons can use in competition and defense. Let us consider competition first.

A baboon group has several reproductively active males and a limited number of receptive females available at any one time. We should expect males to compete with each other for these females. Yet in Pumphouse this competition takes an aggressive form in only 25 percent of the cases where one male gains possession of a female from another male (Strum 1982). In the majority of cases we find successful social maneuvers that rely on a male's social experience, his knowledge of his fellow group members, and his *friendship* with the contested female. Fighting over a female does not, in itself, guarantee reproductive success. Female cooperation plays an important role in whether a male can successfully face up to a challenger, and a female also determines whether the male will be allowed to copulate. An uncooperative female can tire her partner, disrupting both his feeding and his copulations. These costs weigh heavily on the male, who may voluntarily abandon an uncooperative female. In a sense, the female has won the right to choose a male of her liking for her next consort partner. The key to female cooperation appears to be the friendship that forms between males and females; females cooperate more with their male friends than with other males, and friendships become important aspects of male-male competition.

When a male aggressively challenges another male, we expect the defense to be flight or fight. Yet very often the threatened male baboon turns, instead, to a female (or an infant) to use as an agonistic buffer.[9] Bolstered by this unusual ally, the challenged male returns to face his opponent, often successfully averting further aggression. The key to his success, however, is the cooperation of his buffer. Without it, the distressed male faces two problems (an aggressive opponent and a screaming liability, since the distress of an uncooperative partner may bring the wrath of the troop upon the offender) instead of one. Infant or female cooperation, here as in the case of competition, correlates positively with friendship, and friendship becomes an important aspect of male defense.

We can now see why the first order of business for a newcomer male should be to form friendships with females and, through them, with infants. We can also observe that males without such friendships (newcomers during the early days of their residency) are at a disadvantage in both competing with and defending against males who have such ties. Consequently, at least from the male's point of view, friendships appear to be important investments that generate cooperative, predictable partners who can be used in social maneuvers during competition and defense. Why females and infants should cooperate is discussed elsewhere (Strum 1983a, b). Basically, females and infants do not benefit directly in the competitive and defensive interactions between males unless we consider grooming a benefit. Instead they reap complementary benefits before and afterward: active assistance when under attack from conspecifics or external threats, access to limited resources that the male friend possesses, and a general decrease in interference from others when they are with the male friend. Friendships create a delicately balanced system of social reciprocity in which each partner cooperates to the extent that he or she has benefited or hopes to benefit.

Why Is There No Classic Male Dominance Hierarchy?

A new male joins the troop. After he begins to befriend a female, he also begins to follow resident males, one at a time. Continual following, harassment, and aggression by the newcomer occur regardless of what the resident might do. Although resources can be involved, the "winning" newcomer does not claim his prize. Often there is no resource in sight and the goal appears to be both an assessment (Parker 1974) of the other male and a method by which the resident is forced to recognize the newcomer's presence in the troop. The following ends as abruptly as it started, at a point where the resident and newcomer have reached some resolution of their relationship. A similar sequence takes place between adolescent males maturing within the troop and the adult males already resident there (Strum 1982).

At the most basic level, the reason that there is no stable male dominance hierarchy in Pumphouse is that there is a constant influx and exit of males. Because newcomers and maturing adolescents use aggression to "communicate" with residents, to gain information about another male, and to force their recognition and ultimate acceptance, the majority of male agonistic interactions do not relate directly to competition. Whatever traditional type of dominance hierarchy is extracted from these data loses its significance through the attempt to solidify what is basically a dynamic set of male interactions.

When we look specifically at situations of competition over limited resources, for example receptive females and the meat on carcasses of prey that the baboons have captured (Strum 1975b, 1976a, b, c, 1981a), we find that even here aggression plays a somewhat minor role. A good example is when males vie with each other over a sexually attractive female. Friendships with females play a role in a male's success. But other social maneuvers also operate to gain the female for a male. For example, as tension mounts between a consort male and the other males following the consort pair, a change in partners can occur. Often the new consort male is not one of the active followers but rather a male who had remained on the sidelines, unnoticed but closely monitoring the situation. At the right moment, when the other males are involved with each other, he will rush to the female and claim her. Similarly, he might incite other males against the consort male and then back out himself, remaining free to claim the female at the right moment.

In the classic male dominance hierarchy, rank is determined by aggression, is stable, and, more important, predicts a male's ability to gain limited resources. These examples show that aggressive strategies of competition do not always succeed. In Pumphouse, much of male aggression serves no immediate competitive purpose and there are effective, nonaggresive methods to use when competing for critical resources. But the alternative methods rely on experience, skill, and relationships that a male must acquire within the troop, so that the aggressive newcomers find themselves at a disadvantage and the experienced residents have an edge. Since aggressors are often not the winner of limited resources, they abandon aggressive strategies as soon as they have developed the social basis for other options.

Why Is There So Little Male Aggression?

Before we consider why there is so little male aggression in Pumphouse, it is important to note that the rate of aggression in all baboon populations is lower than is generally believed. In the classic DeVore and Washburn studies (Washburn and DeVore 1961; DeVore 1965b; Hall and DeVore 1965), the observers were forced to feed the males in order to elicit enough intermale aggression to form the basis of a dominance hierarchy. In other studies (e.g., Hausfater 1975; Packer 1979) researchers resort to measures other than aggression between males (such as nonaggressive supplantations from feeding sites) when determining the male dominance hierarchy because they, too, have observed so few incidents of real aggression. All baboon studies actually agree about the low frequency of male aggression. Traditionally, the existence of a male dominance hierarchy was used to explain this low rate. The hierarchy was believed to avert aggression, allowing individuals to settle disputes without recourse to actual violence. (A critique of the position can be found in Rowell 1974.)

When we try to explain the infrequent aggression of Pumphouse males, we have a different problem, for there is no stable dominance hierarchy as an intervening variable (Strum 1982). Returning to first principles, we can ask, "What is the function of aggression in baboon society?" The answer should be competition and defense (Marler and Hamilton 1966; Wilson 1975). Yet is it? Most aggression between Pumphouse males is unrelated to resources (Strum 1982) and therefore cannot be viewed as direct competition. Instead, aggression appears to be a means of communication between males when newcomers are trying to enter the troop or when maturing males are trying to change their existing relationship within the group. Furthermore, Pumphouse males have competitive and defensive methods that do not rely on aggression and are as effective as aggressive strategies. Taken together, these data suggest that many of the functions attributed by theorists to aggression in baboon society are as effectively served by nonaggressive alternatives.

Social Strategies

The answer to the questions posed by the Pumphouse data—why are there friendships; why is there no classic male dominance hierarchy; and why is there so little male aggression without a male dominance hierarchy—involves a concept that can be abstracted from the data. This is the idea of "social strategy." Although the concept is not formally developed in the primate literature, Mason (1978) used the phrase to refer to social maneuvers in power relationships among monkeys, and Bernstein (1976) approached the idea when he suggested the primacy of social skills over aggression even for the dominant male in a nonhuman primate group.

A social strategy, as evidenced among Pumphouse baboons, is an integrated set of tactics not directly dependent on aggressive behavior and involving the social "management" or "manipulation" of others for an individual's own benefit (Strum 1979, 1981b, 1982, 1983a, b). There are two broad types of social strategies: those of competition and those of defense (Strum 1982, 1983a, b). When a male baboon, instead of aggressively following a consort pair, watches from the sidelines and successfully claims the female by taking advantage of other males' aggression to the consort male, when a female baboon steals a prey carcass away from a larger male, who earlier was unwilling to share, by grooming him into a stupor, and when a male, instead of facing aggression with aggression, successfully meets the challenge by grabbing an infant or a female to use as an agonistic buffer, these individuals are using social strategies.

We should expect social strategies to exist even if they are absent among Pumphouse baboons. Aggressive competition and defense is dramatic, easy to observe, and probably the major form of overt competition and defense for many animal species. Yet aggression is a high-risk behavior, since fatal injury is always possible. Therefore, should there be a *less risky but equally effective method*, it would have a selective advantage for any individuals must still solve the same problems of competition and defense as their aggressively competent opponents. For these individuals, alternative, nonaggressive strategies should be favored by natural selection.

Thus both on theoretical grounds and from the empirical data on Pumphouse baboons, we should expect social strategies of competition and defense as alternatives to aggressive ways of obtaining limited resources and defending against the aggression of a competitor.

The social strategies of Pumphouse baboons suggest that the functional view of aggression which marked a major advance in the study of animal behavior may, in fact, have overemphasized the role of aggression in daily life. But the potential for alternatives to aggression is greater in some animal species than in others. Social strategies require individuals to assess complex situations and to modify behavioral tendencies on the basis of information from past and present experience. This type of intelligence requires both extensive memory capacity and neural integration of diverse information. We should expect primates to be prime candidates as social strategists. The discovery of social strategies among Pumphouse baboons does have important implications for our characterization of aggression in the primate order. If, for primates, aggression is just *one* strategy among several, and not the sole method available to an individual, and if it is often the least effective and riskiest option, as the Pumphouse data suggest, then selection should have been for a flexible response preparing an individual for the possibility of aggression but not locking him into an aggressive reaction. The previous anthropological perspective clearly recognized this change in aggressive response in *human* evolution. Yet finding this flexibility among baboons implies that no matter how ancient aggression might be, the social alternatives we observe today certainly must predate the hominids. More important, once created, these social strategies must have quickly displaced aggression from its pivotal place as *the* strategy to that of *a* strategy in a much larger array of options. With more evolutionary time and greater selective pressure for the development of flexibility, it becomes increasingly difficult to posit the inevitability and centrality of aggression not just among humans but perhaps among all higher primates.

The implication is not that aggression is evolutionarily unimportant for baboons, for primates, or for mammals. Many of the differences between male and female baboons, and between the sexes of many species, clearly result from the anatomy of aggression in males. Nor am I suggesting that we should expect baboons or humans to be unaggressive. Aggression still has its place as a strategy, but I would like to propose that, once alternatives exist, the social potency of aggression declines, unless one opponent is willing to kill the other. Social strategies allow individuals to circumvent aggression, reverse its outcome, redress grievances, and the like. The original winner, faced with the ineffectiveness of his aggression as the loser switches strategies, is then forced to respond in kind, countering with his own social options. We can observe this phenomenon just as readily among Pumphouse baboons as in modern humans. At times aggression can be a loss of control rather than a planned strategy; in effect the individual loses his ability to employ other options. If social strategies are what they seem, they must rely on what has been called "the social brain" (Wahsburn and DeVore 1961), the newer part of the brain capable of overriding the more primitive responses. Thus we might interpret out-of-control aggression as an evolutionary regression in response.

How Do the Baboons See It?

The empirical and theoretical case for social strategies as alternatives to aggression has just been presented. But how do the baboons see it? Far from being a trivial question, this issue is currently a major challenge in the study of animal behavior.

When evolutionary biologists discuss animals making decisions, formulating tactics of strategies, or behaving so that they "maximize" their reproductive success (e.g., Wilson 1975; Dawkins 1976), they do not assume that the animal is conscious of these actions but merely that the individual has been programmed over evolutionary time and through evolutionary processes to behave in such a way. This reflects a conservative stance initiated by the classical ethologists guarding against the extremes of anthropomorphism that had infused the description and interpretation of animal behavior before the 1930s (Strum and Mitchell 1986). How much awareness do animals have? How conscious are they of their actions and their options, and how much can they plan and control their behavior? The data are difficult to collect, but a wealth of recent information, both from the laboratory and from the field, suggests that animal abilities exceed those which existing ethological and evolutionary models have allowed. (See Griffin 1981, 1984, and the literature on "cognitive ethology.")

It is not yet possible to interview a baboon and ask his or her opinion about either baboon behavior or our interpretations of it. Yet the quantitative data on the Pumphouse troop do yield patterns that suggest principles which, in turn, allow the observer to predict accurately what a baboon is going to do even before it happens. This is a good start, but other types of data exist that give an even better window into the "mind" of the individual. Qualitative data, certain behavioral sequences, "anecdotes," and rare behaviors offer provocative suggestions about baboon abilities which must subsequently, however, be rigorously investigated (Griffin 1981; Strum 1987).

Social strategies have been shown to play an important role in the daily life of Pumphouse baboons. Yet how *aware* are the baboons of their options, and to what extent do they actively create alternatives? In order to illustrate the degree of sophistication and "insight" that baboons can possess, let me present two incidents. The first involves a young adult female of a high-ranking family and an adolescent male of a lower-ranking family. The male was acting like a typical adolescent who tries to establish his rank over all the females by pushing around a select few. At this developmental state he

Shirley C. Strum

is already as large as any female in the troop. Very early on this particular morning, the adolescent male aggressively challenged the female. There were no obvious causes for the aggression. Resources were not implicated, because the female was feeding on grass, a resource that is evenly dispersed and widely available. There was also no social provocation. The female screamed in fright. Normally a relative or friend would respond to her distress, and together they would be able to displace or chase away the bully. But this time, perhaps because she was on the edge of the troop and the wind was blowing in the opposite direction, no one came. The female finally gave way, subordinating herself, perhaps permanently, to the male. Four hours later the male inadvertently approached her again. Both feeding, they paid little attention to each other until the male drew close. Then the female looked up, saw the male, paused to look at her older brother, who was sitting next to her—her brother is dominant to the adolescent male—looked back at the approaching male, and screamed. Her screams alerted the brother, who did not know what was wrong but quickly identified the culprit and chased him through the troop. The brother's support served to nullify the earlier dominance reversal. To an experienced baboon watcher, the salient features of this sequence are that the female "remembered" the previous interaction and later created an opportunity which changed the earlier outcome. Before she could do so, she had to understand the dynamics of dominance and of assistance and the relative ranks of the different participants.

The second incident concerns the highest-ranking female in the troop and an adult male who had just captured, and was eating, an infant Thomson's gazelle. This female had a keen liking for meat but had limited opportunities to get meat for herself. (See Strum 1975b, 1976b, 1981a.) In previous years, male friends had shared carcasses with her, but this particular male was not so inclined. She approached the male and sat reasonably close, hoping to get some meat. When this tactic failed, she moved even closer and started to groom him. Grooming is a very relaxing activity for the animal being groomed, and the male soon loosened his hold on the carcass, falling into a typical grooming stupor. Just at that moment, the female reached in front of him and ran off with the carcass! Several days later the two were engaged in a repeat performance, the male with another gazelle, the female grooming him. This time, however, whenever the female made even the slightest pause in grooming, the male's hand quickly gripped the carcass. After several minutes, the female stopped, looked around, and suddenly, without any provocation, rushed off to attack another female. The innocent victim was a female friend of the predatory male, who was now in his own situation of conflict. He should support and reassure his friend, but the carcass was too large and cumbersome to drag with him. After a brief hesitation, he did

342

leave the meat, heading for his friend, and just at that moment, the meat-seeking female ran to claim the carcass.

These sequences and numerous others lend support to the idea that baboons have tactical insight. Armed with such abilities, social strategies may not be just interpretive abstractions. A newcomer male certainly acts as if he understands the need for alternatives to aggressive strategies and the importance of friendships if he is to make his way successfully through daily life. Adolescent males act as if they do not entirely understand the requirements but appear to learn from their failures and slowly shift to the adult (and socially skillful) pattern (Strum 1987). And the subtle "tit for tat" we can clearly observe between friends implies that each partner does some type of cost-benefit adjustment.

Further evidence of strategic awareness among baboons is found in the "rules" for agonistic buffering. Infants and females are both effective as buffers but in different situations, and males appear to know this. Yet males do not always behave appropriately. Some males do not use any agonistic buffers even when they should; some males use females all the time even when infants would be better; some males use both infants and females but as they are available rather than as they are effective. Closer examination (Strum 1983b) shows that there is a principle at work: the use of an infant or female as an agonistic buffer depends, for its success, on the existence of a prior friendship between the male and the "buffer." Newcomer males initially have no friendships and thus cannot and do not use this social strategy; later they form friendships with females, and still later, as they become short-term residents, with infants through their friendships with an infant's mother. Male choices reflect a compromise, the best tactic of those available at the time (Strum 1983a, b). Males should therefore change behavior as they change residency classes, and Pumphouse males do exactly this (Strum 1983b).

These data make a strong case for social strategies, and other descriptive information suggests that baboons are aware of the social intricacies surrounding them, that they actually create relationships which provide them with alternatives to use during competition and defense, and that they "manage" social relationships and social situations. The question of "consciousness" depends, to a great extent, on how consciousness is defined *and* on how much consciousness we can legitimately attribute to the daily actions of the average conscious human. Humans "want" friends. They create a system of reciprocity with these friends and rely on friends in a number of important situations. They feel they can depend on these friends' predictability, availability, and cooperation because of the history of their interaction. To what extent is this sequence conscious? To what extent is the subtle "tit for tat" within a human friendship viewed as a conscious management of cost and benefits?[10] And to what extent is this different from what baboons do?

CONCLUSIONS

The baboon case history has raised some critical issues, even for those whose interest is human behavior. It suggests that aggression may not be the only option for nonhuman animals. This possibility does not suggest an unambiguous interpretation of human aggression, but it certainly implies that the adaptationist scenario incorporated into various interpretations, whether psychological, social, or biological, may need revision. With the appearance of social alternatives, aggression becomes just one tactic rather than the primary strategy in competition and defense. Equally important, social strategies seem to alter both the effectiveness and the inevitability of aggression when it is used.

The traditional evolutionary scenario emphasized a shift in the role of aggression in society which came with the advent of language as a more effective means of social communication. While this argument remains valid, the baboon data imply that there was an even earlier shift, one that, just like the later one, placed a premium on intelligence, learning, and the development of social skills. We might envision the following sequence. The first steps could have been foraging shifts which themselves were preadaptive for social strategies. Foraging strategies vary with habitat and food resources among mammals. Fruit-eating primates have relatively larger brains than primates who eat leaves, likely the result of selection for the greater memory and integrative capacity associated with their lifestyle. Since foraging skills depend on neural traits similar to those required for social strategies, selection leading to sophisticated foraging may well have contributed to the evolution of social skills among primates. Another catalyst in the evolution of social strategies may have been the formation of large, multimale, matrilineal groups in response to the greater predation risks associated with a shift to ground living in primates. Here we find the social conditions with both greatest potential and greatest need for social strategies. Since it is not a long or complex step from selection for foraging skills to selection for social skills which enhance reproduction, we might expect to find such skills among a number of primate species.

In this scenario, as in the earlier ones, language still plays a vital role in the evolution of human aggression, but it is part of a process that, I suggest, began earlier. Social strategies themselves, if they are adaptive and rely on special skills closely tied to the level of encephalization, may have played an important role in the evolution of the primate brain. Other investigators have suggested that there is a relationship between social complexity and brain size. Trivers (1971) linked human brain size to the evolution of reciprocal altruism, and Humphrey (1976) has suggested that the intellectual faculties in the higher primates reflect an adaptation to the complexities of social living. The idea of social strategies suggests additional evolutionary avenues in the development of the brain and the history of aggression.

I hope that cultural anthropologists will be intrigued by baboon social strategies and the animal abilities that they imply. Psychological anthropologists may want to take the next step, inquiring about the psychological processes that might be at work in the individual animal. Unfortunately, current methods are inadequate and provide only the sparest information, making speculation difficult. Yet we should not assume that such phenomena do not exist just because we cannot measure them. Our first question, albeit a rhetorical one at this point, is whether baboons display any of the elements of the human psyche. Freudians and biologists would certainly agree that baboons must possess an "id." Most animal ethologists would also argue that baboons certainly have an "ego." The greatest controversy would surround the question of the existence of a baboon "superego," yet any dog owner and any observer of Pumphouse baboons would certainly argue in favor of such a proposition, although the data are unavoidably anecdotal.

We cannot progress further except to observe that, along with our reassessment of evolutionary models of human aggression and our reassessment of the cognitive abilities of the higher primates, we might also need to consider psychological factors. As animals appear more human and humans appear less distinct from animals, the division between species is not erased, but we may begin to wonder where the great "psyche" divide actually resides.

NOTES

The fifteen years of research on which this chapter is based were funded by the following organizations: Fyssen Foundation (Paris), L. S. B. Leakey Foundation, National Geographic Society, National Science Foundation, New York Zoological Society, University of California, San Diego, Wenner Gren Foundation, and World Wildlife Fund–U.S. I thank the government of Kenya for permission to conduct research and the Institute of Primate Research, Nairobi, for local sponsorship. I am also grateful to Roy D'Andrade, Robert Hinde, Bruno Latour, Melford Spiro, and Jonah Western, who provided many helpful comments on an earlier draft of this chapter.

1. I define a tactic as any skillful method used to gain an end. See Western and Strum (1983).

2. For examples, see DeVore (1965a, 1965b), DeVore and Hall (1965), Rowell (1966), Washburn and Hamburg (1968), Rowell (1972, 1974), Hausfater (1975), Seyfarth (1975), Hamilton (1978), Packer (1979), and Popp and DeVore (1979).

3. For example, Cheney (1977), Kaplan (1978), Silk (1980), Walters (1980), de Waal and van Hooff (1981), and de Waal (1982).

4. On females as they influence their choice of partners and the copulatory success of a partner, see, for example, Saayman (1971), Taub (1978), Packer (1979), and Tutin (1979).

5. Strum (1975a, b, 1976a, b, c, 1981a, b, 1982, 1983a, b, c, 1987), Strum and Western (1982), Western and Strum (1983), Strum and Mitchell (1986), and Strum and Latour (1987).

6. A friend is someone with whom an individual is affiliated without being biologically related.

7. Aggression is usually defined as the act of inflicting bodily harm on another individual or the intention of doing so.

8. The winner is the one who, at the end of the exchange of communication signals, makes no submissive gestures, whereas the loser makes only such gestures; interactions in which either or both actors give mixed signals are classified as undecided in outcome.

9. "Agonistic buffering," a frequent occurrence among some primate species, denotes the act in which a male takes an infant onto his belly in the midst of an aggressive interaction with another male. Often this action stops the adversary's attack. See Deag and Crook (1971) for the first description/definition. For further description and discussion, see Ransom and Ransom (1971), Gilmore (1977), Popp (1978a, b), Packer (1980), Taub (1980), Busse and Hamiltion (1981), Strum (1983a, b).

10. See Trivers (1971) for an interesting evolutionary treatment of human emotions such as trust and shame.

16
Whatever Happened to the Other Eye?

F. G. BAILEY 〜〜

"With affection beaming in one eye and calculation shining out of the other."
—a description of Mrs. Todgers in Charles
Dickens's *Martin Chuzzlewit*

Erikson (1963:329), speaking of Hitler's Oedipal troubles, remarks, "But it
obviously takes much more than an individual complex to make a successful
revolutionary." This essay, which is not about revolutionaries but about the
reasons that some leaders are transformed into gods, follows Erikson's implicit suggestion and explores certain explanations which lie outside the
universal truths of psychoanalysis.

NUMENIFICATION

One definition of religion asserts, among other things, that "the core
variable" is a belief in "superhuman beings." In the present chapter I will
use this definition (Spiro 1966b:94) to explore one type of relationship between leaders and their followers. My analysis will focus upon the image of
the leader which is conveyed to the *mass* of his followers. Consideration of
his standing with his entourage, who know him in the round, raises other
issues, and I will address that relationship only as it is necessary to do so.

All leaders present themselves, in varying degrees, as being superior
to their followers. Indeed, this is a matter of definition, for a leader who
excelled those whom he led in no way whatsoever would not be a leader.

The image presented may include attributes which belong in the domain of the superhuman.

This attribute—being superhuman—is indeed a variable. It may be symbolized, at one somewhat crass extreme, in acts of physical prowess. Theodore Roosevelt enjoyed flexing his muscles in public. Dom Mintoff, the Maltese leader, used to take his entourage swimming in the Mediterranean, and it was considered foolish to reach the finishing line before him. Bravery, endurance, or determination may also form part of the image. De Gaulle, that massive target for assassination, did not hesitate to go among crowds. Failure of nerve, as with Edward Kennedy, is a disqualification. Churchill was said (falsely, according to the memoirs of his physician) to have the gift of instant sleep (the catnap) and so could work for hours beyond the normal human capacity. The drowsy Senator Hayakawa was labeled incompetent. Chairman Mao, at a time of life when others need a wheelchair, was photographed bobbing down the Yangtse in a marathon feat of buoyancy.

These examples reflect the superhuman only metaphorically. But there are sometimes more explicitly religious features. A leader's image usually includes a quality which transcends reason. It is coded in a variety of words: luck, destiny, flair, genius, or, in the prosaic phrases of selection boards, "leadership quality." This is how General Montgomery made the point: "I hold that a Commander-in-Chief of great armies in the field must have an inner conviction which, though founded closely on reason, transcends reason" (Montgomery of Alamein 1961:51). In other words, while ordinary mortals must calculate their way toward a decision and find themselves blocked when the complexity of the situation defies computation, a true leader is gifted with a mystical quality—intuition—which gives him "inner conviction" and enables him to make difficult decisions in a manner denied to the common man.

A faith in one's own (or anyone's) superhuman capacity is, reasonably to my mind, deemed religious. But a third category of image satisfies more commonplace notions of what constitutes religion. With varying degrees of directness, political and military leaders may present themselves in a manner that connotes mystical power. Many parade asceticism: Montgomery himself, Franco, de Gaulle, Nasser, and above all Gandhi. In addition, they, and others whose style of life was far from ascetic—for example, Churchill— show themselves to be inspired by a vision, a transcending goal against which all else is measured and the rightness of which is never doubted: Nkrumah and Pan-Africanism, de Gaulle and the glory of France, Churchill and the destiny of Britain to win the war and to rule its Empire. They are "true believers." Finally—in the ultimate category—there are leaders who themselves are presented as divinities. Gandhi, despite his promulgated humility, found that status almost thrust upon him. Nkrumah manufactured it, especially in the closing period of his rule; he was known as the "Redeemer." Augustus Caesar was proclaimed a god, becoming, like his great-uncle before him and all his successors, part of the pantheon officially recognized by the Roman state.

These examples show that a belief by followers in the superhuman attributes of leaders is indeed, as Spiro pointed out, a variable. What varies is the leader's *reputation* for being able to transcend the limit of human capacities (especially reason). Obviously this variable is not, in any objective way, an attribute of the individual, as is height or girth. Rather it refers to the attitudes of the leader's followers and their varying disposition to abandon rationality and to refrain from demands for accountability to have a blind faith in the leader's capacities. This—the leader's charisma—is a variable, and I assume that it can be manipulated.

The act of manipulation is "numenification." It differs from charisma, which Weber (1978:241) defined as "a certain quality of an individual personality by virtue of which he is considered extraordinary and treated as endowed with supernatural, superhuman, or at least specifically exceptional powers or qualities." Numenification, however, is not a "quality" but a strategy, a method for creating or enhancing charisma.

It should be possible to predict the level of numenification by identifying appropriate contexts.

NEEDS AND THE FAILURE OF NERVE

The first context is a purported universal feature of human nature. We all have a tendency, when we are frightened, to surrender ourselves to a protector. This is the Leviathan of Hobbes, "that *mortal god*, to which we owe under the *immortal God*, our peace and defence" (1946:112; emphasis in the original). The alternative, in those famous phrases, is the "war of everyman against everyman" and a life that is "solitary, poor, nasty, brutish and short" (1946:82). Others, less pessimistic and more prosaic, transform the "natural condition of mankind" into a stress variable. Weber (1978:1111; emphasis in the original) implies that it is a stress variable when he writes, "All *extra*ordinary needs, that is, those which *transcend* the sphere of everyday economic routines, have always been satisfied . . . on a *charismatic* basis."

An elegant description of *"extra*ordinary need" is provided by Gilbert Murray (1951:119). He calls it "failure of nerve." Comparing the writing of classical Athens with that which emerged in the Christian period, he explains,

> There is a change in the whole relation of the writer to the world about him. The new quality is . . . a rise of asceticism, of mysticism, in a sense, of pessimism; a loss of self-confidence, of hope in this life and of faith in a normal human effort; a despair of patient enquiry, a cry for infallible revelation; and indifference to the welfare of the state, a conversion of the soul to God.

The outcome, Gilbert Murray says, is the rise of asceticism and mysticism, the desire for an "infallible revelation" and "conversion of the soul to God." I suggest that the feelings that cause these beliefs ("a loss of self-confidence . . . and of faith in normal human effort; a despair of patient enquiry") may also lead to the emergence and acceptance of a leader who is expected literally or figuratively to work miracles.

This hypothesis, that the strategy of numenification is made possible by a general failure of nerve, deserves one simple positive illustration before its limitations are discussed. Germany after the First World War suffered a decade and a half of political and economic chaos. Parliamentary institutions were threatened by extremists on both the Right and the Left. Violence and intrigue replaced debate, and politicians backed by private armies were no more effective than their more constitutionally minded colleagues at bringing about order and security. Then came the depression and further evidence of institutional incapacity to cope with the nation's problems. All of these factors, so it is said, produced that failure of nerve which made possible not only the seizure of power by Hitler but also the quite extravagant cult of leadership which flourished in Germany down to the end of the Second World War (Fest 1975).

But there are difficulties with this argument. First, one need not search far to find instances which point in the other direction: there can be a failure of nerve and no deified leadership. Germany, at the end of the Second World War, had been invaded and conquered, its cities and its industries destroyed, civilians and soldiers alike dying in great numbers. Expectations had been shattered, and institutions which had recently brought spectacular success now had produced a cataclysmic disaster. But as everyone knows, fifteen years later (matching the decade and a half between 1918 and Hitler's assumption of power) the Germans had a car in every garage, an immensely muscular currency, and a growing say in European affairs, and—this is the point—a reasonably robust form of representative government which virtually excluded the cult of personalities (apart from exemplifications of bourgeois respectability, as in the case of Konrad Adenauer) and certainly did not seek legitimacy through that mystique of leadership which buttressed Hitler.

How does one explain this outcome? If the "failure of nerve" hypothesis is correct—if failure of nerve is a sufficient condition for numenification—nothing of the kind should have happened in Germany after the Second World War.

Apart from problems with particular examples, this hypothesis is inadequate in other respects. It does not explain why failure of nerve should encourage numenification rather than, for example, merely the search for personal salvation described by Gilbert Murray or, alternatively, the frontier situation described by the phrase "every man his own protector." Nor does it address the alternative favored by Thomas Hobbes, that centralized authority alone, accepted rationally by "covenant" and without the trappings of mysticism, could remedy failure of nerve.

Such considerations bring our inquiry to another level. The "failure of nerve" hypothesis might rest too much on the assumption that people in general are rational: we devise institutions, we see whether they are satisfying our needs, and we discard them for something better when they fail. These needs are not only those of biological continuation; they include also subtler things, such as the need for self-respect, for a sense of identity, or for an assurance that by and large the world is a predictable place. "Failure of nerve" in fact, refers not only or even mainly to starvation or other physical suffering but rather to the *emotional* stress which arises when one realizes that one cannot comprehend and therefore cannot control one's situation. Since the dependent variable (susceptibility to numenification) is exactly the level of *emotional* attachment to a leader (the suspension by the followers of their rational and critical faculties), then perhaps one should look for the independent variable also in the field of nonrational motivation.

One way of doing so is to invoke yet another need: that for affiliation in its extreme form of total dependency. Of course, merely to say that one gives oneself over blindly to the guidance of another because of a need for dependency is to explain nothing. But if one derives the dependency (or whatever other psychological need or drive is in question) from childhood experiences, then one has not a tautology but a causal explanation (Spiro 1967:76–80). The tendency to personalize one's world (of which susceptibility to numenification is an instance) remains present in the psyche, because one's early experiences were with persons and not with institutions; and when one is reduced to the condition of a child—helplessness—then one is reduced to the childhood solution, which is blind dependency on a parent or parental substitute (Freud 1927).

This reasoning brings us a step forward. It explains (partly) why numenification centers upon the *person* of leaders rather than upon institutional engineering and experiment. It also explains why the frontier solution—every man for himself—is inappropriate, because it would not satisfy the need for simple affiliation, let alone dependency. But it does not

351

explain why the outcome should not be only a purely religious "conversion of the soul to God." That would eminently meet the dependency need without the numenification of any human leader.

The hypothesis is open also to other objections. It cannot deal with variations in an individual at different times or even (assuming standardized patterns of socialization) within cultures. While differences in socialization undoubtedly help to explain different adult reactions to situations of stress (in this case different propensities to accept numenification), they seem unlikely *by themselves* to account for different reactions by the same individual in different situations. If childhood experiences *alone* tell the story, then a given individual should remain constant in his or her reactions to stress (Shweder 1979:272–275).

Reactions vary, as the "failure of nerve" hypothesis suggests, according to the level of stress. To proceed further, one must ask what stress means and how it comes to vary.

"NORMAL HUMAN EFFORT"

The word "stress" may refer to physical suffering, to pain or hunger or exhaustion. It may also signify anguish: for example, guilt or grief. Gilbert Murray's "failure of nerve" clearly indicates mental anguish but not any specific emotion attached to a particular event—like fear arising from an illness or remorse over a wickedness or grief at a bereavement. Rather it suggests a generalized anxiety aroused by anticipated incapacity to protect oneself from harm. It is, as he puts it "a loss of self-confidence . . . , of faith in normal human effort" (1951:119).

The phrase "normal human effort" makes certain assumptions about what is normal in a polity. The features of a normal polity turn out to be (as one might expect from Gilbert Murray) characteristic of a rationally ordered liberal democracy. Such a polity (idealized) has three main tendencies. First an effort is made to disperse power rather than to concentrate it. Second, there is an assumption that those citizens who are given a measure of power to participate in the direction of their own lives will not only exercise that power responsibly but will also more willingly serve the public interest (i.e., they are not "indifferent to the welfare of the state"). They are active citizens, ready to serve, evaluate, and criticize. Third, institutional safeguards ensure that those entrusted to command are held accountable and cannot be corrupted into authoritarianism.

The entire apparatus of such a polity rests upon an unquestioning faith that people are moved more strongly by reason than by emotion and that reason, debate, and compromise can deal with all problems, including practical problems requiring action. There are, it assumes, no questions for which reason will not provide an answer, and therefore every question has a right answer, and if those concerned cannot agree upon what is to be done, then someone's reasoning must be at fault. Manifestly, this assumption is mistaken. Reason alone will not resolve a debate between antagonists who cannot accept a common axiom from which to begin the argument. Pure reason cannot solve a conflict of interests. Furthermore, even when a common axiomatic foundation is accepted, the situation may be so complicated and so beyond computation that reason cannot be used to provide an answer.

But since it is in the nature of some practical problems not to wait, decisions must be taken by means other than reasoning. These means include voting, consultation with oracles, or—the solution which concerns us here—the abandonment of the ordinary man or woman's right to share in power (by offering an opinion on what is to be done) and the handing over of the problem to a leader who will make the decision and take the action.

Such abnegation of one's right to exercise reason, coupled with an implied admission of one's incapacity to do so effectively, is not in itself an irrational act. If reason cannot supply the decision, then spin a coin: otherwise Buridan dies of starvation between the equidistant hamburger joints. The institution of the Roman dictatorship, with the six-month time limit, is a rational solution to the problem of the temporary failure of participatory government, and many political systems contain such devices for meeting a crisis. But such actions, although rational, do not further the cause of rationality inasmuch as they deny the main axiom that all problems yield to collective discussion and reasoning.

The argument, moreover, takes no account of the passions. Like the Roman consul appointing a dictator to meet a particular emergency, people in general, it seems to imply, look objectively at their surroundings, assess their present experience in relation to their hopes or expectations or memories, and decide that there is nothing for it but to hand over the problems and let the dictator solve them. That course of action works well enough (at least in legal theory) for Greek tyrants or Roman dictators or the Defence of the Realm Act in Britain or a State of Emergency in India. But in all these instances the decision is taken by one person or by a select few; it is not taken by the average person-on-the-street. Figuring out and rationally accepting his or her own incapacities and "covenant" for a leader is, to my mind, a thoroughly idealized and implausible description of such a person's activity. He is moved by impulse and panic. In any case, the notion will not explain why, during periods of stress, the leader is sometimes elevated to the company of the superhuman and sometimes not. Furthermore, while it is perfectly rational to recognize one's own limitations or the institutional limitations of participatory democracy (it has difficulties in taking timely action) and hand over power to one person who can do the job, it is not at all rational to believe that he or she is endowed with superhuman capacities and can work miracles.

So where do people learn such irrationality? An answer is to be found partly in the dispositions that come from childhood experiences and affect behavior in conditions of stress. The rest of the answer is that leaders, through rhetoric and manipulation, *encourage* irrationality. The proposition is very simple. Other things being equal, numenification increases when a leader sees an advantage in increasing it and can do so.

The other source of discontent, apart from the failure (or obsolescence) of a vision, is mundane incompetence—failure to deliver what was promised. Third World countries which won independence after the Second World War, especially when there had been a long struggle, seem to have been especially susceptible to this visionary disenchantment. Independence turned out not to be the millennium. The problems faced by their leaders— raising the standard of living, combating corruption, containing factionalism, and so forth—lack the millenarian charm of a freedom fight. They are internally divisive because, whatever the outcome, some people will be losers. Third, they are likely to drive matters down to that point where existing institutions, including existing leadership, are exposed to a failure of nerve.

Since there is no vision to move the mass, to raise their readiness for service and self-sacrifice and to stifle their propensity to grumble and withdraw, then, raising the level of numenification is a sensible tactic for a leader who thinks he is failing to "deliver the goods" and who intends to remain in power.

The conscious use of this tactic suggests that leaders hold a view of human nature which in general accords with the "failure of nerve" theory. When the level of anxiety rises, people succumb to a state of unquestioning dependency. But it must not be the "failure of nerve" contemplated by Gilbert Murray, in which each man finds his individual comfort in devoted allegiance to one or another of a variety of gods or cult leaders. The propensity to worship must be focused upon the one leader, and failure of nerve must be stopped short of the point at which inert meditation replaces a desire to serve. In other words, if the leader is to stay in power, he must make sure that the anxiety is controlled and focused. The technique for doing so is (1) to render the mundane failings less visible by inhibiting rationality, and (2) to provide an explanation for those failings which cannot be concealed. The messages must be simple, direct, and asserted rather than argued. The appeal is to the heart and not the head, and it is designed to inhibit analytic and critical faculties. "National Socialist ideology is to be a Sacred foundation. It is not to be degraded by detailed explanation" (quoted in Erikson 1963:343). Second, the messages concern persons, not structures or processes. If the issue is corruption, for example, then there will be no diagnostic analysis of the organization of government to discover what makes corruption possible and no reasoned program of suggested remedies but only a straightforward indictment of those said to be responsible—privileged classes, neocolonists, immigrant businessmen, or anyone else. Third, the withdrawal from the complexity of the real world may also be achieved by staging political dramas to demonstrate that virtue (namely the leader) is victorious, while virtue's enemies are defeated and punished. Plots and conspiracies are discovered, and the conspirators are named and exterminated. The leader's victory proves, in an agreeably conclusive way, that he or she has superhuman qualities. The hunting down of traitors, like one kind of theatrical performance, diverts attention from the frustrations and deprivations of everyday life. It also provides someone on whom to pin the blame.

Of course, there is likely to be a reckoning. This tactic is, so to speak, addictive, and it is difficult to stabilize, let alone reverse, once it has been started. It has a tendency to eliminate other types of following and does not permit accommodation and a judicious balance in the pattern of loyalties and incentives. Second, the tactic is based upon an unrealistic assumption that an abnormal level of dependency can be maintained indefinitely in a sufficiently large segment of the population, the level of adulation being high enough to shut out either the experience of deprivation or the connection between that experience and the incompetence of the leader. The tactic, pushed to the extreme, implies that the testing of reality can be postponed sine die.

Are we arguing, then, that to raise the level of numenification is to act irrationally, in contradiction to what was said earlier? I think not: it is perfectly rational for someone intent on holding or gaining power to use other people's propensity for irrational behavior. To raise the level of numenification is no more irrational than to treat a disease with particular medication, although it is known to have dangerous side effects. Nevertheless it must also be said that raising the level of numenification does involve two strands of irrationality. First it may close off commentary and criticism from the entourage, and no leader is in fact superhuman enough to do without them. Second, in certain cases one suspects that the leader, taken in by his own image, forgets that God helps mostly those who help themselves. The leader then departs entirely from the habits of pragmatic thought which led him in the first place to manipulate the level of numenification.

RELIGION AND LEADERSHIP

Religion, including that version which emerges in charisma and which is exploited in numenification, consists of illusions with a limited future. I do not mean that it will in the long run yield to logic and science. Even if

355

Weber (1948:155) is correct in perceiving a gradual *Entzauberung* of the world, the terminal point of that process is unthinkable, for the illusion—beliefs placed beyond empirical testing and values held as ends in themselves—is a psychological necessity (and a logical requirement). I refer rather to the short run and to a continuing contrariety between emotion and prudent calculation. What is emotionally gratifying is not necessarily practically useful or even healthy. So the values and beliefs, from time to time, are rubbed hard against reality, and their shape is changed.

Much the same can be said about a leader. Leaders must nourish in others the illusion that they are gifted with superhuman talents. As may be remarked (especially by the French, who are given to talking in this way), the question is one of "personification, significance, authenticity," and the process is one of "mythical incarnation" (Lacouture 1970:11). But at the same time leaders must be practical and must cope with the real world: that is, while they and their entourages must do their best not to destroy the illusions which for others are a psychological necessity, at the same time they themselves must penetrate beyond these illusions to the real world. They have the difficult task of ensuring that the reality never gets so far out of line that it cannot be represented as conforming with the illusion. Failures must be concealed or, if not, at least satisfactorily explained.

Leaders who rely increasingly on charisma run the risk of being caught in a kind of positive feedback: the more they struggle, the tighter become the bonds. Numenification has the effect of inhibiting rationality in the followers. On the good side this effect helps to conceal from them the leader's failings and inadequacies. But at the same time it raises their expectations: they look for miracles. As Weber (1978:1114) puts it, "his divine mission must prove itself by *bringing well-being* to his faithful followers; if they do not fare well, he obviously is not the god-sent master" (emphasis in the original). Given everyone's inability to perform miracles, and given also the failure often to run even a reasonably tidy administration because all the messianic expectations hinder necessary routine work, there is a temptation to intensify the numenification. The problem with charisma is not only that it must be routinized when the time comes to hand control over to noncharismatic successors but also that such a leader, long before that time, may drown himself in a sea of messianic fantasy.

It seems clear that in the last resort the controlling factor is being able to bring to the followers a sufficient level of "well-being." But the well-being is not a simple material matter of food, shelter, and safety, as Weber's words might suggest. Material well-being is offset against psychological and spiritual well-being—a sense of identity, a vision and a purpose in life, and so on—which in turn is compounded with devotion for the leader. Certainly

356

that devotion will to a point compensate for material discomforts and may be the main source of spiritual comfort.

For this reason charisma is indispensable. It would not make sense for a leader, perceiving the dangers of all-consuming numenification, to eschew any charismatic presentation whatsoever. Indeed I have argued that it is impossible to do so and still be a leader. There are, however, some strategies for controlling the situation. One is for leaders to insist on their human qualities from time to time and to bring off the supreme trick of identification in which the masses see the leader not only as an ideal above them but simultaneously as one of them *and* an ideal. Then, the leader is both a comrade and a commander. Castro seems to have been successful at that (Lacouture 1970:25). Public confessions of failure and offers to step down—Castro has made them, and so did Nasser—reflect this strategy and are symbolic denials of godlike capacities. This is a fraternal form of charisma rather than a paternal one.

The other strategy is manifestly paternal. It is to routinize the charisma by subjecting the devotees to the discipline and order of organized worship. Such organizations, although their proclaimed reason for existence is the adoration of some divinity, are very rational and follow the rules of orderly bureaucratic behavior. They domesticate the excesses of devotees, eliminating especially demands for a quick miraculous fix of whatever has broken down. Miracles become part of history: success today comes from hard work and good planning. This routinization leaves room for the leader to work in the real world. An example is the public worship of the Roman emperors as gods.

My discussion in this essay has continually alternated between reason and the emotions. My object has been to show that behavior (in this case, dependency) which is based on an illusion and is an emotional necessity can itself be, in part at least, the product of calculation and design. In other words, not only is there a method in using other people's madness; the madness itself is also in part a product of that method.

NOTE

I am grateful to Fitz John Poole, Mary K. Olsen, and the editors of this volume for their constructive comments. An expanded version of this essay is to be found in Bailey 1988.

Works Cited

Adair, J. 1775. *The History of the American Indians: Particularly Those Nations Adjoining to the Mississippi, East and West Florida, Georgia, South and North Carolina, and Virginia.* London: E. and C. Dilly.

Ahern, Emily M. 1973. *The Cult of the Dead in a Chinese Village.* Stanford: Stanford University Press.

Alcock, J. 1975. *Animal Behavior: An Evolutionary Approach.* Sunderland, Mass.: Sinauer.

Anscombe, G. E. M. 1957. *Intention.* Oxford: Basil Blackwell.

Avruch, Kevin. 1982. "On the 'Traditionalization' of Social Identity: American Immigrants to Israel." *Ethos* 10: 95–116.

Bailey, F. G. 1988. *Humbuggery and Manipulation: The Art of Leadership.* Ithaca: Cornell University Press.

Baity, Philip Chesley. 1975. *Religion in a Chinese Town.* Taipei: Orient Cultural Service.

Barry, Herbert, III, Irvin L. Child, & Margaret K. Bacon. 1959. "Relation of Child Training to Subsistence Economy." *American Anthropologist* 61: 51–63.

Barth, Fredrik. 1967. "On the Study of Social Change." *American Anthropologist* 69: 661–669.

Bartlett, F. C. 1932. *Remembering.* Cambridge: Cambridge University Press.

Bartram, W. 1853. "Observations on the Creek and Cherokee Indians." *Transactions of the American Ethnological Society* 3: 1–81. [Originally written in 1789]

Becker, Ernest. 1973. *The Denial of Death.* New York: Free Press.

Benedict, Ruth. 1946. *The Chrysanthemum and the Sword.* New York: Freedman.

Benveniste, Emile. 1971. *Problems in General Linguistics.* Coral Gables: University of Miami Press.

Berg, F. J. 1968. "The Swahili Community of Mombasa, 1500–1900." *Journal of African History* 9: 35–56.

Berger, Peter L. 1970. *A Rumor of Angels: Modern Society and the Rediscovery of the Supernatural.* Garden City, N.Y.: Doubleday Anchor.

Bernstein, I. S. 1976. "Dominance, Aggression, and Reproduction in Primate Societies." *Journal of Theoretical Biology* 60: 459–472.

Bettelheim, Bruno. 1962. *Symbolic Wounds: Puberty Rites and the Envious Male.* Rev. ed. New York: Collier Books.

———. 1975. *The Uses of Enchantment: The Meaning and Importance of Fairy Tales.* New York: Vintage.

Bilu, Yoram. 1980. "The Moroccan Demon in Israel: The Case of 'Evil Spirit Disease.'" *Ethos* 8: 24–39.

Birdwhistell, R. L. 1970. *Kinesics and Context: Essays on Bodily Motion Communication.* Philadelphia: University of Pennsylvania Press.

———. 1983. "A Longitudinal Study of Three Apache Brothers." *Journal of Psychoanalytic Anthropology* 6: 125–162.

Bohannan, Paul. 1960. "*Conscience Collective* and Culture." In Kurt Wolff (ed.), *Emile Durkheim et al.: Essays on Sociology and Social Philosophy, with appraisals of Durkheim's life and thought.* New York: Harper and Row. Pp. 77–96.

Borish, Steven. 1982. *Stones of the Galilee: A Study of Culture Change on an Israeli Kibbutz.* Ph.D. diss., Stanford University.

Bourguignon, Erika. 1968. "World Distribution and Patterns of Possession States." In Raymond Prince (ed.), *Trance and Possession States.* Montreal: R. M. Bucke Memorial Society. Pp. 3–34.

———. 1973. "Introduction: A Framework for the Comparative Study of Altered States of Consciousness." In Erika Bourguignon (ed.), *Religion, Altered States of Consciousness, and Social Change.* Columbus: Ohio State University Press. Pp. 3–39.

———. 1974. *Culture and the Varieties of Consciousness.* Module in Anthropology No. 47. Reading, Mass.: Addison-Wesley.

———. 1976. *Possession.* San Francisco: Chandler & Sharp.

———. 1979. *Psychological Anthropology.* New York: Holt, Rinehart & Winston.

———. 1984. "Belief and Behavior in Haitian Folk Healing." In P. B. Pedersen, N. Sartorius, & A. J. Marsella (eds.), *Mental Health Services: The Cultural Context.* Berkeley: Sage Press. Pp. 243–266.

———. 1987. "Alternierende Persönlichkeit, Besessenheitstrance, und die psychische Einheit der Menschheit." In Hans Peter Duerr (ed.), *Die Wilde Seele: Zur Ethnopsychoanalyse von Georges Devereux.* Frankfurt: Suhrkamp.

Bourguignon, Erika, & T. L. Evascu. 1977. "Altered States of Consciousness within a General Evolutionary Perspective: A Holocultural Analysis." *Behavioral Science Research* 12: 197–216.

Bowes, Alison M. 1978. "Women in the Kibbutz Movement" *Sociological Review* 26: 237–262.

Boyer, Bryce, George De Vos, & Orin Borders. 1978. "The Burnt Child Reaction among the Yukon Eskimos." *Journal of Psychological Anthropology* 1(1): 7–16.

Boyer, Bryce, George De Vos, & Ruth Boyer. 1983. "On the Acquisition of Shamanistic Status: A Clinical and Rorschach Study of a Specific Case." In Hans Peter Duerr (ed.), *Die Wilde Seele: Zur Ethnopsychiatris von Georges Devereux*. Frankfurt: Suhrkamp.

Bridgman, P. W. 1936. *The Nature of Physical Theory*. Princeton: Princeton University Press.

Bruner, J. S. 1951. "Personality Dynamics and the Process of Perceiving." In R. Blake & G. Ramsey (eds.), *Perception and Approach to Personality*. New York: Ronald Press.

Burrows, E. G., & Melford E. Spiro. 1953. *An Atoll Culture*. New Haven: HRAF Press.

Busse, D., & W. Hamilton III. 1981. "Infant Carrying by Male Chacma Baboons." *Science* 212: 1281–1283.

Cahill, Suzanne E. 1982. *The Image of the Goddess Hsi Wang Mu in Medieval Chinese Literature*. Ph.D. diss. University of California, Berkeley.

Calvin, William H. 1983. *The Throwing Madonna: Essays on the Brain*. New York: McGraw-Hill.

Casson, Ronald W. 1983. "Schemata in Cognitive Anthropology." *Annual Review of Anthropology* 12: 429–462.

Caudill, William. 1949. "Psychological Characteristics of Acculturated Wisconsin Ojibwa Children." *American Anthropologist* 51: 409–427.

Cheney, D. 1977. "The Acquisition of Rank and the Development of Reciprocal Alliances among Free-Ranging Immature Baboons." *Behavior Ecology and Sociobiology* 2: 303–318.

Chiao, Chien. 1981. "Chinese Strategic Behaviors: A Preliminary List." In *Proceedings of the International Conference on Sinology (Academia Sinica, August 15–2, 1980)*, Section on Folklore and Culture. Taipei: Academia Sinica. Pp. 429–440.

Cook, Edwin. 1982. Review of *Gender and Culture* by M. E. Spiro. *American Anthropologist* 84:422–424.

Culler, Jonathan. 1982. *On Deconstruction: Theory and Criticism after Structuralism*. Ithaca: Cornell University Press.

D'Andrade, Roy G. 1961. "Anthropological Studies in Dreams." In F. K. Hsu (ed.), *Psychological Anthropology*. Homewood, Ill.: Dorsey Press. Pp. 296–332.

————. 1981. "The Cultural Part of Cognition." *Cognitive Science* 5: 179–198.

————. 1984. "Cultural Meaning Systems." In R. Shweder & R. LeVine (eds.), *Culture Theory: Essays on Mind, Self, and Emotion*. New York: Cambridge University Press. Pp. 88–119.

————. 1987. "A Folk Model of the Mind." In D. Holland & N. Quinn (eds.), *Cultural Models in Language and Thought*. Cambridge: Cambridge University Press. Pp. 112–148.

————. n.d. "Some Propositions about the Relations of Culture and Cognition." Unpublished ms.

D'Aquili, Eugene G., & Charles D. Laughlin, Jr. 1979. "The Neurobiology of Myth and Ritual." In Eugene G. d'Aquili, Charles D. Laughlin, Jr., & John McManus, *The Spectrum of Ritual: A Biogenetic Structural Analysis*. New York: Columbia University Press. Pp. 152–182.

Dauber, Roslyn, & Melinda L. Cain (eds.). 1981. *Women and Technological Change in Developing Countries*. American Association for the Advancement of Science Selected Symposium No. 53. Boulder: Westview Press.

Davidson, Richard J. 1984. "Hemispheric Asymmetry and Emotion." In Klaus R. Scherer & Paul Ekman (eds.), *Approaches to Emotion*. Hillsdale, N.J.: Lawrence Erlbaum Associates. Pp. 39–57.

Dawkins, R. 1976. *The Selfish Gene*. New York: Oxford University Press.

Day, Richard, Bryce Boyer, & George De Vos. 1975. "Two Styles of Ego Development: A Cross Cultural Longitudinal Comparison of Apache and Anglo School Children." *Ethos* 3: 345–379.

Deag, J., & J. H. Crook. 1971. "Social Behaviour and 'Agonistic Buffering' in the Wild Barbary Macaque, *Macaca sylvana* L." *Folia Primatologica* 15: 183–280.

De Grazia, Sebastian. 1948. *The Political Community*. Chicago: University of Chicago Press.

Deliusin, Lev. 1972. "The I-kuan Tao Society." In Jean Chesneaux (ed.), *Popular Movements and Secret Societies in China, 1840–1950*. Stanford: Stanford University Press. Pp. 225–233, 277–278. [Originally published, 1970]

Derrida, Jacques. 1976. *Of Grammatology*. Baltimore: Johns Hopkins University Press.

————. 1978. *Writing and Difference*. Trans. (A. Bass.) London: Routledge & Kegan Paul.

————. 1982. "Plato's Pharmacy." In *Dissemination*. Chicago: University of Chicago Press.

Devereux, George. 1974. "Trance and Orgasm in Euripides' *Bakchai*." In A. Angoff & D. Barth (eds.), *Parapsychology and Anthropology*. New York: Parapsychology Foundation.

DeVore, Irven. 1965a. "Male Dominance and Mating Behavior in Baboons." In F. Beach (ed.), *Sex and Behavior*. New York: Wiley.

———. 1965b. *Primate Behavior: Field Studies of Monkeys and Apes*. New York: Holt, Rinehart & Winston.

DeVore, Irven, & K. R. L. Hall. 1965. "Baboon Ecology." In I. DeVore (ed.), *Primate Behavior*. New York: Holt, Rinehart & Winston.

DeVorsey, L., Jr. (ed.). 1971. *De Brahm's Report of the General Survey in the Southern District of North America*. Columbia, S.C.: University of South Carolina Press.

De Vos, George A. 1973. *Socialization for Achievement: Essays on the Cultural Psychology of the Japanese*. Berkeley: University of California Press.

———. 1974, "Cross Cultural Studies of Mental Disorder: An Anthropological Perspective." In G. Caplan (ed.), *American Handbook of Psychiatry*, vol. 3. New York: Basic Books.

———. 1975a. "Apprenticeship and Paternalism: Psychocultural Continuities Underlying Japanese Social Organization." In Ezra Vogel (ed.), *Modern Japanese Organization and Decision-Making*. Berkeley: University of California Press.

———. 1975b. "The Dangers of Pure Theory in Social Anthropology." *Ethos* 3: 77–91.

———. 1978. "Selective Permeability and Reference Group Sanctioning: Psychocultural Continuities in Role Degradation." In Milton Yinger & Stephen Cutler (eds.), *Major Social Issues: A Multidisciplinary View*. New York: Free Press.

———. 1980. "Ethnic Adaptation and Minority Status." *Journal of Cross-Cultural Psychology* 11: 101–125.

———. 1982. "Adaptive Strategies in American Minorities." In E. E. Jones & S. Korchin (eds.), *Minority Mental Health*. New York: Praeger. Pp. 74–117.

———. 1983a. "Adaptive Conflict and Adjustive Coping: Psychocultural Approaches to Ethnic Identity." In Theodore R. Sarbin & Karl Scheibe (ed.), *Studies in Social Identity*. New York: Praeger. Pp. 204–230.

———. 1983b. "Ethnic Identity and Minority Status: Some Psycho-Cultural Considerations in Identity: Personal and Socio-Cultural." In Anita Jacobson-Widding (ed.), *Identity: Personal and Socio-Cultural: A Symposium. Acta Universitatis Upsaliensis* (Stockholm), no. 5.

———. 1985. "Dimensions of the Self in Culture." In Anthony Marsella, George De Vos, & Francis L. K. Hsu (eds.), *Culture and Self: Asian and Western Perspectives*. New York: Methuen.

———. 1986. "Insight and Symbol: Dimensions of Analysis in Psychoanalytic Anthropology." *Journal of Psychoanalytic Anthropology* 9:191–233.

De Vos, George A., & Orin Borders. 1979. "A Rorschach Comparison of Delinquent and Non-Delinquent Family Members." *Journal of Psychoanalytic Anthropology* 2: 425–442.

De Vos, George A., & Marcelo Suarez-Orozco. 1987. "Sacrifice and the Experience of Power." *Journal of Psychoanalytic Anthropology* 10:309–339.

De Vos, George A., & Hiroshi Wagatsuma. 1966. *Japan's Invisible Race.* Berkeley: University of California Press.

De Waal, Frans. 1982. *Chimpanzee Politics: Power and Sex among Apes.* London: Jonathan Cape.

De Waal, Frans B. M., & J. van Hoof. 1981. Side-Directed Communication and Agonistic Interactions in Chimpanzees. *Behavior* 77: 164–198.

Dolgin, Janet, David Kemnitzer, & David Schneider. 1977. "Introduction." In *Symbolic Anthropology: A Reader in the Study of Symbols and Meanings.* New York: Columbia University Press.

Doolittle, Justus. 1865. *Social Life of the Chinese: With Some Account of Their Religious, Governmental, Educational, and Business Customs and Opinions, With Special but Not Exclusive Reference to Fuchau.* New York: Harper & Brothers.

Douglas, Mary. 1966. *Purity and Danger.* London: Routledge & Kegan Paul.

———. 1973. *Natural Symbols: Explorations in Cosmology.* Harmondsworth: Penguin Books.

———. 1981. *Edward Evans-Pritchard.* New York: Penguin Books.

Durkheim, Emile. 1915. *The Elementary Forms of the Religious Life.* New York: Macmillan. [Originally published 1912]

———. 1933. *The Division of Labor in Society.* New York: Macmillan. [Originally published 1893]

———. 1938. *Rules of the Sociological Method.* Glencoe, Ill.: Free Press. [Originally published 1895]

———. 1947. *The Elementary Forms of the Religious Life.* Glencoe, Ill.: Free Press. [Originally published 1912]

———. 1954. *The Elementary Forms of the Religious Life.* Glencoe, Ill.: Free Press. [Originally published, 1912]

———. 1960. *Les formes élémentaires de la vie religieuse: Le système totémique en Australie.* Paris: F. Alcan. [Originally published 1912]

———. 1961. *The Elementary Forms of the Religious Life.* New York: Collier Books. [Originally published 1912]

———. 1964a. *The Division of Labor in Society.* Trans. George Simpson. New York: Free Press. [Originally published 1893]

———. 1964b. "The Dualism of Human Nature." In Kurt Wolff (ed.), *Essays on Sociology and Philosophy.* New York: Harper & Row. Pp. 325–340. [Originally published 1914]

————. 1966. *Suicide: A Study in Sociology.* Trans. John A. Spaulding & George Simpson. New York: Free Press. [Originally published 1897]

————. 1974. "Individual and Collective Representations." In *Sociology and Philosophy.* Trans. D. F. Pocock. New York: Free Press. Pp. 1–34. [Originally published 1898]

Edgerton, Robert B. 1971. *The Individual in Cultural Adaptation.* Berkeley: University of California Press.

Eggan, Dorothy. 1961. "Dream Analysis." In B. Kaplan (ed.), *Studying Personality Cross-Culturally.* Evanston: Harper & Row.

Eister, Allan W. 1974. "Introduction." In A. Eister (ed.), *Changing Perspectives in the Scientific Study of Religion.* New York: Wiley.

Ekman, Paul. 1970. "Universal Facial Expressions of Emotion." *California Mental Health Research Digest* 8: 151–158.

Elliott, Alan J. A. 1955. *Chinese Spirit-Medium Cults in Singapore.* Monographs on Social Anthropology n.s. 14. London: London School of Economics.

Ellison, Gaylord D. 1979. "Chemical Systems of the Brain and Evolution." In David A. Oakley & H. C. Plotkin (eds.), *Brain, Behavior, and Evolution.* London: Methuen. Pp. 78–98.

Erikson, Erik H. 1963. *Childhood and Society.* New York: Norton.

————. 1968. *Identity, Youth, and Crisis.* New York: Norton.

Evans-Pritchard, E. E. 1965. *Theories of Primitive Religion.* Oxford: Oxford University Press.

Exner, John, & Irving Weiner. 1982. *The Rorschach: A Comprehensive System.* Vol. 3: *Assessment of Children and Adolescents.* New York: Wiley.

Fest, Joachim C. 1975. *Hitler.* New York: Random House.

Festinger, L., H. W. Riecken, & S. Schachter. 1956. *When Prophecy Fails.* Minneapolis: University of Minnesota Press.

Field, Margaret. 1969. "Spirit Possession in Ghana." In John Beattie & John Middleton (eds.), *Spirit Mediumship and Society in Africa.* New York: Africana.

Fillmore, Charles. 1977. "Topics in Lexical Semantics." In R. Cole (ed.), *Current Issues in Linguistic Theory.* Bloomington: Indiana University Press. Pp. 76–138.

Firth, Raymond. 1959. "Problems and Assumption in an Anthropological Study of Religion." *Journal of the Royal Anthropological Institute* 89: 129–148.

————. 1974. "Faith and Skepticism in Kelantan Village Magic." In William R. Roff (ed.), *Kelantan: Religion, Society, and Politics in a Malay State.* Kuala Lumpur: Oxford University Press. Pp. 190–224.

Fisher, Helen. 1982. *The Sex Contract: The Evolution of Human Behavior.* New York: Quill.

Fogelson, Raymond D. 1971. "The Cherokee Ballgame Cycle: An Ethnographer's View." *Ethnomusicology* 15: 327–338.

———. 1977. "Cherokee Notions of Power." In R. D. Fogelson & R. N. Adams (eds.), *The Anthropology of Power.* New York: Academic Press. Pp. 185–194.

———. 1978. *The Cherokees: A Critical Bibliography.* Bloomington: Indiana University Press.

———. 1980. "Windigo Goes South: Stoneclad among the Cherokees. In M. M. Halpin & M. M. Ames (eds.), *Manlike Monsters on Trial.* Vancouver: University of British Columbia Press. Pp. 132–151.

Fox, Robin. 1979. "The Evolution of Mind: An Anthropological Approach." *Journal of Anthropological Research* 35: 138–156.

Frake, Charles. 1964. "Notes on Queries in Ethnography." *American Anthropologist* 66(3.2): 132–145.

Freud, Anna. 1937. *The Ego and Mechanisms of Defense.* London: Hogarth Press.

Freud, Sigmund. [Works cited in text by date of writing]

———. 1900. *The Interpretation of Dreams.* [In *The Standard Edition of Freud's Complete Psychological Works*, vols. 4–5 (London: Hogarth Press and the Institute of Psycho-Analysis, 1953–1975).]

———. 1907. "Obsessive Actions and Religious Practices." [In *The Standard Edition of Freud's Complete Psychological Works* (London: Hogarth Press and the Institute of Psycho-Analysis, 1953–1975), 9:115–128.]

———. 1908. " 'Civilized' Sexual Morality and Modern Nervous Illness." [In *The Standard Edition of Freud's Complete Psychological Works* (London: Hogarth Press and the Institute of Psycho-Analysis, 1953–1975), 9:181–204.]

———. 1910a. "The Antithetical Meaning of Primal Words." [In *The Standard Edition of Freud's Complete Psychological Works* (London: Hogarth Press and the Institute of Psycho-Analysis, 1953–1975), 11:153–162.]

———. 1910b. *Leonardo da Vinci and a Memory of His Childhood.* [In *The Standard Edition of Freud's Complete Psychological Works* (London: Hogarth Press and the Institute of Psycho-Analysis, 1953–1975), 11:63–137.]

———. 1913. *Totem und Tabu.* [*Gesammelte Werke*, vol. 9 (London: Imago Publishing, 1940–1952]

———. 1914. "On Narcissism." [In *The Standard Edition of Freud's Complete Psychological Works* (London: Hogarth Press and the Institute of Psycho-Analysis, 1953–1975), 14:73–102.]

————. 1918. *Totem and Taboo: Resemblances between the Psychic Lives of Savages and Neurotics*. [Reprint ed., New York: Vintage Books, 1946.]

————. 1923. "A Neurosis of Demoniacal Possession in the Seventeenth Century. [In Philip Rieff (ed.), *Studies in Parapsychology*. New York: Collier, 1963. Pp. 91–125.]

————. 1925. "Negation." [In *The Standard Edition of Freud's Complete Psychological Works* (London: Hogarth Press and the Institute of Psycho-Analysis, 1953–1975), 19:235–242.]

————. 1927. *The Future of an Illusion*. [In *The Standard Edition of Freud's Complete Psychological Works* (London: Hogarth Press and the Institute of Psycho-Analysis, 1953–1975), 21:3–56.]

Fromm, Erich. 1968. *Escape from Freedom*. New York: Avon.

Funnell, Robert, & Richard Smith. 1981. "Search for a Theory of Cultural Transmission in an Anthropology of Education: Notes on Spindler and Gearing." *Anthropology and Education Quarterly* 12: 275–300.

Fürer-Haimendorf, Cristoph von. 1964. *The Sherpas of Nepal: Buddhist Highlanders*. Berkeley: University of California Press.

Fyffe, W. 1761. "Letter to Brother John, February 1, 1761." Manuscripts Collection of the Thomas Gilcrease Institute of American History and Art.

Galin, David. 1976. "The Two Modes of Consciousness and the Two Halves of the Brain." In Philip R. Lee et al., *Symposium on Consciousness*. New York: Penguin. Pp. 26–52.

————. 1977. "Lateral Specialization and Psychiatric Issues: Speculations on Development and the Evolution of Consciousness." In Stuart J. Dimond & David A. Blizard (eds.), *Evolution and Lateralization of the Brain. Annals of the New York Academy of Sciences* 299:397–411.

Gearing, F. O. 1962. *Priests and Warriors: Social Structures for Cherokee Politics in the Eighteenth Century*. Memoir No. 93. Washington, D.C.: American Anthropological Association.

Geertz, Clifford. 1966. "Religion as a Cultural System." In Michael Banton (ed.), *Anthropological Approaches to the Study of Religion*. London: Tavistock. Pp. 1–46.

————. 1973a. "The Impact of the Concept of Culture on the Concept of Man." In *The Interpretation of Cultures*. New York: Basic Books.

————. 1973b. *The Interpretation of Cultures*. New York: Basic Books.

————. 1983. *Local Knowledge*. New York: Basic Books.

Gellhorn, Ernst, & William F. Kiely. 1972. "Mystical States of Consciousness: Neurophysiological and Clinical Aspects." *Journal of Nervous and Mental Disease* 154:399–405.

Gerber, Eleanor. 1985. "Rage and Obligation: Samoan Emotion in Conflict."

In G. White & J. Kirkpatrick (eds.), *Person, Self, and Experience.* Berkeley: University of California Press. Pp. 121–167.

Gibbons, Don, & James De Jarnette. 1972. "Hypnotic Susceptibility and Religious Experience." *Journal for the Scientific Study of Religion* 11: 152–156.

Gilmore, H. 1977. "The Evolution of Agonistic Buffering in Baboons and Macaques." Paper presented at the annual meeting of the American Association of Physical Anthropologists, Seattle.

Gladwin, Hugh. 1972. "Semantics, Schemata, and Kinship." Paper presented at the Mathematics in the Social Sciences Board Conference, Riverside, Calif.

Glaser, Gilbert H. 1978. "Epilepsy, Hysteria, and 'Possession': A Historical Essay." *Journal of Nervous and Mental Disease* 166(4): 268–274.

Goldschmidt, Walter, & Robert Edgerton. 1961. "A Picture Technique for the Study of Values." *American Anthropologist* 63: 26–45.

Goodenough, Ward H. 1965. "Rethinking 'Status' and 'Role': Toward a General Model of the Cultural Organization of Social Relationships." In M. Banton (ed.), *The Relevance of Models for Social Anthropology.* American Sociological Association Monographs No. 1. London: Tavistock. Pp. 1–24.

―――. 1981. *Culture, Language, and Society.* Menlo Park, Calif.: Benjamin/Cummings.

Graham, David Crockett. 1961. *Folk Religion in Southwest China.* Smithsonian Miscellaneous Collections, vol. 142, no. 2. Washington, D.C.: Smithsonian Institution Press.

Griffin, D. 1981. *The Question of Animal Awareness.* 2nd ed. New York: Rockefeller University Press.

―――. 1984. *Animal Thinking.* Cambrigde, Mass.: Harvard University Press.

Grootaers, Willem A. 1946. "Une société secrète moderne: I-kuan Tao: Bibliographie Annotée." *Folklore Studies* 5: 316–352.

Grünbaum, Adolf. 1984. *The Foundations of Psychoanalysis.* Berkeley: University of California Press.

Haan, Norma. 1977. *Coping and Defending: Processes of Self-Environment Organization.* New York: Academic Press.

Hale, K. L. 1971. "A Note on the Walbiri Tradition of Antonymy." In D. D. Steinberg & L. A. Jakabovits (eds.), *Semantics: An Interdisciplinary Reader in Philosophy, Linguistics, and Psychology.* New York: Cambridge University Press. Pp. 472–482.

Hall, K. R. L., & I. DeVore. 1965. "Baboon Social Behavior." In I. DeVore (ed.), *Primate Behavior.* New York: Holt, Rinehart & Winston.

Hallowell, A. Irving. 1942. "Acculturation Processes and Personality

Changes as Indicated by the Rorschach Technique." *Rorschach Research Exchange* 6: 42–50.

———. 1955a. "Acculturation and Personality of the Ojibwa." In *Culture and Experience*. Philadelphia: University of Pennsylvania Press. Pp. 345–357. [Originally published 1951]

———. 1955b. "Aggression in Saulteaux Society." In *Culture and Experience*. Philadelphia: University of Pennsylvania Press. Pp. 277–290. [Originally published 1940]

———. 1955c. *Culture and Experience*. Philadelphia: University of Pennsylvania Press.

———. 1955d. "The Self and Its Behavioral Environment." In *Culture and Experience*. Philadelphia: University of Pennsylvania Press. Pp. 75–110.

———. 1959–1963. "Personality, Culture, and Society in Behavioral Evolution." In Sigmund Koch (ed.), *Psychology: A Study of a Science*, vol. 6. New York: McGraw-Hill. Pp. 429–509.

———. 1976. *Contributions to Anthropology: Selected Papers of A. Irving Hallowell*. Ed. R. Fogelson. Chicago: University of Chicago Press.

Halverson, John. 1987. "Art for Art's Sake in the Paleolithic." *Current Anthropology* 28(1): 63–89.

Hamilton, W. D. 1964. "The Genetical Theory of Social Behaviour (I & II)." *Journal of Theoretical Biology* 7: 1–16, 17–32.

Hamilton, W. J. 1978. "Sex Differences in Cooperative Behavior of Free-ranging Savannah Baboons." In *Papers Presented at Wenner-Gren Conference: Baboon Field Research: Myths & Models, June, 1978*. New York: Wenner Gren.

Harrell, C. Stevan. 1974. *Belief and Unbelief in a Taiwan Village*. Ph.D. diss. Stanford University.

Hausfater, G. 1975. *Dominance and Reproduction in Baboons: A Quantitative Analysis (Contributions to Primatology)*. Basel: Karger.

Hay, David. 1979. "Religious Experience amongst a Group of Post-Graduate Students: A Qualitative Study." *Journal for the Scientific Study of Religion* 18: 164–182.

Hay, David, & Ann Morisy. 1978. "Reports of Ecstatic, Paranormal, or Religious Experience in Great Britain and the United States: A Comparison of Trends." *Journal for the Scientific Study of Religion* 17: 255–268.

Helm, June, George De Vos, & Therese Carterette. 1960. *Variations in Personality and Ego Identification within a Slave Indian Kin Community*. National Museum of Canada Bulletin No. 190, Contributions to Anthropology.

Hempel, Carl G. 1952. *Fundamentals of Concept Formation in Empirical Science*. Chicago: University of Chicago Press.

———. 1965. "The Logic of Functional Analysis." In *Aspects of Scientific Explanation and Other Essays*. New York: Free Press.

Henry, James L. 1982. "Possible Involvement of Endorphins in Altered States of Consciousness." *Ethos* 10: 394–408.

Herskovits, Melville J. 1948. "The Contributions of Afroamerican Studies to Africanist Research." *American Anthropologist* 50: 1–10.

Hertz, Neil. 1979. "Recognizing Casaubon." *Glyph* 6: 24–41.

Hilgard, Ernest R. 1968. *The Experience of Hypnosis*. New York: Harcourt, Brace & World.

Hilgard, Ernest R., & Josephine R. Hilgard. 1975. *Hypnosis in the Relief of Pain*. Los Altos, Calif.: William Kaufmann.

Hirst, Paul Q. 1975. *Durkheim, Bernard, and Epistemology*. London: Routledge & Kegan Paul.

Ho, David Y. F. 1986. "Chinese Patterns of Socialization: A Critical Review." In Michael H. Bond (ed.), *The Psychology of the Chinese People*. Hong Kong: Oxford University Press. Pp. 1–37.

Hobbes, Thomas. 1946. *Leviathan*. Oxford: Blackwell. [Originally published 1651]

Hogbin, I. 1970. *The Island of Menstruating Men: Religion in Wogeo, New Guinea*. Scranton: Chandler.

Holland, Dorothy, & Debra Skinner. 1987. "Prestige and Intimacy: The Cultural Models behind Americans' Talk about Gender Types." In D. Holland & N. Quinn (eds.), *Cultural Models in Language and Thought*. Cambridge: Cambridge University Press. Pp. 78–111.

Holzinger, C. H. 1960. "Some Observations on the Persistence of Aboriginal Cherokee Personality Traits." In W. N. Fenton & J. Gulick (eds.), *Symposium on Cherokee and Iroquois Culture. Smithsonian Institution Bureau of American Ethnology Bulletin* 180: 229–237.

Hood, Ralph W., Jr. 1974. "Psychological Strength and the Report of Intense Religious Experience." *Journal for the Scientific Study of Religion* 13: 65–71.

Horton, Robin. 1960. "A Definition of Religion and Its Uses." *Journal of the Royal Anthropological Institute* 90: 201–226.

———. 1967. "African Traditional Thought and Western Science." *Africa* 37: 50–71, 155–187.

Hsiao Ching-fen. 1972. "The Current Situation of New Religion in Taiwan." *Theology and the Church* 10(2): 1–24.

Hsu, Francis L. K. 1985. "The Chinese Concept of Self." In Anthony Marsella, George De Vos, & Francis Hsu (eds.), *Culture and Self*. London: Methuen. Pp. 24–55.

Hudson, Charles. 1977. "James Adair as Anthropologist." *Ethnohistory* 24: 311–328.

Huizinga, J. 1955. *Homo Ludens: A Study of the Play Element in Culture.* Trans. R. F. C. Hull. Boston: Beacon Press. [Originally published 1949]

Humphrey, N. K. 1976. "The Social Function of Intellect." In P. Bateson & R. Hinde (eds.), *Growing Points in Ethology.* Cambridge: Cambridge University Press.

Hutchins, Edwin. 1987. "Myth and Experience in the Trobriand Islands." In D. Holland & N. Quinn (eds.), *Cultural Models in Language and Thought.* Cambridge: Cambridge University Press. Pp. 269–289.

Jacobs, J. Bruce. 1980. *Local Politics in a Rural Chinese Cultural Setting: A Field Study of Mazu Township, Taiwan.* Canberra: Contemporary China Centre, Research School of Pacific Studies, Australian National University.

Jacobs, Sue Ellen. 1982. "Women in Development (A Review Essay)." *American Anthropologist* 84: 365–371.

Jaynes, Julian. 1976. *The Origin of Consciousness in the Breakdown of the Bicameral Mind.* Boston: Houghton Mifflin.

Jerison, Harry J. 1975. "Evolution of the Brain and Intelligence." *Current Anthropology* 16: 403–426.

Joffe, Natalie F. 1940. "The Fox of Iowa." In Ralph Linton (ed.), *Acculturation in Seven American Indian Tribes.* New York: Appleton-Century.

Jordan, David K. 1972. *Gods, Ghosts, and Ancestors: The Folk Religion of a Taiwanese Village.* Berkeley: University of California Press.

———. 1981. " 'Causes and Effects' Tales in Sectarian Revelation." In *Proceedings of the International Conference on Sinology, Academia Sinica, August 15–20, 1980, Section of Folklore & Culture.* Pp. 73–99.

———. 1982. "The Recent History of the Celestial Way, a Chinese Pietistic Association." *Modern China* 8: 435–462.

———. 1983a. "Chinese Pietism: Syncretic Movements in Modern Taiwan." In C. R. Das (ed.), *Folk Culture: Proceedings of the International Seminar on Folk Culture, Cuttack, Orissa, India, December 19–23, 1979,* vol. 2. Cuttack: Institute of Oriental & Orissan Studies. Pp. 49–67.

———. 1983b. "The Repression of Hostility and the Representation of Hell in South Taiwan Religious Processions." In Ruth-Inge Heinze (ed.), *Asian Concepts of Hell, I.* Berkeley: Folklore Institute. Pp. 17–31, 82–83.

Jordan, David K., & Daniel L. Overmyer. 1986. *The Flying Phoenix: Aspects of Sectarianism in Taiwan.* Princeton: Princeton University Press.

Kakar, Sudhir. 1982. *Shamans, Mystics, and Doctors: A Psychological Inquiry into India and Its Healing Traditions.* New York: Knopf.

Kant, I. 1929. *Critique of Pure Reason*. Trans. N. Kemp Smith. London: Macmillan. [Originally published 1781]

Kaplan, J. 1978. "Fight Interference in Rhesus Monkeys." *American Journal of Physical Anthropology* 49: 241–250.

Kardiner, Abram. 1946. *The Psychological Frontiers of Society*. New York: Columbia University Press.

———. 1948. "The Concept of Basic Personality Structure as an Operational Tool in the Social Sciences." In Douglas Haring (ed.), *Personal Character and Culture Milieu*. Syracuse: Syracuse University Press. Pp. 431–448.

Kardiner, Abram, & E. Preble. 1961. *They Studied Man*. Cleveland: World Publishing.

Keesing, Roger M. 1974. "Theories of Culture." *Annual Review of Anthropology* 3: 73–97.

Kenny, M. G. 1986. *The Passion of Ansel Bourne: Multiple Personality in American Culture*. Washington, D.C.: Smithsonian Institution Press.

Kerboull, Jean. 1973. *Le vaudou: Magie ou religion?* Paris: Robert Laffont.

Kernberg, Otto. 1975. *Borderline Conditions and Pathological Narcissism*. New York: Aronson.

Kerr, Madeline. 1963. *Personality and Conflict in Jamaica*. London: Collins.

Kilborne, Benjamin. 1981. "Pattern, Structure, and Style in Anthropological Studies of Dreams." *Ethos* 9: 165–185.

King, Ambrose Y. C., & Michael H. Bond. 1985. "The Confucian Paradigm of Man: A Sociological View." In Wen-Shing Tseng & David Y. H. Wu (eds.), *Chinese Culture and Mental Health*. Honolulu: University of Hawaii Press. Pp. 29–45.

Klink, C. F., & J. J. Talman (eds.). 1970. *The Journal of Major John Norton, 1816*. Toronto: Champlain Society.

Kluckhohn, Clyde. 1952. "Universal Values and Anthropological Relativism." In *Modern Education and Human Values*. Pitcairn-Crabbe Foundation Lecture Series. Pittsburgh: University of Pittsburgh Press. Pp. 87–112.

———. 1953. "Universal Categories of Culture. In A. L. Kroeber (ed.), *Anthropology Today*. Chicago: University of Chicago Press. Pp. 507–523.

———. 1955. "Ethical Relativity: Sic et Non." *Journal of Philosophy* 52: 662–677.

———. 1960. "Recurrent Themes in Myth and Myth Making." In H. A. Murray (ed.), *Myth and Myth Making*. New York: George Braziller. Pp. 46–60.

Kluckhohn, Clyde, & W. H. Kelly. 1945. "The Concept of Culture." In

Ralph Linton (ed.), *The Science of Man in the World Crisis*. New York: Columbia University Press. Pp. 78–105.

Kroeber, Alfred Lewis. 1948. *Anthropology: Race, Language, Culture, Psychology, Pre-History*. Rev. ed. New York: Harcourt, Brace.

La Barre, Weston. 1938. *The Peyote Cult*. New Haven: Yale University Press.

———. 1962. *They Shall Take Up Serpents: Psychology of the Southern Snake Handling Cult*. Minneapolis: University of Minnesota Press.

Lacouture, Jean. 1970. *The Demigods: Charismatic Leadership in the Third World*. New York: Knopf.

Lakoff, George. 1987. *Women, Fire, and Dangerous Things*. Chicago: University of Chicago Press.

Leach, Edmund R. 1967. "Virgin Birth." *Proceedings of the Royal Anthropological Institute* 3: 39–50.

Lessa, William A. 1961. "Sorcery on Ifaluk." *American Anthropologist* 63: 817–820.

LeVine, Robert. 1973. *Culture, Behavior, and Personality*. Chicago: Aldine.

Lévi-Strauss, Claude. 1963. "The Structural Study of Myth." In *Structural Anthropology*. New York: Basic Books. Pp. 206–231.

Levy, Jerre. 1977. "The Mammalian Brain and the Adaptive Advantage of Cerebral Asymmetry." In S. J. Dimond & D. Blizard (eds.), *Evolution and Lateralization of the Brain*. Annals of the New York Academy of Sciences 299:264–272.

Levy, Robert I. 1984. "Emotion, Knowing, and Culture." In R. Shweder & R. LeVine (eds.), *Culture Theory: Essays on Mind, Self, and Emotion*. New York: Cambridge University Press. Pp. 214–237.

Lewis, I. M. 1971. *Ecstatic Religion: An Anthropological Study of Spirit Possession and Shamanism*. Harmondsworth: Penguin Books.

Lex, Barbara W. 1975/76. "Psychological Aspects of Ritual Trance." *Journal of Altered States of Consciousness* 2(2): 109–122.

———. 1978. "Neurological Bases of Revitalization Movements." *Zygon* 13(1): 276–312.

Li, Yih-yuan. 1976. "Shamanism in Taiwan: An Anthropological Inquiry." In William P. Lebra (ed.), *Mental Health Research in Asia and the Pacific*. Vol. 4: *Culture-Bound Syndromes, Ethnopsychiatry, and Alternate Therapies*. Honolulu: University Press of Hawaii. Pp. 179–188.

———. 1985. "Social Change, Religious Movements, and Personality Adjustment: An Anthropological View." In Wen-Shing Tseng & David Y. H. Wu (eds.), *Chinese Culture and Mental Health*. Honolulu: University of Hawaii Press. Pp. 57–66.

Lifton, Robert. 1970. *History and Human Survival*. New York: Random House.

Lii Shyh-yu. 1948. *Shianntzay Hwabeei Bihmih Tzongjiaw.* [*Contemporary Secret Religions of North China.*] Chengtu: Studia Serica Monographs, series B, No. 4.

Linton, Ralph. 1936. *The Study of Man.* New York: Appleton-Century-Crofts.

Liou Jy-wann. 1975. "Dooki no Sekai: Taiwan no Shiyamanizumu." ["The World of the Medium: The Shamans of Taiwan."] *Etonosu* 3: 56–67.

Longe, A. 1969. "A Small Postscript on the Ways and Manners of the Indians called Charikees." *Southern Indian Studies* 21: 3–49. [Originally written 1725]

Lorenz, K. Z. 1964. "Ritualized Fighting." In D. Carthy & F. J. Ebling (eds.), *The Natural History of Aggression.* New York: Academic Press. Pp. 39–50.

———. 1966. *On Aggression.* London: Methuen.

Louis-Philippe, King of France. 1977. *Diary of My Travels in America.* Trans. S. Becker. New York: Delacorte Press.

McClelland, David. 1951. *Personality.* New York: Dryden Press.

McCreery, John L. 1979. "Potential and Effective Meaning in Therapeutic Ritual." *Culture, Medicine, and Psychiatry* 3: 53–72.

McElroy, Ann. 1979. "The Negotiation of Sex-Role Identity in Eastern Arctic Culture Change." In A. McElroy & C. Matthiasson (eds.), *Sex Roles in Changing Cultures.* Occasional Papers in Anthropology No. 1. Buffalo: State University of New York. Pp. 49–60.

McElroy, Ann, & C. Matthiasson, eds. 1979. *Sex Roles in Changing Cultures.* Occasional Papers in Anthropology No. 1. Buffalo: State University of New York.

MacLean, Paul D. 1978. "The Evolution of Three Mentalities." In S. L. Washburn & Elizabeth R. McCown (eds.), *Human Evolution: Biosocial Perspectives.* Menlo Park, Calif.: Benjamin/Cummings. Pp. 32–57.

———. 1955. *Sex and Repression in Savage Society.* Cleveland: Meridian Books. [Originally published 1927]

Mandell, Arnold J. 1980. "Toward a Psychobiology of Transcendence: God in the Brain." In Julian M. Davidson & Richard J. Davidson (eds.), *The Psychobiology of Consciousness.* New York: Plenum. Pp. 379–464.

Mandler, George. 1984. *Mind and Body.* New York: W. W. Norton.

Marler, P., & W. J. Hamilton. 1966. *Mechanisms of Animal Behavior.* New York: John Wiley & Sons.

Maslow, Abraham H. 1970. *Religions, Values, and Peak Experiences.* New York: Viking.

Mason, W. 1978. "Ontogeny of Social Systems." In D. Chivers & J. Herbert (eds.), *Recent Advances in Primatology*, vol. 1. London: Academic Press.

Masson, J. Moussaieff. 1983. *The Assault on Truth: Freud's Suppression of the Seduction Theory.* New York: Farrar, Straus & Giroux.

Maynard, Eileen. 1979. "Changing Sex Roles and Family Structure among Oglalla Sioux." In A. McElroy & C. Matthiasson (eds.), *Sex Roles in Changing Cultures.* Occasional Papers in Anthropology No. 1. Buffalo: State University of New York. Pp. 11–20.

Mead, Margaret. 1932. *The Changing Culture of an Indian Tribe.* New York: Columbia University Press.

———. 1956. *New Lives for Old.* New York: William Morrow.

Mednick, Martha T. Shuch. 1981. "The Revolution That Never Was." Review of *Gender and Culture* by M. E. Spiro. *Contemporary Psychology* 26: 101–102.

Merton, Robert K. 1949. "Manifest and Latent Functions." In *Social Theory and Social Structure.* Glencoe: Free Press.

Metraux, Alfred. 1972. *Voodoo in Haiti.* New York: Schocken.

Metzger, Duane, & Gerald Williams. 1966. "Some Procedures and Results in the Study of Native Categories: Tzeltal 'Firewood.'" *American Anthropologist* 68: 389–407.

Mill, John Stuart. 1856. *A System of Logic.* Vol. 2. 4th ed. London: John W. Parker & Son.

Miner, Horace, & George De Vos. 1960. *Oasis and Casbah: Algerian Culture and Personality in Change.* Anthropology Papers, University of Michigan Museum of Anthropology, No. 15. Ann Arbor: University of Michigan.

Miron, Steven. 1984. "Education and Enculturation in Taiwan." *Journal of the Chinese Studies Student Organization [U.C.S.D.].* 1: 12–56.

Moen, Elizabeth, Elise Boulding, Jane Lillydahl, & Risa Palm. 1981. *Women and the Social Costs of Development: Two Colorado Case Studies.* Social Impact Adjustment Series No. 5. Boulder: Westview Press.

Montgomery of Alamein. 1961. *The Path to Leadership.* London: Collins.

Mooney, J. 1900. "Myths of the Cherokees." *Smithsonian Institution Bureau of American Ethnology, Nineteenth Annual Report, 1897–98,* pt. 1: 3–576.

Morgan, Lewis Henry. 1877. *Ancient Society; or, Researches in the Lines of Human Progress from Savagery through Barbarism to Civilization.* New York: Henry Holt.

Muramatsu, T., et al. 1962. *Nipponjin-Bunka to Pasonariti no Jissho-Teki Kenkyu. [The Japanese: An Empirical Study in Culture and Personality.]* Tokyo: Reimei Shobo.

Murphy, Yolanda, & Robert Murphy. 1974. *Women of the Forest.* New York: Columbia University Press.

Murray, Gilbert. 1951. *Five Stages of Greek Religion.* New York: Doubleday.

Murray, Henry. 1938. *Explorations in Personality.* New York: Oxford University Press.

Naquin, Susan. 1976. *Millenarian Rebellion in China: The Eight Trigrams Uprising of 1813.* New Haven: Yale University Press.

Nash, Manning. 1965. *The Golden Road to Modernity.* New York: Wiley.

Nisbet, Robert A. 1974. *The Sociology of Emile Durkheim.* New York: Oxford University Press.

Oakley, David A. 1979. "Cerebral Cortex and Adaptive Behavior." In David A. Oakley & H. C. Plotkin (eds.), *Brains, Behavior, and Evolution.* London: Methuen. Pp. 154–188.

Obeyesekere, Gananath. 1981. *Medusa's Hair.* Chicago: University of Chicago Press.

Olbrechts, F. 1931. "Cherokee Belief and Practice with Regard to Childbirth." *Anthropos* 26: 17–33.

Ornstein, Robert E. 1972. *The Psychology of Consciousness.* New York: Penguin.

Ortner, Sherry B. 1970. "Food for Thought: A Key Symbol in Sherpa Culture." Ph.D. diss., University of Chicago.

———. 1973. "On Key Symbols." *American Anthropologist* 75: 1338–1346.

———. 1978. *Sherpas through Their Rituals.* Cambridge: Cambridge University Press.

———. 1981. "The White-Black Ones: The Sherpa View of Human Nature." In James Fisher (ed.), *Himalayan Anthropology: The Indo-Tibetan Interface.* The Hague: Mouton. Pp. 263–286.

Overmyer, Daniel L. 1976. *Folk Buddhist Religion: Dissenting Sects in Late Traditional China.* Cambridge, Mass.: Harvard University Press.

———. 1977. "A Preliminary Study of the Tz'u-hui T'ang." *Bulletin of the Society for the Study of Chinese Religions* 4: 19–40.

———. 1981. "Alternatives: Popular Religious Sects in Chinese Society." *Modern China* 7: 153–190.

———. 1985. "Values in Chinese Sectarian Literature: Ming and Ch'ing Pao-chüan." In David Johnson, Andrew J. Nathan, & Evelyn S. Rawski (eds.), *Popular Culture in Late Imperial China.* Berkeley: University of California Press. Pp. 219–254.

Packer, C. 1979. "Male Dominance and Reproductive Activity in *Papio anubis.*" *Animal Behavior* 27: 37–45.

———. 1980. "Male Care and Exploitation of Infants in *Papio anubis.*" *Animal Behavior* 28: 512–520.

Parker, G. A. 1974. "Assessment Strategy and the Evolution of Fighting Behaviour." *Journal of Theoretical Biology* 47: 223–243.

Parsons, Talcott. 1937. *The Structure of Social Action.* Glencoe, Ill.: Free Press.

———. 1960. "Durkheim's Contribution to the Theory of Integration of

Social Systems." In Kurt Wolff (ed.), *Essays in Sociology and Philosophy*. New York: Harper & Row. Pp. 118–153.

Paul, Robert A. 1970. "Sherpas and Their Religion." Ph.D. diss. University of Chicago.

———. 1982. *The Tibetan Symbolic World: Psychoanalytic Explorations*. Chicago: University of Chicago Press.

———. 1988. "Fire and Ice: The Psychology of a Sherpa Shaman." In *The Psychoanalytic Study of Society* 13: 95–132.

Peters, Larry G. 1978. "Psychotherapy in Tamang Shamanism." *Ethos* 6: 63–91.

———. 1981. *Ecstasy and Healing in Nepal: An Ethnopsychiatric Study of Tamang Shamanism*. Vol. 4: *Other Realities*. Malibu: Undena Publications.

———. 1987. "The Tamang Shamanism of Nepal." In Shirley Nicholson (ed.), *Shamanism: An Expanded View of Reality*. Wheaton, Ill.: Theosophical Publishing House. Pp. 159–180.

Peters, Larry G., & Douglass Price-Williams. 1980. "Towards an Experiential Analysis of Shamanism." *American Ethnologist* 7: 397–418.

Pfeiffer, John E. 1985. *The Emergence of Humankind*. 4th ed. New York: Harper & Row.

Piaget, Jean. 1927. *La causalité physique chez l'enfant*. Paris: Alcan.

———. 1932. *The Moral Judgment of Children*. London: Routledge & Kegan Paul.

———. 1953. *The Origin of Intelligence in the Child*. London: Routledge & Kegan Paul.

Pocock, D. F. 1961. *Social Anthropology*. London: Sheed & Ward.

Poole, Fitz John. 1987. "Personal Experience and Cultural Representation in Children's 'Personal Symbols' among Bimin-Kuskusmin." *Ethos* 15: 104–135.

Popp, J. 1978a. *Male Baboons and Evolutionary Principles*. Ph.D. diss., Harvard University.

———. 1978b. "Kidnapping among Male Anubis Baboons in Masai Mara Reserve." Paper presented at the Wenner-Gren Conference "Baboon Field Research: Myths & Models." New York

Popp, J., & I. DeVore. 1979. "Aggressive Competition and Social Dominance Theory: Synopsis." In D. Hamburg & E. McCown (eds.), *The Great Apes*. Menlo Park, Calif.: W. A. Benjamin.

Popper, Karl R. 1963. *The Open Society and Its Enemies*. Vol. 2. New York: Harper & Row.

Postman, L. 1951. "Toward a General Theory of Cognition." In J. Rohre & M. Sherif (eds.), *Social Psychology at the Crossroads*. New York: Harper.

Potter, Jack M. 1974. "Cantonese Shamanism." In Arthur P. Wolf (ed.),

Religion and Ritual in Chinese Society. Stanford: Stanford University Press.

Prince, Raymond H. 1974. "The Problem of 'Spirit Possession' as a Treatment for Psychiatric Disorders." *Ethos* 2: 315–333.

———. 1979/80. "Religious Experiences and Psychosis." *Journal of Altered States of Consciousness* 5: 167–181.

———. 1982a. "The Endorphins: A Review for Psychological Anthropologists." *Ethos* 10: 303–316.

———. 1982b. "Shamans and Endorphins: Hypotheses for a Synthesis." *Ethos* 10: 409–423.

Quinn, Naomi, & Dorothy Holland. 1987. "Culture and Cognition." In D. Holland & N. Quinn (eds.), *Cultural Models in Language and Thought.* Cambridge, Mass.: Cambridge University Press. Pp. 3–40.

Rabinow, Paul, & William M. Sullivan, eds. 1979. *Interpretive Social Science: A Reader.* Berkeley: University of California Press.

Radcliffe-Brown, A. R. 1935. "On the Concept of Function in Social Science." *American Anthropologist* 37:394–402.

———. 1940a. "On Joking Relationships." *Africa* 13: 195–210.

———. 1940b. "On Social Structure." *Journal of the Royal Anthropological Institute* 70:1–12.

———. 1948. *A Natural Science of Society.* New York: Free Press.

———. 1949. "A Further Note on Joking Relationships." *Africa* 14: 133–140.

———. 1952. "Introduction." In A. R. Radcliffe-Brown, *Structure and Function in Primitive Society.* Glencoe, Ill.: Free Press. Pp. 1–14.

———. 1958. *Method in Social Anthropology.* Ed. M. Srinivas. Chicago: University of Chicago Press.

Ransom, T., & B. Ransom. 1971. "Adult Male-Infant Relations among Baboons (*Papio anubis*)." *Folia Primatologica* 16: 179–195.

Rappaport, Roy A. 1968. *Pigs for the Ancestors.* New Haven: Yale University Press.

———. 1971. "The Sacred in Human Evolution." *Annual Review of Ecology and Systematics* 2: 23–44.

———. 1979. *Ecology, Meaning, and Religion.* Berkeley: North Atlantic Books.

Reisman, David, et al. 1958. *The Lonely Crowd: A Study of the Changing American Character.* New Haven: Yale University Press.

Restak, Richard. 1984. *The Brain.* New York: Bantam.

Ricoeur, Paul. 1970. *Freud and Philosophy: An Essay on Interpretation.* New Haven: Yale University Press.

———. 1974. *Conflict of Interpretations: Essays on Hermeneutics.* Evanston: Northwestern University Press.

————. 1976. *Interpretation Theory: Discourse and the Surplus of Meaning.* Fort Worth: Christian University Press.

Roberts, John. 1951. *Three Navaho Households: A Comparative Study in Small Group Culture.* Papers of the Peabody Museum of American Archaeology & Ethnology, vol. 40, no. 3. Cambridge, Mass.: Peabody Museum.

Rogers, B. 1981. *The Domestication of Women: Discrimination in Developing Societies.* London: Tavistock.

Rowell, T. E. 1966. "Forest Living Baboons in Uganda." *Journal of Zoology* 149: 344–364.

————. 1972. *Social Behavior of Monkeys.* Kingsport, Tenn.: Penguin.

————. 1974. "The Concept of Social Dominance." *Behavioral Biology* 11: 131–154.

Rumelhart, David, James McClelland, & the PDP Research Group. 1986. *Parallel Distributed Processing: Explorations in the Microstructure of Cognition.* Cambridge, Mass.: MIT Press.

Ryan, E. Dean, & Robert Foster. 1967. "Athletic Participation and Perceptual Augmentation and Reduction." *Journal of Personality and Social Psychology* 6: 472–476.

Saayman, G. 1971. "Grooming Behavior in a Troop of Free-Ranging Chacma Baboons (*Papio ursinus*)." *Folia Primatologica* 16: 161–178.

Sahlins, Marshall. 1976. *Culture and Practical Reason.* Chicago: University of Chicago Press.

Salim, A. I. 1973. *The Swahili-Speaking Peoples of Kenya's Coast.* Nairobi: East African Publishing House.

Sangren, P. Steven. 1987. *History and Magical Power in a Chinese Community.* Stanford, Calif.: Stanford University Press.

Sarbin, Theodore R., & Karl Scheibe (eds.). 1983. *Studies in Social Identity.* New York: Praeger.

Sargant, William. 1959. *Battle for the Mind.* New York: Harper & Row.

Schafer, Roy. 1980. "Narration in the Psychoanalytic Dialogue." *Critical Inquiry* 7: 29–53.

Scheff, T. J. 1979. *Catharsis in Healing, Ritual, and Drama.* Berkeley: University of California Press.

Schneider, David M. 1976. "Notes Towards a Theory of Culture." In K. Basso and H. Selby (eds.), *Meaning in Anthropology.* Albuquerque: University of New Mexico Press.

Schneider, David M., & Lauriston Sharp. 1969. *The Dream Life of a Primitive People: The Dreams of the Yir Yoront of Australia.* Anthropological Series No. 1. Washington, D.C.: American Anthropological Association.

Schutz, A. 1970. *Phenomenology and Social Reality.* The Hague: Nijhoff.

Seaman, Gary. 1978. *Temple Organization in a Chinese Village*. Taipei: Orient Cultural Service.

Seyfarth, RM. 1975. "The Social Relationships among Adults in a Troop of Free-Ranging Baboons (*Papio cynocephalus ursinus*)." Ph.D. diss., Cambridge University.

Sheau Ling-i [pseudonym]. 1977. *Torngji Juotour jy Yanjiow*. [*Researches into Mediums and Their Interpreters*.] Tainan: Renguang.

Sheu Dih-shan. 1941. *Fwujih Mishinn de Yanjiow*. [*Researches into the Superstition of Planchette Divination*.] Changsha: Shangwuh Yinnshugoan.

Shweder, Richard A. 1979. "Rethinking Personality and Culture." *Ethos* 7: 255–279.

———. 1980. "Rethinking Culture and Personality Theory, Part 3." *Ethos* 8: 60–94.

Silk, J. 1980. "Kidnapping and Female Competition in Captive Bonnet Macaques." *Primates* 21: 100–110.

Silverman, Julian. 1975/76. "Altered States of Consciousness: Positive and Negative Outcomes." *Journal of Altered States of Consciousness* 2: 295–317.

Simeons, A. T. W. 1962. *Man's Presumptuous Brain*. New York: E. P. Dutton.

Skeat, W. W. 1967. *Malay Magic, Being an Introduction to the Folklore and Popular Religion of the Malay Peninsula*. New York: Dover. [Originally published 1900]

Skorupski, John. 1976. *Symbol and Theory: A Philosophical Study of Theories of Religion in Social Anthropology*. Cambridge: Cambridge University Press.

Smith, Arthur H. 1914. *Proverbs and Common Sayings from the Chinese*. Shanghai: American Presbyterian Mission Press.

Song Weizhen. 1985. "A Preliminary Study of the Character Traits of the Chinese." In Wen-Shing Tseng & David Y. H. Wu (eds.), *Chinese Culture and Mental Health*. Honolulu: University of Hawaii Press. Pp. 47–55.

Sonq Her. 1976. "Torngji Shyh Shernma?" ["What Is a Medium?"] *Jiannkang Shyhjieh* [*Health World*] 5: 35–41.

Spencer, Robert F. (ed.). 1969. *Forms of Symbolic Action*. Seattle: American Ethnological Society.

Spiegel, Herbert, & David Spiegel. 1978. *Trance and Treatment: Clinical Uses of Hypnosis*. New York: Basic.

Spindler, George D. 1955. *Sociocultural and Psychological Processes in Menomini Acculturation*. Culture & Society Series No. 5. Berkeley: University of California Press.

————. 1974a. "From Omnibus to Linkages: Models for a Study of Cultural Transmission." *Council for Anthropology and Education* 1: 2–6.

————. 1974b. "Schooling in Schönhausen: A Study in Cultural Transmission and Instrumental Adaptation in an Urbanizing German Village." In George Spindler (ed.), *Education and Cultural Process: Toward an Anthropology of Education.* New York: Holt, Rinehart & Winston. Pp. 230–272.

Spindler, George D., & Walter Goldschmidt. 1952. "Experimental Design in the Study of Culture Change." *Southwestern Journal of Anthropology* 8: 68–83.

Spindler, George D., & Louise S. Spindler. 1965a. "The Instrumental Activities Inventory." *Southwestern Journal of Anthropology* 21: 1–23.

————. 1965b. "Researching the Perception of Cultural Alternatives: The Instrumental Activities Inventory." In Melford E. Spiro (ed.), *Context and Meaning in Cultural Anthropology.* New York: Free Press. Pp. 312–337.

————. 1978a. "Die Vermittlung von kulturellen Werten und spezifischen Anpassungsmechanismus in einem Dorf mit zünehmenden städtischen Gepräge." *Rheinisches Jahrbuch für Volkskunde* 22(2): 85–96.

————. 1978b. "Identity, Militancy, and Cultural Congruence: The Menominee and Kanai." *Annals of the American Academy of Political and Social Sciences* 436: 74–85.

————. 1979. "Discussant Commentary." In A. McElroy & C. Matthiasson (eds.), *Sex Roles in Changing Cultures.* Occasional Papers in Anthropology, No. 1. Buffalo: State University of New York. Pp. 89–93.

————. 1981. Comment on "Search for a Theory of Cultural Transmission in an Anthropology of Education: Notes on Spindler and Gearing," by Robert Funnell & Richard Smith. *Anthropology and Education Quarterly* 12: 275–300.

————. 1982. "From Familiar to Strange and Back Again: Roger Harker and Schönhausen." In G. Spindler (ed.), *Doing the Ethnography of Schooling: Educational Anthropology in Action.* New York: Holt, Rinehart & Winston. Pp. 14–20.

————. 1984. *Dreamers with Power: The Menomini.* 2nd ed. Prospect Heights, Ill.: Waveland Press.

————. 1987. "In Prospect for a Controlled Cross-Cultural Comparison of Schooling: Schönhausen & Roseville." In G. Spindler (ed.), *Education and Cultural Process: Anthropological Approaches.* Prospect Heights, Ill.: Waveland Press. Pp. 389–400.

Spindler, Louise S. 1962. *Menomini Women and Culture Change.* Memoir No. 91. Washington, D.C.: American Anthropological Association.

————. 1975. "Researching the Psychology of Culture Change." In T. R.

Williams (ed.), *Psychological Anthropology*. The Hague: Mouton. Pp. 137–162.

———. 1976. "The Menominee." In Bruce Trigger (ed.), *Handbook of North American Indians*, vol. 15. Washington, D.C.: Smithsonian Institution. Pp. 708–724.

———. 1978. "Researching the Psychology of Culture Change and Modernization." In George D. Spindler (ed.), *The Making of Psychological Anthropology*. Berkeley: University of California Press. Pp. 174–198.

———. 1979. "Changing Women in Men's Worlds, Part I." In A. McElroy & C. Matthiasson (ed.), *Sex Roles in Changing Cultures*. Occasional Papers in Anthropology No. 1. Buffalo: State University of New York. Pp. 35–41.

Spindler, Louise S., & George D. Spindler. 1958. "Male and Female Adaptations in Culture Change." *American Anthropologist* 60: 217–233.

———. 1979. "Changing Women in Men's Worlds, Part II." In A. McElroy & C. Matthiasson (eds.), *Sex Roles in Changing Cultures*. Occasional Papers in Anthropology No. 1. Buffalo: State University of New York. Pp. 41–63.

Spiro, Melford E. 1951. "Culture and Personality: The Natural History of a False Dichotomy." *Psychiatry* 14: 19–46.

———. 1952. "Ghosts, Ifaluk, and Teleological Functionalism." *American Anthropologist* 54: 497–503.

———. 1953. "Ghosts: An Anthropological Inquiry into Learning and Perception." *Journal of Abnormal and Social Psychology* 48: 376–382.

———. 1954. "Human Nature in Its Psychological Dimensions." *American Anthropologist* 56: 19–30.

———. 1956. *Kibbutz: Venture in Utopia*. Cambridge, Mass.: Harvard University Pres.

———. 1958. *Children of the Kibbutz*. Cambridge, Mass.: Harvard University Press.

———. 1959. "Cultural Heritage, Personal Tensions, and Mental Illness in a South Sea Culture." In M. K. Opler (ed.), *Culture and Mental Health*. New York: Macmillan.

———. 1961a. "Culture and Personality: An Overview and a Suggested Reorientation." In Francis L. K. Hsu (ed.), *Psychological Anthropology*. Homewood, Ill.: Dorsey. Pp. 459–493.

———. 1961b. "Social Systems, Personality, and Functional Analysis." In Bert Kaplan (ed.), *Studying Personality Cross-Culturally*. Evanston, Ill.: Row, Peterson. Pp. 93–127.

———. 1961c. "Sorcery, Evil Spirits, and Functional Analysis." *American Anthropologist* 63: 820–824.

———. 1963. "Causes, Function, and Cross-Cousin Marriage: An Essay in

Anthropological Explanation." *Journal of the Royal Anthropological Institute* 94: 30–43.

———. 1964. "Religion and the Irrational." In Melford E. Spiro (ed.), *Symposium on New Approaches to the Study of Religion*. Seattle: University of Washington Press. Pp. 102–115.

———. 1965a. "Religious Systems as Culturally Constituted Defense Mechanisms." In Melford E. Spiro (ed.), *Context and Meaning in Cultural Anthropology: Papers in Honor of A. I. Hallowell*. Glencoe, Ill.: Free Press. Pp. 100–113.

———. 1965b. "A Typology of Social Structure and the Patterning of Social Institutions." *American Anthropologist* 67: 1097–1119.

———. 1966a. "Buddhism and Economic Action in Burma." *American Anthropologist* 68: 1163–1173.

———. 1966b. "Religion: Problems of Definition and Explanation." In Michael Banton (ed.), *Anthropological Approaches to the Study of Religion*. London: Tavistock. Pp. 85–126.

———. 1967. *Burmese Supernaturalism: A Study in the Explanations and Resolution of Suffering*. Englewood Cliffs, N.J.: Prentice-Hall.

———. 1968a. "Culture and Personality." In David L. Sills (ed.), *International Encyclopedia of the Social Sciences*, vol. 3. New York: Macmillian/Free Press. Pp. 558–563.

———. 1968b. "Virgin Birth, Parthenogenesis, and Physiological Paternity: An Essay in Cultural Interpretation." *Man* 3: 242–261.

———. 1968c. Review of *Purity and Danger* by Mary Douglas. *American Anthropologist* 70: 391–393.

———. 1969a. "The Psychological Functions of Witchcraft Belief: The Burmese Case." In W. Caudill & T. Lin (eds.), *Mental Health in Asia and in the Pacific*. Honolulu: East-West Center Press.

———. 1969b. "Summary Analysis." In R. Spencer (ed.), *Forms of Symbolic Action*. Seattle: American Ethnological Society.

———. 1970. *Buddhism and Society: A Great Tradition and Its Burmese Vicissitudes*. New York: Harper & Row.

———. 1972. "Culture and Personality: An Overview and Suggested Reorientation." In Francis L. K. Hsu (ed.), *Psychological Anthropology*. Cambridge, Mass.: Schenkman. P. 573–607. [Originally published 1961]

———. 1973. "Social Change and Functional Analysis: A Study in Burmese Psychocultural History." *Ethos* 1: 263–297.

———. 1976. "A. Irving Hallowell." *American Anthropologist* 78: 608–611.

———. 1977. *Kinship and Marriage in Burma: A Cultural and Psychodynamic Analysis*. Berkeley: University of California Press.

————. 1978a. *Burmese Supernaturalism: A Study in the Explanation and Resolution of Suffering.* Expanded ed. Philadelphia: ISHI.

————. 1978b. "Culture and Human Nature." In George Spindler (ed.), *The Making of Psychological Anthropology.* Berkeley: University of California Press. Pp. 331–360.

————. 1979a. *Gender and Culture: Kibbutz Women Revisited.* Durham: Duke University Press.

————. 1979b. "Symbolism and Functionalism in the Anthropological Study of Religion." In Lauri Honko (ed.), *Science of Religion: Studies in Methodology.* The Hague: Mouton.

————. 1979c. "Whatever Happend to the Id?" *American Anthropologist* 81: 5–13.

————. 1980. "A. Irving Hallowell." In *International Encyclopedia of Social Sciences.* Biographical Supplement Volume. New York: Macmillan/Free Press. Pp. 261–262.

————. 1982a. *Buddhism and Society: A Great Tradition and Its Burmese Vicissitudes.* Rev. ed. Berkeley: University of California Press.

————. 1982b. "Collective Representations and Mental Representations in Religious Symbol Systems." In Jacques Maquet (ed.), *On Symbols in Anthropology.* Malibu, Calif.: Undena. Pp. 45–72.

————. 1982c. *Oedipus in the Trobriands.* Chicago: University of Chicago Press.

————. 1984. "Some Reflections on Cultural Determinism and Relativism with Special Reference to Emotion and Reason." In R. Shweder & R. LeVine (eds.), *Culture Theory: Essays on Mind, Self, and Emotion.* New York: Cambridge University Press.

————. 1986. "Cultural Relativism and the Future of Anthropology." *Cultural Anthropology* 1: 259–286.

Spiro, Melford E., & Roy G. D'Andrade. 1958. "A Cross-Cultural Study of Some Supernatural Beliefs." *American Anthropologist* 60: 456–466.

Springer, Sally P., & George Deutsch. 1981. *Left Brain, Right Brain.* San Francisco: W. H. Freeman.

Stanner, W. E. H. 1956. "The Dreaming." In T. A. G. Hungerford (ed.), *Australian Signpost.* Melbourne: F. W. Cheshire. Pp. 51–65.

Stroebel, Margaret. 1979. *Muslim Women in Mombasa, 1890–1975.* New Haven: Yale University Press.

Strum, Shirley C. 1975a. "Life with the Pumphouse Gang." *National Geographic* 147: 672–691.

————. 1975b. "Primate Predation: Interim Report on the Development of a Tradition in a Troop of Olive Baboons." *Science* 187: 755–757.

————. 1976a. "Primate Predation and Bioenergetics: A Reply." *Science* 191: 131–154.

————. 1976b. "Predatory Behavior of Olive Baboons (*Papio anubis*) at Gilgil, Kenya. Ph.D. diss., University of California, Berkeley.

————. 1976c. "Primate Predation and Bioenergetics: A Reply." *Science* 191: 314–317.

————. 1979. "Social Strategies and the Evolutionary Significance of Social Relationships." Unpublished ms.

————. 1981a. "Processes and Products of Change: Baboon Predatory Behavior at Gilgil, Kenya." In Robert S. O. Harding and Geza Teleki (eds.), *Omnivorous Primates*. New York: Columbia University Press. Pp. 255–302.

————. 1981b. "Baboon Behavior." *Swara* 4: 24–26.

————. 1982. "Agonistic Dominance in Male Baboons: An Alternative View." *International Journal of Primatology* 3: 175–202.

————. 1983a. "Why Males Use Infants." In David Milton Taub (ed.), *Primate Paternalism*. New York: Van Nostrand Reinhold. Pp. 146–185.

————. 1983b. "Use of Females by Male Olive Baboons." *American Journal of Primatology* 5: 93–109.

————. 1983c. "Baboon Cues for Eating Meat." *Journal of Human Evolution* 12: 327–336.

————. 1987. *Almost Human: A Journey into the World of Baboons.* New York: Random House.

Strum, Shirley C., & Bruno Latour. 1987. "Redefining the Social Link: From Baboons to Humans." *Social Science Information* 26:783–802.

Strum, Shirley C., & W. Mitchell. 1986. "Baboon Models and Muddles." In Warren G. Kinzey (ed.), *The Evolution of Human Behavior: Primate Models*. Albany: State University of New York Press.

Strum, Shirley C., & Jonah D. Western. 1982. "Variations in Fecundity with Age and Environment in Olive Baboons (*Papio anubis*)." *American Journal of Primatology* 3: 61–76.

Su Ming-dong. 1979. *Tian Daw Gayluenn.* [*Overview of the Celestial Way.*] 2nd ed. Kaohsiung: privately published.

Swartz, Marc J. 1969. "The Cultural Dynamics of Blows and Abuse among the Bena of Tanzania." In R. Spencer (ed.), *Forms of Symbolic Action*. Seattle: University of Washington Press. Pp. 16–34.

————. 1982a. "Cultural Sharing and Cultural Theory: Some Findings of a Five Society Study." *American Anthropologist* 84: 314–338.

————. 1982b. "The Isolation of Men and the Happiness of Women: Sources and Use of Power in Swahili Marital Relationships." *Journal of Anthropological Research* 38: 26–44.

————. 1983. "Culture and Implicit Power: Maneuvers and Understandings in Swahili Nuclear Family Relations." In M. Aronoff (ed.), *Culture*

Change: Political Anthropology, vol. 2. New Brunswick, N.J.: Transaction Press. Pp. 19–38.

———. 1988. "Shame, Culture, and Status among the Swahili of Mombasa." *Ethos* 16: 21–57.

Swartz, Marc J., & David K. Jordan. 1976. *Anthropology: Perspectives on Humanity.* New York: Wiley.

———. 1980. *Culture: The Anthropological Perspective.* New York: Wiley.

Taub, D. 1978. *Aspects of the Biology of the Wild Barbary Macaque.* Ph.D. diss., University of California, Davis.

———. 1980. "Testing the 'Agonistic Buffering' Hypothesis." *Behavioral Ecology and Sociobiology* 6: 187–197.

Tiger, Lionel, & Joseph Shepher. 1975. *Women in the Kibbutz.* New York: Harcourt Brace Jovanovich.

Timberlake, H. 1948. *Lieut. Henry Timberlake's Memoirs, 1756–1765.* Ed. S. C. Williams. Marietta, Ga.: Continental Book Company. [Originally published 1765]

Tinbergen, N. 1953. *Social Behavior in Animals.* London: Methuen.

Trivers, R. 1971. "The Evolution of Reciprocal Altruism." *Quarterly Review of Biology* 46: 35–57.

Trowbridge, C. C. n.d. Unpublished manuscript in the Shea Collection, Georgetown University Library, Washington, D. C. [Circa 1825.]

Tseng Wen-shing (Tzeng Wen-hsing). 1972. "Psychiatric Study of Shamanism in Taiwan." *Archives of General Psychiatry* 26: 561–566.

Tsurumi, Kazuko. 1970. *Social Change and the Individual.* Princeton: Princeton University Press.

Tu Wei Ming. 1984. "On Neo-Confucianism and Human Relations." In George De Vos (ed.), *Religion and the Family in East Asia.* Senri: National Museum of Ethnology.

Turner, Victor. 1957. *Schism and Continuity in an African Society: A Study of Ndembu Village Life.* Manchester: Manchester University Press.

———. 1967. *The Forest of Symbols: Aspects of Ndembu Ritual.* Ithaca: Cornell University Press.

———. 1969. *The Ritual Process: Structure and Anti-Structure.* Chicago: Aldine Press.

———. 1978. "Encounter with Freud: The Making of a Comparative Symbologist." In G. Spindler (ed.), *The Making of Psychological Anthropology.* Berkeley: University of California Press.

Tutin, C. 1979. "Mating Patterns and Reproductive Strategies in a Community of Wild Chimpanzees." *Behavioral Ecology and Sociobiology* 6: 29–38.

Tylor, Edward Burnett. 1871. *Primitive Culture: Researches into the Development of Mythology, Philosophy, Religion, Language, Art, and Custom.* London: John Murray.

———. 1958. *Religion in Primitive Culture*. New York: Harper. [Reprint of volume 2 of Tylor 1871]

Tzeng Wen-shing (Wen-shing Tseng). 1972. "Tsorng Renger Fajaan Kann Jonggworen Shinqger." ["Viewing Chinese Character from the Perspective of Human Development."] In Lii Yih-yuan & Yang Gwo-shu (eds.), *Jonggworen de Shinqger: Kejih Tzonqhershinq de Taolenn [The Character of the Chinese: An Interdisciplinary Approach]*. Monograph Series B, No. 4. Nankang: Institute of Ethnology, Academia Sinica.

Underhill, Ruth Murray. 1979. *Papago Woman*. New York: Holt, Rinehart & Winston.

Von Wright, Georg H. 1971. *Explanation and Understanding*. Ithaca: Cornell University Press.

Walker, Sheila. 1972. *Ceremonial Spirit Possession in Africa and Afro-America*. Leiden: E. J. Brill.

Wallace, Anthony F. C. 1956. "Mazeway Resynthesis: A Biocultural Theory of Religious Inspiration." *Transactions of the New York Academy of Sciences* 18: 626–638.

Walters, J. 1980. "Interventions and the Development of Dominance Relationships in Female Baboons." *Folia Primatologica* 34: 61–89.

Wang Yih-jia. 1976. "Shernyuh yeu Torngji." ["Spirit Communication and Meduims."] *Jiannkang Shyhjieh [Health World]* 5: 41–44.

Washburn, Sherwood L., & I. DeVore. 1961. "The Social Behavior of Baboons and Early Man." In S. Washburn (ed.), *Social Life of Early Man*. Chicago: Aldine.

Washburn, Sherwood L., & David A. Hamburg. 1965. "The Study of Primate Behavior." In Irven DeVore (ed.), *Primate Behavior: Field Studies of Monkeys and Apes*. New York: Holt, Rinehart & Winston. Pp. 1–13.

———. 1968. "Aggressive Behavior in Old World Monkeys and Apes." In P. Jay (ed.), *Primates*. New York. Holt, Rinehart & Winston. Pp. 458–478.

Washburn, Sherwood L., P. Jay, and J. Lancaster. 1965. "Field Studies of Old World Monkeys and Apes." *Science* 150: 1541–1547.

Webber, Mark, Christopher Stephens, & Charles D. Laughlin. 1983. "Masks: A Re-examination; or, 'Masks? You Mean They Affect the Brain?'" In N. Ross Crumrine & Marjorie Halpin (eds.), *The Power of Symbols: Masks and Masquerade in the Americas*. Vancouver: University of British Columbia Press. Pp. 204–218.

Weber, Max. 1948. *From Max Weber: Essays in Sociology*. Ed. H. H. Gerth, H. H. Mills, & C. Wright Mills. London: Routledge & Kegan Paul. [U.S. edition 1946]

———. 1949. "'Objectivity' in Social Science and Social Policy." In Edward A. Shils & Henry A. Finch (eds.), *The Methodology of the Social Sciences*. New York: Free Press. Pp. 49–112. [Originally published 1904]

————. 1978. *Economy and Society.* Ed. Guenther Roth & Claus Wittich. Berkeley: University of California Press.

Wedenoja, William A. 1978. *Religion and Adaptation in Rural Jamaica.* Ph.D. diss., University of California, San Diego.

————. 1980. "Modernization and the Pentecostal Movement in Jamaica." In Stephen D. Glazier (ed.), *Perspectives on Pentecostalism: Case Studies from the Caribbean and Latin America.* Washington, D.C.: University Press of America. Pp. 27–48.

————. 1988. "The Origins of Revival: A Creole Religion in Jamaica." In George R. Saunders (ed.), *Culture and Christianity: The Dialectics of Transformation.* Westport, Conn.: Greenwood. Pp. 91–116.

Weller, Robert P. 1987. *Unities and Diversities in Chinese Religion.* Seattle: University of Washington Press.

Wen Tzong. 1977. "Jenpoh Shyejiaw Iguann Daw Jiechuan Chyi Huangmiow Inmow." ["Cracking the Case of the Heterodox Unity Sect and Exposing Its Preposterous Conspiracy."] *Shyhjy Bawchyng [Intelligence Knowledge]* 18 (11): 10–15.

Werner, E. T. C. 1932. *A Dictionary of Chinese Mythology.* Shanghai: Kelly & Walsh.

Werner, Oswald. 1985. "Folk Knowledge without Fuzz." In J. Doughtery (ed.), *Directions in Cognitive Anthropology.* Urbana: University of Illinois Press. Pp. 73–90.

Western, J. D., & Shirley C. Strum. 1983. "Sex, Kinship, and the Evolution of Social Manipulation." *Ethology and Sociobiology* 4: 19–28.

Whiting, John W. M. 1941. *Becoming a Kwoma.* New Haven: Yale University Press.

————. 1961. "Socialization Process and Personality." In Francis L. K. Hsu (ed.), *Psychological Anthropology: Approaches to Culture and Personality.* Homewood, Ill.: Dorsey Press. 1961. Pp. 355–380.

Whiting, John W. M., & Irvin L. Child. 1953. *Child Training and Personality: A Cross-Cultural Study.* New Haven: Yale University Press.

Williams, S. C. 1928. *Early Travels in the Tennessee Country.* Johnson City, Tenn.: Watauga Press.

Wilson, Edward O. 1975. *Sociobiology: The New Synthesis.* Cambridge, Mass.: Belknap Press.

Wilson, Richard W. 1973. "Shame and Behaviour in Chinese Society." *Asian Profile* 1: 431–447.

Witkin, Herman A. 1967. "Cognitive Styles across Cultures." *International Journal of Psychology* 2: 233–50.

————. 1969. "Social Influences in the Development of Cognitive Style." In D. A. Goslin (ed.), *Handbook of Socialization Theory and Research.* New York: Rand McNally. Pp. 687–706.

————. 1978. *Cognitive Styles in Personal and Cultural Adaptation.* Worcester, Mass.: Clark University Press.

Witthoft, J. 1947. *Green Corn Ceremonialism in the Eastern Woodlands.* Occasional Contributions No. 13. Ann Arbor: Museum of Anthropology, University of Michigan.

Wu, David Y. H. 1985. "Child Training in Chinese Culture." In Wen-Shing Tseng & David Y. H. Wu (eds.), *Chinese Culture and Mental Health.* Honolulu: University of Hawaii Press. Pp. 113–134.

Yeats, W. B. 1956. "He Wishes for the Cloths of Heaven." In *The Collected Poems of W. B. Yeats.* New York: Macmillan.

Yengoyan, Aram A. 1970. "Demographic Factors in Pitjantjatjara Social Organization." In Ronald M. Berndt (ed.), *Australian Aboriginal Anthropology: Modern Studies in the Social Anthropology of the Australian Aborigines.* Perth: University of Western Australia Press. Pp. 70–91.

————. 1979. "Economy, Society, and Myth in Aboriginal Australia." *Annual Review of Anthropology* 8: 393–415.

Yongerman, Barry. 1981. "Kibbutz Backsliders." *Jerusalem Post Magazine,* April 17, p. 26.

Contributors

KEVIN A. AVRUCH is associate professor of anthropology at George Mason University. He is the author of *American Immigrants in Israel: Social Identities and Change*.

F. G. BAILEY is professor of anthropology at the University of California, San Diego, and a fellow of the American Academy of Arts and Sciences. His most recent book is *The Tactical Uses of Passion: An Essay on Power, Reason, and Reality*.

ERIKA BOURGUIGNON is a leading authority on possession and trance. A professor of anthropology at Ohio State, she is the author of *A World of Women: Anthropological Studies of Women in the Societies of the World*.

ROY G. D'ANDRADE is the author of numerous papers in the field of cognitive anthropology. A founding officer of the Society for Cultural Anthropology, he is professor of anthropology at the University of California, San Diego.

GEORGE DE VOS, a professor of anthropology at the University of California, Berkeley, is a major figure in the study of psychological anthropology. His most recent book is *Heritage of Endurance: Family Patterns and Delinquency Formation in Urban Japan*.

RAYMOND D. FOGELSON is professor of anthropology at the University of Chicago. He is an authority on the Cherokee and a student of the history of anthropological theory. He is the author of *The Cherokees: A Critical Bibliography*.

DAVID K. JORDAN specializes in the study of popular religion and ritual in Taiwan. A professor of anthropology at the University of California, San Diego, he is the author of *The Flying Phoenix: Aspects of Chinese Sectarianism in Taiwan*.

MICHAEL E. MEEKER is professor of anthropology at the University of California, San Diego. His special interests include cultural theory, symbolism in folk literature, and Islam, particularly in Turkey.

MANNING NASH is professor of anthropology at the University of Chicago. A specialist in economic anthropology, he has written *Unfinished Agenda: The Dynamics of Modernization in Developing Nations*.

GANANATH OBEYESEKERE's specializations include psychological anthropology and religion, with special reference to Sri Lanka and South India, as well as the history of social theory. He is professor of anthropology at Princeton University.

ROBERT A. PAUL is the editor of *Ethos*, one of the two journals of psychological anthropology. A professor of anthropology and liberal arts at Emory University, he is the author of *The Tibetan Symbolic World: Psychoanalytic Explorations.*

GEORGE SPINDLER is the founding editor of the Holt, Rinehart, and Winston series of ethnographies and formerly editor of the *American Anthropologist.* He is professor of anthropology at Stanford University.

LOUISE SPINDLER specializes in cross-cultural psychology and culture change. A lecturer in anthropology at Stanford University, she is the author of *Menomini Women and Culture Change* and *Culture Change and Modernization: Mini-Models and Case Studies.*

SHIRLEY C. STRUM is associate professor of anthropology at the University of California, San Diego. She has published many field studies of free-ranging baboons and is now finishing a book on the behavior of baboons.

MARC J. SWARTZ has been a Guggenheim Fellow and an officer of the American Anthropological Association. A professor of anthropology at the University of California, San Diego, he is known for his work in political anthropology and, more recently, culture theory.

WILLIAM WEDENOJA specializes in transcultural psychiatry and religion, with special emphasis on Jamaica and the Caribbean, but his interests include the culture of the Southern United States. He is associate professor of sociology at Southwest Missouri State.

ARAM YENGOYAN specializes in culture theory and sociolinguistics. His special field areas are Southeast Asia and Australia, and his books include *The Imagination of Reality: Essays in Southeast Asian Coherence Systems.*

Index

Aborigines: Australian, 94, 207, 217, 218; religion of, 63–78
Acculturation, 38
Adair, James, 164–65, 171, 175,
Adenauer, Konrad, 350
Aggression, 9–10, 203, 212–15, 225, 267, 292, 311, 313; definition of, 212
Aggression, baboon, 9, 329, 335; and primate anatomy, 330–32; traditional view of, 331–32, 338, 340, 345; competition and defense, 336–37, 339, 344; case studies, 342–44; definition of, 346 (n. 7). *See also* Baboons
Aggressive speech (Swahili), 116, 117, 129, 140, 142 (n. 5); definition(s) of, 118; and joking and avoidance behavior, 118; similarities between types, 133–34, 139; differences between types, 134–35, 139. *See also* Badtalk; Curses; Reproaches
Agonistic buffer, 336, 339, 346 (n. 9); rules of, 343. *See also* Aggression, baboons
Allen, Woody, 223
Altered state of consciousness (ASC), 284–85
American Revolutionary War, 168
Animism, 249
Anthropology: American, 16, 42, 276; British, 16, 17–19, 42; as history or science, debate over, 46; relation between culture and behavior, 146–47; as a science, 162, 270; ability to generalize, 202. *See also* Cognitive anthropology; Functionalism; Psychoanalytic anthropology; Psychological anthropology; Social anthropology
Antirelativism, 308
Aristotelian tradition, 45
"A Rumor of Angels" (P. Berger), 253

Asceticism, 348, 350
Augustus Caesar, 349
Australia. *See* Aborigines: Australian; Pitjantjatjara
Automatic writing (Taiwan), 100, 105–10
Avruch, Kevin, 2, 15
Aztec, 252

Baboons, 9, 329, 330; traditional (functional) view of aggression in, 331–32, 338, 340, 345; troop, structure of, 332–33, 344; friendships of, 333, 335–37, 343; communication of, 334–35, 344; grooming by, 335, 336, 342; social strategies of, 339–43; awareness, consciousness of, 341, 343. *See also* Aggression, baboon
Badtalk (Swahili aggressive speech), 133, 134, 135, 136, 140, 141 (n. 1, 2); definition of, 118; and female sexuality, 121–24; targets of, 123–29; users of, 123–29; uses of, 129–31
Baha'i, 252
Bailey, F. G., 10, 42, 347
Barth, Fredrik, 42
Bartram, William, 168
Basic personality structure, 82, 94–95, 296
Bauernhaus (German "great house"), 191, 194
Bayluan (Taiwanese sectarian society), 100, 101, 104, 105
Becker, Ernest, 273
Becoming a Kwoma (J. Whiting), 181 (n. 8)
Behavior, guide(s) for, 2, 129, 147, 150, 237. *See also* Role; Status
Behavioral environment, 50, 52, 292; in Burma, 28

Index

Behaviorism, 151–52

Belonging, sense of, 222, 229, 230, 235–36, 237

Benedict, Ruth, 308

Benveniste, Emile, 203, 204–05, 219

Bernstein, I. S., 339

Bettelheim, Bruno, 175, 220

Bible, The, 279, 280

Bilu, Yoram, 323

Biological determinism, 183, 184, 198

Biology, human, 223–24; relationship to culture, 275

Birdwhistell, R. L., 225

Blood (Kanai), 185, 186, 187, 188–89, 194, 196; male-female differences, 189

Boas, Franz, 16, 201

Bohannan, Paul, 86

Borish, Steven, 200

Bourguignon, Erika, 8, 283, 296, 308

Bridgman, P. W., 94

Bruner, J. S., 24

Buddha, 251

Buddhism, 239, 268, 274; Therevada, 28, 36, 251, 254; Burmese, 80–81, 157, 248, 310, 312, 314; Taiwanese, 103, 104; and Burmese supernaturalism, 312, 314. *See also* Monks

Buddhism and Society (M. Spiro), 28, 53, 254, 276

Burma, 26–28, 36, 40, 81, 222, 246–47, 249, 251, 289–90, 313, 314, 316, 317, 319, 322, 324. *See also* Buddhism

Burmese Supernaturalism (M. Spiro), 19, 28, 57 (n. 7), 276, 290–91. *See also* Exorcism; Nats (Burma); Shamanism, Burmese; Witchcraft

Caesar, Sid, 223

Cass, Lewis, 170

Castro, Fidel, 357

Catharsis, 286, 289–94, 303; collective, 290

Cathexis, 31, 39, 158; of social sanctions, 35; of goals, 157; object, definition of, 241 (n. 11)

Causal/functional relationships, 153

Celestial Way (Taiwan), 100, 107–10, 112 (n. 9); as "White Lotus" sect, 112 (n. 15)

Celibacy, 260, 263

Ceremonies, use of masks in, 291

Changing Perspectives in the Scientific Study of Religion (A. Eister, ed.), 45

Charisma, 10, 349, 355–57; problem with, 356

Cherokee, men, 172, 175; father-son relationship, 177; mother's brother—sister's son relationship, 177–79

Cherokee, women: and adultery, 164–65, 169–70; status of, power of, 164–76, 179; marriage of, 166, 167, 170, 171; mother-child relations, 166, 176–79; pollution in, 173; and Oedipus complex, 176–79

Chickasaw, 164

Child, Irvin L., 58 (n. 10)

Children of the Kibbutz (M. Spiro), 182

China, 99, 111

Choctaws, 164

Chomsky, Noam, 201

Christianity, 104, 165, 252, 278

Church of Jesus Christ of Latter Day Saints, 252

Churchill, Winston, 348

Churinga, 65, 76, 246

Clan: Aboriginal, 64–65, 66, 70, 71–72; definition of, 71

Cognitive anthropology, 4, 155, 305

Cognitive dissonance, theory of, 106

Cognitive ethology, 341

Collective conscience, 86, 90

Collective consciousness, 85–88, 90, 92–93

Collective motivation, 84, 87–88, 94, 95; and suicide, 88, 90

Collective representations, 19, 42, 51, 64, 72–73, 91–93, 250; of myth and religion, 53, 70, 72; as culture (E. Durkheim), 91

Communitas, 285, 298

Compassion Society (Taiwan), 100, 101

Cook, Edwin, 183

Coping mechanisms, 222, 227–34, 237, 240 (n. 3); types of, 226. *See also* Denial; Ego defense mechanisms; Introjection; Projection

Corruption, 354–55

Creeks, 164

Cro-Magnon man, 300, 302–03

Culler, Jonathan, 79 (n. 8)

Cultural determinism, 15, 29, 51, 146, 161, 182, 183, 184, 198, 276

Cultural ecology, 44

Cultural evolution, 146

Cultural heritage, 147, 151, 248; learning of, 148–50, 153–54

Cultural idealism, 146, 147

Index

Index

Latent function, definition(s) of, 33, 34
Laughlin, Charles, 286
Leach, Edmund, 36, 37, 49, 57 (n. 6)
Leaders, 350–53; superhuman attributes of, 347–49, 355–56; charisma of, 349, 355–57; and failure of nerve hypothesis, 354; and "mythical incarnation", 356. *See also* Numenification
Le Bon, Gustave, 86, 92
Leonardo (S. Freud), 96
Lessa, William, 22–23
Lesser, Alexander, 57 (n. 3)
Leviathan, 349
Le Vine, Robert, 153, 154
Levirate, 171
Lévi-Strauss, Claude, 42, 49, 84, 86, 94, 201, 203, 205
Levy, Jerre, 301
Levy, Robert I., 157
Lex, Barbara, 286
Lifton, Robert, 240 (n. 2)
Limbic system, 291, 294, 300
Linton, Ralph, 117, 140
Little Hans (S. Freud), 95
Longe, Alexander, 165

McClelland, David, 159
MacLean, Paul, 291, 292
Magical thought, 229
Making of Psychological Anthropology, The (G. Spindler, ed.), 15, 58 (n. 18)
Malaysia, 249
Malinowski, Bronislaw, 3, 43, 54, 57 (nn. 2, 6), 62; and Oedipus complex, 60–61, 162–63
Mandalay, 247
Mandel, Arnold, 287
Manifest function, definition(s) of, 33, 34
Manus, 154
Mao Zedong, 348
Marriage, cross-cousin, 209
Marx, Karl, 245
Maslow, Abraham, 306
Mason, W., 339
Masson, J. Moussaieff, 95
Matriarchy, 172
Matrilineal complex, in Trobriands, 60–61
Matrilocal residence, 163, 171
Maya, 252

Maymyo, 247
Mead, Margaret, 154
Mechansims of defense. *See* Coping mechanisms; Culturally constituted defense mechansims
Medium, writing (*tâng-ki*), Taiwan, 105–10
Mediums, speaking: in Taiwan, 105–06, 113 (n. 21); in Singapore, 113 (n. 21)
Meeker, Michael, 3, 60
Melanesia, 180 (n. 8)
Menomini, 185, 186, 189, 194, 196; male-female differences, 187–88
Merton, Robert K., 19, 21, 22, 32, 33, 98
Methodological monism, 46
Mill, John Stuart, 91–92
Mintoff, Dom, 348
Miracles, Taiwan, 106; definition of, 99
Mistassini Cree, 185, 186, 187, 189, 194, 197; male-female differences, 190
Mohammed, 252
Mombasa, 119, 121, 124, 136, 140, 142 (n. 4)
Monks, Buddhist, Burmese, 2, 8, 28, 81, 96, 97, 116, 254, 314; psychology of, 259; and culturally constituted defense mechanisms, 312
Monks, Buddhist, Sherpa, 8, 256–74; sexual abstinence of, 255, 258, 261, 262, 263, 264; economic motivation of, 256–57; officiating at funerals by, 256, 258, 261; courses of study, 259; parental death of, 265–67, 270; early marriage of, 268–69
Monks, Buddhist, Tamang, 322
Montgomery, Bernard Law, 348
Morality, 3, 30, 35, 51, 62, 64, 69, 71, 132–33
Morgan, Lewis H., 79 (n. 1), 172
Morisy, Ann, 306
Moses, 252
Motivation, 3, 10, 82, 90, 150, 254, 272, 325; and religion, 24, 52, 76, 256–57, 277, 313, 315, 318; as variable in analysis of social systems, 29, 31; and social sanctions, 30; and intent, 33–34 unconscious, 34–35, 99, 111 (n. 2); and totemism, 77; collective, 84, 87–88, 94, 95; and E. Durkheim, 84, 88; deep, 95–96; and goals, 157–59
Multiple personality syndrome, 315
Murray, Gilbert, 349–50, 351, 352, 354
Murray, Henry, 159

Index

Protestant Ethic and the Spirit of Capitalism, The (M. Weber), 37
Psyche and culture, "generative" model of, 254
Psychic economy, 262
Psychic fixation, 75, 76
Psychic unity of mankind, 309
Psychoanalysis, 54, 63, 75–77, 79 (n. 6), 83, 94, 95, 203, 206, 218, 223, 225, 230, 347; theory of, 27, 31, 53, 60–61, 230, 231, 276
Psychoanalytic anthropology, 80, 97
Psychobiology, 275, 277, 283, 291, 299; of ritual trance, 288, 294, 302, 305
Psychodynamics, 267; theory of, 49, 150, 162
Psychological anthropology, 10, 16, 41, 49, 161, 254, 275, 345
"Psychological Functions of Witchcraft Belief: The Burmese Case, The" (M. Spiro), 26–28
Psychological reductionism, 91, 162
Psychological theories of learning, 24.
Psychology, psychoanalytic, 222
Psychotherapy, 289, 298
Pumphouse Gang, 332–45 passim. See also Aggression, baboon; Baboons
Purity and Danger (M. Douglas), 58 (n. 17), 128, 173

Radcliffe-Brown, A. R., 29, 30, 38, 41–42, 43, 47, 54, 118; and social anthropology, 17–19, 26, 36; and functionalism, 18–19, 23, 32, 34, 37, 41–42, 57 (nn. 2, 3); and E. Durkheim, 86, 92; on religion, 93
Reaction formation, 228
Reciprocal altruism, 331, 345
Redfield, Robert, 16
Reincarnation, 251
Reisman, David, 237
Religion, 28–29, 44, 100, 101–05, 203, 236, 238, 275, 279, 299; definition(s) of, 7, 36–37, 43, 51, 58 (n. 14), 93, 246, 347; symbols of, 45, 72, 246, 248, 250–53, 273, 274, 313–15; primitive, 62–63, 65–78, 94, 305; nineteenth-century view of, 74, 79 (n. 1); as culturally constituted defense mechanism, 80–82, 313–14, 324; as projective system, 83; as system, 99, 277, 309; three constraining matrices of, 245; derivations of, 248–52; roles, 255, 258–59, 297; and suffering, 277–78; ecstatic, 283–84, 286, 288, 289, 292,

306; emergence of, 303; attributes of, 347–49; and leadership, 355–57. See also Buddhism; Monks; Sectarian societies; Supernaturalism, Burmese; Trance
"Religion: Problems of Definition and Explanation" (M. Spiro), 111 (n. 1)
"Religious Systems as Culturally Constituted Defense Mechanisms" (M. Spiro), 83
Remstäler (Germany), 185, 186, 187, 190, 197–98, 200; male-female differences, 191, 193–95; modernization in, 192
Repression, 218, 220, 240 (n. 4), 241 (n. 5), 291, 302
Reproaches (Swahili aggressive speech), 133–35, 140; definition of, 118; users of, 131–32
Resonance, 223–26, 234, 239
Revivalism (Jamaican trance cult), 278, 279–83, 285, 286, 288, 290, 293, 295, 298, 306; ceremony of, 280; expression of sexuality in, 292; motives of members, 296–97. See also Trance, ritual
Ricoeur, Paul, 54, 95–96
Ritual trance. See Trance, ritual
Role, 31, 32, 224, 225, 276; performance of, 6, 38, 116, 150, 182, 197–98, 212–13; definition of, 30; religious, 255, 258–59, 297, 315–18; choices of, 256, 269, 271, 272
Roosevelt, Theodore, 348
Rorschach, 6, 81, 186, 187–88, 189, 195–96, 222, 231, 239, 240 (n. 1), 241 (n. 10), 296; kinesthetic perceptions of, 223
Rules (E. Durkheim), 85, 86, 87, 88, 90, 93, 94, 95
Rules: prescriptive, 206, 211, 215, 217, 218, 219, 220; proscriptive, 206, 220

Sahlins, Marshall, 58 (n. 16)
St. Augustine, 59 (n. 18)
Sartre, Jean-Paul, 237
Scheff, T. J., 289–90, 292, 293–94, 305
Schemata, cognitive, 230, 234
Schemata, cultural, 4, 155–60; definition of (characteristics of), 155–56; lower-level, 158; upper-level, 158
Schizophrenia, 285
Schneider, David M., 44, 208
Secondary-process thought, 51–52, 277
Sectarian societies: membership in, 101; functional analysis of, 101–05; and writing medium (tâng-ki), 105, 106–10

400